BraveTart

BraveTart

ICONIC AMERICAN DESSERTS

Stella Parks

Foreword by J. Kenji López-Alt

Photography by Penny De Los Santos

W. W. Norton & Company
Independent Publishers Since 1923
New York | London

Pictured on the front cover: Homemade Oreo® Cookies

Copyright © 2017 by Stella Parks
Foreword copyright © 2017 by J. Kenji López-Alt
Photographs copyright © 2017 by Penny De Los Santos

All rights reserved
Printed in China
First Edition

For information about permission to reproduce selections from this book,
write to Permissions, W. W. Norton & Company, Inc.,
500 Fifth Avenue, New York, NY 10110

For information about special discounts for bulk purchases, please contact
W. W. Norton Special Sales at specialsales@wwnorton.com or 800-233-4830

Manufacturing by RR Donnelley Shenzhen
Book design by Toni Tajima
Production manager: Anna Oler

ISBN 978-0-393-23986-7

W. W. Norton & Company, Inc.
500 Fifth Avenue, New York, N.Y. 10110
www.wwnorton.com

W. W. Norton & Company Ltd.
15 Carlisle Street, London W1D 3BS

1 2 3 4 5 6 7 8 9 0

To midnight snacks

CONTENTS

II CLASSIC AMERICAN BRANDS*

* Homemade versions of the brand-name products referred to are my own recipes, not provided or endorsed by the owners of those brands.

III CLASSIC AMERICAN ICE CREAM

FOREWORD

by J. Kenji López-Alt

GREETINGS TO THE LUCKY FINDER OF THIS BOOK. In your wildest dreams you cannot imagine the marvelous surprises that await you.

Several years ago, Stella Parks served me a bowl of cereal at Table 310, a trendy restaurant in Lexington, Kentucky, where she was running the pastry kitchen (pastry *dungeon*, as she affectionately called it) at the time. I'd read her blog, BraveTart. I'd worked with her on pieces for Serious Eats. I cheered when she was named one of America's Best New Pastry Chefs by *Food & Wine* magazine, but I'd never actually tasted her food.

Oh man, she really gets *it*, I thought to myself as I took the first bite. The dessert was a play on Lucky Charms®, complete with crunchy diamond-shaped multicolored marshmallows and a delicate panna cotta made to taste just like cereal milk. If you ate your Lucky Charms the right way (cereal bits first, semi-soaked marshmallows next, oat-flavored cereal milk to wash it down), you already know what this dessert tastes like in your mind.

What's incredible, though, is that if you were to go home right afterward and pour yourself a bowl of Lucky Charms, you'd find them to be unpalatably sweet, the marshmallows more Styrofoam-like than crunchy. Stella had managed to make a bowl of Lucky Charms that tasted more like Lucky Charms to me than actual Lucky Charms. Think about that!

If Stella had a superpower (which I'm convinced she does), it's her ability to tap directly into those parts of our brains that store our childhood taste memories, unlocking them and stimulating desires that we never even knew we had, hidden away like the creme in the middle of a Hostess® CupCake (see page 247 for Stella's version). Remember that awe, wonder, and unbridled joy you experienced as a toddler, peering out from behind your mom's or dad's legs in the boxed cake aisle of the supermarket, your eyes glazed like a pair of Honey Buns (page 271) as they took in the rows of double chocolate brownies and angel's food and buttercream? Reading and baking from *BraveTart* is like this, but better, because you're an adult now and nobody's gonna tell you how much frosting to put on those cakes.

But to imply that all of Stella's research takes place in the candy aisle would be doing her a huge disservice. You will not find a more thoroughly researched treatise on the history of classic American home baking than what is within the pages of this book. Stella's recipes are more than just recipes; they're thesis papers, informed not only by her own palate and skills, but by the hundreds of historic recipes, newspapers, advertisements, and books she unearthed in her studies.

When was the last time you saw a book on baking with a seventeen-page notes section?

I am convinced that Stella is the result of a biological accident where a lab technician dropped Betty Crocker, Ernie the Keebler Elf, Mr. Wizard, and Fannie Farmer's DNA samples into an incubator and out emerged a living, breathing pastry goddess. A genetic experiment gone horribly, horribly right.

Despite what reality TV shows might have you believe, great desserts are not about size or complexity or fancy decorations (though Stella's got no problem getting fancy when she needs to). They're not about breathtaking feats of culinary wizardry (though Stella's got plenty of those). They're not even about knowing how to make the lightest buttercream (marshmallows!) or the fluffiest yellow cake (potato flour!). They're about striking that balance between comfort and quality. They're about feeding friends and family and reminding them what they loved about desserts in the first place. And most important, they're about making and serving the desserts that speak to *you*, in the way that *you* want to make them.

By the time you're done reading *BraveTart*, you'll not only know how to make Stella's favorite brownies (page 56) or her version of Little Debbie's® favorite Oatmeal Creme Pies (page 234), you'll have been sufficiently schooled in the underlying science and technique to be able to make your *own* favorite brownies, whether you like them fudgy or cakey (and, because of Stella's infectious infatuation with history, you'll note that the cake-fudge paradigm shift occurred sometime in 1929).

Where Willy Wonka relied on magic to bring his creations to life, Stella relies on science, history, and fanatical testing and devotion to her craft. This is good news for us. You have to be born with magic, but science, history, and technique are lessons we can *all* learn.

BraveTart

INTRODUCTION

I BELIEVE IN THE POWER of fudge frosting, rainbow sprinkles, and warm cherry pie. I like sticky buns for breakfast, and strawberry shortcake for dessert. I'm all about layer cakes, mile-high meringue, and cookie dough straight from the bowl. There's a sleeve of Thin Mints in my freezer, and a jar of Skippy on the shelf. I set marshmallows on fire, I fry doughnuts in oil, I steal Santa's cookies, and I always lick the spoon.

That's the resume that matters most, what I think you should know about me before buying this book. Anyone can go to culinary school and pretend pastry cream is puddin', but that doesn't make it so. There's real magic in a box of instant Jell-O, one that can't be matched with egg yolks and butter, and you've got to respect your roots more than your training to admit it. Look. I've been to culinary school. I've worked in fancy restaurants, and I've been named one of the best pastry chefs in America. Not for being fancy, but for what *Food & Wine* called a collection of "homey" desserts.

And that's my deal—I love American dessert, in all its cozy splendor, every messy, unpretentious bite. So this isn't a cookbook about making anything *fancy*, it's about making everything from scratch. Not because you have to, but because it's fun. Or, at least, it can be, with the right recipe; one that cares about the process as much as the result. Because what's the use in making your best friend a birthday cake if you're totally frazzled when it's done?

I've spent five years of my life with these recipes, testing and retesting to make sure my methods are as simple and reliable as they can be, looking for the unexpected variables that might derail you along the way. I might not always opt for the ingredients and techniques you'd expect, but know that the flavors will never be anything but what you remember, iconic in every way. I'm not here to "upgrade" or "fix" American desserts because I don't believe they're broken, I'm just here to make them more like the things they ought to be: apple pie that doesn't dirty every dish in your kitchen, sturdy chocolate sandwich cookies that twist apart just like the real deal, glossy brownies with a paper-thin crust, and layers of golden yellow cake as thick and fluffy as the kind from a box.

Most of the desserts in this book date back more than a hundred years, making them an essential part of American culture and cuisine. Doesn't matter when or where you grew up, you've had a slice of devil's food cake and know the shape of a Fig Newton by heart. These desserts are a thread running through our history, well worth untangling from urban legends and corporate propaganda, because that history should not be lost. For that reason, most of my recipes begin with a bit of culinary time travel—an origin story, if you will. I've also included reproductions of the vintage advertisements I've collected over the years, because they're what unified the notion of American dessert from coast to coast, and every place in between.

I hope you bake like crazy. I hope you scribble in the margins, and splatter the pages, and adapt my recipes to make each dessert your own.

A PINT ISN'T A POUND

I'D LIKE TO GO BACK IN TIME and punch the guy who decided to give two entirely different systems of measurements the same name. Consider the *ounce*, a measurement of weight—how heavy something is. Now consider the *fluid ounce*, a measurement of volume—how much space something takes up.

We understand the difference between weight and volume intuitively. Imagine helping a friend on moving day and finding two identical boxes, one labeled "Stuffed Animals" and the other "Cast-Iron Skillets." It doesn't matter that they're the same size, you know the one filled with teddy bears won't break your toes if you drop it. That intuitive understanding flies out the window when we read a recipe, in part because we've been taught a lie: A pint's a pound the world around. By conflating pints (a measurement of volume) with pounds (a measurement of weight), the rhyme suggests the terms are interchangeable, when they most certainly are not.

The fluid ounce was specifically designed to measure the space occupied by a single ounce of water. Establishing a one-to-one relationship between the weight and volume of water allowed for standard container sizes such as pints, quarts, and gallons to regulate the sale of beer, milk, cider, and other fluids with a water-like density.

Now, back in the nineteenth century, American cookbooks employed a hodgepodge of measurements, from pounds and ounces to pints and quarts, along with folksy approximations like "knobs" of butter, "glugs" of molasses, and "handfuls" of cornmeal. While some recipes called for standardized volume measurements such as the gill (4 fluid ounces), others relied on variable tin cups, teacups, tumblers, saucers, and wineglasses.

Influential American cookbook authors like Maria Parloa and Fannie Farmer brought order to chaos in the 1890s by establishing the half-pint *cup* as the basic unit of measure for their recipes. Though inherently less accurate than weight, cups eliminated confusing terms and allowed folks who couldn't afford a balance scale to bake with confidence.

Things didn't get screwy until the twentieth century, when companies introduced glass measuring cups with thin red hashmarks to indicate the number of liters, milliliters, cups, and ounces. It was as egregious a mistake as a compass labeled North, South, East, and Left. With "2 cups" and "16 ounces" marked off side by side, such measuring cups reinforced the misguided notion that "a pint's a pound."

That's a disastrous notion in the kitchen, because if a recipe calls for 8 ounces of honey and you use a measuring cup instead, you're going to wind up with 12 ounces of honey. The difference isn't semantics—it's a quarter pound. Variations that extreme result in failure, wasted ingredients, disappointment, and frustration. Now do you see why I want to punch that guy?

While some bakers have turned to the metric system, weighing in grams and measuring in milliliters, I think we can embrace the cultural quirks inherent to American baking while saving our sanity at the same time. To that end, my recipes will always use ounces to indicate weight and cups to indicate volume. The dreaded "fluid ounce" will not appear again in this book.

SO WHY WEIGHT?

People who bake as a hobby love their gadgets: ice cream machines, blenders, stand mixers, food processors, Bundt pans, waffle irons, rolling pins, cake-pop makers (seriously?), silicone baking mats, brownie corner pans, lollipop molds, cookie cutters, copper pots, and hundreds of other highly specialized tools. Yet the overwhelming majority of American bakers won't purchase the most basic kitchen tool of all: a scale. Many think it's pretentious, overly technical, unnecessary, or a total drag. I like to say it's the telescope of the kitchen.

If you want to see the stars, you don't *need* a telescope. They're right there in the sky for anyone to see. But if you had a telescope, you could explore the craters of the moon, see the rings of Saturn, and make out the individual points of light in an otherwise blurry nebula. Necessary? Not at all. A lot of fun? Heck, yeah.

Unlike a telescope, a scale doesn't cost hundreds of dollars. In fact, you can get a reliable kitchen scale for about twenty-five bucks, and top-of-the line models only cost about fifty. You don't need a scale to make the recipes in this book, but why choose to limit yourself to nineteenth-century technology? Baking with a scale offers a lot of benefits you may have never considered.

A SCALE CUTS PREP TIME AND CLEANUP IN HALF. It takes two seconds to shake a pound of flour into a bowl. How long does it take to measure out 3½ cups of flour? Then multiply that by every ingredient in a recipe. Baking isn't a race, but measuring stuff isn't exactly the fun part.

A SCALE GUARANTEES CONSISTENT RESULTS. Let's go back to those 3½ cups of flour. Did you spoon flour into the cup, or dip the cup straight into the bag? Thanks to density, that matters. A scoop of flour can weigh over 6 ounces, while spooning it out results in about 4½. With cup measurements, any ingredient that can be compacted is vulnerable to variation, a problem that disappears with a scale.

A SCALE PUTS US ON THE SAME PAGE. Scales eliminate the problem of variations in cup sizes, as "1 cup" will vary considerably depending on whether you reach for a liquid measuring cup, a dry measuring cup, or a novelty measuring cup shaped like a heart. With a scale, you never have to worry about what a "heaping cup of peanut butter" looks like, or how "firmly" you should pack the brown sugar.

A SCALE ELIMINATES LOSS. When you measure out 1 cup of honey, the amount you actually put into a recipe depends on whether you filled it almost to the brim or stopped shy to avoid dribbling—or perhaps it overflowed a bit. Oh, and how well did you scrape the cup? With a scale, there's no question that all 8 ounces go directly into the bowl.

A SCALE MAKES IT EASY TO CUSTOMIZE. Want a half batch? What about one fifth? Just divide each weight measurement and let the scale do the rest. Now try dividing cup measurements the same way. How do you accurately determine 0.375 or 0.15 cups? You can eyeball it or convert to tablespoons and get pretty close, but that's a lot of work for cakes that come "pretty close" to rising, fudge that turns out "pretty close" to creamy, or ice cream that's "pretty close" to frozen.

A SCALE LETS YOU SEE THE MATRIX. When you think in cups, you think in code. If a recipe calls for a cup of oatmeal and a cup of honey, a one-to-one ratio stares you in the face. It's all too easy to think, "This recipe uses equal parts honey and oatmeal." But when you deal with weight, you'll see that recipe actually calls for three times as much honey as oatmeal. Weight shows you what's actually happening rather than what *seems* to be happening.

All of my recipes include cup measurements because I want everyone to jump on in, bake something tasty, and have fun in the kitchen using whatever equipment feels most comfortable. That said, cups can't replicate the precision of a scale unless I resort to obnoxious measurements like "1 cup minus 2¼ teaspoons," for example, to match 6½ ounces of sugar. For that reason, I often round cup measurements to the nearest logical amount, making the previous example "1 cup," so don't be alarmed if you notice the volume and weight of an ingredient don't line up. But this is only done in recipes that will tolerate such variation. Whenever success depends on precision, I always provide the information you need. For example, my Homemade Oreo® dough has to nail a specific pH or the brown dough will not turn black in the oven; hence, I call for "⅓ cup plus 1 tablespoon" so you can precisely measure 1¼ ounces cocoa powder.

NOTES ON INGREDIENTS AND EQUIPMENT

INGREDIENTS

ALL-PURPOSE FLOUR. With a name like "all-purpose flour," you'd think that any brand would do, but the term isn't actually regulated, meaning the behavior can vary wildly from brand to brand, as different wheats yield flours with different ratios of starch and protein. White Lily starts with chlorinated soft white wheat, for a uniquely mild flour that produces ultratender biscuits. King Arthur favors unbleached hard red wheat, for a heartier flour that works especially well with chewy breads.

While I adore these flours in specific applications, they also represent the extreme ends of the all-purpose label, and I've found that makes them less versatile with recipes that live in the middle: cookies, cakes, and pastries. For that reason, my favorite is Gold Medal's bleached all-purpose flour, made from both white and red wheat. That blend allows it to strike a perfect balance between the two styles, for a truly *all-purpose* flour that's suitable for everything from delicate scones and flaky pie crust to chewy English muffins and tender cookies.

Don't let the "bleached" moniker scare you away, no one's dumping bottles of bleach into the flour; rather, such flour is treated with a process that lightens the wheat's color, leaving only a trace amount of benzoic acid behind. For context, benzoic acid occurs naturally and abundantly in foods like cranberries and cinnamon, presenting no health concerns at all. So, you can use whatever brand of all-purpose flour you prefer, but bear in mind that those made from 100 percent red or 100 percent white wheat may excel in some areas but cause trouble in others.

BROWN SUGAR. With only 10 percent added molasses, light brown sugar has a mild color and flavor that won't obscure the natural browning of cookies and cakes—one of the most important signs of doneness. Unless it is specifically called for, avoid dark brown sugar, as its deeper color and pH may change how some recipes behave.

BUTTER. Salted butter forces a baker to relinquish the important (and highly personal) job of seasoning to factory formulas that vary from brand to brand. For that reason, my recipes were developed with unsalted American butter (not European style), giving me full control of the sodium content in every dessert. Instead of calling for soft or room-temperature butter, I've also made an effort to include specific temperatures, for clarity.

BUTTERMILK. To the uninitiated, nonfat buttermilk may sound about as legit as fat-free half-and-half, but it's no dieting gimmick. In fact, you should avoid full-fat versions touted as gourmet—buttermilk is what's left over after churning cream into butter, so it's naturally low-fat. If buttermilk isn't sold in your neck of the woods, use plain unsweetened fat-free yogurt (not strained or Greek) instead.

CAKE FLOUR. Cake flour is a soft white-wheat pastry flour that's naturally low in protein and high in starch. American cake flour is traditionally bleached, a process that lowers its pH, alters its starch, and mellows its flavor, for a remarkably delicate flour in every sense of the word. My favorite brand is Swans Down, which comes in a bright red box. It is sold in most supermarkets, alongside other baking flours. Despite what you may read online, cake flour can't be faked with a blend of all-purpose flour and cornstarch (a life hack that utterly misses the point of this uniquely unabsorbent flour).

Unbleached cake flour was unheard of until a few years ago. While it's comparatively low protein, this new flour behaves differently because of its unneutralized starch and high pH. For that reason, unbleached cake flour *cannot* be used in Effortless Angel's Food Cake (page 98), Boston Cream Pie (page 105), or Homemade Twinkies® (page 244).

CHOCOLATE AND COCOA POWDER. Despite their iconic logos and trusted reputations, most national brands offer nothing but harsh and acidic chocolate or cocoa that tastes lackluster at best (they're often skimmed of cocoa butter as a cost-saving measure). For more luscious brownies, devil's food cake, and chocolate pudding, the single most important thing you can do is ditch those mass-market brands. The quality of your desserts will improve dramatically, and you can buy in bulk online to offset the higher cost.

My favorite dark chocolate for baking is Endangered Species' 72%; for tempering, it's Valrhona's 72% couverture. My favorite milk chocolate for baking is Endangered Species' 48%; for tempering, it's Callebaut's 33.6%. My favorite white chocolate for baking *and* tempering is Republica del Cacao's 31% Acera—often sold by third parties as "31% white chocolate from Ecuador."

COCONUT MILK. Because its balance of water and fat makes it an ideal substitute for milk or cream in most cakes and candies, I always keep a few cans of unsweetened full-fat coconut milk on hand for emergencies, though its mellow tropical flavor makes for a fun variation anytime. It cannot be replaced by the thin, watery coconut "beverage" sold in refrigerated cartons as a milk substitute.

COCONUT OIL. This nonhydrogenated oil is solid at room temperature, so you can use it like butter or shortening. Refined coconut oil is neutral in flavor, with a high smoke point that makes it my favorite frying oil for doughnuts (see page 189). Virgin coconut oil tastes like fresh coconut, but those very aromatic compounds make it a bad choice for high-heat applications. It's creamy and soft at what most anyone would consider "room temperature," but below 65°F, it turns rock hard, and at 76°F, it begins to melt. You can find pint jars of coconut oil alongside other oils at the grocery store, but in warehouse clubs or online, you can buy a quart for a few dollars less, and with its three-year shelf life, you'll have plenty of time to use it up!

CORN SYRUP. This invert sugar gets a bad rap because of its evil twin, high-fructose corn syrup (HFCS), which is processed to convert roughly half of its natural glucose to fructose. It's not that fructose itself is scary (honey is 40 percent fructose, while agave nectar clocks in at 90 percent), but that HFCS puts sugar where you'd least expect it: salsa, potato chips, beef stew, whole wheat bread. That can wreak havoc on our daily sugar intake, making it hard to avoid even on days when we skip dessert.

Sugar belongs in dessert, so there's no reason to avoid regular unmodified corn syrup. It has a neutral flavor, color, and pH that no other syrup can match. It serves as a binding agent in eggless doughs like that for Homemade Pop-Tarts® (page 274), prevents crystallization in Buttered Vanilla Marshmallows (page 65), and ensures that my Fluffy Cocoa Nougat (page 302) stays creamy and light. I use regular Karo Syrup, but if you're concerned about GMOs, try an organic brand called Wholesome Sweetener.

EGGS. Most cakes and cookies don't mind the subtle fluctuation in the weights of "large" eggs (about 1¾ ounces each), so I generally call for eggs by number rather than weight. When it comes to whites or yolks alone, I prefer weight measurements, which make it easy to use up leftovers from other projects without having to guess how many I've collected in a jar.

FREEZE-DRIED FRUIT. Unlike moist and chewy dried fruits, freeze-dried fruits are bone-dry—like astronaut ice cream. They're easily crushed or ground into a fine powder that can be used to thicken and flavor Homemade Rice Krispies Treats® (page 316), Homemade Pop-Tarts® (page 274), Homemade McDonald's®-Style Baked Apple Turnovers (page 288), and Homemade Vanilla Oreo® Filling (page 215). Look for pouches of freeze-dried fruit at grocery stores such as Whole Foods, Trader Joe's, and Fresh Market, or from brands like Nature's All Foods, Crispy Green, Just Tomatoes Etc!, and Crunchies online.

GELATIN. While most pastry chefs prefer sheet gelatin, I've adapted my recipes for the more readily available powdered variety. It's easier to use in small-batch recipes, and its strength is consistent from brand to brand (sheet gelatin's power is more variable). Most supermarket brands of unflavored gelatin are excellent and affordable.

Gelatin's behavior depends on a surprising number of factors, from pH to the concentration of sugar in a solution, and even the length of time it's allowed to "bloom" in cold water. It can also be weakened by temperatures above 212°F, the enzymes in many tropical fruits, and exposure to high-proof alcohol. For these reasons, deviating from the recipe is always a hit-or-miss proposition.

KINAKO. This golden flour is made from full-fat roasted soybeans, so it has more in common with almond flour than with pale soy flour, which is made from defatted raw soybeans to better mimic lean, mild, all-purpose flour. Plain soy flour is also gritty and a little bitter, totally unlike the sweet and nutty flavor of melt-in-your-mouth kinako (it's so delicious it's a straight-up dessert topping in Japan). I love incorporating this toasty ingredient into my gluten-free flour blends, where it stands in for barley malt (White Chocolate Butterscotch Blondies, page 58) or whole wheat (Graham Crackers, page 202). Look for kinako in Japanese shops and online, or in Korean markets, where it is called *bokkeun konggaru*.

KOSHER SALT. I've got a tiny kitchen with an even smaller pantry, so I don't have space for all sorts of salt. Since I like cooking with a dish of kosher salt by the stove, I reach for it when baking as well. I use Diamond Crystal, one of the few 100-percent-pure salts on the market. Most other brands contain yellow prussiate, aka sodium ferrocyanide, as an anticaking agent, an additive that wreaks havoc in candy making by interfering with crystallization. For its purity and ease of use, I highly recommend making the switch to Diamond Crystal. With other brands of kosher salt, which pack more salt into every teaspoon, use only two-thirds as much as my recipes call for. With fine-grained table salt, use half the amount.

LAVENDER. Dried flowers are popular for crafting hanging bouquets and homemade potpourri, so make sure the lavender you buy is meant for culinary use! Other grades may be treated with chemicals that are not safe to eat. Look for dried lavender with other herbs and spices in health food stores or natural markets, or order online from organic brands.

MALT. The toasty, butterscotch sweetness of our favorite brand-name cakes and cookies comes from barley malt—a thick, sticky syrup made from fermented grain. You'll find it in the health food aisle of many grocery stores, or wherever home-brew and bread-baking ingredients are sold. In some recipes, such as Homemade Wonder® Bread (page 242) and Homemade Crunch Bars (page 296), I prefer using malted milk powder instead. As a dry ingredient, it's much easier to handle, with a rich but mild flavor. It's easy to find in the hot cocoa aisle, from brands like Ovaltine and Carnation—just don't grab the chocolate variety by mistake. Note that malt, in any form, is not gluten-free.

MATCHA. Thanks to Japanese restaurants that put green tea ice cream on the menu, matcha-flavored desserts have developed something of a cult following. But *matcha* isn't Japanese for "green tea," it's the name of a specific product made from shade-grown *gyokuro* leaves that have been destemmed, deveined, and stone ground into a floury powder with an intense flavor and dissolving quality unlike any other type of tea. My favorite tea shop imports a special grade of matcha formulated especially for baking (Matcha Jade Bliss), sold online at essencha .com.

MILK. While dairy-forward desserts like pudding and ice cream require whole milk for a rich mouthfeel and full flavor, butter-heavy cakes and cookies only need milk to regulate the texture of the batter or dough. My recipes always let you know when the percentage isn't important, so that you can use whatever milk you have on hand. When recipes do call for whole milk, accept no substitutions.

MOCHIKO. Although it is sometimes called "sweet rice flour" or "glutinous rice flour," this flour contains neither sugar nor gluten. Its English names come from awkward translations, which is why I prefer to stick with the original—mochiko. It's a fine white flour made from the type of rice reserved for mochi, the sticky/sweet Japanese dessert. While it's easy to find in stores or online from brands like Bob's Red Mill, I generally buy a small box at the Japanese market whenever I need to pick up ingredients like matcha or kinako.

OAT FLOUR. I love oat flour in whole-grain variations of Homemade Wonder® Bread (page 242), Top-Shelf Muffin Mix (page 284), and Graham Crackers (page 202), but it's also the secret to thick and chewy Triple-Oatmeal Cookies (page 39). Look for brands like Bob's Red Mill and Arrowhead Mills, which are more finely ground than DIY alternatives. Some brands are certified gluten-free, although many celiacs still find oats problematic.

POWDERED SUGAR. Up until recently, all powdered sugars were alike: hypersweet, with a strange tinny flavor and a subtle grit from cornstarch. Thanks to the recent push for organic, a whole new breed has emerged, made from raw cane sugar and tapioca starch. The subtle flavor of sugarcane mellows the sweetness of these organic brands, adding some much-needed dimension to what was formerly a one-note ingredient. Even better, tapioca starch dissolves more readily in uncooked applications, making gritty, starchy frostings a thing of the past.

SUGAR. Because sweetness is sugar's least important role in almost any recipe, using less will unleash all manner of unforeseen problems, causing custards to curdle, cakes to collapse, and pies to weep. Cutting back on sugar will also prevent proper spreading, browning, whipping, and freezing, while encouraging excess gluten development and faster bacterial growth. If a dough, batter, custard, or candy tastes too sweet, don't cut back on the sugar—add a little salt.

TAPIOCA STARCH. Also known as tapioca flour, this fine powder is one of my favorite ingredients for thickening fruit pies, where it creates a light, translucent gel that's never gloppy or cloudy. It cannot be used interchangeably with cornstarch, or even instant tapioca granules. Tapioca comes from cassava root, but some Asian countries manufacture it from similar plants, such as sago. Unfortunately, these alternatives aren't true tapioca and don't behave the same way, leading to soupy pies. For that reason, look for packaging that mentions cassava by name; brands like Bob's Red Mill are easy to find in most supermarkets.

VANILLA. Supermarket vanilla beans are abysmal—withered, brittle, difficult to cut, and astronomically expensive. And those tiny bottles of vanilla extract are, ounce for ounce, one of the priciest ingredients around and often chock-full of filler rather than flavor. Abandon ship! If you buy in bulk online, you can have plump vanilla beans for as little as a buck each, or top-notch vanilla extract for only a dollar an ounce. Even fancier vanilla may cost twice as much online, but that's still half the price of what you pay in stores. Head to beanilla.com for beans, and look for extract from brands like Rodelle and Better Body.

EQUIPMENT

BAKING SHEETS. Save your money for chocolate; the gimmicky features touted by the makers of so-called "specialty" cookie sheets don't do anything but attempt to justify their absurd price tags. From the best restaurant in New York City to the darkest pastry dungeon in Kentucky, pastry chefs share one thing in common: cheap aluminum sheet pans. What you want at home is what we'd call a half sheet, a simple 18-by-13-inch slab of standard-duty 18-gauge aluminum rolled at the edges to form a rim. At wholesale clubs like Sam's or Costco, you should expect to pay about six bucks a pop, and maybe a little more from some name brand online.

BROWNIE PANS. Glass or ceramic baking dishes radiate heat long after they're pulled from the oven, making it easy to overbake brownies and blondies. I prefer lightweight 9-by-13-by-2-inch aluminum baking pans, which are deep enough for thick sheet cakes too. My favorite manufacturer is Fat Daddio, because their anodized (i.e., nonreactive) pans are perfect for lasagna as well, with removable bottoms to boot!

CAKE PANS. Nothing can ruin dessert faster than flimsy cake pans. They're thin, dark, and shallow, resulting in overbaked cakes that rise poorly and have a dark heavy crust. And, they're almost always more expensive than my favorite 8-inch anodized aluminum pans, $12 from Fat Daddio online. At 3 inches deep, they allow the recipes you already love to rise higher and flatter (minimizing the amount of domed crust that needs to be trimmed away), with less browning too. These pans let me create the ultra-thick layers depicted on boxes of cake mix (which actually rely on food styling slight of hand), and they're fantastic for cinnamon rolls and sticky buns as well.

CAST-IRON TURNTABLE. If you enjoy arriving to parties with a showstopping layer cake in hand, or simply baking birthday cakes for friends and family, I can't say enough about how much you'll love Ateco's 612 turntable. Its ultra-heavy cast-iron base simply can't be toppled, and its stainless steel plate spins with frictionless speed so you can sculpt buttercream into a mirror-smooth finish in a matter of seconds. Take the time to find a retailer that offers free shipping online, and you can nab one for about fifty dollars.

CHEESECAKE PAN. For my New York Cheesecake, I use an 8-by-3¾-inch round pan. It's an unusual depth, but you can find such pans online from brands like Browne Foodservice, and Parrish Magic makes a similar 9-inch pan that can be used instead. I prefer removable-bottom cheesecake pans over traditional springform pans because there are no moving parts—the latch of a springform pan once caught on my oven mitt, exploding half-cooked cheesecake batter over the bottom of my oven.

COOKIE CUTTERS. For most baking tasks, you don't need anything more than a nested set of plain round cutters (Ateco is my favorite brand), but if you're feeling fancy, a fluted set is nice as well. Beyond that, it's all about your personal style. For me, that means having a set of Chicago Metallic's circus animal "plunger cutters," which stamp out tigers and giraffes, among others, complete with stripes and spots.

COOKIE DOUGH SCOOP. A stainless steel scoop with a spring-loaded trigger is a baker's best friend, making short work of cookie doughs and portioning muffin or cupcake batter with less mess. If you get only one, grab a #40 scoop. It dishes up roughly 2 tablespoons of dough, the perfect amount for a 3-inch cookie.

DIGITAL SCALE. I've been using the same OXO Good Grips stainless steel scale for more than ten years, and it's what I always buy to give friends and family ready to ditch their measuring cups. It toggles between ounces and grams, with a backlight so you can read the numbers even in a dimly lit kitchen. The plate is removable for easy cleaning, and the pull-out display means oversized bowls won't block your view. I recommend their eleven-pound model, which won't be maxed out by heavy glass or ceramic bowls that can unexpectedly gobble up half the weight allotment of a five-pound model.

DIGITAL THERMOMETER. With features such as "shattering glass" and "mercury poisoning," I can't fathom a single benefit to an old-fashioned candy thermometer, whose markings can fade with use or fog with steam. Digital thermometers offer lightning-fast readouts accurate to the decimal, and programmable alerts that let me walk away from the kitchen confident I'll hear the chime when my candy's ready. I adore Polder's oven-safe thermometer/timer, which can handle anything from peanut brittle to pot roast—an invaluable tool even for those who don't often make candy at home.

FOOD PROCESSOR. While you don't need a food processor to shred carrots or grind cookie crumbs, it's essential for the fine-textured homemade flours that give many of my recipes their intensity. If you don't have one, team up with a friend who does—the flours can be stored in airtight containers for up to a month at room temperature, so you can grind now and bake later.

MESH SIEVES. For anything from sifting flour to straining caramel, I rely on the same 8-inch sieve. It's big enough to accommodate any recipe, with a long sturdy handle that keeps it from falling into wide pots or bowls. Whatever the shape, look for sieves made from stainless steel, which won't impart wonky flavors to lemon desserts. Finer grades of mesh are great for straining out tiny particles or plant fibers from syrups, stocks, and fruit purees, but they're a real pain when it comes to a thickened custard.

OVEN THERMOMETER. Few ovens run true to temp, so if the estimated bake times in your favorite recipes never quite pan out, set the record straight with a five-dollar oven thermometer. With a little patience, you can work out an easy chart to remind yourself what the temperature on the dial *actually* means (at my parents' house, I preheat the oven to 375°F when I need it at 350°F).

ROLLING PIN. Regardless of what anyone says, the best rolling pin is the one that feels comfortable in your hands. I love the maple French pins made by J. K. Adams, which are both elegant and affordable, but there's nothing wrong with a Shaker-style handle. For cut-out cookies like Homemade Oreo® Cookies (page 212), nothing beats the paisley design of Sun Craft's embossed rolling pin, available on Amazon.

SPATULA, FLEXIBLE. In my experience, good spatulas are strangely hard to find. Most are too rigid and thick, or wonderfully flexible but easily melted. And don't get me started on the slimy texture of a wet silicone handle. My favorites come from Good Cook, offering the best of both worlds: colorful spatulas that are thin and flexible yet heat-resistant, with easy-to-grip bamboo handles that won't turn slick with steam (a common problem in custard and candy making). I'm not a spokesperson, it's just hard to shut up when you're in love.

SPATULA, OFFSET METAL. This is one of the most important tools I own, and not just for cake decorating! My 8-inch spatula is thin enough to slide under a sticky dough to free it from the counter but strong enough to "knead" Baltimore Fudge (page 74). Its offset handle keeps your knuckles away from messy projects, and it can double as a cake or pie server too.

STAINLESS STEEL SAUCIERS (1/16-INCH-GAUGE). Balloon whisks and spatulas have no trouble scraping the gently rounded corners of a saucier, compared to the sharp corners of a straight-sided pot. They're designed to facilitate stirring and scraping, making creamy custards and perfectly condensed milk a breeze. If you don't have a saucier, make sure you're using the right whisk (see below).

My recipes specify size in terms of quart capacity, so you never have to guess how my idea of medium, for example, compares to yours. It's okay if you don't have the exact size, but don't use anything smaller, or you may risk overflow. When going a size up, be aware that the increased surface area may allow custards and candies to cook faster than indicated. Candies and custards should never be made in cast-iron or enameled cookware, which will radiate heat and continue cooking well past the desired temperature.

STAND MIXER. If you're serious about baking, investing in a stand mixer will provide a lifetime of satisfaction. I've had the same KitchenAid for more than ten years, and despite my full-time job as a pastry chef, it's still going strong. Aside from the joy (and efficiency) of working hands-free, its extra horsepower will get any job done faster while guaranteeing lighter cakes, fluffier marshmallows, and chewier breads. So, in my recipes, the times listed for mixing and creaming are based on a stand mixer—it may take up to twice as long to achieve the same results with the lower wattage and smaller beaters of a hand mixer.

WHISKS. I have an collection of whisks in every size and shape, but the truth is that I really only ever use one: the 8-inch six-wire stainless steel balloon whisk that came in my tool kit when I enrolled at the Culinary Institute of America. It's simple and elegant, easy to clean, and perfect for reaching into bowls and sauciers alike. Yet while it's everything I could ever need at work or at home, it's absolutely useless with the straight-sided pots and pans of my parents' kitchen. There I reach for a ball whisk—the sort that looks as if its wire loops have been cut and capped with little ball bearings. Because they're not constrained to the arc of a metal loop, the tines are able to reach into the tightest corners of any pot. Stainless steel ball whisks generate a remarkable clatter and can scratch up enamel, so I prefer the sort with silicone tips.

Part I

Classic American Desserts

No scoop? Use a pair of spoons to round the cookie dough for Chopped Chocolate Chip Cookies (page 34).

Chapter I

COOKIES & CANDY

This chapter is dedicated to sweet snacks nibbled out of hand—warm chocolate chip cookies, chewy snickerdoodles, crisp graham crackers, and creamy fudge and other classic candies.

CHOCOLATE CHIP COOKIES

At the turn of the twentieth century, the falling price of chocolate kicked off an era of innovation. It was a time when drugstores served up the first chocolate sodas, sundaes, and shakes; when Rockwood & Company produced the world's first chocolate sprinkles, in Brooklyn; when Milton Hershey gave America its first milk chocolate bar.

On the home front, affordable chocolate gave housewives a chance to experiment and splurge, dreaming up the sort of in-your-face chocolate desserts Americans still love today: devil's food cake, brownies, and fudge. In that uberchocolatey climate, it seems only natural that bakers would puzzle out a cookie as simple as chocolate chip, but culinary historians disagree.

Apparently the combination was so far-fetched that Americans would go on to manufacture full-fledged candy bars like Butterfinger®, Snickers®, and Milky Way® before it would occur to a single soul that chocolate + cookie dough might be a good idea. According to the official story, chocolate chip cookies weren't invented until 1938, the year Ruth Wakefield published her recipe for Toll House® Chocolate Crunch Cookies.

Apocryphal accounts insist she stumbled onto the recipe by accident, while modern arguments favor the notion of intelligent design. (I'd expect no less from a college-educated dietician, home economics expert, restaurateur, and best-selling cookbook author.) Yet either version of the story suggests Toll House Cookies were invented in a vacuum, that Ruth wasn't influenced by the culinary climate of her day, and that American bakers didn't even have the wherewithal to stick some chopped chocolate in a cookie.

I don't buy it, so let's go back in time, to the late 1800s, when American cookies were built to last: rolled thin and baked to a crisp. The most popular sort were called jumbles—thin ring-shaped cookies flavored with whatever a baker had on hand, like a dash of cinnamon, lemon zest, grated coconut, or minced almonds. With extra milk or eggs, the stiff dough could be softened enough to drop from a spoon. These so-called "soft jumbles" were still baked until crisp; the technique simply eliminated the hassle of rolling.

As chocolate became less expensive in the latter half of the nineteenth century, it became yet another way to flavor a batch of jumbles. Recipes rarely called for more than an ounce or two, melted in a pan over a teakettle or else finely shaved—techniques that diffused a small amount of chocolate through the entire dough. By the 1870s, stand-alone recipes for chocolate jumbles emerged as more than a simple variation.

My favorite example is a recipe that appeared in newspapers across the country throughout 1877.[1] These "Chocolate Jumbles" called for a cup of butter,

World War II–era advertisements encouraged American housewives to bake chocolate chip cookies for the troops.

two cups of sugar, three cups of flour, four eggs, and two full cups of grated chocolate.

Sound familiar? The ratios are nearly identical to the recipe found on every bag of chocolate chips today, but with twice as many eggs and *a lot* more work. Forget easy-grip Microplanes, try grating a block of chocolate on a nineteenth-century rasp. I bought one at an auction, and while it was sharp enough to take the skin off my knuckles whenever I slipped, the awkward device produced only a few spoonfuls of chocolate shavings in ten minutes. Ample time for the chocolate to begin melting against the palm of my hand, slippery conditions that caused me to lose my grip more than once.

Despite this messy, frustrating, time-consuming, and potentially bloody technique, grated-chocolate jumbles were all the rage during the 1880s and '90s, with virtually identical recipes appearing in countless American cookbooks, newspapers, and magazines, including *Good Housekeeping* and *Ladies' Home Journal.*[2]

At a time when bakers relied on intuition over explicit instruction, I think the recipe's popularity hinged on an unspoken shortcut: grabbing a knife. It's the type of common-sense adjustment that would occur to anyone without a grater, or those simply frustrated by the tedium (and pain) involved. And why not? So long as they converted a block of chocolate into a pint of tiny bits, harried cooks had no reason to care how it was done.

Thing is, the *how* actually makes a big difference. Two cups of grated chocolate weigh a mere four ounces, while two cups of finely chopped chocolate can tip the scale at twelve (exactly how many ounces you find in a bag of chocolate chips). Thanks to falling prices and chocolate sold by the pound, it was a mistake bakers in 1877 could afford to make.

To test my theory, I sought out locally milled flour, freshly laid eggs, and salted Amish butter (for that nineteenth-century flair), then traded my KitchenAid for a wooden spoon. Aside from chopping the chocolate, I followed that 1877 recipe to the letter, which resulted in a bowl of soft, sticky dough that brought about my next inescapable conclusion: ain't no way folks tried to roll it out. Maybe a few determined souls kept shoveling

in more flour, but the practical solution would have been to shrug and grab a spoon. Those who did would have baked up America's first chocolate chip cookies, some twenty-six years before Ruth Wakefield was even born. It's no stretch to imagine; in the early 1900s, eerily similar recipes, called "Chocolate Drops," appeared in newspapers nationwide.

The trend wasn't limited to kitchens at home. In 1928, the R. W. Keyes general store in Oshkosh, Wisconsin, advertised chocolate chip cookies by the pound.[3] Far from some isolated aberrance, chocolate chip cookies appeared by name in supermarket advertisements throughout the early 1930s, including Buy Rite markets in Iowa, IGAs in Indiana, Bennett's in New York, and Krogers throughout Ohio.[4] In 1937, a full year before Toll House Cookies made their debut, corporate bakery distributors like Colonial (Pennsylvania), Salerno (Michigan), and Flavor Kist (Illinois) had begun manufacturing chocolate chip cookies as well.

To me, that's a mountain of evidence pointing to the fact that Ruth Wakefield didn't invent chocolate chip cookies—she adapted them. Her 1938 recipe relied on the exact ratio of butter, sugar, flour, and chocolate established by nineteenth-century chocolate jumbles, but with half as many eggs and a fifty-fifty blend of white and brown sugar.

Those tweaks gave Ruth's version a butterscotchy flavor and more impressive crunch, but what truly set her recipe apart was the unprecedented media blitz that came with it. To promote the fourth edition of *Toll House Tried and True Recipes*, Ruth's publisher, M. Barrow & Company, secured a corporate sponsor. Reporting on the deal in 1940, *Publishers' Weekly* explained:

> To further national interest, arrangements have been completed with the Nestlé Chocolate Company for the use of the Toll House Chocolate Crunch Cookie recipe. The recipe and the book will be featured on all of Nestlé chocolate wrappers [and] newspaper advertising that is scheduled to appear in fifty-five principal cities.[5]

This agreement simply escalated one established the year before, which Ruth had hammered out with a smaller company licensed to manufacture Nestlé's chocolate in New York. The cookies were exactly what the Swiss upstart needed to break into the American market, with two whole bars of chocolate in every batch.

Of course, folks at home were free to grab whatever chocolate they preferred, giving established brands like Baker's or Hershey's an edge. To prevent their competitors from swooping in (swooping is bad), Nestlé introduced "Toll House Morsels." While ostensibly designed to eliminate the hassle of chopping, their distinctive name ensured Nestlé chocolate would always be integral to the Toll House recipe.[6]

While that polka-dotted presentation has become emblematic of chocolate chip cookies, it defies the origin of their name—*chips* being an apt description for the pile of shards and shavings produced by chopped chocolate. Commercial chips also prevent chocolate from flavoring the dough, confining it to intense but isolated bites.

My recipe gets back to chopped chocolate, replicating what I believe to be the nineteenth-century shortcut that made chocolate jumbles a hit. Chopping chocolate creates a blend of chunky nuggets, slender shards, and fine, powdery bits, marbling the dough with fudgy streaks and pockets of pure chocolate.

Freed from the constraints of a twelve-ounce bag, I can pick and choose among different types of chocolate to create my own custom blend. Whether that's a trio of milk chocolates from three different brands or a yin-yang blend of dark and white, mixing things up means every batch of "chips" will offer something new.

Get the most flavor for Chocolate Chip Cookies (page 34) with a variety of chopped chocolates.

CHOPPED CHOCOLATE CHIP COOKIES

A pinch of nutmeg and a sprinkling of salt amplify the butterscotchy flavor of chocolate chip cookies, while a blend of milk and dark chocolate chunks provide alternating bites of creamy sweetness and bitter intensity. You can bake the cookies until they're golden brown and crunchy, but I prefer to pull them while they're still a wee bit pale so they stay soft and fudgy, crisp only around the very edges. *See photos on pages 28 and 33.*

YIELD: thirty-two 3-inch cookies or sixty-four 2-inch cookies | **ACTIVE TIME:** about 25 minutes

2½ cups | 14 ounces roughly chopped mixed dark, milk, and/or white chocolate (not chips)

2¾ cups | 12½ ounces all-purpose flour, such as Gold Medal

2 sticks | 8 ounces unsalted butter, soft but cool—about 65°F

1 packed cup | 8 ounces light brown sugar

1 cup | 7¼ ounces white sugar

2 teaspoons Diamond Crystal kosher salt (half as much if iodized), plus more for sprinkling

1 teaspoon baking soda

½ teaspoon baking powder

1 tablespoon vanilla extract

⅛ teaspoon grated nutmeg

1 large egg, straight from the fridge

Adjust oven rack to middle position and preheat to 350°F. Set a handful of chopped chocolate aside. Place remainder in a medium bowl, sift flour on top (if using cup measures, spoon flour into the cups and level with a knife before sifting), and toss to combine.

Combine butter, brown sugar, white sugar, salt, baking soda, baking powder, vanilla, and nutmeg in the bowl of a stand mixer fitted with a paddle attachment. Mix on low speed to moisten, then increase to medium and beat until light and fluffy, about 5 minutes. With the mixer running, crack in the egg and continue beating until smooth. Reduce speed to low, add flour/chocolate, and mix to form a stiff dough.

Divide into thirty-two 1½-ounce (2-tablespoon) portions or sixty-four ¾-ounces (1-tablespoon) portions. Arrange on parchment-lined aluminum baking sheet, leaving 2 inches between them. Sprinkle with reserved chocolate and a pinch each of kosher salt. Bake until the cookies are puffed and pale gold around the edges but steamy in the middle, about 15 minutes for large, 12 minutes for small. Or, for crunchy cookies, continue baking until golden, 3 to 5 minutes more.

Cool on the baking sheets until set, about 5 minutes. Enjoy warm, or store in an airtight container for up to 2 days at room temperature.

MAKE AHEAD

Divide the portioned dough among several heavy-duty zip-top bags and refrigerate for up to 1 week, or freeze for up to 6 months. Let stand at room temperature until quite soft (about 70°F), and bake as directed.

→ Mix it up!

BROWN BUTTER: Ready for a total knockout? Up the butter to 10 ounces (2¼ sticks) and use 2 eggs. In a 2-quart stainless steel saucier, melt the butter over medium-low heat. Increase to medium and simmer, stirring with a heat-resistant spatula, while the butter hisses and pops. Continue cooking and stirring, scraping up any brown bits that form on the bottom of the pan, until butter is golden yellow and perfectly silent. Pour into the bowl of a stand mixer, making sure to scrape up all the toasty brown bits, and cool until semi-solid and opaque. Proceed with the recipe as directed, incorporating the second egg after the first.

DOUBLE CHOCOLATE: For soft cookies with a brownie-like chocolate intensity, reduce flour to 6 ounces (1⅓ cups) and sift with 6 ounces (2 cups) Dutch-process cocoa powder, such as Cacao Barry Extra Brute. Prepare dough as directed, but flatten each portion into a ¾-inch disc. Bake 8 minutes for small cookies, 10 minutes for large.

HOMEMADE FAMOUS AMOS®: Hypercrisp and crunchy, these bite-sized cookies get an extra layer of flavor and crunch from 4 ounces (1 cup) toasted pecans. Chop along with the chocolate, and proceed with the recipe as directed. Divide into 1 tablespoon (¾ ounce) portions and bake until golden, about 15 minutes. Makes 64 cookies.

MALTED MILK CHOCOLATE: This variation is best with a blend of milk chocolates, one fairly intense and the other a touch milky, such as a mix of Endangered Species 48% and Valrhona's 32% Dulcey. Increase white sugar to 14 ounces (2 cups) and omit brown sugar. Along with butter, add 1 ounce (4 teaspoons) barley malt syrup and 2¼ ounces (½ cup) malted milk powder.

MAPLE WALNUT: Toss 6 ounces (1½ cups) toasted walnut pieces with the flour and chocolate. Increase white sugar to 10½ ounces (1½ cups) and omit brown sugar. Along with the butter, add ¾ teaspoon ground cinnamon and 3 ounces (¼ cup) grade B maple syrup. For either size cookie, bake about 2 minutes longer than directed.

WHITE CHOCOLATE MACADAMIA NUT: Reduce chocolate to 9 ounces (1⅔ cup) of your favorite white chocolate, mixed with 7 ounces (1½ cups) lightly toasted macadamia nuts.

GLUTEN-FREE: Replace the all-purpose flour with 4 ounces (¾ cup) white rice flour, 4 ounces (1 cup) oat flour, and 4 ounces (1 cup) teff flour.

OATMEAL COOKIES

You'd think a cookie made from oats and raisins would date back to some ancient Scottish kitchen, but the recipe's actually rather modern. For most of human history, millers ground or chopped oat kernels into a coarse meal. By nature, those hard little niblets of grain restricted oats to slow-cooked preparations such as porridge.

But Americans had zero interest in toiling over the stove for a bowl of mush, so they relegated oats to a trough in the barn. That view didn't begin to change until the 1850s, when a German immigrant named Ferdinand Schumacher established a mill in Akron, Ohio. Instead of grinding or chopping the kernels, he rolled the oats flat with heavy steel pins, crushing each grain into a delicate flake.

These "rolled oats" cooked in a fraction of the time, amassing a faithful following during the years of the Civil War. Soon enough, other local mills adopted the novel technique as well—including the Quaker Mill Company.[1] These competing mills (including a few in Illinois and Iowa too) merged into various configurations over the years, ultimately forming the American Cereal Company in 1891. The conglomerate chose to maintain the Quaker Mill's mascot, a jolly version of William Penn in a wide-brimmed hat, feeling it best embodied their ideals of wholesome nourishment.

In an effort to expand the market for rolled oats beyond their snug pocket of the Midwest, the American Cereal Company commissioned the Quaker Oats Special in 1892. This spiffy train had fourteen boxcars, each painted like a tin of Quaker Oats. It traveled only during daylight hours, a moving billboard that cut through a thousand backyards in its trek from Cedar Rapids to Portland, Oregon. The Quaker Oats Special stopped at every major depot along the way, serving as a mobile oatmeal museum and distributing free samples of rolled oats to all who came. Newspapers followed its progress across the country, and on April 6, 1892, the *Cedar Rapids Gazette* declared it "the most artistic and thoroughly decorated train ever seen."[2] Once the oatmeal express finally reached Portland,

every family awoke to a trial-sized package of rolled oats stuffed in their mailbox.

Technically speaking the stunt ended there, but rail schedules show the Quaker Oats Line on track through 1897.[3] Two years after that, industry rags like the *The Railway Conductor* joked that the only freeloader never thrown from a train was Mister Quaker Oats, if only because he was firmly painted on.[4] Like a passenger with an expired ticket, the Quaker man lingered for years longer, thanks to a state-of-the-art waterproof finish.

Although the American Cereal Company's repertoire of promotional recipes seemed to begin and end with a back-of-the-box recipe for a loaf of bread, that decade of exposure and excitement set the stage for bakers to experiment with rolled oats at home. Unlike steel-cut oats, thin rolled-oat flakes readily absorb moisture from a dough, making any cookie more thick and chewy by default.

Rolled-oat cookies seemed to multiply throughout cookbooks of the 1890s, and while few recipes called for Quaker Oats by name, they didn't have to—the American Cereal Company virtually controlled the market.[5] Those early oatmeal cookies would have tasted a lot like the ones we make today, with plenty of butter, brown sugar, and cinnamon, but they were raisinless and sadder for it.[6]

See, the raisin train wouldn't get rolling until 1912. No, seriously. An actual "Raisin Train" set out from Fresno in 1912, making its way toward Chicago to spread the gospel of Sun-Maid and the California Associated Raisin Company.[7] And they had good news indeed; in contrast to the dried grapes imported from Spain or Turkey, the short journey from California kept domestic raisins plump, juicy, and *cheap*. Much like the Quaker Oats Special, the Raisin Train prompted a spike in popularity for the humble fruit.

I wish I could say the story ended with a Reese's-style collision of the two trains ("You got raisins in my oatmeal!"), but the popularity of the combo seems more strategic. As it turns out, Sun-Maid and Quaker

Oats once shared the services of Lord and Thomas, one of America's first advertising agencies.[8] I can't help but imagine that when they arranged to publish Sun-Maid's *Souvenir California Raisin Recipe Book* in 1915, some hotshot ad man suggested "Oatmeal Cookies" with Quaker in mind.

Whether by coincidence or design, this recipe added half a pound of California raisins to an otherwise classic oatmeal cookie. The recipe appeared in cookbooks throughout the tumultuous years marked by World War I, the Great Depression, and World War II, perhaps because sweet raisins and starchy oats created a wholesome cookie that could scoot through the lean years with less sugar and flour.[9]

Though they seem undeniably old-fashioned today, oatmeal raisin cookies were once on the cutting edge, relying on a new method for milling oats, a cooperative of California farmers that overthrew an Old World monopoly, a national advertising campaign, and a cross-promotional recipe to boot. With that history in mind, I'm not shy about updating the recipe to include new ingredients like oat flour and cranberries. By reducing the need for traditional all-purpose flour, oat flour keeps the cookies especially tender while playing up their essential flavor. Unlike raisins, dried cranberries are a uniquely American fruit, adding a burst of tart flavor and cheery color that helps my oatmeal cookies stand out.

Dried cranberries add a burst of color and tart flavor to my oatmeal cookies.

TRIPLE-OATMEAL COOKIES

These buttery brown sugar cookies may be loaded with crunchy pecans and tart cranberries, but they're all about the oats: rolled for the heartiness of a granola bar, steel-cut for a toothsome chew, and flour for a tender crumb. Pick up a bag of oat flour online or in stores, usually in the baking aisle. Whole wheat flour will do in a pinch.

YIELD: thirty-two 3-inch cookies | **ACTIVE TIME:** about 20 minutes

⅔ cup | 3 ounces all-purpose flour, such as Gold Medal

¾ cup | 2½ ounces oat flour, such as Bob's Red Mill or Arrowhead Mills

1⅔ cups | 6 ounces old-fashioned rolled oats (not quick-cooking or instant)

¼ cup | 1½ ounces steel-cut or Irish oats

1¼ cups | 5 ounces pecan pieces, toasted

1 cup | 6 ounces dried cranberries

2 sticks | 8 ounces unsalted butter, soft but cool—about 65°F

⅔ packed cup | 5 ounces light brown sugar

½ cup | 3½ ounces white sugar

1½ teaspoons Diamond Crystal kosher salt (half as much if iodized), plus more for sprinkling (optional)

1¼ teaspoons baking soda

½ teaspoon ground cinnamon

1 tablespoon vanilla extract

1 large egg, straight from the fridge

Adjust oven rack to middle position and preheat to 350°F. Sift flour into a medium bowl (if using cup measures, spoon into the cups and level with a knife before sifting). Add oat flour, rolled oats, steel-cut oats, toasted nuts, and dried fruit. (Stored in an airtight container, this mix will keep for 2 months at room temperature.)

Combine butter, brown sugar, white sugar, salt, baking soda, cinnamon, and vanilla in the bowl of a stand mixer fitted with a paddle attachment. Mix on low speed to moisten, then increase to medium and beat for about 30 seconds. With the mixer running, crack in the egg and continue beating until smooth. Reduce speed to low, add the dry ingredients, and mix to form a stiff dough.

Arrange thirty-two 1-ounce (2-tablespoon) portions of dough on parchment-lined aluminum baking sheets, leaving 2 inches between them. Flatten into ½-inch discs; if you like, sprinkle each with a pinch of a salt. Bake until puffed and light gold around the edges but pale and steamy in the middle, about 12 minutes. Cool on the baking sheet until set, about 5 minutes.

Enjoy warm, or store in an airtight container for up to 2 days at room temperature.

MAKE AHEAD
Divide the portioned dough among several heavy-duty zip-top bags and refrigerate for up to 1 week, or freeze for up to 6 months. Let stand at room temperature until quite soft (about 70°F) and bake as directed.

continued ↓

→ Mix it up!

APRICOT–WHITE CHOCOLATE: Tart bursts of chewy apricot, creamy bites of white chocolate, and buttery pistachios make for a sophisticated variation. Replace dried cranberries with 6 ounces (1 cup) dried apricots diced into ¼-inch pieces and swap the pecans for 5 ounces (1 cup) toasted pistachios, roughly chopped. Add 6 ounces (1 cup) white chocolate chunks or chips.

GERMAN CHOCOLATE: With chewy oats and crunchy pecans already in the mix, all you need is a handful of dark chocolate and coconut to turn these cookies into mini–German chocolate cakes. Simply replace the cranberries with 6 ounces (2 cups) sweetened shredded coconut, and toss flour/oat mixture with 12 ounces (2 cups) finely chopped dark chocolate, such as Valrhona's 72% Araguani. Bake until lightly golden all over, about 15 minutes. If you like, drizzle the finished cookies with Chewy Caramel (page 306), cooled until thick but still warm. This variation yields 48 cookies.

TRAIL MIX: To capture the salty-sweet flavor and crunch of trail mix in cookie form, reduce the butter to 6 ounces (1½ sticks) and add 2 ounces (a generous ¼ cup) creamy peanut butter. To complete the illusion, stir in 6 ounces (1 cup) M&M's®.

GLUTEN-FREE: Replace the all-purpose flour with 2 ounces (½ cup) tapioca flour or arrowroot and 2 ounces (½ cup) coconut flour. Prepare the dough as directed, but flatten each portion into a disc prior to baking.

SNICKERDOODLES

When it comes to a name as gooftastic as *snicker-doodle*, I imagine a nonsense word pulled from some lost stanza of *Jabberwocky*. " 'Twas a krinkled puffers cookie / Did shoog and a butter poodle / All fluffled, crisp cinna chewie / And baked ye snickerdoodle." After all, Lewis Carroll insists the vorpal blade went snicker-snack!

Snickerdoodles are indeed a fantastic snack—a particularly thick sort of sugar cookie dusted with cinnamon and baked until crisp around the edges but still soft and chewy in the middle. For obvious reasons, *snickerdoodle* is often dismissed as a nonsense word.[1] Writing about snickerdoodles for the *Philadelphia Times* back in 1902, home economics expert Martha Wentworth mused, "perhaps, though, the very oddity of their name increases their value."[2]

As it turns out, Snickerdoodles may have a perfectly legit linguistic heritage—if not the one most commonly told. The original theory, put forth by James Beard himself, suggested that *snicker* was a prefix akin to the German word *schnecken,* which means "snail." More important, he claimed, it was short for *schneck-ennudeln,* a type of Pennsylvania Dutch cinnamon bun twirled up like the profile of a snail.

Ostensibly, *schneckennudeln* gave way to snick-erdoodles . . . somehow? Sure, both treats are round and involve a dash of cinnamon, but a connection that tenuous is like concluding bagels were named after baguettes simply because they're both a type of bread. The *schnecken* connection seems even less likely once you realize that snickerdoodles evolved from nineteenth-century coffee cakes called Snip Doodles.

The Melrose Household Treasure, a Boston cookbook published in 1877, described the "Snip Doodle" as a cinnamon-scented cake, rich with milk and butter, dusted in sugar, and then baked as a thin sheet to be cut into squares while still warm.[3] That being the case, it seems to me that snip coincides with *shnit,* "to slice," or *shnipla,* "to snip," in old Pennsylvania Dutch.

Thumbing through an 1895 dictionary of Pennsylvania Dutch, I found a few possible origins for the word *doodle* as well: *hoodle* and *doomel.*[4] Both translate as "hurry," which proved to be a common theme throughout the years.[5] "Easy to make when hurried," proclaimed *The Home Maker* magazine of its recipe for snickerdoodles in 1889.[6] Another, from *The Idaho Statesman* in 1901, called snickerdoodles "quickly made little cakes."[7] For informal gatherings, the *Zanesville Signal* suggested a "quick coffee cake, such as the Snickerdoodle," in 1932.[8] A decade after that, *American Notes & Queries* would define snip- and snicker-doodles by their "hasty dusting" of cinnamon sugar.[9]

Regardless of the etymology, snip- and snicker-doodles were meant to be eaten in a hurry as well;[10] with four cut sides exposed to open air, the squares of unfrosted cake would have rapidly staled. So it seems only natural that they evolved into drop cookies by the turn of the century[11]—not that it was a universal switch. Recipes for both snip- and snicker-doodle coffee cakes would persist well into the 1940s and beyond, but the cookie variation was invariably a snickerdoodle.

As early as 1923, Crisco began a national advertising campaign centered around "Mrs. T's Snicker Doodles," a peculiar sort of cupcake chock-full of nuts, spices, and dried fruit and topped with a mace-flavored frosting. The campaign continued through the Great Depression, but needless to say, the recipe was a dud. Yet it introduced America to the idea of snickerdoodles without butter, a trick that took off at the onset of World War II.[12]

Without Crisco toeing the line, bakers settled on snickerdoodles made with a blend of butter and shortening. Thanks to its superior creaming properties and higher fat content, shortening produced a thicker, richer cookie than butter alone. At the same time, less butter made the cinnamon flavor seem more pronounced. Together these changes gave snickerdoodles a unique identity, distinct from simple sugar cookies with cinnamon on top.

The pillowy-soft and chewy snickerdoodles of my

I-love-the-'80s childhood were most certainly made with shortening, but it's hard to get on board with the idea of hydrogenated fat. In my quest for an alternative, I tried everything from ghee to almond oil before settling on a blend of butter and coconut oil. Coconut oil is solid at room temperature, so it creams up light like shortening, with a similar richness.

While my initial experiments centered on refined coconut oil, which tastes completely neutral, I eventually discovered that virgin coconut oil made my snickerdoodles even better. Instead of tasting overtly nutty or tropical, it functions as an aromatic, coaxing out more flavor from both cinnamon and vanilla.

As a bonus, I found that a splash of milk is all it takes to turn my snickerdoodle dough into a snip doodle batter. It's the fluffy coffee cake that started it all, with the added richness of coconut oil to prevent it from staling so fast. It's light, tender, and rich, with a sweet and spicy flavor. What's more, it comes together just as quickly as the old-timey recipes suggest.

The earliest recipes for snip- and snickerdoodles call for baking powder. In fact, snickerdoodles were used in national advertisements for Cleveland Baking Powder as early as 1891.[13] But baking powder wouldn't become a reliable pantry staple for another twenty years, prompting folks at home to create a DIY version with cream of tartar and baking soda, resulting in more pronounced cracks and a slightly sour flavor. For some, this would become the cookie's defining feature, but my recipe is true to the baking powder found in the original.

Chewy cookies or fluffy cake: you decide (see pages 44 and 47).

SNICKERDOODLES

There's nothing quite like the smell of cinnamon sugar wafting from the kitchen, except perhaps discovering its source: a warm tray of snickerdoodles. Their crinkled tops and pillowy thickness come from a blend of butter and coconut oil—a natural alternative to shortening (see pages 41–42). Shape big bakery-style snickerdoodles if you want to invest more real estate in their rich and chewy centers, or downsize if you'd prefer a higher ratio of crispy edges. *See photo on page 43.*

YIELD: thirteen 5-inch cookies or twenty-six 3½-inch cookies | **ACTIVE TIME:** 30 minutes

Cookies:

2⅓ cups | 10½ ounces all-purpose flour, such as Gold Medal

1 stick | 4 ounces unsalted butter, pliable but cool—about 60°F

½ cup | 3½ ounces refined or virgin coconut oil, solid but creamy—about 70°F

1½ cups | 10½ ounces sugar

1¼ teaspoons Diamond Crystal kosher salt (half as much if iodized)

1 teaspoon baking powder

⅛ teaspoon grated nutmeg

1 tablespoon vanilla extract

1 large egg, straight from the fridge

Cinnamon Sugar:

¼ cup | 2 ounces sugar

2 teaspoons ground cinnamon, or to taste

2 teaspoons grated cinnamon, or to taste

Make the dough:

Adjust oven rack to middle position and preheat to 400°F. Sift flour into a medium bowl (if using cup measures, spoon into the cups and level with a knife before sifting).

Combine butter, coconut oil, sugar, salt, baking powder, nutmeg, and vanilla in the bowl of a stand mixer fitted with a paddle attachment. Mix on low speed to moisten, then increase to medium and beat until light and fluffy, about 5 minutes, pausing to scrape with a flexible spatula halfway through. With the mixer running, crack in the egg and continue beating until smooth. Reduce speed to low, add flour, and mix to form a stiff dough.

Divide into thirteen 2½-ounce (¼-cup) portions or twenty-six 1¼-ounce (2-tablespoon) portions.

Dust and bake the cookies:

Mix sugar with ground and grated cinnamon in a small bowl; add more spice if you prefer. Roll each portion of dough into a smooth ball, tumble in Cinnamon Sugar until fully coated, and arrange on parchment-lined aluminum baking sheets, leaving 2½ inches between each. Flatten into ½-inch discs and generously sprinkle with the remaining Cinnamon Sugar.

Bake at 400°F until the Snickerdoodles begin to spread, about 6 minutes for either size, then rotate baking sheet and reduce oven temperature to 350°F. Continue baking until the cookies are firm around the edges but still puffy in the middle, about 5 minutes for small, 8 minutes for large. Cool on the baking sheet until the edges crisp, about 10 minutes.

Enjoy warm, or store in an airtight container for up to 2 days at room temperature.

TROUBLESHOOTING

Older ovens may wildly overshoot 400°F, so use an oven thermometer to ensure the Snickerdoodles won't scorch.

MAKE AHEAD
Divide the portioned dough among several heavy-duty zip-top bags and refrigerate for up to 1 week, or freeze for up to 6 months. Let stand at room temperature until quite soft (about 70°F) and bake as directed. Freeze leftover Cinnamon Sugar in an airtight container up to 2 months, for use in future Snickerdoodles or Snip Doodles (page 47).

→ *Mix it up!*

BACON-BACON: Cook 12 ounces bacon (1 package or 12 strips) on a griddle over medium-low heat until fat is rendered and bacon is golden and chewy, but not yet crisp, about 10 minutes. Transfer to a bed of paper towels, then roughly chop. Cool 3½ ounces (½ cup) bacon fat until solid and creamy, about 70°F, and use in place of coconut oil to make the dough. After rolling the cookies in cinnamon sugar, top the flattened cookie dough with chopped bacon. Otherwise, bake and cool as directed.

BANANA BREAD: Sift flour with 1 ounce (¼ cup) oat flour. Mash 5 ounces (⅔ cup) ripe banana with ¼ teaspoon ground cloves to add after the egg. Fold 6 ounces (1½ cups) toasted walnut pieces into the finished dough. Portion and roll in cinnamon sugar, but do not flatten, as this dough will spread nicely on its own. Bake as directed.

COOKIES AND CREAM: My favorite ice cream in cookie form. Roughly chop 8 ounces Homemade Oreo® Cookies (page 212; about 20 sandwich cookies) and freeze until hard, about 2 hours. Stir into the dough after adding the flour. Portion and shape as directed, but skip the Cinnamon Sugar. Bake at 350°F until firm around the edges but pale and steamy in the center, about 12 minutes for small cookies, 15 minutes for large.

OATMEAL STREUSEL: After flattening the sugar-dusted cookies, top with a sprinkling of frozen Snickerstreusel (page 48). You'll need about one teaspoon per small cookie, or two teaspoons per large (5 ounces or 1 cup total). Otherwise, bake as directed.

TAHITIAN COCONUT: Make the dough with virgin coconut oil and a teaspoon of pure coconut extract in addition to the vanilla. For the topping, omit the cinnamon and blend the sugar with the seeds from Tahitian vanilla bean, split lengthwise and scraped with a paring knife.

GLUTEN-FREE: It takes an arsenal of gluten-free flours to give Snickerdoodles the same chewy/crisp texture, but the results are identical to the original. Replace the all-purpose flour with 4 ounces (1 cup) almond flour, 3 ounces (¾ cup) tapioca flour or arrowroot, 2 ounces (½ cup) mochiko, 1 ounce (¼ cup) coconut flour, and ½ ounce (1 tablespoon) teff flour. This variation is not suitable for Snip Doodles.

Custom Snickerdoodles

In my research, I occasionally ran across snickerdoodles coated in brown sugar, or white sugar flavored with lemon zest or cocoa powder. I consider these historical variations a sign that no recipe is set in stone, so feel free to pick and choose from the options below to create your own custom blend. Toss everything together in the bowl of a food processor and pulse until well combined.

Sugar Sprinkle. Start with 1½ ounces (¼ cup) sugar.	*Roasted Sugar* (page 102) to mellow the sweetness with a hint of caramel
	Light or dark brown sugar to deepen the flavor of malt and spice (see below)
	Maple sugar to bring an earthy sweetness to coffee, chocolate, and/or spice (see below)
	White sugar to allow subtle flavors like vanilla and lavender to shine
	Turbinado or *demerara sugar* to give the cookies a crunchy shell
Primary Flavor. Add one of these bold ingredients to establish a base note, or skip to Aromatics.	1½ teaspoons matcha (see page 22)
	1½ teaspoons Dutch-process or natural cocoa powder
	¼ cup (¾ ounce) malted milk powder (this is not gluten-free)
	2 tablespoons (⅛ ounce) dried lavender buds, preferably organic
	1 teaspoon instant espresso powder, such as Medaglia d'Oro
Aromatics. Add one aromatic top note.	Seeds from 1 vanilla bean (pod reserved for another use)
	2 teaspoons orange zest or 1 teaspoon lemon zest
	2 teaspoons pumpkin pie spice
	1½ teaspoons ground ginger

Snip Doodles

Snip Doodles are a snap. A splash of milk transforms my Snickerdoodle dough into a thick batter that's spread onto a baking sheet and sprinkled with cinnamon sugar—a casual coffee cake that puffs up soft and tender under a crinkly crust. No scooping, no rolling, no fuss. It's best warm from the oven with a mug of coffee, or dressed up with a dollop of silky Make-Ahead Whipped Cream (page 89). *See photo on page 43.*

YIELD: 20 pieces, roughly 3 inches square │ **ACTIVE TIME:** 20 minutes

1 tablespoon all-purpose flour or cornstarch for dusting

1 recipe Snickerdoodle dough (page 44), prepared up through the addition of the egg

1 cup | 8 ounces milk (any percentage will do)

1 recipe Cinnamon Sugar or any Sugar Sprinkle (page 46)

Adjust oven rack to middle position and preheat to 350°F. Lightly grease an aluminum baking sheet, dust with flour, and tap out the excess.

Prepare the Snickerdoodle dough according to the recipe, pausing after the egg. Mixing on low, sprinkle in a third of the flour, followed by a third of the milk, alternating between the two until fully incorporated and smooth. Fold once or twice with a flexible spatula to ensure the batter is well mixed from the bottom up, then scrape onto the prepared baking sheet. Spread into a 15-by-11-inch layer and dust with Cinnamon Sugar. Bake until the cake is puffed and firm, about 15 minutes; a toothpick inserted into the center should emerge with a few crumbs attached. Cool for roughly 10 minutes to set the crumb, then "snip" into squares with a pizza wheel or knife. Serve warm.

Wrapped tightly in foil, Snip Doodles will keep for up to 3 days at room temperature.

Snickerstreusel

As it turns out, the ratio of cinnamon and sugar I prefer in Snickerdoodles adds just the right balance of sweetness and spice in buttery oatmeal streusel. What's more, so will any of my Custom Snickerdoodle Sugar Sprinkles, offering exponential possibilities. Start with lavender-vanilla sugar and finish with almonds for a delicate topping on blueberry muffins, or combine ginger-maple sugar with pecans to scatter over a loaf of banana bread or Butternut Pumpkin Pie (page 166).

YIELD: about 1½ cups (8 ounces) | **ACTIVE TIME:** 15 minutes

1 recipe Cinnamon Sugar or any Sugar Sprinkle (page 46)

¼ teaspoon Diamond Crystal kosher salt (half as much if iodized)

¼ cup | 1 ounce all-purpose or whole wheat flour (use oat flour or kinako for gluten-free)

½ cup | 2 ounces old-fashioned rolled oats (not quick-cooking or instant)

3 tablespoons | 1½ ounces unsalted butter, very soft—about 70°F

⅓ cup | 2 ounces chopped almonds, hazelnuts, or pecans

Combine Cinnamon Sugar (or Sugar Sprinkle), salt, flour, oats, and butter in the bowl of a stand mixer fitted with a paddle attachment and mix on low until mealy and fine. Fold in nuts by hand. Divide evenly between two pint zip-top bags (about ¾ cup | 4 ounces each) and freeze for up to 6 months. Use frozen. Each bag is enough to cover a 9-by-5-inch loaf of quick bread, a dozen muffins, or a 9-inch pie.

PEANUT BUTTER COOKIES

It's tempting to think the invention of peanut butter cookies must have hinged on the debut of grocery store peanut butter in the twentieth century, but American bakers are a determined lot. Our first recipes appeared in the 1890s, calling for a cup or more of peanuts minced with a knife, pounded fine, or fed through a meat grinder.[1]

These techniques crammed a ton of peanut flavor into every bite but didn't express any of the natural oils, so the peanuts functioned more like a flour than a fat. While a few recipes took advantage of that fact with crispy cut-out cookies, others added milk until the dough was soft enough to drop from a spoon.[2]

Even as peanut butter became more widely available at the turn of the century, it was slow to catch on as an ingredient, probably because it wasn't the cheap treat we know today.[3] At the Simpson Crawford department store in Manhattan, peanut butter went for thirty cents a pound—three cents more than butter itself (nearly a buck more, once you adjust for inflation).[4] But the price came down quickly enough, and by 1909, the *Indianapolis Star* featured a batch of "Peanut Cookies" made with an entire jar.[5]

Such recipes took hold during World War I, when the United States Department of Agriculture issued regular bulletins on the "Food Value of Peanut Butter" to help households get more protein on "Meatless Tuesday" (Uncle Sam wouldn't catch on to the power of alliteration until the next world war, with Meatless Mondays).[6] These pamphlets were packed with some pretty kooky recipes (peanut butter omelets, anyone?)

but their peanut butter cookies were spot on, relying on peanut butter to mask the flavor of nonrationed flours like barley and rye.[7]

Whether in cookies or simple sandwiches, peanut butter remained a family favorite after the end of the war, leading to a boom in peanut-centric snacks in the 1920s (see pages 216 and 297). At the same time, manufacturers worked to improve peanut butter's shelf life and eliminate the oily layer that always rose to the top of the jar. Their solution involved blending peanut butter with hydrogenated oil, creating a smooth emulsion with a higher melting point that kept the peanut oil solid at room temperature—and beyond, as it turned out. With the addition of hydrogenated fat, doughs made from peanut butter melted more slowly in the oven, making the cookies more chewy and thick.[8]

Peanut butter would go on to be a staple of the Great Depression, when the cookies were stripped down to the bare essentials: a cup of sugar, a cup of peanut butter, an egg, and a cup of flour.[9] It's the recipe most of us know today, chubby, soft, and rich. While there's no arguing with its economy and convenience, I couldn't help but wonder if we weren't missing out on what older recipes had to offer.

My recipe brings butter back into the equation, but only enough to help the peanut butter cream up fluffy and light. That aeration offsets the dense, sometimes oily texture of pure peanut butter to give the cookies a more open crumb. I've also adopted the ground peanuts so common to nineteenth-century recipes for a boost in flavor and tenderness (no meat grinder required).

HONEY-ROASTED PEANUT BUTTER COOKIES

These salty-sweet cookies are chewy and intense, with a double dose of flavor from the honey-roasted peanut flour—a thirty-second project that keeps them tender and rich. They're one of those rare cookies that improve with age, making them one of my favorite options for cookie jars and care packages alike. *See photo on page 52.*

YIELD: thirty-four 3-inch cookies | **ACTIVE TIME:** about 25 minutes

1 cup | 4½ ounces all-purpose flour, such as Gold Medal

1¼ cups | 6 ounces salted honey-roasted peanuts

1¼ cups | 10 ounces creamy peanut butter

1 stick | 4 ounces unsalted butter, soft but cool—about 65°F

1½ cups | 10 ounces sugar

¾ teaspoon Diamond Crystal kosher salt (half as much if iodized)

¾ teaspoon baking soda

½ teaspoon baking powder

2 teaspoons vanilla extract

1 large egg, straight from the fridge, well beaten

3 tablespoons | 1½ ounces milk (any percentage will do)

Adjust oven rack to middle position and preheat to 350°F. Sift flour into the bowl of a food processor (if using a cup measure, spoon into the cup and level with a knife before sifting). Add peanuts and pulse until fine, about 1 minute. (In an airtight container, this mixture will keep at room temperature for up to a month.)

Combine peanut butter, butter, sugar, salt, baking soda, baking powder, and vanilla in the bowl of a stand mixer fitted with a paddle attachment. Mix on low speed to moisten, then increase to medium and beat until soft and light, about 3 minutes. With the mixer running, add the egg in two additions, mixing until each one is well incorporated. Reduce speed to low and add the peanut flour, followed by the milk, mixing to form a very soft dough.

Divide into thirty-four 1⅛-ounce (2-tablespoon) portions. Arrange on a parchment-lined aluminum baking sheet, leaving 2 inches between them. Bake until the edges are firm and just barely beginning to brown but the cookies are still puffed and steamy in the middle, about 16 minutes. Cool on the baking sheet until the crumb is set, about 10 minutes.

Enjoy warm, or store in an airtight container for up to 1 week at room temperature.

MAKE AHEAD

Refrigerate the portioned dough on a wax paper–lined cutting board until firm, about 30 minutes. Divide among several heavy-duty zip-top bags and refrigerate for up to 1 week, or freeze for up to 6 months. Let stand at room temperature until quite soft (about 70°F) and bake as directed.

→ Mix it up!

COCONUT WHITE CHOCOLATE: This variation adds the nutty, chewy texture of coconut to the already nutty cookies, along with pockets of creamy white chocolate. Simply stir 6 ounces (2 cups) sweetened shredded coconut and 6 ounces (1 cup) finely chopped white chocolate into the finished dough.

E.T. COOKIES: Back in the 1980s, our local supermarket sold peanut butter cookies with Reese's Pieces® to cash in on the popularity of America's favorite extraterrestrial. When I'm craving that nostalgic combination, I stir one 10-ounce bag (1⅓ cups) Reese's Pieces into the dough. Portion and bake as directed.

PB&J: Okay, so there's no actual J in this variation, but chewy dried cherries add a sweet-tart flavor reminiscent of that childhood classic. Stir about 6 ounces (1 cup) dried cherries into the dough.

SNICKERDOODLE STYLE: The chewy/crisp dynamic of a peanut butter cookie reminds me of Snickerdoodles (page 44), a vibe you can play up by rolling the portioned dough in 6 ounces (¾ cup) of Vanilla Bean Sugar Sprinkle, one of the Alternative Snickerdoodle Sprinkles on page 46. Otherwise, bake as directed.

GLUTEN-FREE: Replace the all-purpose flour with 1¾ ounces (½ cup) oat flour, 1 ounce (¼ cup) coconut flour, and ½ ounce (2 tablespoons) tapioca flour or arrowroot.

Thick, chewy, and super peanut buttery Honey-Roasted Peanut Butter Cookies (page 50).

BROWNIES AND BLONDIES

In the 1880s, way before every party had to be Pinterest-worthy, magazines like *Good Housekeeping* and *Ladies' Home Journal* popularized "Brown Dinners," the blandest of all possible theme parties, complete with such drabtastic delights as brown soup, brown bread, browned potatoes, turkey with brown sauce, and brownies.[1] And before you get too excited, I should explain "brownies" was nineteenth-century slang for panfried mushrooms.

These monochromatic meals morphed into Brownie Banquets during the 1890s,[2] birthday buffets filled with kid-friendly browns: graham crackers, chocolate ice cream, and brownies too—this time in the form of chewy molasses cakes.[3] A typical recipe, this one pulled from the Boston Cooking School's 1896 cookbook, called for equal parts butter, powdered sugar, and molasses, three parts bread flour, and an egg. Like gingerbread, but without any spices. Yum.

But the guests of honor were a different sort of Brownie—the potbellied, pointy-eared gnomes created by Canadian author and illustrator Palmer Cox. Brownies attended each banquet in the form of paper dolls and figurines, available from general stores or the five-and-dime. That's also where you'd find the Brownies' adventures, for sale in children's magazines or anthologies like *The Brownies at Home*.

Brownies were so popular that the Chicago World's Fair commissioned Palmer to send the Brownies to the Columbian Exposition via a special edition of their adventures published in 1893.[4] This early take on viral marketing built buzz for the Fair to bolster attendance of the Children's Pavilion,[5] where chefs prepared meals in the "kitchen-garden" and astronomy expert Mary Proctor taught a class on "Brownies in the Sky."[6]

It's as likely a place as any for a treat like chocolate brownies to emerge, particularly when you consider their origin is historically credited to a chef at Chicago's Palmer House Hotel. According to legend, socialite Bertha Palmer demanded that the hotel prepare some dainty treat her high-society friends could nibble without forks. Rising to the occasion, the chef invented a simple chocolate cake so rich it required no frosting.

While Bertha was no frivolous debutante, she did co-own the hotel and distinguished herself as a feminist, philanthropist, and public speaker. She also chaired the 1893 World's Fair Board of Lady Managers, overseeing the development and implementation of both the Women's and Children's Pavilions.[7]

So between Bertha Palmer, Palmer Cox, and Brownies at every turn, it's hard to resist the notion that chocolate brownies were born in Chicago around 1893. While there's nothing to definitively tie brownies to the Fair, a Chicago cookbook published a recipe for unleavened chocolate cake in 1899[8]—the oldest proto-brownie I know.

The first recipe to call brownies by name, though, was published on January 22, 1904, in the *Lowell Sun*. It called for a cup of sugar, a half cup of butter, two eggs, two squares of chocolate, and a half cup of flour, without any added liquids or leavening. It's the very ratio of ingredients we use in brownies today, and that same recipe appeared at least twice more in 1904: once as an anonymous contribution to Chicago's *Service Club Cook Book*,[9] and again in *Home Cookery*, a community cookbook assembled by the Laconia Woman's Club in New Hampshire.[10]

Given the timeline and diverse locations, it seems less likely that these recipes borrowed from each other than that they drew from a common source. Until someone can uncover an older recipe, I'd like to imagine the missing link had something to do with the Chicago World's Fair. The recipe for brownies in *Home Cookery* was submitted by Eleanora Quinby, whose relative Senator Henry Quinby oversaw New Hampshire's participation at the Fair.[11] The book itself was edited by Laura Hibbard, whose brother Charles had a photography exhibit at the fair entitled "Old Man of the Mountain," incidentally housed at the Smithsonian today. Even if those connections didn't take Eleanora and Laura to Chicago in 1893, both women were in prime position to have heard firsthand accounts, or to have received some souvenir. The plot thickens in 1905, when the Laconia Woman's Club hosted baking expert Fannie Farmer.[12] Perhaps they welcomed her to town with a batch of Eleanora's brownies, because in 1906, chocolate brownies appeared in Fannie Farmer's *Boston Cooking School Cook Book* for the very first time.

That 1906 recipe was fundamentally unlike the molasses brownies of previous editions, and much closer to Eleanora's, with half as much butter, a bit more flour, and only one egg (enough tweaks that any baker could feel comfortable calling the recipe her own). It was this recipe that brought brownies to the national stage, and recipes multiplied through newspapers, cookbooks, and advertisements in the early 1900s.

These were invariably made by creaming the butter and sugar together as for a traditional cake, but Swans Down changed the game with an all-new recipe for brownies in its 1929 mail-order cookbooklet, *Home Baked Delicacies*. The ratio of ingredients matched Eleanora's recipe, but the directions called for whipping the eggs with sugar and for melting the butter and chocolate into a sort of ganache. This made brownies more fudgy than cakey, and it remains the most common method today.

My brownies share roughly the same ratio of sugar, eggs, chocolate, and butter as Eleanora's recipe, and the same amount of dry ingredients. But instead of using flour alone, I traded about forty percent of it for cocoa powder to create an even more intense flavor. The ingredients are assembled according to that old Swans Down recipe, with a twist—brown butter. Aside from adding a nutty flavor to complement the brown sugar and chocolate, it reduces the water content for a brownie that's more fudgy, tender, and rich.

I've also included a recipe for blondies, a word that entered the vernacular with Duncan Hines Blonde Brownie Mix in the 1940s. The very idea of brownies without chocolate made them seem like something of an oxymoron, and folks ever since have been defining (and rejecting) blondies over what they lack: chocolate. My recipe rescues blondies from that reputation by making them equal to brownies in every way, based on the same recipe but loaded with white chocolate instead of dark, and with malted milk powder in place of cocoa. The result is a blondie with the same chewy texture and a crinkly crust but a powerhouse butterscotch flavor all its own.

Dark chocolate for brownies (page 56) with a glossy, paper-thin crust. White chocolate for blondies (page 58) with a rich, butterscotchy chew.

GLOSSY FUDGE BROWNIES

I'm obsessed with that fragile, crinkly, paper-thin brownie crust. It's the sign of a well-balanced recipe, and a solid indicator of the goodness to come. I'm naturally biased, but my brownies live up to the hype implied by their shimmery crust. They're chewy but tender, and impossibly dark because where most brownies start with cocoa or chocolate, I grab both. *See photo on page 55.*

YIELD: twenty-four 2½-inch squares | **ACTIVE TIME:** 40 minutes

1 cup | 4½ ounces all-purpose flour, such as Gold Medal

1⅓ cups | 4 ounces Dutch-process cocoa powder, such as Cacao Barry Extra Brute

3 sticks | 12 ounces unsalted butter

1 cup | 6 ounces roughly chopped dark chocolate, about 72%

2¼ cups | 16 ounces white sugar

¼ cup packed | 2 ounces light brown sugar

1¾ teaspoons Diamond Crystal kosher salt (half as much if iodized)

6 large eggs, straight from the fridge

1 tablespoon vanilla extract

1 teaspoon instant espresso powder, such as Medaglia d'Oro (optional)

Get ready:

Adjust oven rack to middle position and preheat to 350°F. Line a 9-by-13-by-2-inch aluminum baking pan with two crisscrossed sheets of foil so that the bottom and long sides are covered, leaving an overhang on the long sides, and grease lightly. Sift flour and cocoa together (if using cup measures, spoon into the cups and level with a knife before sifting).

In a 2-quart stainless steel saucier, melt butter over medium-low heat. Increase to medium and simmer, stirring with a heat-resistant spatula while the butter hisses and pops. Continue cooking and stirring, scraping up any brown bits that form in the bottom of the pan, until the butter is golden yellow and perfectly silent. Remove from heat and stir in chocolate; the mixture will seem quite thin.

Make the brownies:

Combine white sugar, brown sugar, salt, eggs, vanilla, and instant espresso, if using, in the bowl of a stand mixer fitted with the whisk attachment. Whip on medium-high speed until thick and fluffy, about 8 minutes. Reduce to low and pour in warm chocolate-butter. Once incorporated, add flour/cocoa and continue until well combined. Fold with a flexible spatula, to ensure the batter is well mixed from the bottom up.

Pour into the prepared pan and bake until the brownies are glossy and just barely firm (like the soft part of your forearm), about 25 minutes (or 205°F). Cool to room temperature.

Tug the foil loose and lift the brownies from the pan. Cut into twenty-four 2½-inch squares. Store in an airtight container with a sheet of wax paper between each layer for up to 1 week at room temperature. Leftover brownies can be chopped into bite-sized pieces and frozen for up to 6 months, a fantastic mix-in for your favorite homemade ice cream.

will be fine, albeit with a more deeply toasted flavor.

While warm, these brownies may seem cakey and light (which is easy to mistake for

overbaked), but as they cool, their crumb becomes more dense, compact, and fudgy.

→ *Mix it up!*

CREAM CHEESE: With nuggets of cream cheese studded throughout the batter, this variation cuts the chocolate intensity with bursts of tangy freshness. Freeze an 8-ounce block of cream cheese until firm, then cut into ½-inch chunks and freeze for 30 minutes more. Fold the frozen cream cheese into the batter and bake as directed.

DANGER BROWNIES: This variation ensures every brownie has a few crispy edge pieces, making each more dangerously alluring. While the brownies are cooling, bring 4 ounces (½ cup) heavy cream to a gentle simmer; off heat, whisk in 3 ounces (½ cup) finely chopped dark chocolate. Transfer cooled brownies to a cutting board, trim a ½-inch strip off the outer edges, and dice into ½-inch chunks; set aside in a large bowl. Cut the remaining brownie into about sixteen pieces, topping each with a small mountain of gooey brownie chunks.

HAZELNUT BROWNIES (GLUTEN-FREE): Without flour, the brownies bake up remarkably like a European torte, with a sophisticated flavor perfect for any dinner party. Replace the all-purpose flour with 7 ounces (1¾ cups) hazelnut flour or an equal weight of toasted, skinned hazelnuts pulsed with the cocoa in a food processor until powdery and fine, about 1 minute.

MILKY SWIRL: In the oven, condensed milk thickens to a gooey caramel-like consistency that's firm enough to slice but still creamy and soft. Spread the batter in the pan as directed, then use the back of a spoon to create 15 shallow wells. Fill each with a tablespoon of chilled Quick Condensed Milk (page 169), then drag a dull knife through the center of each to create gentle swirls. Bake as directed.

WHITE CHOCOLATE BUTTERSCOTCH BLONDIES

My blondies aren't exactly typical fare. They're loaded with brown butter, white chocolate, and malted milk powder, giving them a flavor reminiscent of a butterscotch milkshake crossed with a malt ball. They're as chewy and rich as any brownies, with the same glossy, crinkly crust, which comes from cocoa butter—so be sure not to skimp on the quality of the white chocolate. *See photo on page 55.*

YIELD: twenty-four 2½-inch squares │ **ACTIVE TIME:** 40 minutes

2½ cups │ 11½ ounces all-purpose flour, such as Gold Medal

2 sticks │ 8 ounces unsalted butter

1¼ cups │ 7 ounces chopped 31% white chocolate, such as Republica del Cacao or Caramelized White Chocolate (page 60)

2 packed cups │ 16 ounces light brown sugar

½ cup │ 3½ ounces white sugar

½ cup │ 2 ounces malted milk powder

1¾ teaspoons Diamond Crystal kosher salt (half as much if iodized)

6 large eggs, straight from the fridge

1 tablespoon vanilla extract

Get ready:

Adjust oven rack to middle position and preheat to 350°F. Line a 9-by-13-by-2-inch aluminum baking pan with two overlapping sheets of foil so that the bottom and long sides are covered, and grease lightly. Sift flour into a medium bowl (if using cup measures, spoon into the cups and level with a knife before sifting).

In a 2-quart stainless steel saucier, melt butter over medium-low heat. Increase to medium and simmer, stirring with a heat-resistant spatula while the butter hisses and pops. Continue cooking and stirring, scraping up any brown bits that form in the bottom of the pan, until the butter is golden yellow and perfectly silent. Remove from heat and stir in white chocolate; the mixture will seem quite thin.

Make the blondies:

Combine brown sugar, white sugar, malted milk powder, salt, eggs, and vanilla in the bowl of a stand mixer fitted with the whisk attachment. Whip on medium-high speed until thick and fluffy, about 8 minutes. Reduce speed to low and pour in warm chocolate-butter. Once incorporated, add flour and continue until well combined. Fold with a flexible spatula to ensure the batter is well mixed from the bottom up.

Pour into the prepared pan and bake until the blondies are golden, glossy, and just barely firm (like the soft part of your forearm), about 35 minutes (or 210°F). Cool 1 hour to room temperature.

Tug the foil loose and lift the blondies from the pan. Cut into twenty-four 2½-inch squares. Store in an airtight container with a sheet of wax paper between each layer for up to 1 week at room temperature. Leftover blondies can be chopped into bite-sized pieces and frozen for up to 6 months, a fantastic mix-in for your favorite homemade ice cream.

TROUBLESHOOTING
See Brownies, page 56.

→ *Mix it up!*

DANGER BLONDIES: This variation ensures every blondie has a few crispy edge pieces, making each more dangerously alluring. While the blondies are cooling, bring 2 ounces (¼ cup) heavy cream to a gentle simmer; off heat, whisk in 4 ounces (⅔ cup) finely chopped Caramelized White Chocolate (page 60). Transfer cooled blondies to a cutting board, trim a ½-inch strip off the outer edges, and dice into ½-inch chunks; set aside in a large bowl. Cut the remaining blondie into about sixteen pieces, topping each with a small mountain of gooey blondie chunks.

PEANUT BUTTER SWIRL: The blonde-on-blonde swirl is almost invisible, but you can't miss the burst of salty goodness in every bite. Spread the batter into the pan as directed, then use the back of a spoon to create 15 shallow wells. Fill each with a tablespoon of creamy peanut butter, preferably commercial, then drag a dull knife through the center of each to create gentle swirls. Bake as directed.

GLUTEN-FREE: Omit the malted milk powder and replace the all-purpose flour with 4 ounces (¾ cup) white rice flour, 4 ounces (1 cup) tapioca flour, 2 ounces (½ cup) cornstarch, and 2 ounces (⅔ cup) kinako (see page 21).

Caramelized White Chocolate

In the gentle heat of a low oven, white chocolate turns to molten gold, taking on a malty complexity far superior to bagged butterscotch chips. Cooled and crumbled into pieces, Caramelized White Chocolate is one of my favorite additions to Chopped Chocolate Chip Cookies (page 34) and White Chocolate Butterscotch Blondies (page 58), but it can also be melted and whipped into Marshmallow Buttercream (page 114) or turned into a butterscotch variation of my Homemade Magic Shell (page 355).

YIELD: about 2 cups (12 ounces) │ **ACTIVE TIME:** 90 minutes, largely unattended

2¼ cups | 12 ounces pure white chocolate (not chips), such as Valrhona's 35% Ivoire

Preheat the oven to 250°F. Roughly chop the white chocolate and scatter into an 8-inch glass or ceramic baking dish. "Roast" the white chocolate until golden and thick, pausing to stir every 10 minutes. It will take roughly 65 minutes total, though you won't notice much change in color or texture until after the 30-minute mark.

Scrape the melted chocolate onto a sheet of parchment and refrigerate until hard, 15 minutes, then chop or crumble into ¼-inch pieces. Store up to 6 months in an airtight container at room temperature. Use in place of butterscotch baking chips, or to replace plain white chocolate in cakes, cookies, and custards. Caramelized White Chocolate can't be the "seed" when tempering chocolate, though it can be tempered with other methods.

→ Let's get crazy!

GANACHE: bring 6 ounces (¾ cup) heavy cream to a full boil in a 2-quart stainless steel saucier. Add 12 ounces (2 cups) Caramelized White Chocolate and whisk until smooth. Use to glaze Homemade Hostess®-Style Cupcakes (page 247) or Boston Cream Pie (page 105).

S'MORES

The strange tradition of combining warm marshmallows, chocolate, and graham crackers comes from an even stranger tradition, the "Marshmallow Marguerite." This decidedly old-fashioned "dainty" was popularized by the Boston Cooking School's cookbooks and magazines, which featured the recipe and its many variations throughout the years.

Most involved saltines topped with buttered marshmallows, toasted together in the oven to serve with cocoa or tea. Like peanut butter crackers or ants on a log, it was the sort of low-key recipe that didn't need to be written down, yet somehow appeared in magazines again and again, including a graham cracker variation from *Good Housekeeping* in 1910.[1]

Marguerites wouldn't get a major upgrade until 1913, when the January issue of *Table Talk* suggested spreading warm chocolate over sweet crackers or saltines before adding the melted marshmallows.[2] The recipe must have been something of a grassroots phenomenon, as the National Biscuit Company rolled out its own version ten months later: Nabisco Mallowmars.

Almost overnight, an embarrassingly simple snack became a mass-produced commodity: a single graham cracker kissed with marshmallow "creme" and encased in a chocolate shell. It would be another fourteen years before the combination returned to its DIY roots, with the 1927 publication of "Some More" in the handbook *Tramping and Trailing with the Girl Scouts*.[3] This lighthearted approach to Marguerites transported the recipe to the great outdoors, where the messy shower of graham cracker crumbs, dripping chocolate, and gooey marshmallows could be enjoyed with abandon.

Perhaps because of their fireside reputation, s'mores come around but once or twice a year, according to our own traditions. For me, it's when the weather turns cool enough to justify gathering around a bonfire with friends, a rarity that makes homemade graham crackers and marshmallows worth the extra effort—an autumn ritual as memorable as carving jack-o'-lanterns, visiting an orchard, or raking up the golden leaves.

Fresh from-scratch marshmallows aren't as sweet as the ones you buy at the store, making them a better match for creamy milk chocolate. Better yet, each hand-cut cube provides more surface area for toasting. That gives them a deep caramel-vanilla flavor that stands up to my hearty Whole Wheat Grahams (the secret to a s'more fantastic crunch).

Getting back to the heritage of Marshmallow Marguerites, my method of assembly starts with melted chocolate (tempered so it stays glossy and crisp). Spread onto the bottom of every graham, it delivers the same amount of chocolate you'd get in a Hershey's bar, but split into thin layers that melt more quickly, for extra gooey s'mores.

Marshies

Go ahead, make a mess.

CHOCOLATE-COVERED S'MORES

Smashing roasted marshmallows, chocolate bars, and graham crackers together is easy enough, but there's one thing that's always bothered me more than it should—the chocolate never fully melts. So, instead of whole chocolate bars, I coat my graham crackers with tempered chocolate. It delivers the same amount of chocolate overall, but it's split into two thin layers that quickly melt against the heat of a toasted marshmallow to deliver chocolatey goodness from above and below.

YIELD: eight 2¼-by-4¾-inch sandwiches | **ACTIVE TIME:** about 30 minutes | **DOWNTIME:** 15-minute refrigeration

16 Crispy Whole Wheat Graham Crackers (page 202), or any variation

2 cups | 12 ounces roughly chopped dark, milk, or white chocolate

½ recipe (16 cubes | 8 ounces) Buttered Vanilla Marshmallows (page 65), or any variation

Arrange the grahams, bottom side up, on a baking sheet. Temper chocolate according to the directions on pages 292–93, then spread 1 heaping tablespoon (¾ ounce) over each cracker. Smooth the chocolate from edge to edge with an offset spatula and refrigerate for 15 minutes to harden the chocolate. (The grahams can be stored in an airtight container, with a sheet of wax paper between each layer, for up to a week at cool room temperature or for up to 1 month in the fridge.)

For each S'more slide 2 marshmallows onto a bamboo skewer (or stick). Hold directly over an open flame, turning frequently until golden brown, then sandwich between the chocolatey sides of 2 graham crackers and devour.

→ *Mix it up!*

DESIGNER S'MORES: With chocolate transfer sheets, you can print your S'mores with a flurry of white chocolate snowflakes, golden cocoa butter stars, or even delightfully tacky zebra stripes. You only need two 16-by-10-inch chocolate transfer sheets, available online from brands like Global Sugar Arts and Pfeil & Holing.

Place each transfer sheet textured side up on a cutting board. Coat the grahams in tempered chocolate as described above, then gently press into the transfer sheet (chocolate side down). Refrigerate as directed, and the pattern will transfer to the chocolate as it cools.

REVERSE S'MORES: Prepare Crispy Whole Wheat Graham Crackers according to the Chocolate variation on page 204, coat in tempered white chocolate, and pair with the Graham Cracker Crunch variation of Buttered Vanilla Marshmallows (page 66).

Marshmallows as soft and light as a cloud.

Buttered Vanilla Marshmallows

Fresh marshmallows are unbelievably tender and soft, like an airy vanilla mousse in candy form. Even so, they're sturdy enough to toast over an open flame, where each cube offers more crispy caramelization (if toasting isn't on the agenda, check out the Hot Cocoa variation). In a break with tradition, my marshmallows include a spoonful of melted butter to enhance their aroma and silky-smooth texture.

YIELD: thirty-six ½-ounce cubes, about 1½ inches square | **ACTIVE TIME:** 1 hour | **DOWNTIME:** 2-hour refrigeration

3 envelopes (2 tablespoons plus ¾ teaspoon | ¾ ounce) unflavored gelatin powder

½ cup | 4 ounces cool water to bloom the gelatin

1½ teaspoons vanilla extract and/or 1 vanilla bean

½ cup | 4 ounces water for the sugar syrup

⅓ cup plus 2 tablespoons | 5 ounces light corn syrup

1¾ cups | 12 ounces sugar

Heaping ¼ teaspoon Diamond Crystal kosher salt (half as much if iodized)

1 tablespoon | ½ ounce unsalted butter, melted

⅓ cup | 1½ ounces organic powdered sugar, sifted

Temperature Note: Most marshmallow mishaps are temperature related. They're thick and tough if cooked above 250°F, gooey if not cooled to 212°F, or pitifully dense should the syrup drop below 205°F. Avoid these problems with an accurate digital thermometer, which should register 212°F in a pot of boiling water.

Make the marshmallow base:
In a small bowl, mix gelatin with ½ cup (4 ounces) cool water and vanilla extract, if using. Split a vanilla bean, if using, lengthwise with a paring knife, run the flat of the blade down each half to scrape out the seeds, and add to the gelatin, without stirring.

Combine remaining ½ cup (4 ounces) water, corn syrup, sugar, and salt in a 3-quart stainless steel pot and set over medium heat. Stir mixture with a fork until bubbling, about 5 minutes, then increase heat to medium-high. Clip on a digital thermometer and cook, *without stirring*, until the clear syrup registers 250°F, about 5 minutes.

Transfer the thermometer to the bowl of a stand mixer and pour in the hot syrup all at once, scraping the pot with a heat-resistant spatula. Cool to exactly 212°F, about 6 minutes. Add gelatin. With the whisk attachment, mix on low speed until gelatin is melted, then increase to medium-high and whip until thick, snowy white, roughly tripled in volume, and beginning to ball up around the whisk, about 10 minutes. Reduce the speed to low, add melted butter,

return to medium-high, and beat for a few seconds more.

Scrape the creamy marshmallows into a lightly greased 8-inch square baking pan, spreading it into an even layer. Cover with foil and refrigerate until firm, about 2 hours (or let stand overnight at room temperature).

Cut the marshmallows:
Sift some powdered sugar over the marshmallow, invert onto a cutting board, and pry it loose with your fingers. Rub powdered sugar over the sticky candy, then use a large chef's knife to cut six 1½-inch-wide strips. Working with 2 or 3 strips at a time, cut into 1½-inch cubes and tumble in a large bowl with the remaining powdered sugar.

Once the marshmallows are coated, transfer to an airtight container, with wax paper between each layer. Store for up to 3 weeks at room temperature, or freeze for up to 6 months. Enjoy plain, dunked in hot cocoa, or toasted over an open flame, with Crispy Whole Wheat Graham Crackers (page 202) and chocolate.

continued ↓

In winter months, the hot syrup may harden along the bottom of a chilly mixing bowl. Warm the bowl in hot water to prevent this problem, and dry well before use.

Bloomed in high-proof alcohol or acidic juice, the gelatin may not behave as it should, so exercise extreme caution when experimenting with flavored marshmallows.

→ *Mix it up!*

BROWN BUTTER SAGE: This rich, nutty, and herbaceous variation is fantastic with white chocolate for S'mores, or as a topping for old-school sweet potato casserole. Up the butter to 4 ounces (1 stick), and melt in a 1-quart stainless steel saucier over medium-low heat. Increase the heat to medium and simmer, stirring with a heat-resistant spatula while the butter hisses and pops. Then continue cooking and stirring, scraping up any brown bits that form on the bottom of the pan, until the butter is golden yellow and perfectly silent. Pour into a Pyrex measuring cup, making sure to scrape up all the toasty brown bits, and then slowly drizzle into the marshmallow creme while whipping on medium-low.

GRAHAM CRACKER CRUNCH: Not for toasting, these gently spiced molasses marshmallows taste exactly like an old-fashioned graham cracker, with an irresistibly crunchy coating. Use only ½ ounce (4½ teaspoons or 2 envelopes) gelatin, and reduce the corn syrup to 3½ ounces (⅓ cup); add 1½ ounces (3 tablespoons) unsulfured molasses (not blackstrap). Prepare the syrup in a 4-quart stainless steel pot, to account for foaming, but otherwise proceed as directed. Along with the melted butter, whip ½ teaspoon ground cinnamon into the finished marshmallow creme. In place of powdered sugar, coat the freshly cut marshmallows in 3 ounces (¾ cup) Crispy Whole Wheat Graham Cracker crumbs (page 202).

HONEY: Depending on how strong you'd like the flavor to be, all or part of the corn syrup can be replaced with an equal amount of clover or orange blossom honey (darker types tend to develop unpleasant flavors as they cook). Like the molasses syrup in the Graham Cracker Crunch variation, honey syrup will foam, so this variation should be prepared in a 4-quart stainless steel pot.

HOT COCOA 'MALLOWS: When not required to hold their shape over an open flame, marshmallows can get away with 30 percent less gelatin. This makes them more tender and delicate, perfect for dissolving as an airy foam over hot cocoa (see Homemade Swiss Miss®-Style Cocoa, page 75). Simply reduce the gelatin to ½ ounce (4½ teaspoons or 2 envelopes).

PEANUT BRITTLE

In 1843, a Philadelphia woman by the name of Deborah Fisher advertised "The original Pea or Groundnut Candy" at her shop on Eighth Street, just south of Race.[1] There's no telling what recipe she used, but it's not unreasonable to imagine it might have shared something in common with one published less than a mile away in 1844. That recipe, from Eliza Leslie's *Directions for Cookery in its Various Branches*, called for one part brown sugar and four parts molasses, boiled until "crisp and brittle," then mixed with one part blanched peanuts.[2] The result would have been glassy and lean, bittersweet like the burned sugar topping of a crème brûlée.

Ten years later, cookbook author Sarah Rutledge would improve on that formula in *The Carolina Housewife*, enriching the candy with one part butter, creating something rich and tender but dense, like so-called English toffee (pages 318–19).[3] The airy brittle we know today wouldn't come along until 1865, when a Boston cookbook called *The Art of Confectionery* suggested making molasses candy with baking soda "to render it tender."[4]

"Render it tender" may sound more like a lost Elvis B-side than a pivotal moment in the history of American confections, but that single ingredient changed everything. Reacting to the syrup's acidity, baking soda released enough carbon dioxide to aerate the molten candy as it cooled, resulting in the fragile honeycomb of air and sugar we know as brittle today.

Despite its molasses-laced history, I prefer making peanut brittle with corn syrup. The volatile compounds in molasses begin to smoke and burn at relatively low temperatures, creating a bitter brittle that's not always fully crisp. With corn syrup, the candy can be cooked to a much higher temperature, driving off more water, to guarantee crispy results while developing a complex flavor through caramelization.

It also means you don't need a thermometer—there's no mistaking the golden hue of caramel, which will only appear after the syrup hits 340°F. Since there's no risk of burning until about 360°F, that leaves a 20-degree margin of error. Any temperature in that range will trigger thermal decomposition in the baking soda, producing carbon dioxide without any need for acidic ingredients like molasses. The result is a delicate brittle that's tender and crisp, with a rich caramel flavor and peanutty crunch.

Peanut brittle with a deep, caramel flavor.

CARAMEL-VANILLA PEANUT BRITTLE

Forget molasses, this golden brittle gets its color (and complex flavor) from caramelized sugar. It's so easy to make you don't even need a thermometer—just let the syrup simmer until it develops a tawny hue, indicating that all the water has been driven out.

YIELD: about twenty-four 2-inch (¾-ounce) pieces | **ACTIVE TIME:** 30 minutes | **DOWNTIME:** about 1 hour

1 vanilla bean

⅓ cup | 3 ounces water

½ cup | 6 ounces light corn syrup

1 cup | 7 ounces sugar

4 tablespoons | 2 ounces unsalted butter or refined coconut oil

1 rounded cup | 5 ounces dry-roasted or honey-roasted peanuts (salted if you like)

¾ teaspoon baking soda

¼ teaspoon Diamond Crystal kosher salt (half as much if iodized)

Key Point: Honey, molasses, and maple syrup cannot be used in this recipe.

Split the vanilla bean lengthwise with a paring knife and scrape the seeds from each half; reserve the pod for another project. Combine the water, corn syrup, sugar, butter, and vanilla seeds in a 3-quart stainless steel saucier set over medium-low heat and gently stir with a fork until the clear syrup is bubbling hard around the edges, about 5 minutes. Increase heat to medium-high, clip on a digital thermometer if you like, and cook, *without stirring*, until the syrup is golden, about 10 minutes (or approximately 340°F).

Meanwhile, lightly grease an aluminum baking sheet. Measure baking soda and salt into a ramekin.

When the candy is ready, turn off the heat, remove the thermometer, and stir in the baking soda and salt with a heat-resistant spatula. Stir in the peanuts too, then scrape onto the prepared baking sheet and spread into a roughly 12-by-8-inch layer. Cool to room temperature, about 1 hour (prior to that the brittle will stick mercilessly to your teeth).

Chop or break the brittle into 2-inch pieces; there's something cathartic about whacking it with a kitchen mallet. In an airtight container, peanut brittle will keep for about a month at room temperature, or up to 6 months in the freezer.

continued ↓

→ *Mix it up!*

ALMOND, HAZELNUT, OR PECAN BRITTLE: before getting started, preheat the oven to 350°F and toast 5 ounces (1 cup) almonds, hazelnuts, or pecans until golden and fragrant, about 10 minutes; use a kitchen towel to rub the papery skin from hazelnuts. Cool to room temperature and roughly chop, then proceed as directed.

BACON BRITTLE: If you're Southern (or Southern at heart), there's a ramekin of bacon drippings by the stove just waiting to transform peanut brittle into something wonderfully savory. Replace the butter with an equal amount of bacon drippings that have been warmed and strained through a fine-mesh sieve.

CRISPY PEANUT SPRINKLE: Pulverized in a food processor, peanut (or any other nut) brittle makes a rich, sweet, crunchy garnish for ice cream sundaes, frosted cupcakes, or even a bowl of Silky Chocolate Pudding (page 261). Pulse 6 ounces (about nine 2-inch pieces) brittle in a food processor until powdery and fine. Store in an airtight container exactly as you would the brittle itself, and garnish with it only at the last minute; the brittle may soften over time as it absorbs moisture from the air—or dessert.

FUDGE

You might imagine a captain by the name of Fudge turning up in a rousing game of Candyland, somewhere past the Chocolate Swamp but before the Gumdrop Mountains. Far from the likes of Lord Licorice, the real Captain Fudge sailed under the reign of Charles II in the mid-1600s. Known for his "knavery and neglect," the captain always returned to port with "a cargo of lies."[1]

Sailors in the English fleet invoked the captain's name to insult liars, cheats, and scalawags, and we've been fudging it ever since.[2] That casual usage makes it hard to determine when exactly we started calling a chocolate candy that name, but most historians trace fudge to Vassar College in 1888. That year, a student named Emelyn Hartridge made thirty pounds of chocolate candy for a fund-raising event, kicking off a full-fledged fudge fad on campus. For the sake of that rich and creamy candy, her classmates allegedly stole ingredients from the cafeteria, crept from dorm to dorm under the cover of darkness, held secret parties, wrote naughty limericks, and otherwise did the captain proud.

Fudge spread among students of the other Seven Sisters colleges, then nationwide via the awkwardly named "women's fraternity" system, where grads couldn't help but share the recipe as they settled into married life.[3] A prime example is found in Susie Wegg, who learned to make fudge as a Delta Gamma at the University of Wisconsin (class of 1891).[4] After

This 1910 advertisement plays to its audience: former college girls now making fudge at home.

wedding Winfield Smith, she moved to Seattle, where her recipe for "Vassar Fudgies" was published in an 1896 cookbook for the Women's Guild of St. Mark's Church.[5] Her story, and countless others like it, show how fudge reached every corner of America in record time.[6]

By 1912, Fudge 101 threatened to bump Latin off the syllabus at Newcomb College (now Tulane University), prompting professor Mary Harkness to write a scathing op-ed for the *Independent* weekly, where she hailed fudge as the death knell of women's education, one of many practices she feared would leap from "the bedroom to the classroom."[7]

Despite all the excitement, fudge wasn't anything new—just its name.[8] Candies made from boiling milk, butter, brown sugar, and chocolate were common enough in the 1860s and '70s, but they were called "chocolate caramels."[9] The misleading name makes it easy to discount these recipes, but having examined the ratio of ingredients and cooking technique, it's clear to me they were a type of fudge.

My favorite example comes from an 1874 farm journal, *The Cultivator and Country Gentleman*, which published a chocolate caramel recipe from "a Baltimore Friend."[10] It called for four ounces butter, six ounces chocolate, eight ounces milk, and twenty-four ounces brown sugar, boiled for twenty minutes. The only difference between that recipe and modern fudge is constant stirring, which would have triggered crystallization of the supersaturated syrup, creating a crumbly texture. Five years later, *The Cultivator* published a nearly identical recipe, described as a crumbly caramel "much used and liked in Baltimore."[11]

What's interesting is that one day, Emelyn Hartridge would explain to former professor Lucy Salmon that the original recipe for fudge came from a classmate whose cousin sold the candy in Baltimore.[12] So how did it go from a crumbly caramel to the creamy confection we know today? Sheer neglect. Instead of being made on a stovetop by a dedicated cook, fudge was relegated to the gentle heat of a chafing dish in the midst of a college party, and likely cooked to a much lower temperature.

What the Vassarites discovered was that fudge didn't need to be boiled or stirred nearly so hard. Their casual approach let it boil and cool in peace, preventing the crystallization that defined the so-called chocolate caramels. When they did get around to stirring the candy, their efforts actually disrupted crystallization, creating smaller and smaller crystals that felt less gritty on the tongue.

That means there's nothing scary about fudge. It's so easy a nineteenth-century college girl could make it in her dorm room without any proper equipment or fancy ingredients. Things are even easier with a digital thermometer, which takes all the guesswork out of boiling and cooling fudge, so you know exactly when to stir . . . and when not to.

My recipe adopts Baltimore's nineteenth-century chocolate caramel ratio, but with a bit of white sugar to tone down the acidity of brown sugar, and dark chocolate for a surprisingly mellow flavor. Instead of stirring the candy, I've found it easier to knead, which means the fudge turns out especially creamy and smooth.

Cut Baltimore Fudge (page 74) into squares with a pizza wheel while the fudge is still warm.

BALTIMORE FUDGE

Packing up a tin of fudge is one of my favorite holiday traditions, but I'm partial to keeping a stash for myself. For that reason, I've scaled this recipe to yield enough to both share and hoard. Once you try a piece, you'll appreciate why: Old-fashioned fudge tastes like a cube of hot cocoa—creamy, sweet, and richly chocolatey. In fact, drop a piece into some steaming milk and it *is* hot cocoa (see my Homemade Swiss Miss®-Style variation). *See photo on page 73.*

YIELD: about forty-eight 1½-inch squares | **ACTIVE TIME:** about 30 minutes | **DOWNTIME:** 1½ hours to cool

1 cup | 8 ounces milk (any percentage will do)

5 tablespoons | 2½ ounces cold unsalted butter, cut into pieces

1 teaspoon Diamond Crystal kosher salt (half as much if iodized)

2 cups gently packed | 16 ounces light brown sugar

2 cups | 14 ounces white sugar

1⅔ cups | 8 ounces finely chopped 72% dark chocolate (not chips)

1 tablespoon vanilla extract

⭐ ─────────────────

Temperature Note: Most fudge fiascoes are temperature related. If the boiling syrup is not cooked to 240°F, the fudge will not set as it should. If it is cooked to a significantly higher temperature, the fudge will have a dry texture, like an after-dinner mint (though this is actually quite nice!). If the boiling syrup is not cooled to 118°F, the fudge will be grainy. Avoid these problems with an accurate digital thermometer, which should register 212°F in a pot of boiling water.

Make the fudge:

Combine milk, butter, salt, brown sugar, white sugar, and chocolate in a 3-quart stainless steel pot set over medium heat. Stir constantly with a fork until chocolate has melted and the syrup has begun to bubble around the edges, about 8 minutes. In a ramekin of water, wet a pastry brush and wipe all around the sides of the pan, wherever you see sugar crystals or splashes of chocolate. Rewet as needed, "washing" the sides until spotless. Be generous! Extra water will not harm the fudge, but sugar crystals will. Clip on a digital thermometer and cook, *without stirring*, until it registers 240°F, about 5 minutes (the syrup will bubble vigorously, but it will not overflow a 3-quart pot). Remove from heat and cool to 118°F, roughly 1½ hours. As the foamy syrup recedes, you may notice flecks of chocolate around the sides of the pot, but this is perfectly fine.

Knead and cut the fudge:

Lightly grease a 12-inch square work space. Cover a large cutting board with parchment (not wax) paper; have a second sheet of parchment and a rolling pin at the ready.

Stir vanilla extract into the thick syrup with a flexible spatula; the chocolate flecks around the pot may feel gritty but will soon disappear. Keep stirring the gooey, glossy fudge until it thickens into a batter-like paste, about 5 minutes. Scrape onto the prepared work space and knead by spreading the fudge into a ½-inch layer with a metal bench scraper, then scraping it back into a lump. Keep spreading and scraping until it loses its gloss, about 5 minutes.

Immediately scrape onto the cutting board, cover with a second sheet of parchment, and roll out into a roughly 9-by-12-inch rectangle, about ½ inch thick. Immediately cut into forty-eight 1½-inch squares. In an airtight container, with a sheet of parchment between each layer, the fudge will keep for up to 3 weeks at room temperature, or up to 2 months in the fridge.

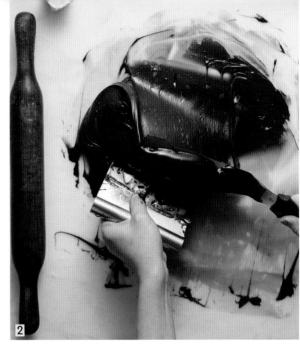

1. Spread and scrape the warm and gooey fudge until it thickens.

2. As it thickens, the fudge will lose its sheen. You're almost done!

3. A beautiful mess.

TROUBLESHOOTING

It's important to stir by hand, as electric mixers are far too powerful, taking the fudge from a liquid to a solid in mere seconds.

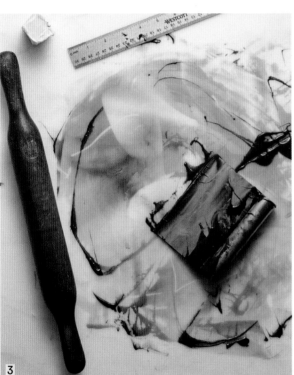

→ Mix it up!

HOMEMADE SWISS MISS®-STYLE COCOA: For a single serving of hot cocoa, dissolve 1½ ounces (¼ cup) fudge in 4 ounces (½ cup) boiling milk (any percentage will do). Season with a pinch of salt, and serve with Buttered Vanilla Marshmallows (page 65).

COCONUT WHITE CHOCOLATE: Replace the dark chocolate, milk, and butter with white chocolate (such as Valrhona's 35% Ivoire), unsweetened full-fat coconut milk, and virgin coconut oil. Proceed as directed.

Boston Cream Pie (page 105).
Proving simple and rustic can be
elegant as well.

Chapter 2

CAKES

This chapter is devoted to cakes in every form: New York Cheesecake (essentially a custard), Strawberry Shortcake (glorified biscuits and jam), Angel's Food Cake (an airy sponge), Pineapple Upside-Down (baked in a skillet), and Boston Cream Pie (a pudding cake with an identity crisis). Then it's on to frosted layer cakes, from those that depend on one part of the egg or another (White and Yellow Cake), shredded vegetables (Carrot Cake), or chemical reactions (Red Velvet) to the Lord of Tricksters himself, Devil's Food. So, whether you want a rustic apple skillet cake or some showstopper for a birthday bash, this chapter has you covered.

CHEESECAKE

Food writers tell us that cheesecake dates back to ancient Greece, but give me a break. Some guy might have shoved globs of cheese and honey into a kiln, but unless he picked up cream cheese and graham crackers at the *agora*, he sure as Hades didn't bake a cheesecake.

Cheesecake, and our love for it, grew from a series of uniquely American conditions: the culture of cheese making in nineteenth-century Pennsylvania, a New York dairyman who successfully laid claim to the trademark Philadelphia, and Depression-era bakers who abandoned pie dough for a cookie crust made from . . . crackers?

It's true that people have been eating cakes of cheese for ages beyond counting. Americans got used to the idea via English recipes for "curd cheese" cake, a tart filled with a custard made from wine-curdled milk.[1] Sure, it sounds awful, but that's just bad copy. Call it "house-made ricotta flan baked in a flaky pastry crust," and you could slap it on any trendy restaurant menu today.

Cheesecake came a step closer to the dessert we know today when Philadelphia cookbook author Eliza Leslie replaced those grainy curds with local cream cheese, then reminiscent of fresh goat cheese, with a creamy but crumbly texture. She called it "Cream Cheese Pudding," a lightly sweetened custard baked in a pastry shell.[2]

It's no coincidence that proto-cheesecake debuted in a city synonymous with cream cheese today. In the 1800s, Pennsylvania dairies developed a reputation for their delicious "full cream" cheese[3]—an umbrella term describing any sort of cheese made from whole milk, unskimmed and therefore "full" of cream.[4] In New York, cheese makers favored a leaner style. Now there's nothing wrong with skim-milk cheese in and of itself (hello, Parmesan), but skim milk made soft cheese seem chalky and dry.

As a result, Pennsylvania cheese makers found it worth the cost of shipping to send their cheese to Manhattan, where New Yorkers were glad to pay more for the luxury of rich, creamy cheese imported from Philly. Even in 1889, the New York State Dairy Commission considered that a longstanding problem to overcome, finding "the great amount of skim cheese made in this State injures the reputation of our makers," and that the average consumer "especially dislikes New York Cheese."[5]

Plenty of New York dairies made top-notch "full cream" cheese, but according to the commission, an even greater number fraudulently sold skim cheese as "full cream," while others went so far as to add artificial dye to hide its pallid color. The industry was in shambles, and cheese makers struggled with the stigma of their own address. That surely included William Lawrence, who got into the cheese business in 1862, when he was just twenty years old.[6] We don't know the details of his upstate operation, only that he'd found success with Neufchâtel (perhaps because of its foreign name) and went on to introduce a line of full-cream cheese in 1872, eventually calling it "Star Brand."

While William was savvy enough to develop his own trademark, it wasn't a particular success. Perhaps seeing its squandered potential, New York distributor Alvah Reynolds contracted with William in 1880, arranging for unmarked packages of cream cheese he would resell under his own label, "Philadelphia." It was a stroke of absolute genius, and immensely profitable from the start. Consumers never dreamed Philadelphia Cream Cheese came from a factory in Chester—if they had, their concerns would have been warranted. When the New York State milk inspector dropped by William Lawrence's factory on November 2, 1883, he found "the milk is skimmed and is run into the emulsifier, where it is [illegally] mixed with lard."[7] The inspector deemed the milk too sour for routine analysis and declared the entire facility a loss.

Whether that crackdown led William to reform his lardy ways, or whether consumers simply couldn't resist the clever brand, Philadelphia Cream Cheese came to dominate the industry. In 1903, Alvah Reynolds sold his brand to the Phenix Cheese Company, which ditched William Lawrence (by then a politician) in favor of establishing a plant of their own.

Well aware that their success hinged on a single word, Phenix vigorously defended their trademark, suing anyone and everyone who dared market cream cheese in conjunction with the word "Philadelphia" or even "Pennsylvania" (!), including actual Pennsylvania cheese makers based in Philadelphia.[8] A decade of such legal shenanigans fundamentally redefined cream cheese, obliterating the wide and varied Philadelphia styles in favor of Phenix's monolithic Philadelphia brand.

On the flip side, Phenix vaulted Philadelphia Cream Cheese to the national stage, changing the way bakers from Minneapolis to Atlanta prepared desserts like cheesecake in the twentieth century. "As formerly made," wrote cookbook author Emma Telford in 1909, "there was a tedious separation of curds and whey, but the housewife of today eliminates that by taking a Neufchâtel or cream cheese as the foundation."[9]

That same year, the *New York Times* published a recipe for "A Good Cheesecake," with a pound of cream cheese, twelve ounces cream, seven ounces sugar, three eggs, lemon zest, and orange flower water.[10] Though today's cheesecakes are more likely to use sour cream, the ratios were remarkably modern, nothing like the eggy custards of English descent. Far from remaining some hush-hush New York secret, newspapers across the country ran that very recipe in 1910[11]—eighteen years before New York deli owner Arnold Reuben would claim to have invented the New York cheesecake.

Regardless of where his recipe came from, we can thank Reuben's constant competition with archrival Leo Lindemann for making cheesecake the title of a Louis Armstrong hit, a plot point for Frank Sinatra and Marlon Brando in *Guys and Dolls*, and a guilty pleasure for late-night talk show hosts, movie stars, and politicians alike. Cheesecake would have been a local favorite in any small town, but in the famed delis of New York, it became a tourist attraction on its own.

Those formative cheesecakes initially relied on the pastry crust traditional to curd-cheese cake and cream cheese pudding, but in 1928, the *New York Post* published a recipe that featured a crushed zwieback crust. This was swiftly replaced by all-American graham crackers in the 1930s, when Nabisco kicked off the "Cracker Cookery" craze (see Graham Crackers, page 201).

My recipe combines the best parts of nineteenth- and twentieth-century recipes, using the same basic ratio of ingredients established by the *New York Times* in 1909, but with a little less cream. In its place, I've added fresh goat cheese, which lightens the heaviness of modern cream cheese. The result is a cheesecake that feels classic in all the important ways (it's rich, creamy, tangy, and thick) but without the gluey density. It's served up on a crisp graham cracker crumb crust, made from Crispy Whole Wheat Graham Crackers (page 202) for an even more pronounced graham flavor.

SOUFFLÉED CHEESECAKE

The basic ratios of my cheesecake are in line with a recipe published in New York City over a hundred years ago, but with a portion of the cream cheese replaced by goat cheese. That combination mimics the texture of old-fashioned cream cheese—tangy, fresh, and a little crumbly too. It makes for a cheesecake that tastes perfectly authentic, but without the gumminess that can plague some recipes. Thanks to an initial burst of high heat, it puffs gently in the oven, creating a uniquely light but creamy consistency. *See photo on page 82.*

YIELD: one 8-by-4-inch cheesecake; 16 servings | **ACTIVE TIME:** about 1 hour |
DOWNTIME: 75 minutes to cool, plus 12-hour refrigeration

Graham Cracker Crust:

1¾ cups | 7 ounces Crispy Whole Wheat Graham Cracker crumbs (page 202)

2 tablespoons | 1 ounce unsalted butter, melted

⅛ teaspoon Diamond Crystal kosher salt (half as much if iodized)

Cheesecake Filling:

2 pounds cream cheese (four 8-ounce packages), softened—about 70°F

1 cup | 8 ounces fresh goat cheese (not precrumbled), softened—about 70°F

1 tablespoon freshly squeezed lemon juice

1 tablespoon vanilla extract

¼ teaspoon Diamond Crystal kosher salt (half as much if iodized)

¼ teaspoon orange flower water

2 cups | 14 ounces sugar

6 large eggs, straight from the fridge

¾ cup | 6 ounces heavy cream

Get ready:

Adjust oven rack to lower-middle position and preheat to 450°F. This recipe requires an 8-by-3¾-inch round pan, whether springform, non-latching with a removable bottom (see page 23), or a traditional cake pan. With a two-piece pan, wrap the bottom in foil before attaching the sides. With a solid pan, line the bottom with parchment paper. In either case, lightly grease the pan.

Add the crumbs, butter, and salt to the prepared pan, stir with a fork until well combined, and then compress into an even layer.

Make the cheesecake filling:

Combine cream cheese, goat cheese, lemon juice, vanilla extract, salt, and orange flower water in the bowl of a stand mixer fitted with a paddle attachment. Mix on low speed until roughly combined, then increase to medium and beat until smooth, about 5 minutes; halfway through, pause to scrape the bowl and beater with a flexible spatula.

Reduce speed to medium-low, add sugar all at once, and mix until well combined. Set a fine-mesh sieve over the bowl, crack in the eggs, and whisk until they pass through; discard any clots that remain. Resume mixing on low until well combined, then scrape the bowl and beater once more.

In a 1-quart stainless steel saucepan, bring the cream to a full boil. Add to batter while mixing on low; this helps release any air pockets introduced in mixing. Use immediately, or refrigerate until needed—up to 1 week (bring to room temperature before baking).

Pour into the prepared pan and place on a baking sheet. Bake until the cheesecake puffs ½ inch over the rim of the pan and is golden on top, about 20 minutes. If necessary, rotate the baking sheet halfway through baking to ensure even browning.

Turn off the oven and open the door to vent for 10 minutes. Close the door, set oven to 250°F, and continue baking until the outer edges of the cheesecake feel firm and the center registers 145°F on a digital thermometer, about 35 minutes.

Cool cheesecake for 15 minutes, then run a thin knife around the sides to loosen (this helps the cake settle evenly as it cools). Cool for an hour more, then cover and refrigerate until cold, at least 12 hours.

Unmold the cheesecake:
Loosen the sides of the cheesecake with a thin knife. For a springform pan, simply pop the latch and remove the sides. For a nonlatching pan, set on a large can of tomatoes or similarly sized object and use both hands to carefully drop the outer ring. For a solid cake pan, let stand in a few inches of scalding water until the pan feels warm. Drape the cake with plastic wrap and invert onto a large flat plate. Remove the pan or the bottom of a two-piece pan, peel off the parchment, and invert onto a serving plate.

Cut with a long thin knife, pausing to clean the blade under hot running water between slices. Tightly wrapped in plastic, leftovers will keep for up to 10 days in the fridge.

TROUBLESHOOTING

Baking at high heat does more than brown the top—it causes the cheesecake to soufflé ever so slightly, creating a more delicate texture inside. If you'd prefer the cheesecake pale and dense, bake it at 250°F for about 75 minutes; use the same temperature to check for doneness.

Many ovens don't run true to temperature. Given the extremes involved, play it safe and keep a close eye on your cheesecake as it browns.

→ *Mix it up!*

COOKIE CRUMB CHEESECAKE: Replace the Graham Cracker crumbs with an equal amount of Homemade Oreo® crumbs (page 214) or Homemade Nutter Butter® crumbs (page 219).

FROMAGE: For a truly cheesy cake, reduce the cream cheese to 24 ounces, omit the goat cheese, and divide the remaining 16 ounces between two or more of your favorite soft, rich cheeses. Some of my favorites include Fromage d'Affinois, Saint-Marcellin, Bûcheron, mascarpone, and even Saint Agur (a particularly creamy blue). Their flavor will shine through clearly, so choose something you know and love.

GREEN TEA CHEESECAKE: The herbal, mossy flavor of Japanese green tea provides a lovely counterpoint to the tangy richness of cream cheese. Simply whisk 2 tablespoons matcha (not bagged or loose green tea; see page 22) into the sugar and proceed as directed.

PUMPKIN CHEESECAKE: Reduce cream cheese to 1½ pounds (3 cups), replace lemon juice with ½ ounce (1 tablespoon) dark rum, and increase kosher salt to ½ teaspoon. Along with sugar, add 2 teaspoons ground cinnamon, 1½ teaspoons ground ginger, and ½ teaspoon ground cloves. Omit heavy cream, and replace with 15 ounces (1⅔ cups) pumpkin puree. If you like, serve with Malted Butterscotch Sauce (page 352) and a sprinkling of toasted hazelnut pieces.

GLUTEN-FREE: Prepare crust with the Gluten-Free variation of my Crispy Whole Wheat Graham Crackers (page 204); thanks to the roasted soybean flour in the dough, they bake up with a nutty richness much like classic whole wheat.

Souffléed Cheesecake (page 80) puffs in the oven, but the interior stays creamy and pale. For blueberry syrup, see page 349.

STRAWBERRY SHORTCAKE

Whether purchased from a supermarket or a farmers' market, strawberries are a strictly modern fruit. Prior to the 1800s, they grew only in the wild—an itsy-bitsy berry sharp eyes might spot in a patch of clover. After transplanting some to his Virginia garden in 1776, Thomas Jefferson noted that it took a hundred strawberries to fill a single cup.[1] Dubbed *Fragaria virginiana*, the curious fruit joined the wild strawberries European botanists collected from around the world. One such variety was a big-but-bland strawberry native to the western coast of South America, *Fragaria chiloensis*. And then, one day, a new sort of strawberry started to grow, by all accounts an accident.

In the close quarters of a humid greenhouse, the Virginia strawberries cross-pollinated with their Chilean counterparts, producing something better than both, something big and flavorful. No botanist ever stepped forward to claim the hybrid, but Philip Miller (director of the Chelsea Physic Garden in London) first mentioned the crossbreed in 1759—a gift from a friend in the Netherlands. Thanks to its fruity flavor and floral aroma, it became known as *Fragaria ananassa*, the "pineapple strawberry."

It was nothing short of a revolutionary development, making strawberries commercially viable for the very first time, but America had a different sort of revolution on its plate. Decades would pass before New England botanists could begin adapting *Fragaria ananassa* to the climate of the New World, methodically introducing more of its hardy parent stock while retaining its size through artificial selection.

Even after they developed "pineapple" strawberries that would thrive in American soil, farmers were hesitant to abandon bankable acres to an untested crop. As a result, strawberry culture didn't begin to take root in America until the 1840s. Oh, but when it did. . . . Newspapers covered the arrival of strawberries like storm trackers following a hurricane. In 1843, the *Baltimore Sun* gleefully reported that strawberries in Charleston were said to be three and a half inches around (rather modest by today's standards).[2]

Strawberries became an obsession for backyard and windowsill gardeners, as well as a booming cash crop—even among livestock farmers and those who'd never before fussed with fruit.[3] Historians call it the era of "Strawberry Fever," a period from roughly 1850 to 1870 when the growth of strawberries exploded across the nation. During that time, growers developed hundreds of cultivars with alluring names: Black Roseberry, Boston Scarlett, MacAvoy's Extra Red.[4]

Most of these would vanish with the season, making each a rare opportunity, and for a time the entire country's social calendar hinged on a single crop.[5] Mary Todd Lincoln held strawberry parties in Springfield to rally supporters to her husband's cause, and it speaks to their success that she chose a strawberry-embroidered gown for her portrait as First Lady.[6]

Political subtext notwithstanding, these parties were meant to show off the best strawberries that money could buy. Instead of mashing or cooking the berries into oblivion, which might disguise an inferior batch, the strawberries were showcased as simply as possible: alongside dishes of sugar and cream. Down south, you could expect a buttermilk biscuit to mop up the juices, but up north, you'd more likely find a pound cake or else a slice of angel's food. Yet all could be properly styled "short" cake thanks to their tender (shortened) crumb.

I suspect that flexibility, or rather, that sense of personalization, is what kept us hot for shortcake long after our Strawberry Fever broke.[7] More often than not, the strawberry shortcake of my childhood was an impromptu affair, Cool Whip and store-bought angel's food cake with oversized supermarket berries. But on certain occasions, perhaps when my folks had the time, shortcake was fresh-picked summer strawberries and whipped cream melting over made-from-scratch biscuits.

I'll never begrudge the former version, light as a feather and candy-sweet, but my heart belongs to those buttermilk biscuits. I can't resist that element of warmth, or the way their flaky tops and crispy bottoms contrast with the softly whipped cream. Despite their fluffy tenderness, biscuits have enough structure to hold up under the juicy berries (or even vanilla ice cream).

Biscuits today usually start from a dough that's relatively lean and wet—roughly one part butter, four parts buttermilk, and five parts flour. Those conditions favor gluten development, which can make biscuits tough if not handled with care. It's worth the risk, however, because gluten is what lets biscuits rise up fluffy and tall. Nineteenth-century recipes, such as the shortcake published in *The Complete Bread and Cracker Baker,* took a different approach. With one part butter, one part cream, and two parts flour, this super-rich, low-moisture formula traded height for a tender crumb and crispy bottom crust.[8]

After months of testing every ratio in between those two styles, I finally hit upon a combination that delivers it all: biscuits that are fluffy and tall, tender and crisp, rich enough to feel indulgent with fresh fruit, but light enough to top with cream. In short, the perfect shortcake.

BUTTERMILK BISCUITS WITH STRAWBERRIES AND CREAM

If you've never made buttermilk biscuits before, don't let their fussy reputation fool you. This crispy, fluffy, flaky Southern tradition couldn't be any easier—you don't even need a rolling pin. In fact, you don't even need to knead. The dough is simply patted out and folded over three times, making the process as easy as 1-2-3. Folding also gives my biscuits beautiful pull-apart layers, perfect for sandwiching with berries and cream. *See photos on pages 14 and 87.*

YIELD: six 2½-inch biscuits | **ACTIVE TIME:** 15 minutes

Buttermilk Biscuits:

2 cups | 9 ounces all-purpose flour, such as Gold Medal, plus more for dusting

1 tablespoon baking powder

2 teaspoons sugar

1½ teaspoons Diamond Crystal kosher salt (half as much if iodized)

1 stick | 4 ounces cold unsalted butter, cut into ½-inch cubes

¾ cup | 6¾ ounces cultured low-fat buttermilk, straight from the fridge

1 recipe Sliced Summer Strawberries (page 88)

1 recipe Make-Ahead Whipped Cream (page 89), or any variation

Key Point: Cast iron ensures that biscuits bake up wonderfully crisp on the bottom, so don't expect the same results with another metal. Placing biscuits close together minimizes spreading, so if you don't have cast iron, a cake pan is preferable to a baking sheet.

Adjust oven rack to lower-middle position and preheat to 400°F. Sift flour into a medium bowl (if using a cup measure, spoon into the cup and level with a knife before sifting). Whisk in baking powder, sugar, and salt. Add butter, toss to break up the pieces, and smash each cube into a thin sheet. Continue smashing and rubbing until the butter has mostly disappeared into a floury mix, although a few larger Cheerio-sized pieces may remain. (This can also be done with 4 or 5 pulses in a food processor.) If you like, the mix can be refrigerated for up to 3 weeks in an airtight container.

Stir in buttermilk with a flexible spatula, stopping as soon as the dough comes together in a sticky ball. Turn out onto a lightly floured surface, sprinkle more flour on top, and gently pat into a 6-inch square (no need to be overly precise), then fold in half; repeat twice for a total of 3 folds. Pat the dough out ¾ inch thick and cut out as many 2½-inch rounds as you can. Arrange close together in an 8-inch cast-iron skillet. Gather scraps into a ball, pat out and fold once, then cut out another few biscuits.

Bake until golden brown on top and along the sides, about 35 minutes.

Split warm biscuits in half and place each bottom in a shallow dessert bowl. Spoon Sliced Summer Strawberries and Make-Ahead Whipped Cream over the shortcakes to taste, and top with the remaining biscuit halves. Serve immediately.

TROUBLESHOOTING

If you're used to shortening, you'll be surprised at how quickly all-butter biscuits begin to brown, but because of their thickness, they need to bake longer than you'd expect.

continued ↓

CREAM SCONES: Reduce kosher salt to 1 teaspoon, and reduce butter to 2 ounces (4 tablespoons). Replace buttermilk with 2 ounces (¼ cup) milk, any percentage will do, and 6 ounces (¾ cup) heavy cream. Stir to form a soft dough, turn onto a lightly floured surface, and pat into a 7-inch round. Cut into 6 wedges with a chef's knife, sprinkle with sugar, and arrange on a parchment-lined baking sheet. Bake until puffed and lightly brown, about 22 minutes. If you like, add up to 6 ounces (1 cup) milk chocolate chips or 4 ounces (⅔ cup) fresh blueberries, tossed in just before the dairy. This variation depends on thick cream, and cannot be made with 100 percent milk.

DROP BISCUITS: Reduce butter to 3 ounces (6 tablespoons), increase buttermilk to 9 ounces (1 cup plus 2 tablespoons), and stir with a flexible spatula to form a soft dough. With a pair of spoons, drop ten roughly equal portions on a parchment-lined baking sheet. Bake until golden brown, about 30 minutes.

EXTRA FLUFFY: My brother doesn't care for crispy biscuits—he wants them fluffy as a cloud. When I bake for him, I reduce the butter to 3 ounces (6 tablespoons), which limits how the biscuits spread in the oven, encouraging them to puff up instead of out.

WHOLE WHEAT: When improvising shortcakes with winter fruit, whole wheat makes for a remarkably hearty but tender biscuit. Simply reduce the all-purpose flour to 6 ounces (1⅓ cups), mixed with 2½ ounces (½ cup) whole wheat flour (not stone-ground).

A spring tradition in Kentucky: buttermilk biscuits, with strawberries and cream.

Sliced Summer Strawberries

In Kentucky, strawberry season lasts only a few weeks, so whether I'm at the strawberry patch or the farmers' market, every basket represents a rare opportunity—shortcake. Even the best strawberries require a bit of sugar to coax out their juices, some more than others. Start on the lower end for naturally sweet and tender berries, and add more for those that are more tart and firm.

YIELD: about 3 cups; 6 servings | **ACTIVE TIME:** about 5 minutes | **DOWNTIME:** 1-hour rest

6 heaping cups | 2 pounds, whole, ripe strawberries

½ to ¾ cup | 3 to 5 ounces sugar

⅛ teaspoon Diamond Crystal kosher salt (half as much if iodized)

Wash and drain the strawberries, then trim their leafy caps with a paring knife. Halve small strawberries, and slice the rest ¼-inch thick. Toss with sugar and salt in a medium bowl, then let stand for about an hour at room temperature, until the berries are swimming in juice.

Leftovers can be refrigerated in an airtight container for up to 2 days. The berries will soften considerably, but warmed on the stovetop, they're a lovely topping for ice cream or cheesecake (page 80).

Make-Ahead Whipped Cream

I developed this low-maintenance recipe in my restaurant days, when I needed a big batch of whipped cream to last through the night in a steamy kitchen. The trick is a bit of extra sugar, which helps the cream whip into a stable foam that can be held for up to eight hours. With a hearty pinch of salt, it's not too sweet, making it the ideal accompaniment for everything from Strawberry Shortcake (page 83) to Butternut Pumpkin Pie (page 166).

YIELD: about 3 cups | **ACTIVE TIME:** 5 minutes

½ cup | 4 ounces sugar

⅛ teaspoon Diamond Crystal kosher salt (half as much if iodized)

1½ cups | 12 ounces heavy cream

2 teaspoons vanilla extract or 1 vanilla bean, split lengthwise with a paring knife

Combine sugar, salt, cream, and vanilla extract, if using, in the bowl of a stand mixer fitted with the whisk attachment. If using a vanilla bean, run the flat of the blade down each half to scrape out the seeds and add them to the cream (reserve the pod for another project). Mix on medium-low speed to dissolve the sugar, about a minute, then increase to medium-high and whip until cream is thick enough to hold firm peaks, about 3 minutes.

Use immediately, or cover and refrigerate until needed, up to 8 hours.

Refrigerate leftovers in an airtight container for up to 1 week; before serving, briefly rewhip the cream to restore its light and silky texture.

→ *Mix it up!*

BASIL: This emerald-green variation has an herbal freshness that's perfect with Strawberry Shortcake. Grind the sugar with 2 ounces (2 cups loosely packed) fresh basil leaves in a food processor until the leaves disappear and the sugar looks wet, like pesto. Proceed as directed.

BROWN SUGAR: Replace the sugar with light or dark brown sugar.

CHERRY PIT: A light cherry-almond flavor that's perfect with a slice of Cherry Pie (page 179). Combine heavy cream with 3¾ ounces (⅓ cup) cherry pits, cover, and steep overnight in the fridge. Strain and whip as directed.

COCOA: Combine the sugar with 1 ounce (⅓ cup) Dutch-process cocoa powder, such as Cacao Barry Extra Brute.

FREEZE-DRIED FRUIT: This variation is as colorful as it is tasty. Grind sugar with ⅓ ounce (⅓ cup) freeze-dried fruit such as bananas, blueberries, cherries, or cranberries in a food processor until powdery and fine, then whip as directed. For a thicker consistency, pulse in the food processor bowl until thick, just 90 seconds or so.

ORANGE: Combine sugar with 1 tablespoon orange zest and ¼ teaspoon orange flower water.

STRAWBERRY: Double Strawberry Shortcake, anyone? Add 2 ounces (¼ cup) chilled strawberry syrup (see Strawberry Ice Cream, page 340) to the cream and proceed as directed.

PINEAPPLE UPSIDE-DOWN CAKE

Contrary to popular belief, a pineapple won't ripen post-harvest. It develops flavor by converting starch to sugar from the parent plant; once picked, it has no starch reserves of its own, so the process grinds to a halt. Over time, its aroma will intensify and its shell may deepen to golden amber as it softens enough to let go of its leaves, but these are just signs of impending rot.

Which is to say, no ripe pineapple could have survived the journey from Hawaii to America in the nineteenth century. That forced growers to pick immature fruits which arrived on our shores tart and tough—better for decor than dessert. When not artfully arranged on the mantelpiece to signal hospitality, those underripe pineapples required lots of cooking and even more sugar—ideal for homemade jams and jellies.[1]

These tropical preserves could be spread over biscuits for a twist on shortcake or spooned into a pastry crust for a pineapple tart, but they more commonly served as a filling for layer cakes.[2] An 1889 recipe from a Milwaukee newspaper stacked its "Pine-Apple Cake" three layers tall,[3] but down south, that number might fly up to seven.[4] Practically speaking, a single layer of buttery yellow cake would do—especially for less formal affairs.

Thanks to the effort and expense, these cakes were something of a rarity, but that would soon change. At the turn of the century, James Dole established canning facilities in Hawaii, allowing growers to harvest and preserve pineapples at their peak: tender, sweet, and aromatic. Nothing like the sour green rocks Americans had previously known, making canned pineapple a smash hit. According to their own figures, the Association of Hawaiian Pineapple Packers went from two thousand cases of pineapple canned in 1901 to nearly six million by 1920.[5]

Where others might have toasted such success with umbrella drinks on the beach, the Pineapple Packers saw a problem. While they were selling literal boatloads of pineapple, their facilities were operating at only a fraction of capacity. In a 1921 interview with *Printers' Ink*, they explained their advertising dilemma. "Our need . . . is to widen the demand. We cannot do this by telling how delicious pineapples are. People know that already."[6]

Despite losing the leafy crown, canned pineapple remained regal and exotic, something people saved for special occasions. If the Packers had any hope of boosting sales, they'd have to change public opinion, and that meant something far more risky: knocking pineapple off its pedestal. If their advertisements struck the wrong note, they'd cheapen its image for years to come, but if things went right? Pineapples would become an everyday fruit, like apples, oranges, and bananas.[7]

That meant they'd need a host of everyday recipes, the premise for their first official cookbook: *Ninety-Nine Tempting Pineapple Treats*.[8] Published in 1924, it was advertised in grocery stores and magazines and through a direct-mail campaign aimed at promoting ideas to serve pineapple "every day in a new way."[9]

Some of these are still familiar today: baked ham covered in pineapple rings and cloves, leaves of iceberg lettuce topped with cottage cheese and pineapple, and crushed pineapple over vanilla ice cream for a simple sundae. Yet the sleeper hit was a recipe called Pineapple Cake Glacé.[10] It streamlined the slow-cooked pineapple marmalade of nineteenth-century pineapple cakes with an all-in-one technique that combined crushed pineapple and brown sugar in the bottom of a cast-iron skillet with a simple cake batter spooned directly on top. In the oven, the pineapple and sugar bubbled into a jammy layer as the fluffy cake baked. When it was done, the cake was gorgeously sauced and ready to serve—upside down.

Pineapple Cake Glacé swept national newspapers in 1925.[11] In Kentucky, the *Middlesboro Daily News* called it a "topsy turvy cake,"[12] and Ohio's *Sandusky Star Journal* reported that hundreds gathered to attend a local demonstration, earning the story a full-page headline: "Frying Pan Cake New Dessert Novelty, and It's Good!"[13]

Decorative rings of canned pineapple dotted with maraschino cherries would be the norm by 1928,[14] but the recipe would otherwise remain virtually unchanged for the better part of a century—surprising for a cake born of adaptation. Nineteenth-century pineapple cakes made clever use of unripened but exotic fruit, and twentieth-century recipes turned the idea upside down with pineapple from a can, so shouldn't twenty-first-century recipes embrace the field-ripened jet-set Hawaiian pineapples found in every grocery store today?

Compared to canned pineapple, which is effectively poached in its own syrup during sterilization or pasteurization, fresh pineapple has a firm texture and natural acidity well suited to baking. And it doesn't actually need to be peeled! Just slice it vertically, and the shell is left around the outer edges, where it's as easy to avoid as the crust on a slice of bread. With a few cookie cutters, all types of fun shapes can be stamped out in no time.

In the spirit of those "everyday" recipes that made upside-down cake so famous, my recipe is simple enough to be a weeknight dessert. The cake itself is a one-bowl affair, made extraordinary with simple touches like coconut milk and dark rum, which highlight its inherently tropical flair. Don't worry; if you don't happen to have these ingredients on hand, regular milk and vanilla will do.

Fresh pineapple cut into stars, for a truly stellar upside-down cake.

UPSIDE-DOWN PINEAPPLE CUTOUT CAKE

Don't let the fresh pineapple deter you—it can be prepped in less time than it takes to preheat the oven. Just follow my lead and slice it vertically, then cut each slab with your favorite cookie cutters, a personal touch that lets you customize the look for any occasion. The cake itself is wonderfully light but heady with the scent of coconut and rum, a perfect match for the gooey brown sugar and pineapple topping.

YIELD: one 12-inch skillet cake; 10 to 12 servings | **ACTIVE TIME:** about 40 minutes

1 large golden pineapple (about 4 pounds)

Cake Batter:

1¾ cups | 8 ounces all-purpose flour, such as Gold Medal

1 cup | 7 ounces sugar

2 teaspoons baking powder

¼ teaspoon Diamond Crystal kosher salt (half as much if iodized)

⅛ teaspoon grated nutmeg

1 stick | 4 ounces unsalted butter, soft but cool—about 65°F

2 large eggs, straight from the fridge

¾ cup | 6 ounces unsweetened coconut milk (full-fat or lite)

1 tablespoon dark rum or vanilla extract

Brown Sugar Topping:

¾ cup packed | 6 ounces light or dark brown sugar

⅛ teaspoon Diamond Crystal kosher salt (half as much if iodized)

¼ cup | 2 ounces unsweetened coconut milk (full-fat or lite)

Prepare the pineapple:
With a chef's knife, cut off the pineapple's leafy top and its thick-skinned bottom so that it stands upright. Starting on one side, slice three or four ½ inch slabs, until you reach the core. Repeat on the opposite side (discard each "heel"), then slice off the remaining "columns" of fruit.

Cut the slabs with stainless steel cookie cutters no more than 2 inches across, using an assortment of shapes and sizes to maximize the yield; or cut into geometric shapes with a knife. The cutouts can be refrigerated in an airtight container for up to 3 days.

Make the cake:
Adjust oven rack to lower-middle position and preheat to 350°F. Line the bottom of a 10-inch cast-iron skillet with a parchment round.

Sift flour into the bowl of a stand mixer (if using cup measures, spoon into the cups and level with a knife before sifting). Add sugar, baking powder, salt, nutmeg, and butter, then mix on low with a paddle attachment until the butter disappears into the floury mix, about 2 minutes.

Add eggs, coconut milk, and rum all at once and mix to form a grainy batter, about 20 seconds. Scrape the bowl and beater with a flexible spatula, then fold once or twice to ensure the batter is well mixed from the bottom up.

For the topping:
In a small bowl, stir brown sugar, salt, and coconut milk together with a fork. Pour into the prepared skillet, then arrange the pineapple cutouts on top, nestling the pieces together as close as you can (they will shrink as they bake). Pour the batter on top. Bake until tawny brown and firm, though your fingertip may leave a faint indentation—about 55 minutes (roughly 210°F).

Loosen the edges of the cake with a knife, place an inverted serving plate on top and, with oven mitts, flip the whole thing over. Remove the skillet and serve warm.

Wrapped tightly in plastic, leftovers will keep for up to 4 days at room temperature.

continued ↓

→ Mix it up!

APPLE CINNAMON: Replace the pineapple with 2 pounds (about 4 large) Granny Smith apples, peeled, cored, and cut into ½-inch wedges. Along with the salt in the Brown Sugar Topping, stir in 1 teaspoon ground cinnamon and ¼ teaspoon ground ginger. This variation works equally well with firm winter pears, like Bosc. If you like, serve with a dollop of Caramel Whipped Cream (page 307).

CRANBERRY: For a seasonal twist, replace the pineapple with 12 ounces (3 cups) fresh cranberries.

MANGO: Replace the pineapple with 2 pounds (4 or 5 large) ripe mangoes, cut from the pit in ½-inch wedges. Pulse flour with 1 tablespoon lime zest in a food processor for 1 minute, but otherwise prepare batter as directed. Along with the salt in the Brown Sugar Topping, stir in ¼ teaspoon ground cardamom. To play up the tropical vibe, serve with the Lemongrass variation of Double Vanilla Ice Cream on page 336.

GLUTEN-FREE: Replace the all-purpose flour with 2½ ounces (½ cup) cornstarch, 2 ounces (½ cup) tapioca flour or arrowroot, 2 ounces (½ cup) oat flour, and 1½ ounces (⅓ cup) white rice flour and increase the baking powder to 1 tablespoon.

ANGEL'S FOOD CAKE

American desserts don't have a reputation for understated elegance. We crave cookie-dough ice cream, marshmallow cereal, chocolate milk, and a cherry on top. Yet somehow we managed to invent angel's food cake, the very portrait of restraint. No butter. No egg yolks. No nuts. No chocolate. Just sweetness and vanilla magicked into a billowy cloud.

Europeans started making sponge cake back in the 1600s—always with whole eggs, often with a drizzle of butter, and generally spiked with sherry or rum. As lovers of both cake and rum, colonial Americans had a natural appreciation for the stuff. What they didn't appreciate was its tendency to collapse. Ever the innovators, they improvised a solution by sticking a glass bottle into the middle of the pan (some experts even suggested weighting the bottles with lead shot).[1] This setup conducted heat to the center of the cake, baking it in an even ring.

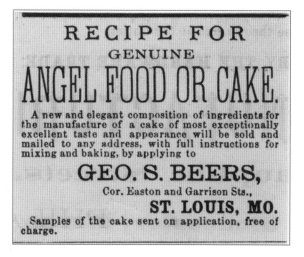

RECIPE FOR
GENUINE
ANGEL FOOD OR CAKE.

A new and elegant composition of ingredients for the manufacture of a cake of most exceptionally excellent taste and appearance will be sold and mailed to any address, with full instructions for mixing and baking, by applying to

GEO. S. BEERS,
Cor. Easton and Garrison Sts.,
ST. LOUIS, MO.

Samples of the cake sent on application, free of charge.

In the earliest days, bakers weren't sure if it was food or cake.

After centuries of European tradition, the first truly American sponge cake came from a Kentucky kitchen in 1839. Unlike most girls in the antebellum South, Lettice Bryan was given an education like her brothers. She went on to pursue a career as an author even after marriage, writing extensively on the subjects of spirituality, language, and domestic science.

In *The Kentucky Housewife*, Lettice introduced readers to an unusual cake made from egg whites whipped with sugar and lemon and orange juice, then folded with just a touch of flour.[2] This clever recipe for "White Sponge" effectively stabilized the meringue with citric acid, and it leaned on a high proportion of sugar, not yolks, to tenderize the otherwise lean cake.

White sponge gained wider recognition in 1864 with the publication of *The Practical Cook Book* in New York.[3] Apparently a purist, Helen Robinson stripped the recipe down to sugar, egg whites, and flour. Despite its clinical name, white sponge captured the imagination of bakers in the 1870s.[4] It appeared frequently in cookbooks of the era, often with added cream of tartar and almond extract to make up for the loss of stability and flavor.[5]

But it wasn't angel's food yet. That phrase originated way back in the sixteenth century with *The Book of Common Prayer*, referencing manna from heaven. It often turned up as a figure of speech in nineteenth-century cookbooks, describing anything sweet but wholesome, including earthly delights such as stewed apples and fruit salad.[6] With its featherlight crumb, gleaming white hue, and fat-free formula, white sponge finally gave believers a dessert that lived up to such a heavenly name.

The first recipe to dub an egg-white sponge "Angel's Food" was *The Home Messenger*, an 1878 fund-raising cookbook for Detroit's Home of the Friendless.[7] The cookbook was littered with advertisements from donors, including the Dover Stamping Company—owners of the newly patented Dover Egg Beater. With a proper name and the right tool for the job, angel's food exploded in popularity through the 1880s and beyond.[8]

With every improvement to hand mixers, particularly as electric mixers took hold, angel's food has enjoyed a resurgence of popularity. Yet despite our ever-increasing horsepower, we still make our recipes the exact same way: adding the sugar in small, painstaking increments. It's the same method used for French meringue. The egg whites are brought to room temperature, beaten until foamy, stabilized with cream of tartar, and then carefully whipped with sugar one spoonful at a time. Problem is, angel's food requires more sugar than a French meringue can handle, so the rest has to be sifted into the flour and folded in at the end. The sheer volume of dry ingredients makes that last step tricky, as overmixing will deflate the fragile meringue (hence many bakers are intimidated by angel's food). That approach, however difficult, was once a baker's best bet, and the easiest method if whipping by hand. But it's needlessly fussy with the horsepower of a modern stand mixer, so I don't fret over angel's food. I throw the cold egg whites in a bowl, add my sugar all at once, and beat it. Just beat it.

No one wants to be defeated by a careless technique, so my no-cook Swiss meringue may raise a few eyebrows, but hear me out. While my angel's food method won't ever reach the lofty heights of a properly made French meringue (or a properly made Swiss one, for that matter), the truth is that it doesn't have to—recipes for angel's food universally call for a softly whipped meringue.

That's because a stiff meringue has gained all the air it can hold, taxing the whites' ability to stretch and expand. They have nothing left to give, so when the entrapped air starts to expand in the oven, their protein chains snap like a rubber band, collapsing the whole thing. But a *softly* whipped meringue hasn't reached its full potential, so it has plenty of strength and elasticity to inflate in the oven like a hot air balloon.

Since I know that's the kind of meringue I need, I can dispense with all the unnecessary precautions, effectively trading potential volume for actual stability, eliminating the risk of collapse, and making angel's food dead easy to prepare.

Effortless Angel's Food Cake (page 98): sweet, simple, and totally angelic.

EFFORTLESS ANGEL'S FOOD CAKE

This is probably the easiest meringue you'll ever make. Just put some cold egg whites and sugar in a bowl, start whipping, and then stop before they're stiff. With a squeeze of lemon for stability, this seemingly underwhipped meringue puffs the angel's food until it's as light as cotton candy. The lemon disappears in the oven, leaving behind a soft, tender vanilla cake.

Aside from my unusual treatment of the meringue, the success of this angel's food hinges on bleached cake flour. It has a super-low protein content that can't be faked with cornstarch or replaced by pastry flour. Look for brands like Swans Down or Softasilk in the baking aisle, and avoid anything marked self-rising or unbleached.

Because this recipe may present a couple of new techniques for the uninitiated, give yourself room to learn. Like a kiss, angel's food only gets better with experience. That's not to say your first time won't be deliciously sweet, only that half the fun is in perfecting your technique.

See photo on page 97.

YIELD: one 10-inch cake; 10 to 12 servings | **ACTIVE TIME:** 30 minutes | **DOWNTIME:** 2 hours to cool

---

1 cup plus 2 tablespoons |
    5 ounces bleached cake flour,
    such as Swans Down

2 cups | 15 ounces egg whites (from a
    dozen large eggs), straight from
    the fridge

2 cups | 15 ounces sugar

1 tablespoon vanilla extract

2 tablespoons | 1 ounce freshly
    squeezed lemon juice

¼ teaspoon Diamond Crystal kosher
    salt (half as much if iodized)

Key Point: The unique behavior of bleached cake flour is vital to this recipe's success; unbleached cake flour will cause the angel's food cake to collapse.

Get ready:
Adjust oven rack to middle position and preheat to 350°F. Have ready an aluminum tube pan with a removable bottom, roughly 10 inches across and 4 inches deep. Nonstick pans will not work. If the pan doesn't have stilts, set out a bottle with a slender neck that will fit into the mouth of the tube.

Sift flour (if using a cup measure, spoon into the cup and level with a knife before sifting).

Make the cake:
Combine egg whites, sugar, and vanilla in the bowl of a stand mixer fitted with the whisk attachment. Mix on low speed to moisten, about 1 minute, then increase to medium-low (4 on a KitchenAid) and whip for 3 minutes; the whites will look very dense, and dark from the vanilla. Add the lemon juice and salt, increase speed to medium (6 on a KitchenAid), and whip for 3 minutes; the meringue will be light but thin, not foamy. Increase to medium-high (8 on a KitchenAid), and continue whipping until the wires leave a distinct vortex pattern in the thick, glossy meringue, another 3 minutes or so, depending on the freshness of the whites. To check the meringue, detach the whisk; when whipped to *very soft peaks*, the meringue will run off the wires but retain enough body to pile up on itself in a soft mound.

Sprinkle cake flour over the meringue and stir gently with a flexible spatula to disperse. Switch to a folding motion and work from the bottom up, cutting through the middle, until no pockets of flour remain. Pour the batter into the pan; if you notice a small patch of unmixed flour as you pour, incorporate it into the surrounding batter with a gentle wiggle of your spatula. The pan should be about two-thirds full.

Bake until the cake has risen well above the rim of the pan, with a firm, golden blonde crust, about 45 minutes (206°F). Immediately invert the pan on its stilts, or over the neck of the bottle, and cool upside down until no trace of warmth remains, at least 2 hours.

Serve:
Turn the cooled cake right side up and loosen the outer edges with a metal spatula. Lift the center tube to remove the cake, then loosen it from the bottom too. Invert onto a serving plate; the cake will slide right off the tube. With a chef's knife or serrated bread knife, cut into 10 or 12 servings with a gentle sawing motion, applying very little downward pressure. Angel's food is mostly air, so the big slices will be less filling than they look.

Wrapped tightly in plastic, leftovers will keep for up to a week at room temperature. You can also drop thin slices of angel's food into a toaster to crisp like a campfire marshmallow.

TROUBLESHOOTING
If a speck of yolk slips into the whites, fish it out with an eggshell. If the yolk can't be removed, save those whites for Tahitian Vanilla Pudding (page 225) or White Mountain Layer Cake (page 110) and start fresh.

Extracts like peppermint and orange, made from essential oils, may cause the meringue to collapse; take care when experimenting with flavorings.

In a kitchen below 68°F, cold air may cause the cake to contract and fall from the pan before its crumb has set. As a workaround, open the oven door and place the inverted cake on the stovetop, where drafts of warm air will stabilize its temperature.

Through trial and error, I've discovered that the highly polished sides of stainless steel angel's food cake pans may cause the cake to fall from the pan as it cools. For best results, use an untreated aluminum tube pan.

→ *Mix it up!*

BROWN SUGAR CINNAMON: A cozy flavor for fall, or to end a heavy holiday meal. Sift the cake flour with 4 teaspoons ground cinnamon, and replace the sugar with an equal amount of light brown sugar (dark will not work as well).

CHOCOLATE: However angelic its texture, this variation turns out as dark as devil's food. Reduce the cake flour to 3 ounces (⅔ cup), sifted with 2 ounces (⅔ cup) Dutch-process cocoa powder, such as Cacao Barry Extra Brute. After cooling the cake, use a slender knife or bamboo skewer to loosen it from the center tube too, as this version tends to stick.

CREAMSICLE: Pulse the cake flour with 2 tablespoons orange zest in a food processor for 1 minute. Replace the vanilla extract with 2 teaspoons orange flower water and the seeds from 1 Tahitian vanilla bean (split and scraped). Trade the lemon juice for 1½ ounces (3 tablespoons) freshly squeezed orange juice.

GREEN TEA: The sweetness of angel's food mellows the bitterness of Japanese matcha, for a mossy-green cake with an earthy but aromatic flavor. Sift the cake flour with 2 tablespoons matcha (see page 22). I love to serve slices alongside Whipped Chocolate Crémeux (page 263) with a scattering of Cocoa Nib Crunch (page 321).

continued ↓

LEMONADE: Grinding lemon zest into the flour helps release its essential oil, making this variation particularly aromatic. Pulse the cake flour with 2 tablespoons lemon zest in a food processor for about 1 minute. Omit the vanilla extract and salt. Increase the lemon juice to 1½ ounces (3 tablespoons). Also lovely with lime juice and zest instead.

ROASTED SUGAR AND VANILLA BEAN: This is, without a doubt, my favorite way to make Angel's Food. It's not my "basic" recipe, because the process of roasting sugar is time-consuming, and not everyone keeps a vanilla bean on hand, but these two upgrades make the cake even more extraordinary. Replace the sugar with 15 ounces (2 cups) Roasted Sugar (page 102). Along with the vanilla extract, use the seeds from 1 Mexican vanilla bean, split and scraped.

GLUTEN-FREE: Sift 2 ounces (½ cup) arrowroot, 1½ ounces (⅓ cup) white rice flour, 1½ ounces (⅓ cup) cornstarch, 1 ounce (¼ cup) coconut flour, and 1 teaspoon baking powder into a medium bowl, then whisk to combine.

ROASTED SUGAR

I once worked in a basement kitchen that could drop down to 50°F in winter, chilling cookie doughs and cake batters to the extent they couldn't be creamed. As a workaround, I often warmed my sugar in a low oven to knock off the chill, bringing it up to about 70°F. One day, sidetracked by a series of phone calls, deliveries, and other office-related duties, I forgot all about it.

Several hours later, the smell of caramel drifted over to my desk and I took off at light speed, expecting to find smoke billowing from the oven and a hotel pan filled with bubbling caramel. When I threw open the oven door, there was nothing but an innocent tray of what looked like turbinado sugar.

It seemed a little lumpy and damp, but to my surprise, the sugar cooled into something powdery and dry, with a toasty, if not outright caramelized, flavor that tasted significantly less sweet than plain sugar. Curious as to how it would behave as an ingredient, I whipped it into a meringue for angel's food. The cake turned out as tender and fluffy as ever, with a intriguing sense of richness and a gentle ivory hue.

Many hours of research later, I've learned that sugar doesn't actually melt. Melting is simply a phase change, when something solid becomes liquid, which has no impact on the chemical composition of a substance. Ice is still water after it melts. Butter is still butter. Chocolate is still chocolate. But "melted" sugar is caramel.

Unlike pure sucrose, $C_{12}H_{22}O_{11}$, caramel has a chemical composition so complex it can't be expressed with a single formula. Within every sample, scientists find hundreds of different compounds, collectively known as caramelins. As it turns out, when you heat sugar up, it doesn't melt—it decomposes.

It seems like a pedantic distinction at first. Regardless of what's technically happening, solid sugar becomes liquid caramel. Who cares? But if you stop to think about it, the implications are huge. If sugar isn't melting, that means thermal decomposition can be initiated at any temperature, given enough time. With the right balance of temperature and time, you can make a light caramel that's powdery and dry.

Unlike caramel powder, which is made from fully caramelized sugar that's cooled and ground fine, "roasted sugar" still contains enough sucrose to behave like plain sugar in any given recipe. Yet because it's not pure sucrose, it tastes less sweet (chemically speaking, it's actually less caloric too), with only a faint hint of caramel.

Those properties make it downright miraculous in hypersweet desserts that rely on sugar for structure (ice cream, meringue, nougat, or marshmallows, even simple syrup) because it tames their sweetness without changing their overall flavor profile, unlike raw or semirefined options such as brown sugar, demerara, and turbinado. It's also pH neutral, so it won't cause any unexpected chemical reactions in recipes that call for baking soda.

Yet of all its potential uses, none can compare to the absolute magic of roasted sugar in angel's food—especially for those who've been put off by the cake's traditional sweetness. Not only does it make the cake demonstrably less sweet, it adds a hint of complexity without overtly deviating from the classic flavor profile.

Roasted Sugar

In a low oven, granulated sugar develops a toasty flavor reminiscent of light caramel or turbinado, yet it remains powdery and dry. That means you can use it to replace white sugar in any recipe, adding a subtle note of complexity to round out the simple sweetness of your favorite dessert. Because of the time involved, you'll want to roast a whole bag of sugar to make it worth your while. Just give it a stir every thirty minutes or so to help it toast more evenly, then cool and store like plain sugar.

YIELD: 4 pounds (9 cups) | **ACTIVE TIME:** about 5 minutes |
DOWNTIME: up to 2 hours in the oven, plus 1 hour to cool

9 cups | 4 pounds refined white sugar

Key Point: This technique will not work with raw or semirefined cane sugar, as its natural molasses content will begin to melt at much lower temperatures, causing the sugar to clump.

Preheat the oven to 325°F. Put the sugar in a 9-by-13-inch glass or ceramic baking dish and roast, stirring well once every 30 minutes, until it darkens to a sandy tan, with a coarse texture like turbinado, about 2 hours. The color change can be strangely difficult to judge in the dim glow of an oven, so scoop out a spoonful to examine in better light.

Let the roasted sugar cool away from any sources of moisture or steam until no trace of warmth remains, about 1 hour. If you notice molten caramel around the edges, pour the hot sugar into a heat-resistant container, leaving the melty bits behind; once cool, the baking dish can be soaked clean. Despite its innocuous appearance, roasted sugar can be dangerously hot, so take care not to touch it.

Store for up to a year in an airtight container at room temperature.

TROUBLESHOOTING
Metal baking pans conduct heat more rapidly, and their corners may harbor traces of grease or moisture, factors that make the sugar more likely to liquefy around the edges.

Given the importance of maintaining a low temperature, use an oven thermometer to verify that yours runs true to dial. Otherwise, the sugar will caramelize too quickly and begin to liquefy.

BOSTON CREAM PIE

Boston cream pie comes from a small but time-honored branch of confusingly named sponge cakes, split and layered with distinctive fillings but almost never frosted. In the 1850s, this included Lafayette Pie (filled with lemon curd), Cream Pie (filled with custard), and Washington Pie (filled with marmalade or jam). These cakes ostensibly took their name from the Washington Pie Plate, variously described as a wide-brimmed pie tin, a one-inch-deep round cake pan, or a scalloped "patty pan."[1]

According to legend, Boston cream pie was first served at the opening of Boston's posh Parker House Hotel in 1856.[2] It was invented by a French-Armenian chef, known only as M. Sanzian, who revolutionized the world of cakes and/or pies with a topping of chocolate fondant—said to have been an unheard extravagance at the time. He called it the "Parker House Chocolate Cream Pie," and it soon became the most famous dessert in Boston, prompting the hotel to officially rename it Boston Cream Pie.

Like any undocumented corporate history, the story isn't quite sound. Why would wealthy guests be impressed by a dab of chocolate at a luxury hotel? If that's what made it famous, why would the hotel later delete *chocolate* from its name? And for that matter, why would any hotel remove its own name from a proprietary dessert in favor of something so generic it could be adopted by any competitor?

In my quest for answers, I turned up an 1852 directory for the city of Boston and found a cook by the name of Augustine Anezin living less than a mile from the Parker House.[3] It's an Armenian surname, so presuming history lost Anezin to a typo, he's the only part of the story I'm willing to believe.

The New York Public Library's collection of historic menus includes "bills of fare" from the Parker House, dating from 1858 to 1946. While nineteenth-century classics like champagne jelly, mince pie, blanc mange, and éclairs turn up aplenty, you won't find any reference to Boston cream pie, chocolate cream pie, chocolate cream cake, or any name that even comes close.

Browsing through stacks of vintage postcards, advertisements, and brochures issued by the Parker House, I found no hint that they had any sort of reputation for dessert at all.

Yet Boston cream pie has, by all accounts, been well loved since the 1870s. The oldest recipe I could find was published in the Methodist Almanac of 1872,[4] but versions turned up everywhere from a rural Michigan community cookbook to North Carolina's *Durham Herald* in 1876.[5] By the 1880s, it was a common sight in newspapers across the country. But even after searching through hundreds of recipes and advertisements published in vintage newspapers, books, and magazines dating from the 1880s straight through World War II, I never once encountered any mention of the Parker House, aside from praise for the hotel's famous dinner rolls.[6]

What's more, not a single one of those sources ever mentioned chocolate. To the contrary, they painstakingly describe a vanilla cream pie—layers of plain sponge cake filled with stiff custard and dusted with powdered sugar—nothing more. It's not that chocolate glaze or frosting was unusual for cakes of that era, only that chocolate was never historically associated with Boston cream pie.

I found no hint of any evidence to the contrary until 1933, when the Glaus Pastry Shop in Salt Lake City advertised "extra special" Boston cream pies in chocolate, vanilla, and butterscotch, but it's unclear whether these were fillings or glaze.[7] The first truly, definitively *chocolate* Boston cream pie appeared in a Pillsbury advertisement in 1934. "Bored with your own cooking? Freshen up your meal."[8] The suggestion was accompanied by a luscious illustration of a Boston cream pie dripping with inky chocolate glaze. There was nothing "fresh" or clever about the standard recipe for sponge cake and custard, leaving me to conclude that the glaze itself was what made an old recipe new.

From 1934 on, that shiny chocolate glaze became something of trend.[9] A cooking column in Ohio's *Sandusky Register* would casually suggest chocolate sauce as an accompaniment to Boston cream pie in 1935,[10] and the following year a Chicago-area grocery chain advertised chocolate-topped Boston cream pie.[11] Yet this was by no means the new norm; an overwhelming majority of recipes published in the 1930s and '40s were as plain Jane as the one printed in 1872.

Flipping through a yellowing copy of the *Oxford University Methodist Church Cookbook*, which my great-great-grandmother helped edit in 1944, I found her Boston cream pie capped with whipped cream. It would be among the last recipes for Boston cream pie published without a glaze; in 1945, the trend took off after a chocolate-drenched Boston cream pie was featured in advertisements for Softasilk cake flour.[12]

The difference between the popularity of Softasilk and of Pillsbury? Betty Crocker.

General Mills introduced Betty in the 1920s, and she (or, rather, a series of actresses) would become America's foremost baking expert. At her suggestion, legions of home cooks and competitors began topping Boston cream pies with chocolate in 1945. And wouldn't you know it, I finally found a reference to such a dessert at the Parker House in 1946, when a Ford Motor Company travel guide mentioned having a slice of chocolate cream pie at the famed hotel.

It's a dubious connection, but I'll give it to them. Who knows, maybe the Parker House has served chocolate-covered Boston cream pie for a hundred years and counting, and it's just that no one ever wrote it down or bothered to mention it in any newspaper, cookbook, or magazine prior to 1946. Not even when the original Parker House was demolished in 1924, prompting a spate of historical retrospectives that somehow neglected to mention any dessert even remotely like Boston cream pie, despite sparing time to wax poetic on the subject of Parker House Rolls.

Considering that recipes didn't include a chocolate topping until the 1930s, it seems to me that wherever Boston cream pie itself originated, it was Pillsbury that introduced the modern version and Betty Crocker who made it America's gold standard. It was their recipes and advertisements that gave the dessert a surge of popularity in the 1940s and '50s, saving an old-fashioned classic from being lost to the sands of time.

My version of Boston cream pie is based on Pillsbury's 1934 recipe for an egg-yolk sponge cake, combining the richness of a yellow cake with the lightness of chiffon. It's easy to whip up, because you don't have to fold in a meringue—the leftover whites go into the vanilla pudding. That gives the filling a fresh, milky flavor and hue to contrast with the custardy yellow cake. The whole thing's slathered in a glossy chocolate ganache, easier to make than Betty Crocker's boiled chocolate glaze, and more intensely chocolatey than any nineteenth-century fondant.

This 1934 ad is the earliest reference to a chocolate-covered Boston cream pie that I could find.

BOSTON CREAM PIE

With layers of custardy yellow cake filled with creamy vanilla pudding and dripping with chocolate ganache, Boston cream pie is cake's answer to a hot fudge sundae. Like ice cream, my Tahitian Vanilla Pudding needs to be chilled, which makes this extravagant dessert easy to tackle in stages. Don't be nervous if you've never made a sponge cake before; I've streamlined the recipe into a one-bowl affair, with a bit of baking powder for backup so it's always tender, light, and fluffy. *See photo on page 76.*

YIELD: one 8-by-4-inch layer cake; 12 servings | **ACTIVE TIME:** 45 minutes |
DOWNTIME: 1 hour to cool, plus 2-hour refrigeration

---

1 recipe Tahitian Vanilla Pudding (page 255), chilled

For the Cake:

2 cups | 8 ounces bleached cake flour, such as Swans Down

2 teaspoons baking powder

1⅓ cups | 9 ounces sugar

¼ teaspoon Diamond Crystal kosher salt (half as much if iodized)

¼ teaspoon grated nutmeg

1 tablespoon vanilla extract

¾ cup | 7 ounces egg yolks (from 12 large eggs), brought to about 70°F

4 tablespoons | 2 ounces unsalted butter, melted

1 cup | 8 ounces milk (any percentage will do), brought to about 70°F

For the Ganache:

⅓ cup | 2½ ounces heavy cream

½ cup | 2½ ounces roughly chopped dark chocolate, about 62%

Key Point: The high pH and starch content of unbleached cake flour will cause this cake to collapse, as will traditional all-purpose flour.

Make the cake:
Adjust oven rack to middle position and preheat to 350°F at least 20 minutes in advance (the batter comes together faster than the preheat cycle). Line two 8-by-3-inch round cake pans with parchment and grease with pan spray. Sift flour into a medium bowl (if using cup measures, spoon into the cups and level with a knife before sifting) and whisk in baking powder.

Combine sugar, salt, nutmeg, vanilla, and egg yolks in the bowl of a stand mixer fitted with the whisk attachment. Mix on low speed to moisten, then increase to medium-high and whip until thick and roughly doubled in volume, with a clear vortex pattern left by the whisk, about 6 minutes. Reduce speed to medium-low and drizzle in butter, followed by milk. Once you've added the last drop, shut off the mixer, detach the bowl, and gently incorporate the cake flour with a balloon whisk. Fold the thin batter with a flexible spatula once or twice from the bottom up, and divide between the prepared pans (about 16 ounces each).

Bake until the cakes are lightly browned and firm, though your fingertip will leave a slight impression in the crust, about 25 minutes. Cool the cakes for 10 minutes, then loosen from the pans with a knife and invert onto a wire rack. Leave the pans on top (to entrap steam) and cool to room temperature, about 1 hour.

Assemble the cake:
Fold a 26-inch-long sheet of foil in thirds lengthwise to create a 4-inch-wide band. Trim top crust from the cakes with a serrated knife (this helps the pudding soak in; see pages 142–44 for details) and place one cut side up on a serving plate. Wrap the foil around the cake to form a snug collar and secure with tape. Stir chilled pudding until creamy, then spread over the cake in an even layer. Add the second cake cut side down, cover with plastic, and refrigerate for at least 2 hours, or up to 12 hours.

continued ↓

Make the ganache:

In a 1-quart stainless steel saucier, bring the cream to a simmer over medium heat. Remove from heat, add chocolate, and whisk until smooth. Pour into a glass measuring cup and refrigerate until thickened but still quite warm, about 25 minutes (or 85°F). Alternatively, the ganache can be made up to a week in advance and refrigerated, then microwaved in a few 5-second bursts until warmed to about 85°F.

Finish the cake:

Discard the foil. Stir the warm ganache and pour onto the dead center of the cake. Spiraling outward from the center with the back of a spoon, spread ganache toward the edges, nudging it over here and there so it drips down in a few places, but otherwise leaving the sides exposed. Let the cake stand at room temperature until ready to serve, at least 30 minutes and up to 3 hours.

Cut into wedges with a chef's knife, rocking from heel to tip (edge to center) to minimize squishing. If you like, serve with a handful of fresh raspberries.

Tightly covered in plastic, leftovers will keep for up to 24 hours at room temperature, or up to a week in the fridge; let stand for 30 minutes at room temperature before serving.

MAKE AHEAD

You can prepare the Tahitian Vanilla Pudding up to a week in advance; refrigerate the leftover egg yolks in an airtight container to use for the cake.

→ *Mix it up!*

BOOZY BOSTON: To add another layer of flavor, prepare a batch of Mexican Vanilla Syrup (page 349) and spike with 2 ounces (¼ cup) dark rum or another liquor of your choosing. After cutting off the top crusts, brush each cake with a few tablespoons of the flavored syrup. Proceed as directed.

GLUTEN-FREE: Replace the cake flour with 2 ounces (½ cup) white rice flour, 2 ounces (½ cup) tapioca flour or arrowroot, 3 ounces (⅔ cup) cornstarch, and 1 ounce (¼ cup) oat flour.

WHITE LAYER CAKE

The *Practical Housekeeper* was published in 1855 as "the young woman's friend," a guidebook to the art of domestic economy.[1] It offered a straightforward approach to household essentials such as baking bread, pickling vegetables, brewing ale, and even the finer points of cheese making. Among these basic necessities, author Marion Scott included eight recipes for butter cake made without egg yolks: White and Light Cake, Carolina Cake, Lady Cake, Premium Starch Cake, and not one but two Delicate Cakes and Silver Cakes.

These represent just a smattering of egg-white-based cakes common to the era. I found other cookbooks jam-packed with such recipes, their simplicity embellished only by fanciful names: Feather Cake, Pearl Cake, Velvet Cake, Perfection Cake, Cream Cake, Lily Cake, Mountain Cake, Merry Christmas Cake, and Ice Cream Cake (no actual ice cream involved). Each called for relatively equal parts refined flour and white sugar; their differences came down to the ratios of butter, egg whites, and dairy, generally milk or sour cream.

In the days before commercial baking powder, some recipes called for baking soda mixed with cream of tartar to leaven the cake, but most relied on whipped egg whites alone. In a spectacular example from 1858, Mary Mann's "Snow Cake" called for "the whites of sixteen eggs, beaten two hours" (as the author of *Christianity in the Kitchen: A Physiological Cook Book*, perhaps she approached it as a meditation).[2]

The sheer effort involved and the highly refined ingredients made white cake a quintessential dinner

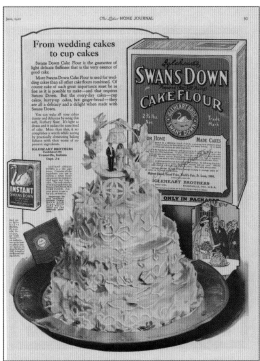

Brands like Swans Down helped popularize the notion of ultra-white cake.

party dessert, elegant and chic thanks to its fine crumb, pristine color, and delicate flavor—generally almond or vanilla. It also took a bit of skill to pull off, making success a point of pride.

Prior to the Civil War, white cakes were often baked as loaves or thick rounds, on occasion split to accommodate a bit of "custard cream." Bakers finished the cake with a layer of meringue as thin and white as frost. That anyone ate such "frosting" was purely incidental; it was simply the nineteenth century's answer to plastic wrap, covering the porous surface of the cake like a second skin, and briefly baked until hard to protect the cake from debris.

As ovens became more reliable, baking powder more common, and egg beaters more effective, white cakes were more commonly layered. My favorite example of this style comes from *Mrs. Elliot's Housewife*, published in 1870.[3] Author Sarah Elliot baked her "White Mountain Cake" in three layers, filled and iced with one of six meringue frostings: a simple paste of egg whites and sugar (the English style we'd call Royal Icing), raw egg whites beaten with sugar (French meringue), egg whites and sugar cooked in a water bath (Swiss meringue), or three different boiled icings of hot sugar syrup whipped with egg whites (Italian meringue).[4]

As their modern names suggest, these frostings have a distinctly European heritage, but something more uniquely American was on the way. In 1896, Janet McKenzie Hill of the *Boston Cooking School Magazine* popularized white layer cakes with marshmallow frosting.[5] Her unusual recipe started with a sugar syrup, like Italian meringue, but was whipped with store-bought marshmallows in place of whites.[6] It effectively created an eggless meringue, a fluffy cloud of sugar and protein so light that twentieth-century newspapers from the *Chicago Tribune* to Missouri's *Springfield Republican* would call the method "Marshmallow Meringue."[7]

At the same time, white cake itself was in the midst of a makeover. Hydrogenated vegetable oil shortening and specially bleached cake flour quite literally paled in comparison to yellow butter and ivory all-purpose flour, inspiring such manufacturers to adopt white layer cakes as a symbol of their refinement and purity. Wesson used three-layer white-on-white cakes in advertisements for liquid oil and shortening alike, while Crisco used a gleaming three-layer cake to promise a "white cake that's really white!"[8] Swans Down used full-color advertisements to prove how genuinely white a cake could be, tempting consumers with a wedding cake under swirls of white frosting. "Make a cake like this? Of course you can, but not with ordinary flour!"

The effects of these two ingredients weren't strictly cosmetic. Cake flour is milled from soft white wheat, naturally low in gluten-forming proteins and milder in flavor and color than heartier red varietals. On the flip side, it was higher in starch, which overthickened batters and prevented cakes from rising as they should. Manufacturers discovered that bleaching cake flour with chlorine gas damaged its starch, negating the bulk of its thickening power. The result was a flour that produced an especially white and tender cake that rose higher than those made from all-purpose.

Likewise, hydrogenated shortening wasn't simply paler than butter, it whipped up lighter during the creaming process while contributing a higher proportion of fat. Not only did that make cakes pale and fluffy, it added a welcome richness that compensated for the lack of egg yolks. Even more, its neutral flavor let the taste of vanilla, rather than butter, take center stage.

Together, cake flour and shortening produced a remarkably light, fluffy, moist, and flavorful vanilla cake with a snowy-white crumb that was a natural match for creamy white marshmallow frosting.[9] Alas, this all-American frosting fell out of favor in the 1930s, when it was replaced by a Swiss or Italian meringue in the guise of seven-minute frosting, which didn't require bakers to have a tin of marshmallows on hand.

In turn, seven-minute frosting gave way to "Butter Cream" in the late 1940s, a simple combination of butter and powdered sugar that took off during America's postwar prosperity. With only two ingredients (three if you count vanilla), these no-cook buttercreams required little time or effort to prepare, delivering a sense of luxury after years of scrimping through recession and war. They also gave Betty Crocker and Duncan Hines a chance to get in on the game, as fatty hydrogenated frostings could be easily packaged in tubs.

It was the beginning of the end for vanilla-on-vanilla cake, once the pinnacle of luxury, good taste, and skill. We see white cake as the lowest common denominator today, but it doesn't have to be. When built on the flavor of top-notch ingredients, the simplicity of white cake and frosting highlight the complexity of vanilla better than any other combination.

My white cake is loosely based on a recipe for "Mountain Cake" printed by the *American Agriculturalist* in 1858.[10] Perhaps because it was a farm journal, it called for buttermilk—a cheap by-product of churning butter that was never in short supply.

I've also updated that recipe with the ingredients that made white cake so phenomenal in the twentieth century: cake flour and snowy white vegetable oil. Instead of the artificially hydrogenated stuff, though, I reach for coconut oil, which is naturally solid at room temperature and every bit as rich. While refined oil has no flavor, the subtle aroma of virgin coconut oil adds a wonderful nuance to white cake, exaggerating the floral notes of vanilla.

I believe Janet Mackenzie Hill's marshmallow frosting stood on the verge of greatness: eggless, airy, and all-American. To bridge the gap between her semi-homemade frosting and tubs of white frosting we know today, I whip soft butter into my own homemade marshmallow creme. It combines the richness of a buttercream and the lightness of meringue, but without any eggy aftertaste to distract from the flavor of pure vanilla.

Light, fluffy, and never, ever dry. This all-vanilla, white-out birthday cake is dedicated to my Momma.

WHITE MOUNTAIN LAYER CAKE WITH MARSHMALLOW BUTTERCREAM

Forget everything you know about "white cake," this recipe's a game changer: rich and velvety to the point of creaminess, heady with vanilla, and almost as fluffy as angel's food cake. The secret is virgin coconut oil, which amplifies the aroma of butter and vanilla while creaming up lighter (and whiter) than butter alone. I top it all off with silky Marshmallow Buttercream, for a cake that's beguilingly complex despite its apparent simplicity. *See photo on page 109.*

YIELD: one 8-by-5-inch three-layer cake; 16 servings | **ACTIVE TIME:** about 45 minutes | **DOWNTIME:** 90 minutes to cool

1 recipe Marshmallow Buttercream (page 114)

Cake Batter:

4 cups | 16 ounces bleached cake flour such as Swans Down

2 sticks | 8 ounces unsalted butter, pliable but cool—about 65°F

⅔ cup | 4 ounces virgin coconut oil, solid but creamy—about 70°F

2¼ cups | 16 ounces sugar

2½ teaspoons baking powder

1 teaspoon baking soda

¾ teaspoon Diamond Crystal kosher salt (half as much if iodized)

1 cup | 8½ ounces egg whites (from 8 large eggs), brought to about 70°F (see note on page 111)

2 tablespoons | 1 ounce vanilla extract

1 teaspoon almond extract

2 cups | 16 ounces cultured low-fat buttermilk, brought to about 70°F

To better synchronize the downtime in both recipes, start the Marshmallow Buttercream before the cake. While it's resting, adjust an oven rack to lower-middle position and preheat to 325°F. Line three 8-by-3-inch anodized aluminum cake pans with parchment and grease with pan spray; if you don't have three pans, the remaining batter can be held at room temperature for up to 3 hours. (The cakes will brown more and rise less in 2-inch pans.) Sift the flour (if using cup measures, spoon into the cups and level with a knife before sifting) and set aside.

Combine butter, coconut oil, sugar, baking powder, baking soda, and salt in the bowl of a stand mixer fitted with a paddle attachment. Mix on low speed to moisten, then increase to medium and cream until fluffy and light, about 5 minutes, pausing to scrape the bowl and beater halfway through. With the mixer running, add the egg whites one at a time,

followed by vanilla and almond extracts.

Reduce speed to low and sprinkle in one-third of the flour, followed by one-third of the buttermilk. Alternate between the two, allowing each addition to be roughly incorporated before adding the next. Once smooth, fold with a flexible spatula to ensure it's well mixed from the bottom up. Divide among the prepared cake pans, about 22 ounces each.

Bake until the cakes are firm but pale, browned only around the very edges, about 40 minutes (or 210°F). A toothpick inserted into the center will emerge with a few crumbs still attached, and your fingertip will leave a slight indentation in the puffy crust.

Cool until no trace of warmth remains, about 90 minutes. Loosen the cakes from their pans with a knife. Invert onto a wire rack, peel off the parchment, and reinvert. Crumb-coat and frost with Marshmallow Buttercream according to the directions on pages 142–44.

Under a cake dome or an inverted pot, the frosted cake will keep for up to 24 hours at room temperature. After cutting, wrap leftover slices individually and store at room temperature for up to 2 days more.

A NOTE ABOUT INGREDIENT TEMPERATURES IN CAKE MAKING: Butter, buttermilk, and egg whites colder than 65°F or warmer than 70°F can produce a range of problems, from mild tunneling and air pockets in the cake to a heavy crumb or even a gummy layer along the bottom. Given that "room temperature" will vary from home to home, there's no standard rule of thumb for how to warm these ingredients, but in my 1000-watt microwave, three 6-second bursts at normal power is perfect for softening two sticks of butter; two 6-second bursts will knock the chill off a cup of egg whites; and a 25-second burst will bring a pint of buttermilk to cool room temperature. Alternately, they can simply be brought to room temperature and monitored with a digital thermometer.

→ *Mix it up!*

APPLE CIDER SPICE CAKE: All the cozy flavor of an apple cider doughnut with none of the frying. Omit the vanilla and almond extracts; add 1 tablespoon ground cinnamon and ¾ teaspoon grated nutmeg to the sugar. Replace the buttermilk with an equal amount of apple cider plus 1½ ounces (3 tablespoons) apple cider vinegar, and proceed as directed. You can't go wrong with classic Vanilla Marshmallow Buttercream, but the butterscotchy Brown Sugar variation (page 115) works well too.

FLUFFY WHITE CUPCAKES: Line cupcake pans with papers. Fill each cup with 1¾ ounces batter—about two-thirds full. Reduce the baking time to 15 minutes, or until a toothpick inserted into the center of a cupcake emerges with only a few crumbs attached. Makes about 36 cupcakes.

HAZELNUT TORTE: This is the cake my brother requested for his wedding, paired with the "Milk" Chocolate variation of my Marshmallow Buttercream (page 115) for a Nutella-esque dessert. Toast 9 ounces (2 shy cups) hazelnuts until golden and fragrant, about 10 minutes in a 350°F oven. Cool completely, then rub with a towel to remove their papery skins. Reduce cake flour to 12 ounces (3 cups), and pulse in a food processor with hazelnuts until powdery and fine. Handled the same way, almonds and pistachios work equally well.

LEMON SUNSHINE: For a bright and refreshing variation, omit the vanilla and almond extracts, add 2 tablespoons lemon zest to the sugar before creaming, and add 1 tablespoon lemon juice along with the buttermilk. Lime, orange, and grapefruit work equally well. I love this variation with tangy Cream Cheese Frosting (page 132).

GLUTEN-FREE: Replace cake flour with 8 ounces (1½ cups) cornstarch, 6 ounces (1¼ cups) white rice flour, 4½ ounces (1 cup) tapioca flour or arrowroot, and 1½ teaspoons potato flour.

MARSHMALLOW BUTTERCREAM

I've never been wild about American buttercream, a thick combination of butter, powdered sugar, and vanilla. While there's no arguing with its sweet simplicity, that convenience comes at a cost. Thanks to undissolved powdered sugar, it quickly crusts over in the open air, leaving a trace of grit in every bite. What's more, its heavy texture makes a mess of delicate layer cakes, churning up a sea of unsightly crumbs. Still, it's a sturdy sort of thing, perfect for sandwich cookies and kid-friendly cupcakes, whipped up in a flash.

Culinary school introduced me to European buttercream, airy concoctions of butter, sugar, and whipped eggs—yolks in the case of French buttercream, whites for Swiss and Italian. They take a little more effort to make, but these light and silky buttercreams glide effortlessly across a cake, making any concern about crumbs a thing of the past. Since the sugar is fully dissolved in the eggs or syrup, it won't recrystallize in a crusty layer, keeping every swirl of frosting lusciously smooth.

I always felt strangely disloyal topping down-home desserts like devil's food cake with fancy Italian buttercream, but it wasn't until I ran across Janet McKenzie Hill's 1896 recipe for "Marshmallow Frosting" that I realized there might be another way. An unabashedly American way. Her recipe, developed at the Boston Cooking School, melted store-bought marshmallows in a soft-ball syrup, then beat the two together until fluffy and soft.

This genius marshmallow maneuver created a cloud of sugar and protein to stand in for meringue—the default frosting of the day. While her recipe ended there, it inspired me to replace the meringue in a classic Swiss buttercream with my own homemade Marshmallow Creme (page 236). The result was as silky and light as anything you'd find in a French café, with the pure vanilla flavor of a classic American buttercream.

Aside from exorcising the inherently eggy aftertaste of a meringue, switching to homemade Marshmallow Creme instantly improved my buttercream's shelf life—up to a week at room temperature. The creme also provides a more versatile foundation, as the basic ingredients (sugar, water, and corn syrup) can be swapped for more flavorful options like brown sugar, coconut milk, and honey. Even better, the gelatin in the Marshmallow Creme creates a super-stable buttercream that can accommodate more liquid ingredients than European styles, letting me whip in an extra helping of fruit puree, melted chocolate, caramel, or liquor.

BUTTERCREAM TROUBLESHOOTING GUIDE

Like their European counterparts, Marshmallow Buttercream (page 114) and Cream Cheese Frosting (page 132) suffer from what I call Goldilocks Syndrome. At roughly 68°F, they have a silky-smooth texture that makes decorating a breeze, but they're thick and sturdy enough to support several layers of cake without refrigeration. Stray too far from that ideal working temperature, and they start to misbehave—turning soft and droopy when warm, or stiffening into a chilly lump.

However frustrating, these problems are as easy to fix as they are to avoid.

This Buttercream's Too Hot!

Scoop up a small spoonful of buttercream and turn it upside down. If it slides off the spoon or flops into a loose peak, it's too warm. The culprit is almost always **butter that's above 68°F**, at which point the buttercream becomes increasingly soft. Even when starting with cool butter, as the recipe suggests, **working in a kitchen warmer than 74°F** will inevitably soften the final buttercream. Warmer temperatures aren't a huge problem for finished cakes (though piped borders may turn droopy), but warm buttercream makes assembling or decorating a cake frustrating and messy.

How to fix it: If your buttercream's a little soft, refrigerate the whole bowl for 15 minutes. If it seems gooey or outright soupy, bump that up to 30 minutes. The buttercream may still look like a milkshake after chilling, but that's okay! Whip for 3 full minutes on medium-high with the whisk attachment, then reevaluate. If it is still too soft, refrigerate for another 15 minutes and try again.

If the buttercream remains soft and soupy despite refrigeration, there's a deeper issue at hand. With Marshmallow Buttercream, this may be a sign the sugar was not cooked or cooled to the correct temperature. With Cream Cheese Frosting, the custard may not have been fully cooked, or the cornstarch may have been mismeasured. In either recipe, experimentation with liquid or acidic ingredients, as well as with alternative fats such as coconut oil or shortening, may also produce unexpected failures.

This Buttercream's Too Cold!

Give the finished buttercream a taste—if it feels greasy or lingers as a buttery lump instead of melting on your tongue, it's too cold. Shy of accidentally mismeasuring an ingredient, the culprit is almost always **butter that's below 65°F**. Cold butter can't entrap air as it should, resulting in buttercreams that seem dense and waxy. Under extreme circumstances, buttercream can even curdle into something lumpy like cottage cheese, particularly when frozen or refrigerated buttercreams aren't fully thawed, or when the temperature in the kitchen drops below 65°F. Cooler temperatures don't create a huge problem for finished cakes (though cold foods rarely taste as good), but cold buttercream will churn up more crumbs during assembly and decoration.

How to fix it: If your buttercream's simply a little stiff, scoop ½ cup of it into a bowl and microwave until fully melted. If it's outright curdled, bump that to 1 cup. Pour the warm melted buttercream back into the bowl and mix on low to incorporate; then increase the speed to medium-high and whip for about 1 minute. If the buttercream remains stiff or dense, melt another portion as before, working until it's silky, smooth, and about 68°F.

Sometimes efforts to adjust a buttercream's temperature overshoot the goal completely, but there's no harm in continued adjustments. After you've fixed your first fussy frosting, future batches will be much easier to handle. As with Goldilocks, experiencing too hot and too cold for yourself makes it easy to recognize when things are Just Right.

Marshmallow Buttercream

If I had to have a signature recipe, this would be it—a frosting as silky as Swiss meringue, as light as a marshmallow, as rich as whipped cream, and sturdy enough to support a layer cake without refrigeration. Simple ingredients make my Marshmallow Buttercream the perfect showcase for a double dose of aromatic vanilla, but don't mistake it for a one-hit wonder. The variations below will get you started, and there are endless other ways to customize the flavor.

YIELD: about 6 cups; enough to fill, crumb-coat, and frost three 8-inch cake layers or 24 cupcakes

ACTIVE TIME: 1 hour | **DOWNTIME:** 2-hour rest

- 1 envelope (2¼ teaspoons | ¼ ounce) unflavored gelatin powder

- ¼ cup | 2 ounces cool tap water to bloom the gelatin

- 1 tablespoon vanilla extract and/or 1 vanilla bean

- ¾ cup | 6 ounces water for the sugar syrup

- ¾ cup plus 2 tablespoons | 10 ounces light corn syrup

- 2 cups | 14½ ounces sugar

- ½ teaspoon Diamond Crystal kosher salt (half as much if iodized)

- 5 sticks | 20 ounces unsalted butter, soft but cool—about 65°F

Make the marshmallow base
In a small bowl, mix the gelatin with 2 ounces (¼ cup) cool tap water and vanilla extract, if using. If using a vanilla bean, split lengthwise with a paring knife, run the flat of the blade down each half to scrape out the seeds, and add to the gelatin without stirring. (Reserve the pod for another project.)

Combine remaining 6 ounces (¾ cup) water, corn syrup, sugar, and salt in a 3-quart stainless steel pot and set over medium heat. Stir mixture with a fork until bubbling, about 5 minutes, then increase heat to medium-high. Clip on a digital thermometer and cook, *without stirring*, until the clear syrup registers 250°F, about 8 minutes.

Transfer thermometer to the bowl of a stand mixer and pour in the hot syrup all at once, scraping the pot with a heat-resistant spatula. Cool to exactly 212°F, about 8 minutes, then add gelatin. With the whisk attachment, mix on low speed until the gelatin is melted, then increase

to medium-high and whip until thick, snowy white, roughly tripled in volume, and beginning to ball up around the whisk, about 10 minutes. Scrape into a greased 4-cup container, cover tightly, and let stand at cool room temperature until thick and firm, at least 2 hours, or up to 1 week.

Make the buttercream:
Transfer marshmallow base to the bowl of a stand mixer fitted with the whisk attachment. Whipping on medium speed, begin adding the butter 1 tablespoon at a time, waiting for about 5 seconds after each addition. The fluffy creme will cling to the whisk at first but loosen as the butter is incorporated. Once combined, scrape the bowl with a flexible spatula and whip a minute more. The buttercream should be light and creamy but thick enough to hang upside down from a spoon. If it seems stiff or dense (feeling greasy rather than melting on your tongue), scoop a cup into a small bowl and microwave until completely melted, about 30 seconds.

Return the melted buttercream to the bowl and whip 15 seconds on medium-high. Conversely, if it seems loose or gooey, refrigerate the entire bowl 15 minutes, then whip 3 minutes on medium-high. For more details, check out the Buttercream Troubleshooting Guide on page 113.

Use according to the directions on pages 110–11, or set aside at cool room temperature for a few hours, until needed, and rewhip before use.

MAKE AHEAD

In an airtight container, the buttercream can be refrigerated for up to 3 weeks, or frozen for 6 months. Soften to about 66°F at room temperature (about 5 hours if refrigerated or 12 hours if frozen), and rewhip before using.

TROUBLESHOOTING

Marshmallow depends on an accurate digital thermometer, so if things go wrong, you can bet the readings were off. This can happen if you misread an analogue thermometer or fail to fully submerge the probe in the syrup, or simply when good thermometers go bad (a sad fact of life). It can also happen when the batteries start to fade. Test the accuracy of your thermometer by making sure it reads 212°F in a pot of boiling water.

In winter months, the hot syrup may harden along the bottom of a chilly mixing bowl. Warm the bowl in hot water to prevent this problem, and dry well before use.

→ *Mix it up!*

BOOZY BOURBON: Whipping the finished buttercream on medium, drizzle in up to 4 ounces (½ cup) of bourbon, tasting along the way to achieve your desired intensity. Alternatively, try applejack, brandy, dark rum, or another flavorful spirit.

BROWN SUGAR: Mild and butterscotchy, perfect for pairing with my Apple Cider Spice Cake (page 111). Replace the white sugar with 15 ounces (1¾ cups) firmly packed dark brown sugar. To add a praline-like flavor and crunch, whip up to 6 ounces (1½ cups) Crispy Pecan Sprinkle (see Crispy Peanut Sprinkle, page 70) into the finished buttercream.

CHERRY ALMOND: Tart, fruity, and beautifully pink. In place of water, bloom the gelatin in 2¼ ounces (¼ cup) pure unsweetened tart cherry juice; omit the vanilla and flavor with ½ teaspoon almond extract. Replace the second portion of water with 12 ounces (1⅓ cups) pure unsweetened tart cherry juice. It will take about 10 minutes longer to reach 250°F, but otherwise proceed as directed. For a more pronounced flavor, drizzle 2 ounces (¼ cup) kirsch or maraschino liquor into the finished buttercream while whipping on medium-low.

DARK OR "MILK" CHOCOLATE: Unlike ganache, which stiffens quickly once it's whipped, this variation has a soft and spreadable consistency that's perfect for decorative flourishes. Melt 12 ounces (2 cups) roughly chopped 72% dark chocolate and whip into the finished buttercream on medium. For a lighter "milk" chocolate flavor, reduce that to 4 ounces (¾ cup) roughly chopped chocolate.

continued ↓

HONEY: Made with delicate clover or orange blossom honey, this gently floral buttercream will underscore the toasty spice of Brown-Butter Carrot Cake (page 138). For something more assertive, try darker honeys like buckwheat or goldenrod. Replace the corn syrup with an equal amount of honey and use a 5-quart pot to accommodate the foaming of the syrup; otherwise, proceed as directed.

PEANUT BUTTER BLISS: One of my favorite frostings for Devil's Food Layer Cake (page 124). Whipping the finished buttercream on medium speed, add 6 ounces (¾ cups) creamy peanut butter 1 tablespoon at a time. For added crunch, whip in up to 6 ounces (1½ cups) Crispy Peanut Sprinkle (page 70).

SALTED CARAMEL: For those who love sweet and savory desserts, try this variation with Devil's Food Layer Cake (page 124) or Apple Cider Spice Cake (page 111). Increase kosher salt to ½ teaspoon and prepare the buttercream as directed. After the final addition of butter, drizzle in up to 11 ounces (1 cup) room-temperature Caramel Sauce (page 306).

STRAWBERRY ROSE: Paired with the Lemon Sunshine version of White Mountain Layer Cake (page 110), this variation tastes like strawberry lemonade. Whipping the finished buttercream on medium, drizzle in up to 6 ounces (⅔ cup) room-temperature Strawberry Syrup (see Strawberry Ice Cream, page 340), followed by 2 teaspoons rose water.

YELLOW LAYER CAKE WITH FUDGE FROSTING

Egg whites were the workhorse of nineteenth-century desserts, an essential ingredient in batters and frostings alike. Elegant cakes such as white mountain and angel's food would plow through the whites, leaving a surplus of second-rate yolks. By virtue of starting with a cast-off ingredient, yellow cake had all the charm of a turkey sandwich after Thanksgiving—loved by all, but enjoyed with less fanfare.[1]

As a vehicle for leftovers, golden yellow cakes weren't shy about their use of yolks.[2] In 1857, South Carolina's *Edgefield Advertiser* published a thoroughly typical recipe that began: "Take yolks of one dozen eggs. . . ."[3] That gave yellow cakes a hearty, custard-like flavor well suited to a bold chocolate frosting. Despite its decidedly yellow heart, that combination was commonly known as chocolate cake (see Devil's Food Layer Cake, page 124).

When the *Chicago Tribune* ran a special on "Chocolate Cake" in 1876, each reader-submitted recipe started with three or four layers of buttery yellow cake filled and topped with chocolate.[4] These frostings ranged from "chocolate jelly" and "chocolate paste" (both a sort of poor man's ganache) to chocolate meringue and a creamy boiled candy made from milk, sugar, and chocolate.

We'd call it fudge frosting today, but in 1876, the term had yet to be invented (see Fudge, page 71). Once it did, this old-fashioned icing came into vogue with the marketing craze surrounding fudge in the early twentieth century.[5] From Calumet baking powder and Jelke Good Luck margarine to Domino powdered sugar, Baker's Chocolate, and Eagle Brand condensed milk, yellow cake with fudge frosting became an advertising goldmine.

Over the years, "fudge" has become synonymous with any sort of chocolate frosting, and I think that's a shame. While I love simple ganache and chocolate buttercream, there's absolutely nothing like the melting richness of genuine fudge. As a patriotic pastry chef, letting a once-classic recipe slip away seems like something of a cultural blow, robbing our cuisine of a uniquely American tradition: frosting cakes with candy (see White Layer Cake, pages 107–8).

To that end, I've retooled the ratio of sugar and butter in my recipe for Baltimore Fudge (page 74), mellowing its sweetness and boosting its intensity for a softly set fudge that's easier to sculpt into those lovely swoops and swirls. But don't worry; if the idea of busting out a candy thermometer seems like too much, you have plenty more options (see the chocolate variations for Marshmallow Buttercream, page 115, and Milk Chocolate Frosting, page 127).

Most yellow cakes today call for whole eggs, and I can't argue with that sort of simplicity and convenience; I even use such a recipe as the foundation for Upside-Down Pineapple Cutout Cake (page 93). But for those of us who love to bake, a ramekin of egg yolks is an all-too-familiar sight, left over from Angel's Food Cake (page 98), Fluffy Cocoa Nougat (page 302), and Tahitian Vanilla Pudding (page 255).

For that reason, I think it's important to balance these desserts with a traditional recipe to polish off their wayward yolks. My Classic Yellow Layer Cake draws on the same ratio given for "Plain Golden Cake" in *The Practical Housekeeper*, written by Marion Scott in 1855.[6] It's roughly equal parts flour and sugar, with an egg yolk for every ounce of butter. The only wild card in my recipe is potato flour.

After my success with mashed potato doughnuts (see page 187), I wanted to see if that sort of fluffiness could translate to yellow cake, and I was absolutely blown away by the results. A single tablespoon of potato flour improved the rise of my Classic Yellow Cake by a full half inch while entrapping enough moisture to extend its shelf life another day. I've kept potato flour as an optional addition, as I had no complaints about my recipe prior to discovering its magic, but it's well worth seeking it out (most supermarkets sell it alongside other specialty flours, from brands like Bob's Red Mill).

CLASSIC YELLOW LAYER CAKE

This is the yellow cake of my childhood, two fluffy layers smothered in Fudge Frosting and just begging for a glass of milk. It's not a family recipe—we grew up on Betty Crocker—but I've managed to capture that same feathery lightness with an unusual trick: potato flour. It's starchy and absorbent, giving the batter the structure it needs to puff up light while allowing me to cut back on the cake flour to keep the cake tender and moist. For the most vibrant golden hue and rich, custardy flavor, be sure to reach for organic eggs.

YIELD: one 8-by-4½-inch layer cake; 12 servings | **ACTIVE TIME:** about 45 minutes | **DOWNTIME:** 2 hours to cool

3⅓ cups | 13½ ounces bleached cake flour, such as Swans Down

2 sticks | 8 ounces unsalted butter, pliable but cool—about 65°F

2 cups | 14 ounces sugar

1 tablespoon baking powder

1 tablespoon potato flour (not potato flakes or starch), such as Bob's Red Mill

1 teaspoon Diamond Crystal kosher salt (half as much if iodized)

½ cup | 5 ounces egg yolks, preferably organic (from about 8 large eggs), brought to about 70°F

4½ teaspoons vanilla extract

1⅓ cups | 13 ounces milk (any percentage will do), brought to about 70°F

1 recipe Fudge Frosting (page 121)

Adjust oven rack to lower-middle position and preheat to 350°F. Line two 8-by-3-inch anodized aluminum pans with parchment and grease with pan spray (the cakes will brown more and rise less in 2-inch pans). Sift the flour (if using a cup measure, spoon into the cup and level with a knife before sifting) and set aside.

Combine the butter, sugar, baking powder, potato flour, and salt in the bowl of a stand mixer fitted with a paddle attachment. Mix on low to moisten, then increase to medium and cream until fluffy and light, about 5 minutes, pausing to scrape the bowl and beater halfway through. With the mixer running, add the egg yolks one at a time, followed by the vanilla.

Reduce speed to low and sprinkle in one-third of the flour, followed by a third of the milk. Alternate between the two, allowing each addition to be roughly incorporated before adding the next. Once it is smooth, fold the batter with a flexible spatula to ensure it's well mixed from the

bottom up. Divide between the prepared cake pans, about 26 ounces each.

Bake until the cakes are golden and firm, about 40 minutes (or 210°F). A toothpick inserted into the center will emerge with a few crumbs still attached, and your fingertip will leave a slight indentation in the puffy crust. Cool until no trace of warmth remains, about 2 hours.

Loosen the cooled cakes from their pans with a knife, invert onto a wire rack, peel off the parchment, and reinvert. Trim the top crust from the cakes with a serrated knife (this helps the cake better absorb moisture from the frosting). Place one layer cut side up on a serving plate. Cover with a cup of frosting, spread it into an even layer with the back of a spoon, and top with the second layer, cut side down. Finish the top and sides of the cake with the remaining frosting, sculpting it into swoops and swirls with the back of the spoon.

continued ↓

This is the birthday cake I bake for myself, with thick fudge frosting spread over every buttery, golden layer.

Under a cake dome or an inverted pot, the frosted cake will keep for up to 24 hours at room temperature. After cutting, wrap leftover slices individually and store at room temperature for up to 2 days more.

TROUBLESHOOTING
See note on page 111 for more information on how ingredient temperature can affect this recipe.

Light and fluffy yellow cake depends on the low protein content of cake flour, so resist the temptation to reach for all-purpose; it will invariably produce a coarse, corn-bread-like cake.

→ Mix it up!

ALMOND TORTE: Reduce the flour to 7½ ounces (1⅔ cups). Toast 6 ounces (1¼ cups) whole unblanched almonds in a 350°F oven until fragrant, about 10 minutes. Cool completely, then pulse with the flour in a food processor until fine. Proceed as directed. This variation works equally well with toasted hazelnuts or pecans.

CLASSIC YELLOW CUPCAKES: Line cupcake pans with papers. Fill each with 1¾ ounces batter, about two-thirds full. Bake for 22 minutes, or until a toothpick inserted into the center of a cupcake emerges with only a few crumbs attached. Makes about 28 cupcakes.

EGGNOG: The custard-like richness of my Classic Yellow Cake makes a natural foundation for the classic taste of eggnog. Add 1 teaspoon grated nutmeg and ½ teaspoon ground cinnamon along with the salt. Replace the vanilla extract with an equal amount of bourbon or brandy. Frost with Boozy Bourbon (or Brandy) variation of Marshmallow Buttercream (page 115).

PUMPKIN SPICE: This autumnal variation has a velvety crumb-like pound cake and a vibrant pumpkin color. Along with salt, add 2 teaspoons ground ginger, 2 teaspoons ground cinnamon, and ½ teaspoon ground cloves. Reduce milk to 6 ounces (⅔ cup), mixed with 12 ounces (1⅓ cups) canned pumpkin puree, but otherwise prepare batter as directed. Divide between the prepared pans, about 30 ounces each, and bake 40 minutes. Cool, level, and finish with Cream Cheese Frosting (page 132). If you like, sprinkle with 5 ounces (1 cup) toasted pecan pieces, and serve with a drizzle of Malted Butterscotch Sauce (page 352).

GLUTEN-FREE: Replace the cake flour with 4 ounces (1 cup) tapioca flour or arrowroot, 4 ounces (¾ cup) white rice flour, 4 ounces (¾ cup) cornstarch, and 2 ounces (½ cup) oat flour. Omit the potato flour; this variation is moist, fluffy, and tender without it.

Fudge Frosting

When I say *fudge*, I'm not waxing poetic about the intensity of my favorite chocolate frosting. I mean honest-to-goodness fudge: milk, brown sugar, and dark chocolate boiled into a soft candy and whipped until creamy smooth. Its old-fashioned flavor, slow melting richness, and genuine *fudginess* are the perfect counterpoint to an all-American, Classic Yellow Layer Cake.

YIELD: about 3 cups; enough to fill and frost two 8-inch cake layers or 24 cupcakes | **ACTIVE TIME:** about 30 minutes |
DOWNTIME: 60 minutes to cool, plus 30-minute rest

1 cup | 8 ounces milk (any percentage will do)

1 cup firmly packed | 8 ounces light brown sugar

1 cup | 7 ounces white sugar

½ teaspoon Diamond Crystal kosher salt (half as much if iodized)

2 cups | 8 ounces roughly chopped 72% dark chocolate (not chips)

1 tablespoon vanilla extract

1 stick | 4 ounces unsalted butter, creamy and soft—about 68°F

Temperature Note: Most fudge fiascoes are temperature related. If the boiling syrup is not cooked to 236°F, the frosting will not set as it should. If it is cooked to a significantly higher temperature, it will be stiff and crumbly. If it is not cooled to 115°F, the frosting will crystallize. Avoid these problems with an accurate digital thermometer, which should register 212°F in a pot of boiling water.

Make the fudge:
Combine milk, brown sugar, white sugar, salt, and chocolate in a 3-quart stainless steel pot. Set over medium heat, and stir constantly with a fork until the chocolate has fully melted and the syrup begins to bubble, about 6 minutes. Then stop stirring.

Wet a pastry brush in a ramekin of water and wipe it all around the sides of the pan, wherever you see sugar crystals or splashes of chocolate. Rewet as needed, "washing" the sides until spotless. Be generous! Extra water will not harm the fudge, but sugar crystals will. Clip on a digital thermometer and cook, *without stirring*, until it registers 236°F, about 6 minutes (the syrup will bubble vigorously, but it will not overflow a 3-quart pot). Remove from the heat and cool to 115°F, roughly 1 hour. As the foamy syrup recedes, you may notice flecks of chocolate around the sides of the pot, but this is perfectly normal.

Whip the frosting:
Scrape the dark, glossy syrup into the bowl of a stand mixer fitted with a paddle attachment. Add the vanilla and mix on low speed to incorporate,

then increase to medium and beat until the fudge is thick and creamy, about 10 minutes. Reduce to medium-low and continue beating until the frosting cools to 68°F, about 5 minutes. Add the butter a tablespoon at a time, waiting until each piece is fully incorporated before adding the next. Scrape the bowl and beater with a flexible spatula, then cover and let stand at room temperature until softly set, about 30 minutes, or up to 12 hours; briefly rebeat before using.

Leftovers can be frozen in a ziptop bag, then melted to use as a chocolate glaze.

TROUBLESHOOTING

Chilly frosting will take on a curdled or oily appearance that's easily corrected with a bit of gentle heat. Simply scoop a cup of frosting into a small bowl and microwave until completely melted, about 30 seconds. Return to the bowl of frosting and beat until glossy and smooth, about 10 seconds.

DEVIL'S FOOD CAKE

Prior to the late nineteenth century, the high cost of chocolate demanded that recipes handle it as a seasoning rather than a building block. So while we think of "chocolate cake" as something with chocolate in it, back then it only needed to have chocolate *on it*.[1] Whether in advertisements for Baker's chocolate or articles in *Good Housekeeping*, recipes for chocolate cake were invariably based on layers of buttery yellow cake (generally made from yolks, though whole eggs were also common).[2]

The frosting portion of the recipe was sometimes referred to as a "paste".[3] When Ohio's *Highland Weekly News* published a recipe for "Chocolate Cake" in 1869, it began with a three-egg yellow cake and ended with a note on paste. This was something of a poor man's ganache, one part chocolate to three parts milk and sugar, boiled until thick and spread between the cake layers.

Of course, recipes more commonly called such a thing chocolate frosting, but the idea of "chocolate paste" was by no means rare. A recipe identical to the one from Ohio was published in *A Dictionary of Everyday Wants* in New York, filed under the heading "Chocolate Paste Cake," in 1872.[4] From 1876 to 1877, syndicated recipes for a spiced chocolate paste appeared in newspapers from Pennsylvania to Kansas, including directions explaining that it was a frosting for cake.[5] In the 1880s, the style was often called a chocolate jelly cake, from instructions that the milk, chocolate, and sugar should be boiled until thick like jelly.[6]

Culinary historians note that the first devil's food cake, intensely chocolate both inside and out, didn't come along until the publication of *Mrs. Rorer's New Cookbook* in 1902.[7] It's the recipe said to have revolutionized chocolate cake in America, but I've discovered that Sarah Rorer didn't dream it up. As early as 1871, some recipes for chocolate jelly cake included two sets of directions: one for using the "jelly" as a frosting, and another for mixing it straight into the cake.[8]

Perhaps because people were more comfortable with traditional frosting, the daredevil idea didn't take hold until 1893, when the April issue of *Table Talk* included a recipe for "Devil's Cake!" (exclamation mark included).[9] At first glance, it seemed identical to any other chocolate cake from that era, with ingredients for a paste of boiled milk and chocolate followed by ingredients for a three-yolk yellow cake. The devil was in the details: explicit instructions for stirring the chocolate paste into the batter, leaving no room for traditionalists to back down.[10] Thanks to the magazine's national circulation (and the recipe's upgrade to brown sugar), word of this devilish cake spread fast; in 1894, the *Frederick Daily News* proclaimed devil's food as "black as only his satanic majesty can be."[11]

Within a decade, devil's food would come to a fork in the road, as recipes began trading the hot milk and chocolate paste for a simpler one made from cold buttermilk and cocoa powder, a path that would eventually lead to red velvet cake (page 130).[12] During the Great Depression, recipes for devil's food traded egg yolks for whole eggs and hot milk for hot coffee, adding a note of bitterness that coaxed out even more chocolate flavor.

Devil's food is so synonymous with chocolate cake today that bakers no longer look to its historical definition, using the name to dress up any old chocolate cake. Browsing through any given cookbook, devil's food seems to be commonly treated as a chiffon cake, made from whipped eggs, sugar, and oil. While fantastically moist and light, such recipes lack the buttery flavor and melting softness of an old-school devil's food cake.

These recipes commonly justify their lack of butter by citing the fact that dairy can mute the taste of chocolate, and while that's true, butter actually contains very little lactose. So long as the recipe doesn't

Advertisements like this helped crystallize the distinction between chocolate and yellow cake.

call for milk or cream, an all-butter chocolate cake can still be fantastically intense. For that reason, I include the hot coffee common to Depression-era recipes, but the remaining ingredients (butter, brown sugar, and melted chocolate) come from the 1873 original.

My recipe has the soft crumb and lingering richness that only butter can provide, with the fudgy richness of brown sugar and melted chocolate.

Historically, that was the only thing used to flavor devil's food, as the expense of chocolate and cocoa forced an either/or approach. But including a few ounces of starchy cocoa powder allows me to cut back on flour. That simple adjustment makes the cake even more tender, flavorful, and dark. Sure, it may fly in the face of tradition, but that's a deal with the devil I'm willing to make.

ONE-BOWL DEVIL'S FOOD LAYER CAKE WITH MILK CHOCOLATE FROSTING

This devilish cake is as black as sin, loaded with coffee, chocolate, cocoa, and butterscotchy brown sugar. The acidity of these deliciously dark ingredients provokes an intensely fizzy reaction from the baking soda for a cake that bakes up fluffy and light, without the need to whip or cream the batter—just stir everything together, and you're done! Paired with mellow Milk Chocolate Frosting, it's a celebration of chocolate in every form.

YIELD: one 8-by-4-inch three-layer cake; 16 servings | **ACTIVE TIME:** about 15 minutes | **DOWNTIME:** 90 minutes to cool

3 sticks | 12 ounces unsalted butter

1½ cups | 12 ounces black coffee, or black tea such as Assam

1 cup | 3 ounces Dutch-process cocoa powder, such as Cacao Barry Extra Brute

1¼ cups | 6 ounces finely chopped dark chocolate, about 72%

2 cups gently packed | 16 ounces light brown sugar

1 tablespoon vanilla extract

1 teaspoon Diamond Crystal kosher salt (half as much if iodized)

6 large eggs, straight from the fridge

3 tablespoons | 1½ ounces egg yolks (from about 3 large eggs)

2 cups | 9 ounces all-purpose flour, such as Gold Medal

1 tablespoon baking soda

1 recipe Milk Chocolate Frosting (page 127)

1 cup | 5 ounces Homemade Oreo® Crumbs (page 214; optional)

Adjust oven rack to lower-middle position and preheat to 350°F. Line three 8-by-3-inch anodized aluminum cake pans with parchment and grease with pan spray; if you don't have three pans, the remaining batter can be held at room temperature for up to 90 minutes. (The cakes won't rise quite as high in 2-inch pans.)

Combine butter and coffee in a 5-quart stainless steel saucier and set over low heat. Once the butter is melted, remove from heat and whisk in the cocoa and chocolate, followed by the brown sugar, vanilla, and salt. Mix in the eggs and yolks. Sift in the flour (if using a cup measure, spoon into the cup and level with a knife before sifting) and baking soda. Whisk thoroughly to combine, then divide among the prepared cake pans (about 23 ounces each).

Bake until the cakes are firm, though your finger will leave an impression in the puffy crust, about 30 minutes (or 210°F). A toothpick inserted into the center will emerge with a few crumbs still attached. Cool until

no trace of warmth remains, about 90 minutes.

Meanwhile, prepare the Milk Chocolate Frosting; note that the frosting must be used as soon as it is made.

Loosen the cakes from their pans with a knife, invert onto a wire rack, peel off the parchment, and reinvert. Trim the top crusts from the cakes with a serrated knife (this helps the cakes better absorb moisture from the frosting). Place one layer cut side up on a serving plate. Cover with a cup of the frosting, spreading it into an even layer with the back of a spoon. Repeat with the second and third layers, cut side down. Finish the top and sides of the cake with the remaining frosting, and coat with cookie crumbs, if you like.

Under a cake dome or an inverted pot, the frosted cake will keep for up to 24 hours at room temperature. After cutting, wrap leftover slices individually and store at room temperature for up to 4 days more.

continued ↓

The best, and easiest, chocolate cake
I know—dark as a moonless night.

→ Mix it up!

CHOCOLATE CHERRY: Like coffee in the basic recipe, cherry juice takes a backseat to dark chocolate in this recipe, but it adds a fruity brightness, compared to coffee's earthy depth. It's a nice way to lighten the cake for summer—especially when paired with pale pink Cherry Almond Buttercream (page 115). Replace the coffee with an equal amount of pure unsweetened tart cherry juice and proceed as directed.

DEVIL'S FOOD CUPCAKES: Line cupcake pans with papers. Fill each with 1¾ ounces of batter, about two-thirds full. Bake for 15 minutes, or until a toothpick inserted into the center of a cupcake emerges with only a few crumbs attached. Makes about 40 cupcakes.

GERMAN CHOCOLATE: This rustic cake won't win any beauty pageants, but with chewy coconut, crunchy pecans, and gooey dulce de leche between every layer, it doesn't have to. Prepare a batch of Quick Condensed Milk according to the Dulce de Leche variation on page 170. Off heat, stir in 8 ounces (2 cups) toasted pecan pieces and 8 ounces (2⅔ cups) sweetened shredded coconut flakes, plus salt to taste. Trim the top crust from each cake and stack on a serving plate with a heaping cup of warm filling spread over each layer, leaving the sides exposed. Serve immediately, or wrap tightly in plastic and store up to 5 days at room temperature.

GRASSHOPPER: In place of coffee, steep 6¾ teaspoons loose-leaf peppermint (or 6 individual teabags) with 12 ounces (1½ cups) hot water for 5 minutes; strain and combine with butter as directed. For the chocolate, try one flavored with natural peppermint, such as Endangered Species 72% Forest Mint (do not use mint chocolate candies). In addition to vanilla, add ¾ teaspoon pure peppermint extract. Reduce salt to ¾ teaspoon, and reduce baking soda to 2¼ teaspoons. Bake as directed.

TOASTED MARSHMALLOW: Instead of Milk Chocolate Frosting, finish the cake with a batch of Seven-Minute Frosting (page 157). After frosting the cake, toast with a small blowtorch (which you can buy on the cheap at the hardware store) to brown and crisp the meringue. Serve immediately.

GLUTEN-FREE: Replace the all-purpose flour with 3¼ ounces (¾ cup) teff flour, 3 ounces (¾ cup) tapioca flour or arrowroot, 1½ ounces (½ cup) coconut flour, and 1½ ounces (⅓ cup) white rice flour.

Milk Chocolate Frosting

Ganache calls to mind an inky black glaze, equal parts cream and chocolate, but with a few tweaks it whips into a light and creamy frosting. Its mellow sweetness pairs perfectly with the intensity of my dark chocolate Devil's Food Cake.

YIELD: about 5½ cups, enough to frost three 8-inch cake layers or 30 cupcakes | **ACTIVE TIME:** 15 minutes | **DOWNTIME:** 90-minute refrigeration

3 cups | 24 ounces heavy cream

3¾ cups | 20 ounces 35% milk chocolate, finely chopped

¼ teaspoon Diamond Crystal kosher salt, or more to taste (half as much if iodized)

In a 3-quart stainless steel saucier, warm the cream over medium heat. When bubbling hard around the edges, pour over chocolate in the bowl of a stand mixer. Whisk by hand until smooth, stir in the salt, and set aside until no longer steaming. Cover and refrigerate six hours, or until thick and cold, around 45°F. Alternatively, cool in a sinkful of ice water, stirring and scraping from time to time with a flexible spatula, about 1 hour. With a whisk attachment, whip on medium-high until thick and silky, with a frosting-like consistency. This can take from 75 to 120 seconds, so watch it closely. Use immediately. Leftovers can be frozen up to 6 months in a pint-sized zip-top bag, then gently warmed to spoon over your favorite desserts.

→ *Mix it up!*

WHITE CHOCOLATE VANILLA: Split a vanilla bean lengthwise with a paring knife, add to the cream, and bring to a simmer as directed. Remove from heat, cover tightly, and steep up to 4 hours. Remove vanilla pod, scrape the flavorful goo back into the cream, and return to a simmer. Finish with 18 ounces (3 cups) finely chopped white chocolate, such as Cacao Barry's 34% Zephyr. Due to the added cocoa butter, this version will whip up a little faster.

RED VELVET CAKE

Red velvet cake is the secret love child of devil's food and a Victorian mistress, equal parts science lesson and urban legend, with a century of culinary heritage overshadowed by decades of chemical and corporate interference. In short, perhaps the most American cake of them all.

Its history begins in 1873, when cookbook author Alvin Wood Chase described America's yearning "to have nice and smooth names applied to things."[1] In his *Second Receipt Book,* Alvin cites "Velvet Cake" as a specific example of the trend. It wasn't any particular type of cake, really, just a name that could be freely applied to anything with a fine and tender crumb.

Twenty years later, the first devil's cake appeared (see page 122), accompanied by a recipe more clearly defined: an all-yolk cake flavored with a hot paste made from hot milk, brown sugar, and chocolate. The two would meet in 1911, with a recipe for "Velvet Cocoa Cake" published in an Ohio newspaper. It was a wee little cake with all the hallmarks of devil's food, made with egg yolk, brown sugar, and hot milk, but cocoa powder in place of chocolate, baked in a loaf or layers to finish with a boiled-milk frosting.[2] Two years later, newspapers in Indiana, Wisconsin, and Pennsylvania printed the same recipe, which continued to circulate for years to come.[3]

As the recipe for velvet cocoa cake drifted farther south, it evolved to incorporate sour milk or buttermilk, which produced a reddish hue, earning it the nickname "Red Devil" as early as 1926.[4] For the most part, "red" simply helped distinguish the cake from the inky-black crumb of a proper devil's food. As far as I can tell, its color became the stuff of legend after a 1931 interview with Delia Garrett, a home economics professor at the University of South Dakota in Vermillion.[5]

Delia spoke without a trace of sensationalism, describing how the chemical reaction between baking soda and buttermilk worked to enhance the natural pigments in cocoa powder to a warm "redbrown" hue.

Apparently the fact that she lived in Vermillion was too much for reporters to ignore, because sensational stories about the "science" of red chocolate cake turned up across the nation, with Delia's conservative description amped up to a flaming red.[6]

By 1933, the color theory had snowballed into the notion that red cakes somehow tasted better, with newspaper kitchen columns treating that as a matter of fact.[7] The pervasiveness of the myth might have been a bit of wishful thinking, as cocoa was far more affordable than chocolate during the Great Depression.[8]

Presumably frustrated with results that didn't live up to the hype, Lynn Chambers popularized doctoring buttermilk-cocoa cakes with a teaspoon of red dye in her syndicated kitchen column in 1942.[9] That kicked off a nationwide trend, with bakers adding anywhere from one to four ounces of artificial dye to punch up the red.[10] Its extravagant color made any comparison to devil's food a thing of the past, and the cake's name finally coalesced into "Red Velvet" in Texas newspapers in 1951.[11]

With every passing year, the emphasis of the recipe shifted further away from softness and flavor to color, leading to recipes in the psychedelic '60s that called for mere teaspoons of cocoa but up to a quarter pound of dye.[12] Red velvet was flat-out tripping by the time tangy cream cheese frosting became de rigueur in the '70s,[13] and today's most popular recipes are typically verbatim reprints of those vintage duds.

Despite my commitment to homemade, from time to time, I'm all about a little dye. A few tiny drops can be stretched into a thousand brilliant sprinkles that are truly a feast for the eyes. But when a recipe reaches the point that it's calling for bottles of dye in a cake that serves eight to twelve, I have to draw the line. As a chef, I just can't invest that heavily in an ingredient that plays no role in the taste, texture, or aroma of my cake.

So I gave up the hype to focus on *velvet,* the silky crumb that once defined an otherwise simple cocoa cake. I also replaced the buttermilk with red wine, which has a lower pH that produces a stronger reaction with the baking soda, making the cake more tender and light. Unconcerned with today's obsession with color, I tested my recipe through more than a dozen different brands of natural cocoa powder to find the most flavorful of them all.

Unsurprisingly, I found high-fat luxe brands to be the most richly chocolate in flavor, yet they all baked up with the same warm mahogany hue. Thanks to the recent push for natural and organic, however, I discovered a new sort of "natural" cocoa powder: raw. Most organic brands of natural cocoa come from roasted cocoa nibs, but raw cocoa powder is just that, raw. Because it's never been exposed to

This 1922 advertisement inspired the look of my own red velvet cake.

high heat, raw cocoa is packed with more anthocyanins—naturally occurring pigments (abundant in red wine as well) that respond to changes in pH.

Technically speaking, anthocyanins turn red when exposed to an acid, but in a plain cake batter, raw cocoa bakes up as brown as any other because the heat of the oven dulls its color. But alkaline ingredients, such as baking soda, have a somewhat mitigating effect. This protects the pigments from turning brown in the oven, resulting in a cake that's far more naturally red. Not exactly *vermillion*, but certainly red enough to send me back to the kitchen, testing and retesting a recipe I thought I'd ironed out long ago.

The result is a red velvet cake I love more than ever, because not only does raw cocoa provide a warmer hue, its bright and fruity flavor pairs brilliantly with my cream cheese frosting.

RED (WINE) VELVET CAKE

This cake's color hinges on the anthocyanins found in red wine and raw cocoa, as even organic brands of "natural" cocoa powder lose their colorful potential in the roasting process. They create a shockingly pale batter, but in the oven it develops a mellow burgundy hue and rich cocoa flavor (plus, these acidic ingredients make for a velvety soft crumb). Paired with light and tangy Cream Cheese Frosting, it's everything red velvet should be. *See photo on page 134.*

YIELD: one 8-by-4-inch layer cake; 16 servings | **ACTIVE TIME:** about 45 minutes | **DOWNTIME:** 90 minutes to cool

1 recipe Cream Cheese Frosting (page 132)

Cake Batter:

2⅔ cups | 12 ounces all-purpose flour, such as Gold Medal

¾ cup | 2¼ ounces raw cocoa powder, such as Navitas Naturals

3½ sticks | 14 ounces unsalted butter, soft but cool—about 65°F

2 cups gently packed | 16 ounces light brown sugar

2¼ teaspoons baking soda

1 teaspoon Diamond Crystal kosher salt (half as much if iodized)

½ teaspoon ground cinnamon

2 tablespoons | 1 ounce vanilla extract

6 large eggs, brought to about 70°F

1½ cups | 12 ounces dry red wine, such as California Cabernet Sauvignon

To finish:

One 3- or 4-ounce block or bar white chocolate

2 tablespoons | ½ ounce cocoa nibs

To better synchronize the downtime in both recipes, make Cream Cheese Frosting before the cake. While it's cooling, adjust oven rack to the lower-middle position and preheat to 350°F. Line three 8-by-3-inch anodized aluminum cake pans with parchment and grease with pan spray. (If you don't have three pans, the remaining batter can be held at room temperature for up to 3 hours.)

Sift flour and cocoa (if using cup measures, spoon into the cups and level with a knife before sifting); set aside.

Combine butter, brown sugar, baking soda, salt, cinnamon, and vanilla extract in the bowl of a stand mixer fitted with a paddle attachment. Mix on low speed to moisten, then increase to medium and cream until fluffy and light, about 5 minutes, pausing to scrape the bowl and beater halfway through. With the mixer running, add the eggs one at a time, mixing until each is fully incorporated before adding the next.

Reduce speed to low and sprinkle in one-third of the flour/cocoa, followed by a third of the red wine. Alternate between the two, allowing each addition to be roughly incorporated before adding the next. Fold batter with a flexible spatula to ensure it's well mixed from the bottom up. Divide among the prepared cake pans (about 22 ounces each).

Bake until the cakes are domed and firm when gently pressed, about 30 minutes. A toothpick inserted into the center will emerge with a few crumbs still attached. Cool until no trace of warmth remains (the domes will level off in time), about 90 minutes.

Loosen the cakes from their pans with a knife, invert onto a wire rack, peel off the parchment, and reinvert.

Crumb-coat and frost the cake with the Cream Cheese Frosting according to the directions on pages 142–44. Slide a dozen 2-inch-wide strips of wax paper under the bottom edge of the cake to shield the plate. Shave the white chocolate with a coarse-bladed

Microplane and use a spoon to sprinkle white chocolate over the top and sides of the cake. When fully covered, scatter the cocoa nibs on top to mimic ermine "spots": If you take a step back and fling the nibs like you would a Frisbee, they'll stick to the sides in a random yet natural pattern (spoiler alert: It's really, really fun).

Under a cake dome or an inverted pot, the frosted cake will keep for up to 24 hours at room temperature. After cutting, wrap leftover slices individually and store at room temperature for up to 3 days more.

STORING
Red (Wine) Velvet Cake scraps make a tasty snack, and an even tastier Ice Cream (page 344). Freeze for up to 6 months in a quart zip-top bag.

→ *Mix it up!*

BUTTERMILK CHOCOLATE: This downy-soft cake is analogous to the "red devil" so popular in the 1920s, with a comforting cocoa flavor mellowed by the addition of dairy. Replace red wine with an equal amount of cultured low-fat buttermilk, brought to cool room temperature, about 65°F.

CRANBERRY VELVET: For those who abstain, replace the red wine with an equal amount of pure, unsweetened cranberry juice—not cranberry cocktail!

RED (WINE) VELVET CUPCAKES: Line cupcake pans with papers. Fill each with 1¾ ounces of batter, about two-thirds full. Bake for 20 minutes, or until a toothpick inserted into the center emerges with only a few crumbs attached. Makes about 40 cupcakes.

GLUTEN-FREE: Replace the all-purpose flour with 4 ounces (1 cup) teff flour, 4 ounces (1 cup) tapioca flour or arrowroot, 2 ounces (½ cup) coconut flour, and 2 ounces (½ cup) white rice flour.

Cream Cheese Frosting

Instead of gritty powdered sugar, this tangy frosting starts with a light vanilla custard made from fresh milk and eggs. That keeps it thick and creamy, but not too rich—perfect for slathering over my Red (Wine) Velvet Cake.

YIELD: about 6 cups; enough to fill, crumb-coat, and frost three 8-inch cake layers or 24 cupcakes
ACTIVE TIME: 45 minutes | **DOWNTIME:** 1-hour refrigeration

1½ cups | 12 ounces milk (any percentage will do)

1 vanilla bean, split lengthwise

1 cup plus 2 tablespoons | 8 ounces sugar

⅓ cup | 1½ ounces cornstarch

3 large eggs, straight from the fridge

1 tablespoon vanilla extract

2 cups | 16 ounces full-fat cream cheese, cool but soft—about 62°F

3 sticks | 12 ounces unsalted butter, cool but soft—about 62°F

2 tablespoons | 1 ounce freshly squeezed lemon juice

Make the custard:

In a 3-quart stainless steel saucier, bring the milk and vanilla bean to a simmer over medium heat. Remove from heat, cover, and steep 30 minutes. Alternatively, cover and refrigerate for up to 24 hours to extract the deepest vanilla flavor.

Whisk the sugar and cornstarch together in a medium bowl, followed by the eggs.

Return milk to a simmer. Remove vanilla bean, scrape the flavorful pulp into the milk, and discard the pod. Ladle ½ cup of hot milk into the eggs, whisking to combine. Repeat with a second and third ladleful, then pour the warmed eggs into the pot and cook over medium heat, whisking constantly, until the custard turns thick and lumpy, about 3 minutes. Once it begins to bubble sluggishly, continue cooking and whisking for *2 full minutes*, to neutralize a starch-dissolving protein found in the yolks; the custard should be very smooth. Remove from heat and stir in vanilla extract.

Pour the custard into a baking dish about 7-by-11 inches to speed the cooling process. Press a sheet of plastic against the surface and refrigerate until thick and cool, about 1 hour (or roughly 68°F). Alternatively, refrigerate for up to 1 week, then let stand at room temperature until warmed to 68°F before proceeding.

Finish the buttercream:

In the bowl of a stand mixer fitted with a paddle attachment, beat the cream cheese and butter on medium speed until fluffy and light, about 5 minutes. Meanwhile, stir the thick pudding until smooth. Scrape the bowl and beater with a flexible spatula, then switch to the whisk attachment. Whipping on medium speed, add pudding a few tablespoons at a time, then drizzle in lemon juice. Scrape the bowl once more and whip for a few seconds to ensure that no lumps remain. The buttercream should be light and creamy, but thick enough to hang upside down from a spoon.

If the buttercream seems stiff or dense (feeling greasy rather than melting on your tongue), scoop a cup of it into a small bowl and microwave until completely melted, about 30 seconds. Return the melted buttercream to the bowl and whip for 15 seconds on medium-high. Conversely, if it seems loose or gooey, refrigerate the entire bowl for 15 minutes, then whip for 3 minutes on medium-high. For more details, check out the Buttercream Troubleshooting Guide on page 113.

Use immediately, or set aside at cool room temperature for a few hours, until needed, and rewhip before use.

MAKE AHEAD

In an airtight container, the frosting can be refrigerated for up to 3 weeks or frozen for up to 3 months. Soften to about 66°F at room temperature (about 12 hours if frozen or 5 hours if refrigerated) and rewhip before using.

STORING

After frosting a cake, you may have a cup or so of Cream Cheese Frosting left over—just enough to drizzle over a batch of Homemade Cinnamon Rolls (page 268). Freeze it in a pint zip-top bag for up to a month, then set out to thaw overnight at room temperature while the dough completes its second rise. In the morning, knead the bag to "remix," and use as directed.

→ *Mix it up!*

COCONUT: Replace the milk with an equal amount of unsweetened full-fat coconut milk.

FRENCH VANILLA FROSTING: For a rich, multipurpose frosting, replace the cream cheese with an equal amount of unsalted butter and omit the lemon juice.

WHITE CHOCOLATE: With cocoa butter to tame the tang of cream cheese and thicken the frosting, this mellow variation is particularly stable. Melt 6 ounces (1 cup) finely chopped 31% white chocolate or Caramelized White Chocolate (page 60). While whipping the finished buttercream on medium, drizzle in the melted chocolate.

Red (Wine) Velvet Cake (page 130).
The original flavor and color of
red velvet came from raw
cocoa powder, not dye.

THE LEGEND OF DEVIL'S FOOD AND
RED VELVET AT THE WALDORF-ASTORIA

In 1949, Pillsbury held its first annual Bake-Off in partnership with the Waldorf-Astoria. After weeding through twenty thousand individual entries, the judges selected a hundred finalists to compete for a fifty-thousand dollar cash prize (nearly half a million dollars today). In the wake of Theodora Smafield's victory, I can't help but wonder if the 19,999 rejected contestants happened to include one sore loser; immediately following the Bake-Off, the Waldorf would hear reports of a dirty rumor.[1]

The story typically went like this: A guest at the hotel enjoyed an unusually delicious slice of devil's food cake. She asked the maître d' for the recipe and he gladly obliged, but sometime later, the woman discovered an astronomical charge on her tab. The hotel wouldn't hear of a refund, saying she'd already seen the recipe and the damage was done. Saddened to see her burdened by such unjustifiable debt, the woman's friends and family contacted newspapers nationwide to share the story (and recipe) behind the "thousand-dollar chocolate cake."[2]

Readers reacted with predictable outrage, retelling the story as if it had happened to their very own friend. Having heard the story firsthand, this next generation of listeners sincerely believed the victim to be the friend of a friend. That sense of connection drove hundreds to call or write the Waldorf in defense of their "acquaintance."

It reached the point that the Waldorf was forced to issue an official statement in 1951, explaining to author Horace Sutton in *Confessions of a Grand Hotel* that "no recipe of ours is a secret," nor would they ever charge for culinary consultations, a longstanding service offered by their concierge.[3]

Yet readers continued to defiantly submit recipes for the Waldorf-Astoria Devil's Food Cake to newspapers and community cookbooks, sustaining the rumor throughout the 1950s.[4] This coincided with a surge of interest in red velvet cake (see page 128), and the two cakes appeared throughout mid-century cookbooks and newspapers, often side by side, creating an element of confusion between the closely related cakes.[5]

The earliest version of this mixed-up tale comes from 1961, when the *San Mateo Times* published an account of a woman from Seattle who visited the Waldorf and enjoyed a slice of unusually delicious red velvet cake. She requested the recipe and the hotel promised to send it along, but when she returned home to Washington she was met with an invoice for three hundred dollars—cash on delivery.[6]

Despite a full decade of identical scuttlebutt surrounding Devil's Food, the utterly ridiculous tale of "Waldorf's Red Velvet" was republished well into the 1970s.[7] Likely as a result of small children hearing their parents tell the tale, it's often repeated today as a bit of family history. I've met more than a handful of people who genuinely believe the story originated with their very own grandmother's best friend, or some such reasonably close yet conveniently distant relation.

CARROT CAKE

According to legend, thrifty English housewives took inspiration from medieval carrot sweetmeats to naturally sweeten their cakes during World War II. Somehow American GIs developed a taste for the stuff (while sipping tea in the trenches, perhaps?) and managed to bring the recipe home. Carrot cake earned its U.S. citizenship in short order, while the recipe faded into obscurity abroad.

The notion of English involvement comes from an honest-to-goodness carrot surplus during World War II, and a short recipe for "Carrot Cake" published by the Ministry of Food in 1943 with "War Cookery Leaflet #4."[1] Granted, those facts sound like a solid origin story, but take one peek at the recipe, and you'll abandon the very notion of cake.

It was a desperate glob of boiled oatmeal, reconstituted egg powder, and a few spoonfuls of grated carrot that barely qualified as food, much less cake, much less something American soldiers would prefer over their stockpile of government-issue Hershey's® Bars, donations of Milky Ways® (see page 300), fresh doughnuts delivered by the Salvation Army (see page 184), and handmade chocolate chip cookie care packages. So outlandish is the idea that historian Jane Fearnley-Whittingstall, author of The Ministry of Food, flat out dismissed the connection.[2]

For a dessert supposedly invented to cope with sugar rationing, the oldest recipes for carrot cake use an obscene amount of the stuff, along with other ingredients rationed in England: fresh eggs, white flour, and oil. Compared to legit wartime recipes issued by the Ministry of Food, scraped together from pan drippings and bread crumbs, vintage carrot cakes demonstrate a suspicious lack of that stiff upper lip.

Carrot cake took root with a different rationing trick from different housewives in a different country during a different world war—the first one. American "war cakes" truly played the part, made with whole wheat or alternative flours like barley and rye. These were moistened with leftover coffee, simmered with currants and raisins to form a sweet paste, and then spiced with whatever happened to be on hand. The recipes were popularized in magazines like Good Housekeeping,[3] proper publications like the War Time Cook Book,[4] and even advertisements for Burnett's Vanilla in 1918.

After the war, newspapers resurrected the recipe as a "Currant Cake," loaded with plenty of butter, sugar, eggs, and nuts.[5] Then a curious thing happened. Perhaps someone misread a batter-smudged recipe, but otherwise identical cakes began calling for simmered carrots and raisins.[6] The Brooklyn Daily Eagle published such a recipe in 1921, complete with cold coffee, carrot-raisin mush, spices, and nuts.[7]

As the recipe circulated through newspapers in California, Ohio, Missouri, Nebraska, New York, Texas, and Wisconsin in the 1930s,[8] two distinct styles of spiced carrot cake emerged: the old-fashioned sort, made from boiled carrot pulp with whipped eggs and melted butter, and one made with grated carrots folded into more traditional batter. My own copy of Best Cake Recipes, published in 1930 by Better Homes & Gardens, includes one of each.

Yet it was an even stranger vegetable dessert that took center stage during the Great Depression—tomato soup cake.[9] Once you recover from that knee-jerk sense of ick, the components sound strangely familiar: a spiced layer cake, chopped nuts, one wacky ingredient, and cream cheese frosting.[10] In August 1935, a syndicated news story noted that "editors throughout the country report a deluge of requests for 'Tomato soup cake.'"[11]

Predictably, Campbell's Soup, Heinz, and Philadelphia Cream Cheese put the recipe to work in advertisements,[12] but tomato soup cake turned up in unexpected places too, from hospital and prison cooking manuals to M.F.K. Fisher's How to Cook a Wolf. Perhaps to avoid snap judgments, the cake adopted aliases such as the Believe It or Not Cake, You'll Be Surprised Cake, Rosy Spice Cake, and Halloween Cake.[13]

Yet carrot cake was still alive and kicking, regularly turning up in newspaper cooking columns throughout the 1940s,[14] taking top honors at the New York Women's International Exposition bake-off in 1946,[15] and serving as Bugs Bunny's official fourteenth birthday cake in 1950. By then, the novelty of tomato soup cake had begun to wane, and America seemed ready to pass the torch (and cream cheese frosting) to carrot cake.

It was just as oil-based chiffon cakes were coming into vogue, which made it easy to put a modern twist on whipped-egg carrot cakes, even if it meant trading butter for oil. My recipe splits the difference between those two styles by using brown butter. Ounce for ounce, it's just as rich as oil, but with a wonderfully nutty flavor to highlight the carrots and earthy spices. In honor of its wartime ancestors, my cake starts with nutty whole wheat flour. Not only does it add a cozy graham flavor, it actually helps the cake bake up especially fluffy because whole wheat can better absorb the water released by shredded carrots. With a homemade cream cheese frosting, it's everything you expect from a carrot cake and more.

BROWN-BUTTER CARROT CAKE WITH CREAM CHEESE FROSTING

To highlight the earthy sweetness of carrots and pecans, my carrot cake starts with brown butter. Its toasty flavor complements the grahamy goodness of whole wheat flour, which also offsets water from the carrots to keep the cake fluffy and light. It's a perennial birthday request in my family, and I generally toast the nuts, shred the carrots, brown the butter, and prepare the buttercream a day in advance.

Knocking these tasks out helps me pull the batter together in a flash, so I can focus on what I love most—decorating the cake with a colorful bouquet of Twisted Carrot Roses (page 141).

YIELD: one 8-by-4-inch layer cake; 16 servings | **ACTIVE TIME:** 60 minutes | **DOWNTIME:** 90 minutes to cool

---

1 recipe Cream Cheese Frosting (page 132)

Cake Batter:

3½ cups | 14 ounces pecan pieces

2 pounds whole, unpeeled carrots (1 small bag)

4 sticks | 16 ounces unsalted butter

2½ cups | 11 ounces all-purpose flour such as Gold Medal

1 cup | 5 ounces whole wheat flour (not stone-ground)

2 cups | 14 ounces white sugar

1 cup gently packed | 8 ounces light brown sugar

4 teaspoons ground cinnamon

4 teaspoons ground ginger

1 tablespoon baking powder

1¾ teaspoons Diamond Crystal kosher salt (half as much if iodized)

1 teaspoon baking soda

1 teaspoon grated nutmeg

¾ teaspoon ground cloves

1 tablespoon vanilla extract

6 large eggs, straight from the fridge

Twisted Carrot Roses (page 141)

Get ready:

To better synchronize the downtime in both recipes, make the Cream Cheese Frosting before the cake. While it's cooling, adjust oven rack to middle position and preheat to 350°F. Toast pecans on a baking sheet until golden brown, about 10 minutes. Cool completely.

Meanwhile, peel, trim, and shred the carrots; measure out 24 ounces (7 cups firmly packed). The carrots can be refrigerated for up to 1 week in a zip-top bag.

In a 2-quart stainless steel saucier, melt the butter over medium-low heat. Increase to medium and simmer, stirring with a heat-resistant spatula while the butter hisses and pops. Continue cooking and stirring, scraping up any brown bits that form in the bottom of the pan, until the butter is golden yellow and perfectly silent. Pour into a Pyrex measuring cup, along with all the toasty brown bits. The brown butter can be

covered and refrigerated for up to 1 week. Remelt before using.

Make the batter:

Preheat the oven to 350°F. Line three 8-by-3-inch anodized aluminum cake pans with parchment and grease with pan spray; if you don't have three pans, the remaining batter can be held at room temperature for up to 3 hours.

Sift the all-purpose and whole wheat flours into a medium bowl (if using cup measures, spoon the flour into the cups and level with a knife before sifting).

Combine the white sugar, brown sugar, cinnamon, ginger, baking powder, salt, baking soda, nutmeg, cloves, vanilla, and eggs in the bowl of a stand mixer fitted with the whisk attachment. Mix on low to moisten, then increase the speed to medium and whip until fluffy and thick, about 5 minutes. Reduce speed to medium-low and drizzle in the

continued ↓

I made this cake for my own wedding, because comfort food and fancy parties should go hand in hand.

brown butter in a steady stream, then add the flours. Once smooth, fold the batter with a flexible spatula to ensure it's well mixed from the bottom up. Fold in the carrots and pecans. Divide among the prepared cake pans (about 33 ounces each).

Bake until the cakes are golden, about 45 minutes (or 210°F). A toothpick inserted into the center will emerge with a few crumbs still attached, and your fingertip will leave a slight indentation in the puffy crust. Cool until no trace of warmth remains, about 90 minutes.

Loosen the cakes from their pans with a knife. Invert onto a wire rack, peel off the parchment, and reinvert. Crumb-coat and frost with Cream Cheese Frosting according to the directions on pages 142–44 and garnish with Twisted Carrot Roses.

Under a cake dome or an inverted pot, the frosted cake will keep for up to 24 hours at room temperature. After cutting, wrap leftover slices individually and store at room temperature for up to 2 days more.

STORING

Brown-Butter Carrot Cake scraps make a tasty snack, and an even tastier Ice Cream (page 344). Freeze for up to 6 months in a quart zip-top bag.

TROUBLESHOOTING

If allowed to cool below 80°F, the brown butter may thicken the batter. While strange to see, this will not change how the batter is handled or baked. Brown butter that's hotter than 110°F will thin the batter, yet produce an otherwise identical cake.

→ *Mix it up!*

BROWN-BUTTER CARROT CUPCAKES: Line cupcake pans with papers. Fill each with 2 ounces batter, about three-quarters full. Bake for 20 minutes, or until a toothpick inserted into the center of a cupcake emerges with only a few crumbs attached. Makes about 48 cupcakes.

CARAMEL APPLE: For an autumnal twist, replace the carrots with 2 pounds (4 large) Granny Smith apples. Wash, core, and shred the unpeeled apples, then wring out in a triple-ply square of cheesecloth to extract 8 ounces (1 cup) juice—a

delicious refreshment on its own. Use the dry shreds as directed, and pair with Salted Caramel Marshmallow Buttercream (page 116). This recipe works equally well with hard winter pears such as Bosc or d'Anjou (soft and juicy varietals will not do).

GLUTEN-FREE: A light nutty variation everyone should try. Replace the flours with 10½ ounces (3 cups) almond flour, 5 ounces (1 cup) cornstarch, and 4 ounces (1 cup) coconut flour.

Twisted Carrot Roses

Carrot cakes are often topped with carrot-shaped squiggles of frosting or marzipan, but you don't need any special ingredients to create these simple carrot roses. For a rainbow bouquet, grab packs of orange, red, and purple "confetti carrots" at the grocery or farmers' market.

YIELD: about 24 roses | **ACTIVE TIME:** about 30 minutes

About six 7-inch carrots (roughly 1 pound) peeled and trimmed

1 cup | 7 ounces sugar

1 cup | 8 ounces water

¼ teaspoon Diamond Crystal kosher salt (half as much if iodized)

Lay a carrot on a cutting board, press a vegetable peeler firmly against the root end, and drag the blade down its length. Discard the first few thin and irregular strips, and continue peeling to amass a pile of thick, even ribbons. Repeat with remaining carrots.

Bring sugar, water, and salt to a boil in a 2-quart stainless steel pot over medium heat. Drop carrot ribbons into the bubbling syrup, simmer 30 seconds, and remove from the heat.

When the carrots are cool enough to handle, fish out a ribbon, letting the excess syrup drip off. Hold the skinny end with your dominant hand, then twist and wrap the ribbon around itself to form a "bud." Continue twisting and wrapping to create petals, then tuck the end of the ribbon underneath itself. If you like, add another ribbon to create a larger rose. Repeat to make a total of about 24 roses, and arrange on the frosted Brown-Butter Carrot Cake (page 138).

← Multi-colored carrots make the most beautiful bouquet.

HOW TO FROST AND DECORATE A SPECIAL-OCCASION LAYER CAKE

You can casually spread some buttercream over a few cake layers for a down-home dessert, but spare an extra moment, and you'll have a showstopper worthy of any pastry case. Whether you're putting together a birthday cake for your best friend, taking dessert to a dinner party, or celebrating New Year's Eve at home, crafting a gorgeous layer cake isn't as hard as you think.

It starts with one simple step: a crumb coat. Just as you'd apply a coat of primer before painting the walls, pastry chefs prime their layer cakes with a crumb coat, which doesn't require any technical skills to master. Fill and stack the cake layers as you normally would, then smear a thin layer of buttercream around the sides and over the top. Pop the whole thing into the fridge till the buttercream is hard.

With the layers and crumbs locked into place, the next layer of buttercream will glide effortlessly over the smooth surface of the crumb coat, creating a beautiful finish. Just don't skimp! Crafting a layer cake with straight sides and crisp edges around the top isn't about putting buttercream on—it's about taking it off. Laying it on thick allows you to sculpt the buttercream into shape without exposing the cake below.

Whether you scrape the buttercream mirror smooth, scratch out a series of pinstripes, or create a groove that spirals around the cake from top to bottom, the results are both gorgeous and functional: The generous layer of buttercream will protect your cake from moisture loss without any need for plastic wrap. If you like, save some of the buttercream (about ¾ cup) to make a shell border (see page 144), or slightly less for a festive inscription—or, if the flavor sounds right, toss it into the freezer for frosting your next batch of Cinnamon Rolls (page 268).

HIP, HIP, HURRAY!

Whether it's your best friend's birthday or New Year's Eve, nothing kicks off a celebration quite like a layer cake. Even if you've never assembled one before, with a bit of patience (and buttercream) I promise your efforts will be rewarded with a totally showstopping affair.

ACTIVE TIME: 45 minutes | **DOWNTIME:** 45-minute refrigeration

Three 8-inch cake layers (from any recipe)

1 recipe Marshmallow Buttercream (page 114) or Cream Cheese Frosting (page 132)

½ cup | 2 ounces of any one of the following: Rainbow Sprinkles (page 325), Chocolate Sprinkles (page 324), finely crushed butterscotch toffee (page 320), Crispy Peanut Sprinkle (page 70), chocolate shavings, cocoa nibs, or finely chopped toasted pecans

Gel paste food coloring (optional)

Level the cakes

Whether the cakes have a pronounced dome or just a gentle bump, trim off the top crust so they stack together neatly. Beginners may find it easier if the cakes are chilled beforehand; just wrap each one in plastic and refrigerate until cold, about 30 minutes. To level each cake, touch the blade of a serrated knife to the point where the cake begins to rise above its outer edges and saw about 2 inches in, then rotate the cake 45 degrees and repeat all the way around. Using those initial cuts as a guide, saw through the center of the dome. Save the tops for snacking (or crumbling into ice cream; see page 344), and take a moment to clean up lest rogue crumbs destroy your hard work.

Stack the cakes

In the bowl of a stand mixer fitted with the whisk attachment, whip the buttercream or frosting until light. If it feels anything other than silky smooth and easy to handle, see the Buttercream Troubleshooting Guide on page 113. Seriously. If you don't find its texture a joy to work with, something's wrong.

Lightly moisten a paper towel with water and lay flat on the center of a cast-iron turntable. Place an 8-inch waxed cardboard cake round on top, dab a tablespoon of buttercream (or frosting) in the center, and place the first layer of cake on top, cut side up. Cover with 1 cup

of buttercream, using an offset spatula to spread it into an even layer that extends ¼-inch beyond the edges. Repeat with the second layer, and end with the third layer *cut side down* (this keeps crumbs away from the surface of your cake); cover with another level cup of buttercream. Pause to clean up any stray crumbs on the turntable or counter, then wash and dry your spatula, which may harbor hidden crumbs.

Crumb-coat

Stand directly in front of the turntable with the offset spatula in your right hand (opposite for lefties). To apply the buttercream, cross your arm over your chest with your elbow slightly elevated, so that the spatula is parallel to the left side of the cake. It may seem awkward at first, but this is the best position for applying buttercream to keep the sides straight and tall. Load a heaping tablespoon of buttercream onto the back of your spatula and spread it over a vertical section of cake, working from bottom to top. Reload the spatula and rotate the turntable as needed to completely cover the sides (this will take about ¾ cup buttercream). Hold the length of the spatula against the side of the cake at a 45-degree angle, then spin the turntable to smooth the sides; this should also push buttercream up toward the top edges of the cake. As excess buttercream piles up on the spatula, scrape it into a ramekin, as it may contain crumbs.

continued ↓

To level the buttercream built up around the top, swipe the spatula from edge to center, rotating the cake as you make your way around. At this stage, the buttercream doesn't need to be pretty or smooth—just roughly even to lock the crumbs in place. Refrigerate the cake, turntable and all, until the buttercream is cold and firm, at least 45 minutes. If you're not ready to finish the chilled cake now, cover with plastic and refrigerate for up to 24 hours. In either case, leave the bowl of buttercream at room temperature so it stays creamy and soft.

Frost and decorate

Stir the buttercream with a flexible spatula to ensure it's creamy and smooth. With the same technique used for crumb coating, thickly cover the top and sides of the cake with all of the remaining buttercream, without any regard to its aesthetic. Then hold the length of the spatula against the side of the cake and briskly spin the turntable to smooth the buttercream (beginners may find this easier to accomplish with a bench scraper). Level the top and scrape the excess buttercream into a ramekin as before.

The cake is now fully frosted and ready to decorate. Try any one of the following techniques:

Old-School Shell Border: Transfer the reserved ¾ cup buttercream to a small pastry bag fitted with a ¼-inch star tip (Ateco #18). Pipe a series of tight swirls with elongated tails around the top edge of the cake, like a row of tiny question marks laid on their side.

Pinstripes: Press the flat tip of a spatula against the base of the cake and drag it straight up, leaving a short spike of buttercream at the top. Repeat all the way around, spacing the pinstripes rather closely to form a mesmerizing pattern of stripes and spikes.

Spiral: Briskly spin the turntable to get it going, place the flat tip of a spatula against the base of the cake, and while continuing to spin the turntable, slowly slowly drag the spatula up toward the top edge of the cake to create a single groove that spirals all the way around, bottom to top.

If you're going to write a message on the cake, leave the top smooth. If not, wipe the spatula clean and spin the turntable as before, slowly dragging the tip of the spatula from the outer edge to the center of the cake.

Swoops and Swirls: Drag the back of a spoon over the cake in series of loops, sculpting the buttercream into swirling shapes. Periodically grab an extra dollop of buttercream to pave the way.

Finishing touches

Place any of the garnishes listed above on a rimmed baking sheet. Run the spatula under the bottom edge of the cake to loosen the buttercream from the turntable, then carefully slide it under the cake round to leverage it up until you can slide your hand underneath and pick it up. With your free hand, scoop up a small handful of garnish and press it against the bottom edge of the cake, letting the excess fall back onto the baking sheet. Work your way around the cake to create a festive band as thin or thick as you desire, then carefully set the cake on a serving plate or cake stand (you may need a helper to hold it steady).

To write a decorative message, put ⅓ cup buttercream in a ramekin. Microwave 1 tablespoon buttercream in a second ramekin until melted and warm. Add a tiny dot of gel paste coloring, and stir to combine. One teaspoon at a time, add to the plain buttercream to achieve your desired hue.

Put 2 tablespoons of tinted buttercream into a parchment cone (see page 324), fold the top edge over to secure, and snip ⅛ inch from the tip. Try practicing your message on an upturned cake pan wrapped in plastic so you can get a feel for how to space the letters, always applying gentle pressure from the top of the bag. When you're ready, this buttercream can be scraped up and reused.

A GAME PLAN FOR ANY CELEBRATION

Like a handwritten thank-you note, old-fashioned layer cakes never fail to impress. No matter the flavor, they always say something special about the occasion—whether it's a birthday or just another Sunday at home. For those of us who enjoy spending time in the kitchen, layer cakes are an immensely satisfying labor of love. I find something incredibly relaxing about whiling away a rainy afternoon with cake layers in the oven and a custard for buttercream bubbling on the stove—no plans, no pressure.

Of course, I don't always have the luxury of lazy-day baking projects. When I want to cash in on the celebratory feeling of a layer cake but find myself short on time, particularly around the holidays, I split the process into a few manageable chunks. Here's my game plan.

One to Six Months in Advance: Any of my buttercreams will keep for 6 months in the freezer or up to 3 weeks in the fridge, so you can tackle it at your convenience (see the recipes for notes on thawing and use). It's also a smart way to take advantage of those rare days when you find unsalted butter on sale. With a batch of buttercream in the freezer, you've already done half the work for any special-occasion cake.

One or Two Days in Advance: With any of my recipes that involve creaming the butter and sugar, you can make the batter one day and bake it the next. That's because my recipes add the leavening agents to the butter and sugar, where creaming has a waterproofing effect that prevents them from reacting until the batter melts in the oven. Prepare the batter and divide it between the pans as directed, then cover with foil and refrigerate for up to 24 hours. This trick can be used with White Mountain Layer Cake (page 110), Classic Yellow Layer Cake (page 118), and Red (Wine) Velvet Cake (page 130).

One Day in Advance: Make the cake from scratch, or set the pans of cold batter out at room temperature for an hour. Bake, cool, assemble, and frost the cake.

A frosted layer cake needs protection only from debris. Store it at cool room temperature under a cake dome or an upturned pot (plastic wrap will stick to soft buttercream). Alternatively, set the cake in a room where it will be safe from curious children or pets.

On the Big Day: If you're playing host, sit back and relax—the cake is done. If you're taking the cake to a party, refrigerate it uncovered for an hour before you depart. This will harden the butter, locking the layers and decorations in place for transit (Fudge Frosting, page 121, does not require refrigeration before travel).

Going the Distance: If you will be traveling for longer than an hour, the cake will need additional preparation for the road. The day before the event, refrigerate the frosted cake for an hour, then loosely wrap it in plastic to prevent it from absorbing odors and return it to the fridge overnight. When it's time to leave, peel off the plastic, place the cake in a cardboard box, and tape it shut (a wine box turned on its side is perfect). The cake will be rock solid, able to withstand up to six hours of travel in an air-conditioned car. After arriving at your destination, let the cake stand at room temperature before serving—it generally takes a total of six hours for the core to warm to room temperature.

Butternut Pumpkin Pie (page 166).

Chapter 3

PIES

Americans love a good apple or cherry pie, but our peculiar sensibilities are best reflected by creamy pudding pies—lemon meringue, coconut, and chocolate, in particular. We're also known for baked custard pastries like pumpkin pie, what Jessup Whitehead called "one of the American specialties." And of course no-bake custards too, like the Key lime pie Craig Claiborne called "the greatest of all regional American desserts."

ALL-AMERICAN PIES

AS AMERICAN AS APPLE PIE. How the heck did a pastry dating back to medieval England become the archetypal American dessert? America didn't even have apples until the colonists brought over the first saplings, and they made their apple pie as we do today: according to Old World traditions. *Pie* was the only thing American about it; the English would have called it a tart.

If anyone could clear up the stylistic difference between pies baked on either side of the pond, it would be Jessup Whitehead. Born in London around 1833, he moved to America as a young man and became a prominent food writer and cookbook author. He didn't confine himself to culinary academia; in his sixties, he became chef de cuisine at Hotel Monte Sano in Huntsville, Alabama.

In 1889, Jessup wrote a culinary encyclopedia entitled *The Steward's Handbook and Guide to Party Catering*. His entry on pie observed the "marked dissimilarity between the English and American idea of pie."[1] He explained that English pies were always sandwiched between two crusts, generally savory, and brought to the table piping hot. Think chicken potpie. American pies, he said, had a sweet filling baked with an "undercrust" alone, and were inevitably cold by the time dessert rolled around.

That isn't to say America doesn't appreciate apple or cherry pie, only that our particular sensibilities are better reflected in pudding pies like lemon meringue, coconut, and chocolate, as well as baked custards such as pumpkin pie—what Jessup called "one of the American specialties." Perhaps the most uniquely American are the no-bake options, like Icebox Vanilla Chiffon or classic Key Lime, dubbed "the greatest of all regional American desserts" by Craig Claiborne.

It wasn't enough that we inherited apple tarts from the English, we borrowed our crust from the French. Traditional recipes for "Puff Paste" commonly appeared in post-revolutionary cookbooks, with thick slabs of butter encased in a soft dough made from a pound of flour. Six or more rounds of rolling and folding created countless flaky layers, adding a welcome richness to our lean fruit pies and crispy contrast to our custard fillings.

New Hampshire–born novelist and poet Sarah Hale (oddly enough, author of "Mary Had a Little Lamb") Americanized the technique in 1852. In *The Ladies' New Book of Cookery*, she wrote that "those who are not practiced in making puff-paste, should work the butter in, by breaking it into small pieces."[2] With the butter in chunks rather than a stiff block, it was easier to roll and fold—a process that developed just the right amount of gluten for a supple but sturdy dough.[3] While it didn't create the "thousand leaves" of *millefeuille*, it was flaky enough for a rustic American pie.

Sarah was the longtime editor of *Ladies' Magazine*, America's first women's-interest publication, and later the *Godey's Lady's Book*, which had over sixty-thousand subscribers in 1850. As she would go on to single-handedly convince Abraham Lincoln to establish Thanksgiving as a national holiday in 1863, her influence in the realm of the domestic arts can't be understated. Her simplified puff paste was echoed and improved upon in American cookbooks through the remainder of the nineteenth century.

We've lost this unpretentious style to recipes that demand a food processor or stand mixer, a freezer, jugs of vodka, spray bottles, zip-top bags, silicone mats, and all sorts of gadgets. I'm all about taking advantage of new ideas and modern equipment, but not when they're unnecessarily convoluted. Try as they might, such gimmicks can't top the sort of flaky crust Sarah Hale could make with her bare hands.

By going overboard to avoid gluten formation, these recipes produce unnaturally weak doughs. You know the sort—the kind that stretch or tear so easily your rolling pin has to double as a stretcher just to move the dough from one place to another. Other recipes obsessively chill the dough, making it crack or crumble rather than conform to the curves of a pie plate. In either case, these tricks turn pie crusts into pure frustration.

Inspired by Sarah Hale's no-nonsense approach to "puff paste," my recipe involves only three pieces of equipment (a bowl, a fork, and a rolling pin), three ingredients (butter, flour, and water), and a technique as easy as folding a beach towel.

NO-STRESS ALL-BUTTER PASTRY CRUST

If you can fold a napkin, you can make an old-fashioned pie crust—no food processor, no pastry knife, no vodka. Most important: no cracking or tearing. The dough is supple, smooth, and strong, so it's easy to handle and shape. It also freezes incredibly well, which is why I always make two. Besides, who doesn't want more pie? Especially one with a crust this tender, flaky, and crisp.

YIELD: two 9-inch pie crusts or one double crust | **ACTIVE TIME:** 20 minutes | **DOWNTIME:** 2-hour refrigeration

1¾ cups plus 1 tablespoon | 8 ounces all-purpose flour, such as Gold Medal, plus more for dusting

1 tablespoon | ½ ounce sugar

1½ teaspoons Diamond Crystal kosher salt (half as much if iodized)

2 sticks | 8 ounces cold unsalted butter, cut into ½-inch cubes

½ cup | 4 ounces cold water

Key Point: If the temperature climbs above 73°F in your kitchen, be aware that everything from your countertop to your rolling pin and the flour itself will act as a heat source to the butter. Combat these conditions by refrigerating your pie plate, rolling pin, and dry ingredients until cool—not cold or frozen. If needed, chill the countertops of a sweltering hot kitchen with bags of ice water.

Making the dough:
Sift flour into a medium bowl (if using cup measures, spoon into the cups and level with a knife before sifting). Whisk in sugar and salt. Cut butter into ½-inch cubes, no smaller, and toss with flour to break up the pieces. Roughly smash each cube flat—nothing more! Stir in cold water and knead until the dough comes together in a ball. With a dough temperature at or below 70°F, it will feel dry to the touch.

Transfer to a generously floured work space, sprinkle with more flour, and roll into a 10-by-15-inch sheet. Fold each 10-inch side toward the middle, and close the packet like a book. Fold top to bottom to make a thick block, then cut in half. Using as much flour as needed, roll one portion into a 14-inch round. Brush off excess flour, drape over a 9-inch tempered glass pie plate, making sure it's flush against the pan.

Trim excess dough into a 1¼-inch overhang all around, then fold over to create a ¾-inch border that sits on the rim of the plate; if positioned inside the rim, the crust will be too shallow to accommodate the filling. Pinch or press the border into a zigzag pattern, and repeat with remaining dough. Wrap in plastic and refrigerate at least 2 hours, or overnight. Alternately, formed crusts can be frozen up to 3 months and thawed in a refrigerator before use.

Baking the crust:
Adjust oven rack to lower-middle position and preheat to 350°F. Line the chilled crust with a large strip of foil (not parchment or wax paper), letting the excess loosely cover the rim. Fill with plain white sugar, a delicious alternative to options like rice or beans (see Roasted Sugar, page 102).

Bake on an aluminum baking sheet until fully set and golden brown, about 1 hour. Remove from the oven and carefully lift out the foil, setting it aside until the sugar has cooled. If the sides of the crust seem puffy or pale, continue baking 10 minutes more. Cool to room temperature. Use immediately, or wrap in plastic and store at room temperature for up to 24 hours.

→ Mix it up!

GLUTEN-FREE: Replace the all-purpose flour with 4 ounces (¾ cup) white rice flour, 2½ ounces (½ cup) cornstarch, 1½ ounces (⅓ cup) tapioca flour, 1 ounce (¼ cup) coconut flour, and ½ teaspoon xanthan gum. Prepare the dough as directed, using a generous amount of cornstarch for dusting. The dough will crack along the creases as it's folded, but that's all right. After portioning the dough, roll to just 12 inches. Cut into quarters and transfer to the pie plate one at a time, pressing the pieces together and then sculpting the border like clay. Chill and bake as directed. (This dough cannot be used for Homemade McDonald's®-Style Baked Apple Turnovers, page 288.)

LEMON MERINGUE PIE

Lemon meringue might not have all the weighty symbolism of an apple pie, but this all-American dessert can be found in kitchens from Ireland to South Africa; *pie de limón con merengue* in Spanish and *remon merenge pai* in Japanese, it's known the world around.

While Brits would like to claim lemon meringue pie as their own, its parentage is in the name. Only in American English were sweet pastries ever called pie.[1]

Some suggest that lemon meringue comes from the French instead, fashioned after a *tarte au citron*, with its shallow, crumbly, cookie-like crust and a rich curd of lemon juice, egg yolks, and sugar. As with Egyptian and Aztec pyramids, barring an alien conspiracy, it seems lemon meringue pie evolved on its own, with a flaky unsweetened deep-dish pastry crust and a light custard made from lemon juice and water.[2]

Water may sound powerfully bland as a basis for dessert, but it's the hallmark of American lemon meringue pie. Consider lemonade. Who wants a tall glass of pure lemon juice and sugar? It's water that makes it crisp and refreshing, and the same is true of pie. Water cuts through the rich lemon custard to keep it zippy and light.

National advertisements, like this one from Sunkist in 1920, helped popularize lemon meringue pie from coast to coast.

My favorite recipe dates back to 1867, published in Pennsylvania's *Harrisburg Telegraph*.[3] It called for the zest and juice of a fresh lemon, two-thirds cup of sugar, and a teacupful of water in a two-yolk custard to match its two-white meringue. Though slim by modern standards, it made for a cheery winter pie.

Over the last hundred and fifty years, the recipe hasn't changed much at all—it's simply grown. My idea of lemon meringue pie comes from the restaurants and diners along the highway, pit stops on one family vacation or another. For some reason, though, I never wanted a slice for myself; I was content to watch the pies twirling around in their merry-go-round display case. Recapturing that memory, the towering meringue and translucent custard of a diner-style pie, is as important to me as nailing its fresh, zippy flavor. As a result, my Lemon Meringue Pie is a monument of mile-high meringue and marigold-yellow custard—both of which rely on plenty of fresh eggs.

The only modern touch in my recipe is a precooked meringue, which eliminates the risk of weeping.

LEMON MERINGUE PIE
WITH MARSHMALLOW MERINGUE

Straight from the fridge, this pie tastes as refreshing as a cold glass of lemonade. It's infused with aromatic lemon zest (strained out at the end), for a full-flavored custard that's silky and light. With a crispy pastry crust and my no-weep, mile-high Marshmallow Meringue, this all-American pie will keep for nearly a week in the fridge—so you can savor it one slice at a time. After juicing the lemons, repurpose those rinds for my easy No-Cook Lemon Syrup (page 158). *See photo on page 154.*

YIELD: one 9-inch pie; 12 servings | **ACTIVE TIME:** about 1 hour | **DOWNTIME:** 4-hour refrigeration, plus 1 hour to cool

Lemon Custard:

1¾ cups | 12 ounces sugar

¼ teaspoon Diamond Crystal kosher salt (half as much if iodized)

½ cup | 2½ ounces cornstarch

½ cup | 5 ounces egg yolks from about 8 large eggs (reserve whites for meringue)

3 tablespoons lemon zest (from 3 large or 6 medium lemons)

1 cup | 8 ounces freshly squeezed lemon juice (from 4 large or 8 medium lemons)

2¼ cups | 18 ounces water

¼ teaspoon orange flower water (optional)

1 fully baked No-Stress All-Butter Pastry Crust (page 150)

1 recipe Marshmallow Meringue (page 156)

Key Point: You must use nonreactive equipment throughout this recipe, or the custard will develop a harsh metallic flavor. Prime culprits can include some old-fashioned whisks and sieves.

Prepare the custard:

Combine sugar, salt, and cornstarch in a 3-quart stainless steel saucier, then whisk in egg yolks, lemon zest, lemon juice, and water. Cook over medium-low heat, whisking gently, until the custard is steaming hot, about 5 minutes (135°F). Increase heat to medium and continue cooking until the custard is thick, about 3 minutes more. Once it begins to bubble sluggishly, whisk 2 full minutes; this is important to neutralize a starch-dissolving protein found in egg yolks.

Remove from heat and strain through a fine-mesh sieve into a bowl, pressing with a flexible spatula to push the custard through. Stir in orange flower water, if using.

Scrape into the prepared crust, spread into an even layer, and cool until a skin forms over the surface, about 30 minutes. Proceed to the next step, or wrap in plastic and refrigerate until needed, up to 24 hours.

Finish the pie:

Adjust oven rack to lower-middle position and preheat to 375°F. Spread Marshmallow Meringue over the custard, working gently if it's still warm; make certain it touches the crust all the way around. Sculpt into swoops and swirls with the tines of a fork.

Nest a wire rack into a baking sheet, place the pie on top, and bake until the whole surface is light gold, with slightly darker peaks, about 20 minutes. Cool for 1 hour at room temperature, then wrap loosely in plastic and refrigerate until cold, about 60°F on a digital thermometer. This can take up to 4 hours if the filling was warm, or just 1 hour if cold to start.

To serve, cut into wedges with a chef's knife, rinsing the blade under running water between each slice. After cutting the first piece, leave it in place to hold its neighbors secure, preventing the meringue from toppling while you slice the rest. Use an angled pie server to lift out each piece.

continued ↓

Lemon Meringue Pie (page 153). As tart, cold, and refreshing as a glass of lemonade. Use a hot, wet knife to cut each slice.

Loosely covered in plastic, leftovers can be refrigerated for up to 1 week.

the technique or ingredients. If you don't own a kitchen scale, measure everything with care.

so extreme freshness isn't as important compared to raw applications.

The custard can be refrigerated for up to 1 week in an airtight container (not metal or plastic). To use, stir with a flexible spatula until creamy, then scrape into the prepared crust and continue as directed.

TROUBLESHOOTING

This recipe relies on a delicate balance of pH, starch, and protein to ensure a fully set custard that's resistant to weeping, so it's not as forgiving as other recipes when it comes to adjusting

MAKE AHEAD

In a glass or ceramic container (not metal or plastic), the lemon zest and juice can be refrigerated for up to 3 days. The most delicate citrus compounds will be altered by the cooking,

→ *Mix it up!*

COCONUT LEMONGRASS: This variation is just as tart, but more aromatic and complex, with a silky richness like Key Lime Pie. Trim the root tip from 2 large stalks (4 ounces) lemongrass and discard any outer layers that feel loose or dry. Split the stalks lengthwise and chop into ¼-inch pieces. Pulse in a food processor with the sugar to bruise the leaves. Replace the water in the custard with 4 ounces (½ cup) bottled coconut water and one 14-ounce can (1⅔ cups) unsweetened full-fat coconut milk. Otherwise, prepare the custard as directed; the lemongrass will be strained out with the zest.

ELDERFLOWER: To give the custard an enchanting floral aroma, reduce water to 16 ounces (2 cups), mixed with 2 ounces (¼ cup) elderflower liquor, such as St. Germain.

LEMON MOUSSE: Prepare the custard as directed, cover, and refrigerate until firm and cold, about 3 hours. Stir with a flexible spatula until creamy, then gently fold in 1 recipe Make-Ahead Whipped Cream (page 89). Spoon into twelve parfait glasses (about 5 ounces | ⅔ cup each) and refrigerate until chilled, or for up to 1 week. Serve with fresh fruit and Homemade Nilla® Wafers (page 197).

Marshmallow Meringue

Forget everything you know about meringue. My recipe couldn't be simpler: Throw all the ingredients into a bowl, warm over a pan of steamy water, and let your stand mixer do the rest. In no time, you'll have a thick and silky meringue that toasts up as beautifully as a marshmallow. Because it's fully cooked on the stovetop, this meringue won't weep or collapse over time, making it the perfect topping for pies and cakes alike (see variations).

YIELD: about 8 cups; enough to generously top a 9-inch pie | **ACTIVE TIME:** about 20 minutes

1 cup | 8 ounces egg whites, from about 8 large eggs

1¾ cups | 12 ounces sugar or Roasted Sugar (page 102)

½ teaspoon Diamond Crystal kosher salt (half as much if iodized)

¼ teaspoon cream of tartar

¼ teaspoon rose water, or seeds from 1 vanilla bean (optional)

★

Key Point: With gently simmering water, the meringue should cook fairly fast. If you find the temperature climbing too slowly, simply crank up the heat.

Fill a 3-quart pot with 1½-inches of water and place over medium-low heat, with a ring of crumpled foil set in the middle to act as a booster seat. In the bowl of a stand mixer, combine egg whites, sugar, salt, cream of tartar, and rose water or vanilla bean (if using). Place over steamy water, stirring and scraping constantly with a flexible spatula until thin, foamy, and 175°F on a digital thermometer, about 10 minutes. Transfer to a stand mixer fitted with the whisk attachment and whip on high until glossy, thick, and quadrupled in volume, about 5 minutes. Use immediately.

TROUBLESHOOTING

If a speck of yolk slips into the whites, fish it out with an egg shell. If the yolk can't be neatly removed, reserve whites for Tahitian Vanilla Pudding (page 255) or White Mountain Layer Cake (page 110), and start fresh, as fat can inhibit both the volume and stability of meringue.

Oil-based extracts, like lemon, orange, and mint can destabilize the meringue. Use sparingly and fold in by hand when the meringue has finished whipping.

MERINGUE COOKIES: Transfer whipped meringue to a pastry bag fitted with a large star tip, and pipe 1-inch kisses onto a parchment-lined aluminum baking sheet, leaving ½ inch between them. Bake at 200°F until firm and dry to the touch, but still quite pale, about 2 hours. When the meringues cool to room temperature, transfer to an airtight container and store up to 1 week. Makes about 100.

SEVEN-MINUTE FROSTING: This meringue whips up just like an old-fashioned seven-minute frosting, but is more stable. It's the perfect amount to generously fill and frost a three-layer cake such as White Mountain (page 110) or Devil's Food (page 124). If you like, toast the meringue with a blowtorch before serving.

SWISS MERINGUE BUTTERCREAM: When time is of the essence, this buttercream comes together faster than any recipe I know. After the meringue is fluffy and light, reduce speed to medium and continue whipping until the bowl feels cool to the touch. Use in place of the marshmallow base, and whip with 20 ounces (5 sticks) butter according to the recipe on page 114.

No-Cook Lemon Syrup

After juicing the citrus for Lemon Meringue Pie (page 153), don't throw away those rinds! Toss them with a little sugar and they'll give up loads of luscious lemon syrup, without any cooking or added water. Drizzle it over pancakes, mix it into a fizzy soda, or even whip it into cream as per the variation below. Whatever you decide, this syrup adds a tangy burst of sunshine to any dessert.

YIELD: just shy of 1 cup (8 ounce) | **ACTIVE TIME:** 5 minutes | **DOWNTIME:** 3 hours

4 cups | 15 ounces "used" lemon rinds, leftover from juicing about 6 medium lemons

1 cup | 7 ounces sugar

Cut rinds into 1-inch chunks, toss with sugar in a nonreactive mixing bowl, and cover tightly. Let stand at room temperature, stirring once every hour or so, until sugar has completely dissolved and the rinds are swimming in pale yellow syrup, about 3 hours, or overnight if you prefer.

Working in batches, press the rinds in a potato ricer (or squeeze in a large piece of triple-ply cheesecloth) so they give up every last drop of juice. Strain into a pint jar through a nonreactive sieve, then seal tightly. Refrigerate up to 3 months. This recipe works equally well with limes.

→ Mix it up!

CRISPY CANDIED PECANS: In a medium bowl, toss 5 ounces (1 cup) pecan halves with 1 ounce (2 tablespoons) lemon syrup. Spread over a parchment-lined aluminum baking sheet and and toast in a 350°F oven until golden brown, about 10 minutes. Immediately transfer to a small bowl, and toss with 1 ounce (¼ cup) powdered sugar. Cool to room temperature, and store in an airtight container up to a month at room temperature.

LEMON CHANTILLY: In the bowl of a stand mixer fitted with the whisk attachment, combine 6 ounces (¾ cup) heavy whipping cream with 3 ounces (⅓ cup) chilled lemon syrup and 1 tablespoon lemon zest. Whip on medium-high until fluffy and thick, about 5 minutes. Use immediately or cover and refrigerate until needed, up to 1 week. Makes 9 ounces (1¼ cups), enough to garnish about 8 desserts.

LEMON SODA: Pour 2 ounces (3 tablespoons) cold lemon syrup over ice, and top with 4 ounces (½ cup) club soda, or more to taste.

DARK CHOCOLATE CREAM PIE

Like a classic coconut cream pie (page 168), the "cream" in this pie is historically unrelated to its topping. Instead, its a reference to the creamy stovetop custard inside, in this case an inky-black chocolate pudding. Its richness and intensity is best countered by a light and toasty vanilla meringue, but if you'd prefer whipped cream, be sure to check out the variations.

YIELD: one 9-inch pie; 12 servings | **ACTIVE TIME**: about 1 hour | **DOWNTIME**: 5 hours to cool

Chocolate Custard:

1⅓ cups | 9 ounces sugar

¾ teaspoon Diamond Crystal kosher salt (half as much if iodized)

½ teaspoon espresso powder (optional)

½ cup | 1½ ounces Dutch cocoa powder, such as Cacao Barry Extra Brute

⅓ cup | 1¼ ounces cornstarch

½ cup | 5 ounces egg yolks, from about 8 large eggs (reserve whites for meringue)

3 cups | 24 ounces milk, any percentage will do

¾ cup | 4 ounces roughly chopped 72% dark chocolate

1½ teaspoons vanilla extract

1 recipe Marshmallow Meringue (page 156)

1 fully baked No-Stress All-Butter Pastry Crust (page 150)

Preparing the custard:
Combine sugar, salt, espresso powder (if using), cocoa powder, and cornstarch in a 3-quart stainless steel saucier, and whisk until no lumps of cocoa remain. Add egg yolks along with a generous splash of milk, and whisk until smooth before incorporating the remaining milk. Cook over medium-low heat, whisking gently until the custard is steaming hot, about 5 minutes. Increase to medium and continue whisking until thick, about 6 minutes more. When it begins to bubble, set a timer and continue whisking exactly 90 seconds to neutralize a starch-dissolving protein found in egg yolks.

Strain into a medium bowl through a single-mesh sieve, pressing with a flexible spatula to push the custard through. Add chocolate and vanilla, then stir until smooth. Cover with a towel to keep warm while you prepare the meringue.

Finishing the pie:
Adjust oven rack to lower-middle position and preheat to 375°F. Prepare meringue as directed; while it whips, scrape the custard into the crust. Top with Marshmallow Meringue, working gently to spread until it touches the crust all the way around. Sculpt into swoops and swirls with the tines of a fork, or place on a cast-iron turntable and spin, using an offset spatula to create a groove that spirals from the outer edge to the center peak.

Set the pie on a wire rack nested in a baking sheet and bake until golden all over, with slightly darker caps here and there, about 20 minutes. Cool for 1 hour at room temperature, then wrap loosely in plastic and refrigerate until cold and firm, about 4 hours or roughly 60°F on a digital thermometer.

Cut into wedges with a chef's knife, rinsing the blade under running water between each slice. After cutting the first piece, leave it in place to hold its neighbors secure, preventing the meringue from toppling while you slice the rest. Use an angled pie server to lift out each piece. Loosely covered in plastic, leftovers can be refrigerated about 1 week.

continued ↓

→ Mix it up!

CHOCOLATE CHERRY PIE: In place of a pastry crust, scrape the filling into a Homemade Oreo® crumb crust, made according to the recipe variation on page 204. Cover with plastic and refrigerate until cold, about 4 hours, then top with a batch of Make-Ahead Whipped Cream prepared according to the freeze-dried cherry variation on page 89. If you like, finish with a handful of shaved chocolate or a sprinkling of cocoa nibs. Serve immediately, or cover loosely in plastic and refrigerate up to 1 week. This variation is equally tasty with a freeze-dried strawberry or freeze-dried banana whipped cream.

S'MORES PIE: In place of a pastry crust, prepare a Graham Cracker Crumb Crust (page 204). Otherwise, proceed as directed.

COCONUT CREAM PIE

In 1843, the recipe for "Cocoanut Pie" in *Mrs. Ellis's Housekeeping Made Easy* begins, "Cut off the brown part of the cocoanut, grate the white part, and mix it with milk. . . ."[1] With that kind of hassle, people didn't bother with *cocoanut* very often, but after the Civil War, a handful of American companies cracked into the market with desiccated coconut flakes.[2]

The convenience came with a catch—the dry, withered coconut needed rehydrating. This meant soaking and simmering the flakes in milk, resulting in bland but chewy coconut and flavorful milk—a natural setup for coconut custard pie.[3]

At the turn of the twentieth century, a Philadelphia flour miller named Franklin Baker acquired a boatload of coconut on the sly when a local merchant was forced to liquidate.[4] He teamed up with his son Frank Jr., a chemist in Chicago, to try desiccating for resale.[5] With their combined experience, the venture was such a rousing success that they abandoned their previous careers to enter the "cocoanut trade" together.

With a brand of their own and some snappy packaging, the Bakers reached out to grocery stores and wholesale distributors, quickly becoming the industry leader despite a major marketing mixup.[6] Their last name, the old-timey spelling of coconut, and a certain brand of American chocolate converged in the etymological showdown of the century, Baker's Cocoa vs. Baker's Cocoanut.[7]

Customers imagined a relationship not only between the two Bakers, but also between the two products. Surely dark cocoa came from the brown part of the cocoanut! Blame a phantom typo from 1755. When compiling his *Dictionary of the English Language*, Samuel Johnson assumed coconut to be a misspelling of cocoa-nut (the cocoa bean).[8] He conflated the two definitions, and by the book's 1833 edition the entry described a nonexistent palm tree that sprouted cocoanuts and cocoa beans alike. Despite the anguished cries of botanists, linguists, and chefs, and despite, you know, fostering a gross misunderstanding among the general public, the dictionary's error persisted until the 1890s, when it threatened the Bakers Frank.

Determined to clear up the confusion, they dropped the "a" in cocoanut and the apostrophe to become Bakers Coconut in 1915.[9] To shore up those changes, Frank Jr. penned an open letter to the confectioners and bakers of America, asking them to "spell it coconut." The pastry peeps supported the idea full force, eliminating *cocoanut* from cookbooks and menus almost overnight. (Ironically, Baker's and Bakers would later be merged under General Foods, making the problem of their similar names entirely moot.)

Two years later, the Baker boys developed a groundbreaking new process: canning flaked coconut with coconut cream (as coconut milk was once styled). Not only did this keep the coconut flakes tender and fresh, it preserved the coconut oil once removed by desiccation, eliminating the need for rehydration.

The Bakers called it "coconut in a tin shell," advertised in the 1920s with recipes for "Coconut Cream Pie."[10] It took its name from the coconut cream, which replaced the traditional milk in the custard, making it a "coconut cream" pie rather than a coconut "cream pie." It was the cat's meow in the Roaring Twenties, but the inclusion of tropical coconut milk disappeared with the Great Depression.

In honor of Frank and Frank, whose coconut changed the English language itself, my recipe is based on theirs, with a creamy coconut milk custard. It's cooked on the stovetop, then spooned into a crispy pastry crust and topped with a thick layer of no-weep Marshmallow Meringue.

FRANKIE'S COCONUT CREAM PIE

Coconut cream pies were historically made with coconut milk—the original "cream" in coconut *cream* pie. It's a no-brainer for an all-natural coconut custard, with a bit of brown sugar to enhance its nutty flavor and a handful of shredded coconut for a macaroon-like chew. Topped with toasted Marshmallow Meringue, it's best served diner-style: with a steaming mug of black coffee.

YIELD: one 9-inch pie; 12 slices │ **ACTIVE TIME:** about 30 minutes │ **DOWNTIME:** 4-hour refrigeration, 1 hour to cool

Coconut Custard:

½ cup | 4 ounces light brown sugar

½ cup | 3½ ounces white sugar

⅓ cup | 1½ ounces cornstarch

½ teaspoon Diamond Crystal kosher salt (half as much if iodized)

⅛ teaspoon ground cardamom or cinnamon

½ cup | 5 ounces egg yolks, from about 8 large eggs (reserve whites for meringue)

3½ cups | 28 ounces unsweetened, full-fat coconut milk

1⅓ cups | 4 ounces sweetened shredded coconut, plus more to garnish

2 teaspoons vanilla extract

1 fully baked No-Stress All-Butter Pastry Crust (page 150)

1 recipe Marshmallow Meringue (page 156)

Prepare the custard:

Whisk brown sugar, white sugar, cornstarch, salt, and cardamom together in a 3-quart stainless steel saucier, followed by egg yolks and coconut milk. Cook over medium-low heat, whisking gently until steaming hot, about 5 minutes. Increase to medium and continue cooking until thick, about 5 minutes more. When the custard begins to bubble, set a timer and continue whisking exactly 2 minutes. This is important to neutralize a starch-dissolving protein found in egg yolks. Off heat, stir in coconut and vanilla.

Scrape into the prepared crust and cool until a skin forms, about 30 minutes. Proceed to the next step, or wrap in plastic and refrigerate until needed, up to 24 hours.

Finish the pie:

Adjust oven rack to lower-middle position and preheat to 375°F. Spread Marshmallow Meringue over the custard (work gently if it's still warm), making certain it touches the crust all the way around. Sculpt into swoops and swirls with the tines of a fork, or place on a cast-iron turntable and spin, using an offset spatula to create a groove that spirals from the outer edge to the center peak. If you like, sprinkle with coconut.

Set the pie on a wire rack nested in a baking sheet and bake until light tan all over, with slightly darker caps here and there, about 20 minutes. Cool for 1 hour, then wrap in plastic and refrigerate until cold and firm, about 60°F on a digital thermometer (this can take up to 4 hours if the filling was still warm, only 2 if refrigerated in advance). Cut into wedges with a chef's knife, rinsing the blade under running water between each slice. After cutting the first piece, leave it in place to prevent the meringue from toppling while you slice the rest. Use an angled pie-server to lift out each piece. Covered in plastic, leftovers can be refrigerated about 1 week.

→ *Mix it up!*

MALTED WHITE CHOCOLATE: Omit white sugar and increase brown sugar to 8 ounces (1 cup). Along with cornstarch, whisk in 2 ounces (⅓ cup plus 2 tablespoons) malted milk powder. Replace coconut milk with an equal amount of plain milk (any percentage). Instead of coconut, finish with 4 ounces (¾ cup) roughly chopped white chocolate, such as Cacao Barry's 34% Zephyr.

Creamy coconut milk makes for a coconut pie like no other.

PUMPKIN PIE

French and English cooks get all the credit for inventing pumpkin pie in the 1600s, but they couldn't have done it without pumpkins brought over from the New World. While merely a novelty across the pond, struggling colonists found pumpkins a necessity. They were easy to grow and easy to store, and even the smallest patch provided a harvest that would last for months.

Aside from soups and stews, hardy pumpkins allowed for fresh pies long after the apple barrel was emptied, perfect for the holidays. Not that making the pie was an easy task. Bakers had to boil or roast the pumpkin, scrape its tender pulp from the shell, sieve out the stringy fibers, and stew the watery pulp until thick. The result was incredibly bland, which meant the puree could serve as a replacement for fresh milk in an otherwise traditional custard pie.

Americans were fond of pies made from winter squash too. Compared to hollow pumpkins, meaty winter squash took up less cellar space and produced more puree. Squash had a similarly mild flavor and rich color, but more natural sweetness, fewer seeds, less water, and creamier flesh. Squash had every advantage over pumpkin but the name, and in 1881, *Arthur's Home Magazine* laid out the details for an all-out bait and switch: "Squash is preferable to pumpkin, and should always be used instead . . . but call it pumpkin pie—that sounds better."[1]

It was no isolated sentiment. American novelist, cookbook author, and poet Emily Leland wrote in 1890, "When I want to make the richest, creamiest, and altogether loveliest pumpkin pies, I use squash. But as squash pies are never celebrated in rhyme . . . I permit them to be called Pumpkin."[2] While bakers at home had no trouble choosing the convenience of squash over pumpkin, a third choice appeared in the 1890s: canned pumpkin puree.

The canned puree offered all the romance of a pumpkin without the hassle of stewing, straining, or simmering. It would have been a death blow for pies made from winter squash except for one tiny detail. Those cans of pumpkin were generally filled with squash. Canners were no more inclined than housekeepers to waste their time stewing, straining, and simmering, while farmers didn't appreciate the bulky pumpkin's low yield per acre. Choosing to can winter squash under the "pumpkin" label was a little white lie that made everyone happy.

The fairy tale came undone when the Pure Food and Drug Act of 1906 established regulations for labeling and fines for misbranded goods.[3] Canners who complied with the law found themselves at a sudden disadvantage; genuine pumpkin puree was both more expensive and less flavorful, a sudden and unexpected disappointment to consumers accustomed to pumpkin purees made from squash.

Some companies adapted by gently condensing the pumpkin into a thick puree, and others condensed it down to a dry, bitter paste. A few, such as Del Monte, went so far as to dehydrate it altogether, and a rebellious minority continued canning squash, chalking up government fines as the cost of doing business.

While canners flailed in the wake of the 1906 act, pumpkin pie found an unexpected patron. That same year, the Chicago beef-canning firm Libby, McNeill & Libby expanded their product line to include canned milk, both evaporated and condensed. To compete with established brands, Libby's marketing focused on recipes that gave consumers a specific reason to reach for their milk. "Libby's Pumpkin Pie" became the centerpiece of their holiday advertising campaign in 1912.[4] Condensed milk created a thick and creamy custard, with a richness that amplified the spicy aromas of cinnamon, ginger, and cloves. Libby called it an "unrivaled" pumpkin pie, but rivals like Borden and Carnation showed off their own recipes the very next holiday season. It was an advertising trifecta that changed the way Americans baked pumpkin pie, but the loser was Libby. Bakers simply preferred a more familiar brand.

After a decade spent fighting for a bigger piece of the proverbial pie, Libby made a grab for the pumpkin itself. In 1929, the firm acquired a three-story pumpkin-canning facility in nearby Morton, Illinois, along with additional plants in Washington and Eureka. It doesn't sound like much, but the tri-city empire belonged to Richard Dickinson—a civil engineer known as the "canning king." He was former president of the National Canners' Association, a one-time chairman of the American Pumpkin Canners, and an avid breeder of cucurbits (the parent family of pumpkin and squash).[5]

Morton and the surrounding areas thus represented a disproportionate number of America's pumpkin growers, so by snatching up Richard's domain, Libby essentially took control of the market. The company gained another decisive victory in 1938 when the FDA erased the legal distinction between pumpkin and squash.

This freed Libby to take advantage of squash, which is exactly what's inside every can of "America's Favorite Pumpkin" today.[6] Though it's cleverly called the Dickinson pumpkin, botanically speaking the vegetable belongs to *Cucurbita moschata*, a species that includes butternut squash, rather than to true pumpkins (*C. pepo* for those keeping score at home). I can't always get on board with such semantic shenanigans, but I've no objections here. Whether in 1881, 1981, or today, America's best pumpkin pies have always come from squash.

Broadly speaking, my recipe looks like any other, but instead of opening cans of this and that, my "pumpkin" puree and condensed milk are made from scratch. The result is a pumpkin pie that tastes exactly like it should, but better in every way: fresh, silky, and surprisingly simple. If you start on the Quick Condensed Milk when you toss the squash into the oven, both'll be done in about forty-five minutes.

BUTTERNUT PUMPKIN PIE

America's favorite pumpkin puree is actually made from squash, so why not turn to the earthy sweetness of fresh butternut squash? It's dead easy to prepare at home and tastes more vibrantly "pumpkin" than anything from a can. By that same token, homemade condensed milk is rich and creamy like no other. Baked together in a crisp and flaky All-Butter Pastry Crust, these DIY ingredients elevate a traditional pie into something more than the sum of its parts.

YIELD: one 9-inch pie; 8 to 12 servings │ **ACTIVE TIME:** 45 minutes (only 5 minutes with components prepared in advance) │ **DOWNTIME:** 45-minute roast, plus 2-hour rest

Butternut Custard:

1 medium butternut squash (about 7 inches long and 4 inches across at the base; at least 24 ounces)

1 recipe (2 cups | 19 ounces) Quick Condensed Milk (page 169), at room temperature

½ cup packed | 4 ounces light brown sugar

1 tablespoon vanilla extract or bourbon

1½ teaspoons ground ginger

1½ teaspoons ground cinnamon

¼ teaspoon grated nutmeg, plus more to garnish if desired

¼ teaspoon Diamond Crystal kosher salt (half as much if iodized)

⅛ teaspoon ground cloves

2 tablespoons | 1 ounce unsalted butter, melted

3 large eggs, straight from the fridge

1 fully baked No-Stress All-Butter Pastry Crust (page 150)

½ recipe (2 cups | 8 ounces) Make-Ahead Whipped Cream (page 89), or any variation (optional)

1 cup | 5 ounces crushed Homemade Heath® Toffee Bits (page 320; optional)

Prepare the squash puree:

Adjust oven rack to lower-middle position and preheat to 400°F. Split the squash lengthways, scoop out the seeds, and place cut side down on a foil-lined aluminum baking sheet. Roast until fork-tender, about 45 minutes.

When the squash is cool enough to handle, use a large spoon to scrape out the pulp. Pulse in a food processor until smooth, or rub through a double-mesh sieve. Measure out 14 ounces (1¾ cups) squash puree. Use warm, or refrigerate in an airtight container for up to 1 week.

Make the pie:

Adjust oven rack to lower-middle position and preheat to 375°F. In a medium bowl, whisk the squash puree, Quick Condensed Milk, brown sugar, vanilla, ginger, cinnamon, nutmeg, salt, cloves, butter, and eggs until smooth. Pour into the baked crust, place on an aluminum baking sheet, and bake until the custard has puffed into a gentle dome, about 25 minutes. Reduce oven temperature to 350°F and continue baking until the custard is firm around the edges but still wobbly in the very center, about 25 minutes more (200°F; 210°F if the probe touches the crust). Let cool at room temperature until the custard is set, about 2 hours.

Cut the pie with a chef's knife. If you like, serve with dollops of whipped cream and a sprinkling of crushed toffee. Wrapped in plastic, leftovers will keep for up to 4 days at room temperature.

continued ↓

Blind baking guarantees a crispy crust and a silky smooth butternut custard, but if you really want to play up that crisp and creamy dynamic, serve with Homemade Heath® Toffee Bits (page 320) and Make-Ahead Whipped Cream (page 89).

MAKE AHEAD

From the No-Stress All-Butter Pastry Crust, which can be rolled, shaped, and frozen months in advance, to the Quick Condensed Milk and squash puree, every element of this recipe can be made well ahead, so don't feel as if you need to tackle it all at once.

If you have any leftover squash puree, it can be refrigerated for up to 1 week and used in your next batch of Five-Minute Muffins (page 282).

→ *Mix it up!*

SNICKERSTREUSEL CRUMBLE: The last-minute addition of crunchy toasted nuts and chewy oatmeal via my buttery Snickerstreusel give this creamy pie a wonderful variety of textures. Make and bake the pie as directed, but after reducing the oven temperature to 350°F, sprinkle the semi-baked pie with 3 ounces (¾ cup) cold or frozen Snickerstreusel (page 48). Continue baking as above, allowing an additional 5 minutes for the streusel to crisp.

Quick Condensed Milk

Homemade sweetened condensed milk traditionally requires ultra-low heat and up to 6 hours of constant stirring, but with a splash of heavy cream added to prevent scorching, I can crank up the heat and be done in 45 minutes. The result is thicker, creamier, and more luscious than anything from a can, with a rich dairy flavor and subtle notes of caramel. If you like chai tea, be sure to try the cinnamon-spiced variation.

YIELD: 2 cups (about 19 ounces) | **ACTIVE TIME:** 45 minutes

4 cups | 32 ounces milk (any percentage will do)

¾ cup | 6 ounces heavy cream

1 cup | 7 ounces sugar

⅛ teaspoon Diamond Crystal kosher salt (half as much if iodized)

Key Point: Even slightly acidic ingredients will cause hot dairy to curdle, including raw cane sugar, brown sugar, coconut sugar, maple syrup, honey, and agave. Take care when experimenting with ingredients not listed in the variations.

Combine milk, cream, sugar, and salt in a 5-quart stainless steel saucier. If using a scale, weigh the pot and ingredients together so you can digitally track the reduction. Place over medium heat, stirring occasionally with a heat resistant spatula, until the milk begins to simmer, about 12 minutes. Continue cooking another 30 minutes more, scraping continuously to prevent a milky buildup from forming around the sides. When the thickened milk-syrup suddenly begins to foam, it's almost done. Keep simmering and stirring until the foam subsides and the dairy has condensed to exactly 2 cups or 19 ounces. If using a scale, the pot will weigh 26 ounces less than when you started.

Pour into an airtight container, seal to prevent evaporation, and refrigerate up to 1 month. To mimic the consistency of canned milk, bring to room temperature before using.

TROUBLESHOOTING

The timing of this recipe may vary considerably depending on the heat output of your stove and the size, shape, and heaviness of your pot. If it takes considerably longer than 12 minutes to bring the milk to a simmer, you can safely increase the heat to medium-high in order to reduce the dairy within the allotted time. Conversely, should the milk begin to simmer much faster, reduce the heat to medium-low to prevent the dairy from cooking too hard.

continued ↓

→ Mix it up!

CHAI SPICE: Along with the sugar, add two 4-inch cinnamon sticks, ½ teaspoon fennel seeds, ½ teaspoon whole allspice berries, 10 whole black peppercorns, 5 whole cloves, and 6 white cardamom pods, gently cracked. Proceed as directed. For an easy chai latte, stir 1 tablespoon of the spiced milk into 6 ounces (¾ cup) hot black tea, such as Assam.

DULCE DE LECHE: This rich and nutty variation owes its caramel flavor and color to baking soda, which raises the dairy's pH, allowing the lactose to brown at lower temperatures than normal. Add ½ teaspoon baking soda to the sugar and proceed as directed; though the mixture will foam more vigorously, there is no risk of overflow. Made with goat's milk in the variation below, dulce de leche is known as *cajeta*. As the browning process will resume with continued exposure to heat, neither dulce de leche or cajeta can be used as an ingredient in baked goods.

FRESH GINGER: Peel and roughly chop a 2-inch piece of fresh ginger; add along with the sugar.

GOAT'S-MILK: This variation is more easily digested by those with lactose intolerance, and because goat's milk won't curdle when it's boiled, there's no need for cream. Trust me, there's nothing "goaty" about it—just gentle creaminess anyone can enjoy. Replace milk and cream with 38 ounces (4¾ cups) goat's milk and proceed as directed. *Note*: This variation requires "ultra-high temperature" pasteurized goat's milk, as raw or low-heat pasteurized versions may turn grainy with prolonged cooking.

LAVENDER: During the cooking process, lavender mellows into something soft and aromatic, without any hint of the soapiness that can so often be its downfall. Add 1 tablespoon dried lavender buds along with the sugar.

ROSEMARY: Wonderfully herbaceous, this variation is my absolute favorite way to make Pumpkin Pie. Add a 4-inch sprig of fresh rosemary along with the sugar.

SOFT-SERVE: This eggless ice cream has an unbelievably pure and creamy flavor, with a silkiness that reminds me of Dairy Queen soft serve. Prepare the Quick Condensed Milk or any variation and pour into a large bowl. Add 10 ounces (1¼ cups) heavy cream, 2 ounces (¼ cup) whole milk, ¼ teaspoon kosher salt (half as much if iodized), and 1 tablespoon vanilla extract and mix well. Chill until cold, about 2 hours, and churn according to the directions for Double-Vanilla Ice Cream (page 334).

VANILLA BEAN: I make this variation whenever I have an empty vanilla bean left over from another project, as the cooking process will extract considerable flavor from even the most withered pod (the sheer volume of seeds in a "fresh" pod can turn the milk gray). Add scraped vanilla pod to the milk and proceed as directed. To deepen the flavor, leave the vanilla pod in the jar of Quick Condensed Milk.

KEY LIME PIE

In the late 1860s, a millionaire by the name of William Curry lived with his wife and children on Caroline Street in Key West. According to tradition, the whole island swooned over a pie made by their family cook, an unusual concoction using canned milk and limes. From the *Chicago Tribune* to *epicurious.com*, food writers have worked this tiny tidbit into a full-blown history lesson without a single historical document to support it.

"Rich Bill" Curry was certainly wealthy enough to have kept a skilled cook in his employ; he famously sailed from Key West to the port of New York to commission a set of flatware from Charles Tiffany himself. As much as I'd love to imagine Bill and his wife, Euphemia, nibbling the first Key lime pie from their solid gold forks, I've found no hint that his family had any penchant for pie.

Nothing in the literature surrounding Key lime pie suggests a connection to Curry at all—or nothing prior to 1995, anyway. That year, a guidebook to the Florida Keys described the Curry Mansion (by then a bed-and-breakfast) as the birthplace of "Aunt Sally's Key Lime Pie."[1] It's the sort of claim that keeps B&Bs alive, but suspiciously late in the game as the first reference to a hundred-and-thirty-year-old legend that should be ripe with lore.

So I reached out to Tom Hambright, archivist at the Monroe County Public Library in Key West. He told me Aunt Sally made a good story, but nothing more. Curious as to how Key lime pie became so famous, I asked more about its history, but despite having presided over the Florida History Department for twenty-five years, Tom couldn't point me to any recipe for the pie prior to one published by the Key West Woman's Club in 1949.

If a respected scholar with virtually unlimited access to firsthand sources couldn't find an earlier reference, the history of Key lime pie had bigger problems than our missing Aunt Sally. Desserts don't just spring into existence fully formed, like Athena. They evolve. Their recipes spread through cookbooks and newspapers, adapting to the climate and needs of a population until they hit a sort of critical mass. Then they go mainstream.

Every recipe starts somewhere, and I refused to believe Key lime pie was an exception. Yet it's universally absent from the vintage Florida cookbooks, newspapers, and magazines I scoured.[2] I didn't limit myself to a literal "Key Lime Pie," but considered anything that might remotely qualify. I hoped for luck with a 1915 copy of the *Florida Tropical Cook Book*, but among eighteen recipes for pie, not a single one called for limes, condensed milk, or graham crackers, much less all three.[3]

It did include a classic recipe for lemon meringue pie, which residents certainly made with local limes (Florida lost its lemon groves to frost in 1895; see page 173). But let's be clear: A lemon meringue pie involves a flaky pastry crust, a water-based stovetop custard, and a layer of baked meringue. Key lime pie has a graham cracker crumb crust, an uncooked dairy-based custard, and a whipped cream topping.

No amount of lime juice can bridge the stylistic difference between the two. One is defined by traditional ingredients and techniques, while the other assembles commercial ingredients with a modern "no-bake" approach. As it turns out, lime meringue pie may be native to Key West, but Key lime was born on Madison Avenue: 352 Madison Avenue, to be specific, in the Borden Dairy experimental kitchen of culinary expert Jane Ellison.[4] Aside from an apparent fondness for Key lime pie, Jane shared something else in common with Aunt Sally—she didn't exist. In 1929, Jane Ellison was Borden's answer to Betty Crocker, a fictitious spokesperson to embody the legion of professional bakers who worked behind the scenes. More to the point, make-believe people like Jane couldn't demand royalties from the endless cookbooks, advertisements, newsletters, and radio programs that bore her name.

From that platform, Jane inducted millions of Americans into the secrets of "shortcut cooking."

In 1931, her bag of tricks included a "Magic Lemon Cream Pie," made with a no-bake condensed milk custard served up in a graham cracker crust and topped with whipped cream.[5] Jane certainly wouldn't have spoiled the fun with science, but that's my favorite part: The magic came from casein, a milk protein that coagulates in the presence of acidity rather than heat.

Condensed milk contains superconcentrated levels of the stuff, but it still takes roughly thirty percent lemon juice for the reaction to work. That much acid would instantly curdle fresh milk, which is to say it's not a concept that would have occurred to home cooks, nor is the ratio of ingredients one a home cook would have the time or inclination to puzzle out. It is, however, exactly the sort of recipe a food scientist would develop.

The recipe was so intriguingly counterintuitive, the reaction so swift, the result so temptingly tart, and the process so educational that Magic Lemon Cream Pie became an instant phenomenon (and perennial favorite) in home economics classrooms and culinary schools, at grocery store demonstrations, and in syndicated recipe columns—in addition to twenty years of Borden radio, television, and print advertisements.

If identical press releases in newspapers from California to Arizona serve as any indication, that lemon pie was a staple of women's club cooking classes in 1932.[6] As a member of the General Federation of Women's Clubs since 1916, the Key West Woman's club surely received whatever "Magic" memo went out through the organization. But even if it didn't, nearly two decades of corporate advertising couldn't have failed to reach an entire state.[7]

I believe Borden's Magic Lemon Cream Pie flourished in Florida just as lemon meringue pie did—with limes. I found the first hint of cross-pollination in 1941, with the May issue of *School and College Cafeteria*.[8] This food-service magazine featured an industrial-sized formula for "Key Lime Pie," with seven cans of condensed milk and an unusual technique for a pastry crust rolled in graham cracker crumbs.

By 1952, the Florida News Service would enshrine Key lime pie as "our most famous treat,"[9] and thirty-five years later, Craig Claiborne's *Southern Cooking* knighted Key lime pie as "the greatest of all regional American desserts."[10] Nearly thirty years on down the road, I have to agree, but for entirely different reasons. Whereas Craig savored the terroir of limes grown in Key West, I see Key lime pie as a stunning reminder of how deeply America's traditions are shaped by advertising.

It's a perfect slice of history, a corporate recipe that found new life with local ingredients in an obscure corner of the country. I wouldn't change a thing about it other than to make my own graham crackers and condensed milk to add a sense of freshness. With Whole Wheat Graham Crackers crushed into crumbs, the crust has a deep graham flavor and more robust crunch. Added to that, the fresh taste and luscious thickness of Quick Condensed Milk create a refreshing and satiny custard for an all-caps declaration of *KEY LIME PIE!*

KEY LIME PRIMER

Without first explaining what Key limes are (and aren't), it's hard to justify my belief that these limes aren't an essential ingredient in Key lime pie. Or at least not for those of us living outside the Florida Keys, where the pie's history is tangled up in the branches of *Citrus aurantiifolia*.

In the nineteenth century, there were no "Key limes," only Mexican limes, a term that applied (and still applies) to the fruit of *C. aurantiifolia* regardless of where it's grown.[1] California farmers in particular had high hopes for Mexican limes. Writing for *The Nation* in 1889, Henry Finck reported that in San Francisco, "lemons are not valued nearly so highly as Mexican limes. . . . I believe that Eastern cities will soon follow the lead of San Francisco in this matter. The lemonade of the future will be made of limes."[2]

While folks on the West Coast raved about Mexican limes, the thorny trees were considered weeds growing wild along the southern coast of Florida, where lemons were more highly prized.[3] With over seven thousand grove-acres in 1890, lemons brought in nearly a million dollars. That'd be over twenty-five million today—not too shabby for a handful of independent farmers.

Everything changed in 1895, when a cold snap known as "The Great Freeze" laid blankets of frost across the Sunshine State.[4] Its commercial lemon groves were destroyed virtually overnight, but way down in the Florida Keys, wild Mexican limes weathered the storm.[5] Following the freeze, farmers planted Mexican lime groves in a fit of desperation, but the gnarly trees seemed to defy cultivation. Their crooked trunks, chaotic branches, and shallow roots sprawled out from their neatly planted rows, and growers complained about wicked thorns and seedy fruit.

Yet those Mexican limes commanded a good price in the lemon-starved market, and in ten short years became a beloved regional crop: the Florida Key Lime.[6] It was still genetically identical to any other Mexican lime, but southern Florida's coral-rich soil and generous rainfall mellowed the fruit's harsh acidity.[7] Thus juicy Key limes became more highly prized than any other.

Acreage grew with every passing year until disaster struck. The Great Miami Hurricane plowed across southern Florida in 1926, ripping their shallow roots from the soil and leaving farmers to start from scratch once more.

Just as they had traded lemons for limes after the frost of 1895, farmers abandoned Key limes and replanted their groves with hardy Persian limes (*C. latifolia*).

Compared to the unruly Mexican "Key" lime, the thornless Persian trees grew in manageable rows and their roots went deep. They produced bigger, lemon-shaped fruits with thick rinds that took the risk out of shipping. What's more, those rinds were less bitter and more aromatic, with a stunning emerald hue—an instant icon of the American supermarket.

The so-called Key lime didn't stand a chance, and today you'll only find it in backyard gardens and isolated patches of the wild; even in the Florida Keys, it's no longer grown on a commercial scale. Those mesh bags of "Key limes" at the store? They're from Central or South America. Even if you made the trek to Key West for a souvenir bottle labeled "100% Key Lime Juice," you still wouldn't get a taste of the real thing: the most famous shop on the island imports limes from Mexico.

That's because "Key" isn't a protected designation of origin. It's a word any producer can use to market *C. aurantiifolia*, whether they have groves in Mexico, Brazil, or Peru. And that's a big deal, right? That's why we distinguish between coffee from Colombia, Java, or Vietnam even though they come from the same bean; why we'd rather have a peach from Georgia than Arizona, or maple syrup from Vermont instead of South Carolina.

Origins matter. Grown elsewhere, the expensive little limes labeled "Key" are bitter, seedy, and dry, which means they're time-consuming to juice and zest. I'd gladly do more work and pay more money if it meant making a more authentic pie, but with imported limes from South America, that isn't the case. All things considered, my vote's for *C. latifolia*, the humble supermarket lime that saved Florida farmers in the 1920s.

It's big and easy to juice, with plenty of fragrant zest, and a balanced lime flavor that's perfectly suited to pie. Some critics complain that "regular" limes are less bitter, but in a well-balanced recipe, that's no problem at all. With homemade condensed milk and graham crackers, my Key lime pie has a mellow sweetness that doesn't require as much acidity to tame.

MAGIC KEY LIME PIE

Homemade graham crackers and stovetop condensed milk give my Key lime pie a freshness you won't find in other recipes, and a more balanced sweetness. From the earthy crunch of the crust to the tangy yet creamy filling, these DIY ingredients take the pie to the next level . . . even without actual Key limes (see page 173).

YIELD: one 9-inch pie; 8 to 12 servings | **ACTIVE TIME:** 15 minutes | **DOWNTIME:** 3-hour refrigeration

Key Lime Custard:

½ cup | 5 ounces egg yolks (from about 8 large eggs)

2 tablespoons lime zest

¾ cup | 6 ounces freshly squeezed lime juice (from 1 pound or 6 to 9 large supermarket limes)

1 recipe Quick Condensed Milk (page 169), at room temperature

1 fully baked Graham Cracker Crumb Crust (page 204)

Whipped Cream:

¼ cup | 2 ounces sugar

⅛ teaspoon Diamond Crystal kosher salt (half as much if iodized)

¾ cup | 6 ounces heavy cream

Prepare the custard:

In a 3-quart stainless steel saucier, whisk together egg yolks, lime zest, juice, and Quick Condensed Milk. Cook over medium-low heat, whisking gently, until the custard is steaming hot, about 5 minutes (or 125°F). Increase heat to medium and continue cooking until custard begins to bubble, about 5 minutes more (it won't seem terribly thick). Pour into the prepared crust and refrigerate, uncovered, until cold and firm, at least 4 hours. (Covered loosely in plastic at this point, the pie can be refrigerated for up to 24 hours.)

Finish the pie:

To make the whipped cream, combine sugar, salt, and cream in the bowl of a stand mixer fitted with the whisk attachment. Mix on medium-low speed for a minute to dissolve the sugar, then increase to medium-high and whip until the cream is thick and stiff, about 5 minutes.

Transfer to a pastry bag fitted with a large star tip and pipe decorative stars or swirls around the edges of the pie. Cut into wedges with a chef's knife, wiping the blade clean between slices. Loosely covered in plastic, leftovers can be refrigerated for up to 3 days.

TROUBLESHOOTING

See Lemon Meringue Pie (page 153).

MAKE AHEAD

In a glass or ceramic container (not metal or plastic), the lime zest and juice can be refrigerated for up to 3 days. The most delicate citrus compounds will be altered by cooking, so extreme freshness isn't as important here compared to raw applications.

Homemade graham crackers and freshly condensed milk, together in one magic pie.

ALL-AMERICAN APPLE PIE

Unlike the simple nineteenth-century recipes that made apple pie America's most famous dessert, today's recipes are bogged down by complicated techniques. From precooking the apples to draining off their juices and even poaching them sous vide, bakers will go to almost any extreme to avoid a watery pie.

Truth be told, watery pie wasn't an issue in the days of yore because it's easy to avoid if you know how. Simply macerate the apples until they shrink before you shape the pie, then avoid cooking them to death. That's it. While old timey bakers relied on intuition, we have something even better: a digital thermometer. With that simple tool, you'll always know exactly when your pie is done—no guesswork or experience required, just cook the pie to 195°F. When the pie cools, the apple filling will be wonderfully gooey and thick.

The key is to keep the internal temperature of the pie from climbing above 200°F, at which point the structure of the apples will begin to break down,

turning to mush as they release their juice and making your pie a soupy mess. But so long as you skirt right beneath that breaking point, those same apple slices will have enough structure to retain their natural water content, keeping the slices tender and juicy for a pie filling that's wonderfully thick. No precooking, special effort, or extra dishes involved.

In fact, no dishes at all! Instead of a large bowl, I prepare the filling in a gallon-sized zip-top bag. It eliminates the mess of spilled sugar and spice when trying to toss several pounds of fruit, and also limits the apples' exposure to the oxidizing effects of air (it's also a nifty make-ahead trick so you can even cut up and macerate the apples overnight). Once the sugar is dissolved and the apples are tender, shake it all up with a bit of tapioca starch, and the pie filling is ready to bake. Don't be alarmed by the cup of liquid that accumulates at the bottom of the bag! That's just the brown sugar, dissolved by a small amount of apple juice, so straining it off won't make a thicker pie.

NO-FUSS APPLE PIE

I take a supremely low-key approach when it comes to apple pie—no precooking the apples or reducing their "juices" on the stove (a misnomer, because the liquid you see is mostly just melted sugar). My method involves simply letting the apples macerate in brown sugar and spice until ultra tender, then tossing in a little tapioca starch just before assembling the pie. It's baked relatively low and slow, giving the crust time to turn golden and crisp without overcooking the apples, which turn to soupy mush at temperatures above 195°F. The result is an apple pie that slices like a dream, with a thick but saucy filling loaded with all kinds of autumnal spice.

YIELD: one 9-inch pie; 12 servings | **ACTIVE TIME:** 45 minutes | **DOWNTIME:** about 5 hours

1 recipe No-Stress All-Butter Pastry Crust (page 150), divided in half

For the Filling:

1 cup packed | 8 ounces light brown sugar

2½ teaspoons ground cinnamon

¾ teaspoon Diamond Crystal kosher salt (half as much if iodized)

½ teaspoon ground ginger

¼ teaspoon ground or grated nutmeg

¼ teaspoon ground cloves

4¼ pounds tart apples, such as Granny Smith, from about 8 large apples

¼ cup | 1 ounce tapioca starch

For the Egg Wash:

1 large egg

1 tablespoon | ½ ounce heavy cream

⅛ teaspoon Diamond Crystal kosher salt (half as much if iodized)

Key Point: I love apple pie à la mode, so mine is seasoned rather generously. If you'd prefer it plain or with slices of cheese, reduce the kosher salt to ½ teaspoon

Preparing the pie:

Roll both portions of dough into 13-inch rounds. Transfer one to a baking sheet, and nestle the other into a 9-inch pie plate, with the excess hanging over the edge. Cover with plastic and refrigerate at least 2 hours, or overnight.

Combine brown sugar, cinnamon, salt, ginger, nutmeg, and cloves in a gallon-sized zip-top bag. Peel, quarter, and core the apples, then slice into ½-inch wedges. Measure 50 ounces (11 rounded cups) into the bag, seal tightly, and tumble until roughly coated. Macerate at room temperature, flipping the bag occasionally to distribute the syrup, until the apples have lost a third of their volume, at least 3 hours. The apples can be held up to 8 hours in the fridge. Immediately prior to assembly, add tapioca starch, re-seal, and toss as before.

Brush the edges of the pie shell with water, then pour in apples and syrup (this is melted sugar, so don't drain it off), nestling the slices into a flattish mound. Stand top-crust at room temperature until pliable like canvas, then drape on top. Pinch to seal both crusts together, trim to ¾-inch, then tuck the dough under itself, so the pie looks something like a bonnet. Don't worry about crimping the edges; pressure from the massive volume of filling will distort the design. Refrigerate the pie until cold and firm, at least 30 minutes. If needed, the pie can be held for up to an hour.

Baking the pie:

Adjust oven rack to lower-middle position and preheat to 400°F. Whisk egg, cream, and salt together in a small bowl, then brush over the chilled pie. With a sharp knife, cut six 3-inch slits around the top, wiggling the blade left and right to open each into a wide vent. Bake on a parchment-lined aluminum baking sheet until golden brown and 195°F in the very center, about 75 minutes.

continued ↓

Cool at least 1 hour before serving, preferably with a scoop of Double Vanilla Ice Cream (page 334), or Cream Cheese Ice Cream (page 343) if you'd like a tangy twist. Wrapped in foil, leftovers will keep 3 days at room temperature. Warm 10 minutes in a 350°F oven to restore the crispy crust.

→ *Mix it up!*

APPLE CRISP: An easy autumnal dessert that can feed a crowd. Instead of a pie shell, pour the filling into a 9-by-13-inch glass or ceramic dish. Bake at 400°F until just starting to bubble around the edges, about 30 minutes. Cover with 8 ounces (1½ cups) Snickerstreusel (page 48), and continue baking until crisp and golden brown, about 25 minutes more. Serves 16.

CLASSIC CHERRY PIE

Fruit pies aren't as mysterious as some folks would have you believe. Cherries, like any fruit, are mostly water, making it quite easy to calculate how much tapioca starch is needed to thicken things up. What most people, even chefs, fail to realize is that sugar determines how that starch will behave, so adjusting it to taste may cause a recipe to fail. Fortunately, I've got everything boiled down to a science, with a fixed ratio of fruit, sugar, and starch, so you can count on a flawless fruit pie every time. To finish things off, try a simple checkerboard design; it's no more complicated than a classic lattice, but it delivers twice as much crispy crust.

YIELD: one 9-inch pie, 12 servings | **ACTIVE TIME:** 45 minutes | **DOWNTIME:** 45-minute roast, 2-hour rest

1 recipe No-Stress All-Butter Pastry Crust (page 150), rolled and folded, but not divided

For the Filling:

6 heaping cups | 2 pounds whole cherries or 5 cups | 28 ounces frozen cherries, thawed but not drained

2 tablespoons | 1 ounce freshly squeezed lemon juice

1 cup | 7 ounces sugar

¾ teaspoon Diamond Crystal kosher salt (half as much if iodized)

⅓ cup plus 1 teaspoon | 1½ ounces tapioca flour, such as Bob's Red Mill

For the Egg Wash:

1 large egg

1 large egg yolk

1 tablespoon | ½ ounce heavy cream

⅛ teaspoon Diamond Crystal kosher salt (half as much if iodized)

½ recipe Make-Ahead Whipped Cream (page 89)

Key Point: This recipe cannot be made with cornstarch, arrowroot, or any other substitution.

Preparing the pie:

Prepare dough as directed on page 150, but instead of dividing in half, aim for a 60/40 split. Roll the larger portion into a 10-by-15-inch rectangle, transfer to a baking sheet, and refrigerate. Roll the smaller portion into a 13-inch round, and transfer to a 9-inch glass pie plate. Fold the excess dough over toward the middle to form a simple border, and refrigerate at least 2 hours. Alternatively, cover in plastic and refrigerate up to 24 hours.

Wash and pit fresh cherries; if you like, reserve pits for Cherry Pit Whipped Cream (page 89). Measure 28 ounces (5 heaping cups) fruit into a medium bowl; add lemon juice, sugar, salt, and tapioca flour, tossing with a flexible spatula to combine. Scrape into prepared pie shell and refrigerate.

With a ruler and pastry wheel, cut chilled dough into thirty 10-by-½-inch strips; use 12 pieces to completely cover the pie. Starting from the very edge, fold back two adjacent strips, peeling them about halfway across the pie. Skip over the next two strips, fold back the following two, and so on until the end.

Lay two strips of dough to form the first horizontal row. Return the folded dough to its original position, then fold back the opposite pairs of dough the same way. Lay down two more strips of dough to form the second horizontal row, then fold the dough back down. Continue, alternating back and forth to cover the entire pie. With a sharp knife, trim the excess dough flush to the edge of the plate, and refrigerate until firm and cold, at least 30 minutes. Meanwhile, adjust one oven rack to the lower-middle position and one to the topmost position; preheat to 400°F.

continued ↓

Baking the pie:

In a small bowl, whisk egg, yolk, cream, and salt; brush over chilled pie. Bake on a parchment-lined aluminum baking sheet until golden brown, with juices starting to bubble through the center, about 75 minutes, or 213°F on a digital thermometer. Halfway through, slide an empty baking sheet onto the top rack to act as a shield and prevent excess browning.

Cool the pie until no warmer than 85°F, about 3 hours in an air-conditioned kitchen, or up to 4 if not. Cut with a chef's knife, and serve with dollops of Make-Ahead Whipped Cream. Wrapped in foil, leftovers will keep 3 days at room temperature; to serve, warm 10 minutes in a 350°F oven to restore the crispy texture of the crust.

TROUBLESHOOTING

Tapioca starch won't gel until cooled to 85°F, so it's imperative to let the pie cool before slicing.

BLUEBERRY PIE: With a small portion of wild blueberries (found in the freezer-aisle of well-stocked supermarkets like Kroger, Whole Foods, and Trader Joe's) mixed into the filling, this pie has an intensity like no other. In place of cherries, use 20 ounces (3¼ cups) fresh blueberries and 8 ounces (2 cups) wild blueberries, fresh or frozen. If you don't have any wild blueberries, increase the amount of fresh blueberries to 28 ounces (6 heaping cups). Decrease salt to ½ teaspoon, but otherwise proceed as directed. Wonderful served with tangy Lemon Chantilly (page 158).

CHERRY OR BLUEBERRY COBBLER: Buttermilk biscuits are a fast, low-key alternative to a traditional crust. Pour filling into a 7-by-11-inch glass or ceramic dish, then prepare a batch of Buttermilk Biscuits (page 85). After folding the dough as directed, roll into a 10-by-6-inch rectangle, cut into 8 pieces with a sharp knife, and arrange over the fruit. Bake at 400°F on a parchment-lined baking sheet until biscuits are golden brown, about 45 minutes. Serve warm, with scoops of Double-Vanilla Ice Cream (page 334). Wrapped in foil and stored overnight at room temperature, leftovers make an excellent alternative to Sunday morning biscuits and jam.

CHERRY OR BLUEBERRY CRISP: For a quick summer dessert, pour filling into a 7-by-11-inch glass or ceramic dish and bake at 400°F until juicy and hot, about 25 minutes. Cover with 8 ounces (1½ cups) Snickerstreusel (page 48), and continue baking until crisp and golden brown, about 25 minutes more.

PEACH COBBLER OR CRISP: Fresh peaches are too soft to withstand 75 minutes in a hot oven for pie, but they're great in comparatively quick-cooking Cobblers or Crisps. Replace cherries with 28 ounces (4⅔ cups) sliced peaches, no need to peel, from about six large peaches or about 36 ounces whole fruit. Proceed as for a Cobbler or Crisp.

Warm, yeast-raised doughnuts dredged in vanilla bean sugar (see page 46).

Chapter 4

DOUGHNUTS

Once but a simple part of the American bread basket, doughnuts have evolved into a distinctly dessert-like affair (even when we insist on serving them for breakfast). Whether yeast raised and as light as cotton candy or sweet and tender like cake, few things taste more wonderful than a doughnut you've fried on your own.

IN THE EARLY NINETEENTH CENTURY, doughnuts fried in vegetable oil were unheard of. Certain circumstances might warrant suet or goose fat (galley cooks preferred blubber), but low cost and widespread availability made lard America's go-to choice. Darn tasty, too. Lard solidified at room temperature, providing a melt-in-your-mouth richness and sealing doughnuts beneath a thin protective layer of fat that kept them fresh for days; doughnuts were commonly kept on hand in an earthenware crock, like cookies in a jar.

While doughnuts could be made plain and cakey with saleratus (an early form of baking soda), prior to the Civil War, most were "raised" with yeast. In the days before individual packets of instant-rise granules, doughnuts called for yeast by the *pint*: bubbling sourdough starters, liquid brewer's yeast, or spongy potato yeast—mashed potatoes and water set aside to collect wild yeast. Each type contributed a different proportion of water to the dough, so recipes required bakers to judge for themselves exactly how much flour they'd need.

By nature, thick potato yeast required the least flour of all, resulting in moist and tender doughnuts that stayed fresh longer than any other type. In 1848, Catharine Beecher (sister of Harriet) noted in her *Domestic Receipt Book* that "Those who use potato yeast like it better than any other."[1] It's impossible to say how many recipes morphed into "potato doughnuts" due to a baker's preference for yeast, but by the turn of the twentieth century, folks seemed to have caught on

to the power of potatoes—even doughnuts leavened with baking powder or newfangled cakes of yeast would often call for plain mashed potatoes.[2]

Another newfangled ingredient revolutionized doughnuts in 1911: hydrogenated cottonseed oil, under the trade name Crisco (ostensibly from **Crys**tallized **C**ottonseed **O**il, but more likely a reference to Crusto, an older brand of shortening).[3] William Procter and James Gamble put doughnut-centric ads in *Good Housekeeping*, the *Saturday Evening Post*, *Ladies' Home Journal*, and *American Cookery* to position Crisco as "a modern, wholesome, vegetable fat."[4]

Frying with Crisco offered some major advantages over lard. It was odorless, tasteless, smokeless (a huge bonus in unventilated kitchens), and certified kosher. Those who suffered from indigestion found Crisco more agreeable than lard, and it cost less too. When meat restrictions made lard scarce during World War I, Crisco swooped in, advertising recipes for "wartime doughnuts." Even the U.S. Department of Agriculture got in on the wartime doughnut craze, issuing a recipe for sweet potato doughnuts in 1918.[5]

Meanwhile, Salvation Army volunteers went to the trenches, frying doughnuts on the front lines to lift the spirits of American soldiers stationed overseas. As the *American Hebrew* magazine put it in 1922, "The Salvation Army lassies with their hot coffee and their doughnuts spelled home and mother and everything

National ads during World War I, such as this one from Crisco, painted doughnuts in a patriotic light.

clean, beautiful and tender to the heartsick."[6] Such was the demand for doughnuts in the midst of war that in the spring of 1918, a Chicago inventor named Walter Tomlinson submitted a patent for the first fully automated doughnut machine.[7]

Prior to that, commercial doughnut machines could rapidly cut and drop doughnuts into hot oil with the turn of a crank, but they still required an element of personal judgement to flip and fry. Walter's machine cut, flipped, fried, and *removed* the doughnuts without any human assistance. It took a year and a half to process the patent, so while Walter missed the wartime boom, he capitalized on its aftermath by providing an exclusive license to the Display Doughnut Machine Corporation of America in 1920.[8]

The company was founded by Adolph Levitt, a Russian Jewish immigrant food historians portray as a mere baker.[9] Yet the nature of his company (a machine manufactory) and Adolph's prior career suggest so much more. Before setting up Display Doughnut, Adolph had owned a series of clothing shops and a dry goods store in Wisconsin before moving to New York at thirty-seven as an investor in the Barker System.[10] These one-room "window bakeries" displayed electric mixers and rotary ovens on Main Streets nationwide, turnkey operations requiring nothing more than an initial investment.

Adolph was no baker, but that didn't stop him from jumping into the business of doughnuts. After getting his feet wet with the Barker System, he set up a corporation of his own, acquired a license to manufacture Walter Tomlinson's machine, and then trademarked his own brand of "Downyflake" cottonseed oil and specialized doughnut flour in 1921. He took out want ads seeking sales associates nationwide, and within a year he had expanded from a single office in Manhattan to branches in Chicago, New Orleans, Boston, San Francisco, Pittsburgh, Portland, and Minneapolis.

With factory-formulated recipes and automated machines, Adolph wasn't equipping bakers, but rather entrepreneurs. Now anyone could open up a doughnut shop, regardless of skill or experience. National doughnuts sales grew from $2 million in 1915 to $93 million in 1933, as mom-n-pop doughnut shops sprang up across the country.[11] Established bakeries and grocery chains added doughnuts to their lineups too, and each business could decide for itself whether to advertise Downyflake or to keep the mix a secret.

Adolph went on to introduce "Mayflower" doughnuts in 1930. Though the company was more famous as a stand-alone doughnut franchise, Mayflower mixes were sold to supermarkets and independent bakeries too, making the brand far more widespread than its eighteen stores would suggest. As franchisees struggled to differentiate themselves while working with identical mixes and equipment, the humble doughnuts became a canvas for colorful sprinkles and flavorful fondant frostings from cherry to vanilla—options that made grandma's doughnuts seem drab.[12]

Adolph created a thriving industry that helped thousands of Americans find work during the Great Depression, but his legacy also helped erase made-from-scratch doughnuts from the majority of our bakeries. I won't deny the appeal of a quick fix at a fast food doughnut chain, or the pleasure of supporting an independent bakery, but I also feel that the tradition of a homemade doughnut is too important (and delicious) to lose.

Potatoes don't just make for the most delicious homemade doughnuts, they actually help them taste a little more like the ones you buy in a fancy shop. That's because potatoes are an all-natural way to mimic industrial dough conditioners, keeping the doughnuts moist, fluffy, and tender. For my Fried Cake Donettes, potato flour creates a soft and velvety crumb, while fluffy Russet potatoes keep my yeast doughnuts as light as cotton candy.

Either way, the trick is to fry with a solid fat to replicate the keeping qualities lard once gave old-fashioned doughnuts (and the lightness modern oils give to store-bought). Instead of hydrogenated shortening, I reach for refined coconut oil. It's naturally solid at room temperature, odorless, flavorless, and stable at temperatures up to 450°F, so it won't stink up the kitchen with that fried-food funk. Coconut oil guarantees doughnuts that fry up light and crisp and are tasty even on the second day (a miracle for Sunday-morning sinkers).

FRIED CAKE DONETTES

This recipe is a cross between my favorite yellow cake and traditional sour cream doughnuts, but made with yogurt so I can enjoy two or three without feeling weighed down by their richness. They're light and fluffy, thanks to a spoonful of potato flour, with a few egg yolks for a more velvety crumb. I love them best with nothing more than a dusting of powdered sugar, but don't hesitate to dredge them in cinnamon sugar if you prefer.

YIELD: about 36 mini doughnuts (1¾ inches) | **ACTIVE TIME:** about 20 minutes

½ cup | 3½ ounces sugar

1 teaspoon baking powder

¾ teaspoon potato flour (not potato flakes or starch), such as Bob's Red Mill

½ teaspoon baking soda

½ teaspoon Diamond Crystal kosher salt (half as much if iodized)

2 tablespoons | 1 ounce unsalted butter, melted

1½ teaspoons vanilla extract

4 large egg yolks (about ¼ cup | 2¼ ounces)

½ cup | 4 ounces plain unsweetened nonfat Greek yogurt

1½ cups | 7 ounces all-purpose flour, such as Gold Medal, plus more for kneading

2 quarts refined coconut oil for frying, see page 189

Combine sugar, baking powder, potato flour, baking soda, and salt in a medium bowl. Add melted butter, vanilla, egg yolks, and yogurt, and stir until well combined. Sift in flour and stir to form a soft dough (if using cup measures, spoon into the cups and level with a knife before sifting). Turn the dough out on a generously floured work surface and knead until no longer sticky.

Roll to a thickness of ⅜ inch. Brush off excess flour with a damp pastry brush and cut into 1¾-inch rounds. Arrange on a paper towel–lined baking sheet and brush away excess flour. Gather scraps, briefly knead, and roll/cut as before.

Press an indentation into the center of each round with a dampened finger, pushing down until you touch the paper towels. Flip the rounds and repeat on the other side. Gently stretch to widen the newly formed holes. Fry according to the directions on page 189.

FLUFFY YEAST-RAISED POTATO DOUGHNUTS

If we Americans know anything, it's that hot oil and potatoes go hand in hand. In this recipe, starchy russet potatoes make doughnuts cotton-candy soft beneath a crispy crust. To prevent waste and minimize handling of the dough, my doughnuts are hand-formed rather than rolled and cut. I love the rustic shapes, which give each doughnut its own unique allure. *See photo on page 182.*

YIELD: sixteen 2½-inch doughnuts | **ACTIVE TIME:** about 45 minutes | **DOWNTIME:** 2½-hour rise

1 medium, 6-ounce russet potato

2¾ cups | 12½ ounces all purpose flour, such as Gold Medal, plus more for kneading

¼ cup | 1½ ounces sugar

1½ teaspoons instant dry yeast (not rapid-rise)

1½ teaspoons Diamond Crystal kosher salt (half as much if iodized)

½ teaspoon grated nutmeg

¼ teaspoon baking soda

½ cup | 4 ounces milk (any percentage will do)

4 tablespoons | 2 ounces unsalted butter, melted and warm— about 115°F

1 large egg, straight from the fridge

2 quarts refined coconut oil for frying, see page 189

Get ready:

Boil, steam, bake, or microwave the potato until tender. When cool enough to handle, peel and press through a fine-mesh sieve or ricer. Measure out 3 ounces (¾ cup gently spooned) potato. This can be refrigerated in an airtight container for up to 1 week; bring to 70°F before using.

Make the dough and first rise:

Combine flour, sugar, yeast, salt, nutmeg, and baking soda in the bowl of a food processor fitted with a metal blade, and pulse until well combined. Add milk, melted butter, egg, and prepared potato. Process until the dough is silky smooth, about 65 seconds. Alternatively, knead the dough on low speed for about 15 minutes on a stand mixer fitted with a dough hook.

Transfer dough to a lightly greased bowl and proof until puffy and light,

though not necessarily doubled, about 75 minutes at roughly 70°F. To test the dough, press gently with a flour-dusted fingertip; if the indentation springs back, let it rise 15 minutes more. The dough is ready when it retains only a shallow impression.

Shape the dough and second rise:

Turn the dough onto a lightly floured work space. Divide into sixteen 1½-ounce portions and round each into a ball. Flatten one and pinch through the center with your thumb and forefinger, then gently stretch into a 3-inch ring. Place on a lightly greased parchment-lined baking sheet and repeat with the remaining dough. Cover with plastic and let rise until roughly doubled, about 75 minutes. Alternatively, refrigerate overnight and then bring to room temperature.

Fry according to the directions on page 189.

→ *Mix it up!*

BANANA: Replace potato with 3 ounces (⅓ cup) mashed banana and increase the flour to 13½ ounces (3 cups).

MISTER MURASAKI: When I lived in Tokyo, I fell in love with *murasaki imo* doughnuts at the

Mister Doughnut chain. Made from purple sweet potatoes, they had a slightly sweeter flavor than most and lovely lilac hue. Seek out purple sweet potatoes from your favorite Asian market. These doughnuts will darken more as they fry, so don't mistake that for burning.

A WORD ON FRYING

To allow for 2 inches of depth and a 2-inch safety margin with the least possible oil, I use a straight-sided stainless steel pot that's 10 inches across and 4 inches deep for frying. You don't have to meet those measurements exactly, but you'll have to use your own judgement to navigate radically different sizes, shapes, and metals.

For example, the rounded corners of a saucier or a Dutch oven will require a greater volume of oil. Lightweight metals like aluminum allow the oil temperature to rocket from one extreme to the other as you fry, while heavy cast-iron is so maddeningly slow adjusting the temperature is a nightmare.

I've found that stainless steel strikes a happy balance between heat retention and responsiveness, so the temperature doesn't fluctuate too wildly when I add the doughnuts or adjust the heat. Regardless of what equipment you choose, spend a few minutes regulating the oil's temperature to get comfortable behind the wheel before you start frying. Clip a digital thermometer to the pot, heat the oil to 360°F, and then turn the dial down to see how long it takes the temperature to drop. Nudge it back up to get a feel for the rebound, then practice maintaining a temperature between 360°F and 370°F. If you like, test the process out with a few cubes of white bread. Familiarizing yourself with the particulars of *your* stovetop, frying pot, and thermometer will demystify the process and give you a boost of confidence—two factors that will make frying doughnuts a lot more fun.

LET'S FRY!

Whether you prefer rich and tender cake doughnuts or lighter-than-air yeast doughnuts, when they're hot and fresh, simplicity speaks for itself. So let your favorite shop fuss with the complicated glazes that make cold doughnuts worthwhile, and enjoy yours warm with cinnamon or vanilla sugar (powdered if you prefer).

YIELD: about 36 mini cake doughnuts or 16 large yeast doughnuts | **ACTIVE TIME:** about 1 hour

2 quarts refined coconut oil, or more as needed

1 recipe Fried Cake Donettes (page 186) or Fluffy Yeast-Raised Potato Doughnuts (page 187)

Powdered or granulated sugar or Cinnamon Sugar (page 44) or Vanilla Sugar Sprinkle (page 46), to taste

Briefly microwave coconut oil to liquefy, then pour oil into a stainless steel pot to a depth of 2 inches. Clip on a digital thermometer and warm to 360°F over medium heat. Meanwhile, line a baking sheet with a double layer of paper towels.

When the oil comes to temperature, slip in a test doughnut and fry until deeply golden, flipping it from time to time to ensure even browning, then carefully remove with a slotted metal spatula or tongs. Cake doughnuts require roughly 60 seconds; yeast doughnuts require about 90. Transfer the test doughnut to the paper towel–lined baking sheet and cool for a moment, then tear it open to check that it's done.

Fry the remaining doughnuts a few at a time, making sure not to overcrowd the pot, adjusting the time accordingly—add a few seconds if the test doughnut was doughy or shave some time off if the crust seemed thick and dark. Drain doughnuts on paper towels, then dredge in whatever sugar you prefer. Plain (unsugared) doughnuts will keep in an airtight container for 24 hours at room temperature; rewarm in the oven and dredge in sugar to serve.

STORING THE OIL

Cool the fry-oil to about 80°F. Meanwhile, secure a piece of 3-ply cheesecloth over the empty oil jar, using a piece of butcher's twine. Pour the fluid oil through the cheesecloth. Refrigerate for up to 6 months.

TROUBLESHOOTING

The flavor and lightness of my doughnuts hinge on refined coconut oil, so don't expect the same results when using liquid vegetable oils or shortening.

Avoid temperature-related problems with an accurate digital thermometer, which should register 212°F in a pot of boiling water.

Part II

Classic American Brands

To stamp and cut your animal crackers (page 199) at the same time, look for a "plunger cutter" in specialty baking stores or online.

Chapter 5

COOKIES & SNACKS

From delicate vanilla wafers to tender cakes stuffed with fig jam, America's "brand made" snacks are often remarkably sophisticated, and well worth the effort of reproducing in variations made at home.

THE TRUE ANCESTOR of Fig Newtons®, Oreo® Cookies, Barnum's Animals® Crackers, Fudge Stripes™, and even Oatmeal Creme Pies wasn't a cookie at all, but a common cracker. Or a biscuit, as we used to say. Cracker making started as a literal cottage industry. One man with an oven could turn a barrel of flour into a few hundred pounds of sea biscuits. These simple crackers lasted for *years*, a staple of the Navy and Merchant Marines. Predictably, bakeries sprang up in port cities like New York and Philadelphia, but Boston in particular made a cracker-jack location.

There, Artemas Kennedy founded the Kennedy Biscuit Company in 1805 to produce pilot's bread and cold-water crackers. A humble biscuit baker by day, Artemas was a Knight Templar by, er, night. But in 1830, he broke rank and spoke out against the murder of noted anti-Mason William Morgan, whose mysterious disappearance still figures prominently in Freemasonry lore. Artemas was then confronted by an unknown Royal Arch Mason, who threatened his life.[1] He reported the incident to his brethren and shortly after giving his testimony, Artemas washed up dead at low tide.[2] Following this in-no-way-conspiratorial turn of events, his son Jason took control of the company and hired his cousin, also named Artemas Kennedy, as factory foreman.[3]

Ten years later, this second Artemas reestablished the family biscuit business in Cambridgeport, Massachusetts. During the years bookended by the

Anola Sugar Wafers, with a delicate canola flower on the box, show Nabisco's fondness for botanical names.

Artemi, demand for crackers rose in lockstep with westward expansion. Where once only salty sea dogs bought boatloads of biscuits, every new wagon setting out for the Oregon Trail packed a cracker barrel of its own.

Demand increased with hungry soldiers fighting the Civil War.[4] Artemas the Younger passed away around that time, leaving the Kennedy Biscuit Company to his son Frank. Overwhelmed by Union ration demands, Frank equipped the factory with industrial dough mixers, rollers, and Ferris wheel–like "reel ovens" to quadruple capacity.

Business boomed, but in a few short years, the war ended, Lincoln was assassinated, the country fell into turmoil, and the biscuit bubble burst. Suddenly America had too many biscuit companies with too much equipment, too many workers, and more hardtack than all the sailors and soldiers in the world could ever choke down. By the 1870s, frontier bakeries popped up along America's roads and railways, eliminating the need for settlers to haul East Coast crackers into the Wild West.

With huge investments and the family business at stake, Frank couldn't afford to abandon biscuits, so he redefined them. By slightly adjusting the Kennedy Biscuit Company's existing recipes, he conjured up a zoo of animal crackers (see page 198), honey grahams (page 200), and delicate vanilla wafers (page 196). He called them "dainty goods," and their success spurred his engineers to design machines that produced ever more fantastic snacks: chocolate wafers filled with vanilla cream (page 209), tender cakes stuffed with fig jam (page 205), and even peanut butter sandwich cookies (page 216).

"Since modern machinery has produced such marvels . . . old-time cookies have rather gone out of fashion."[5] It sounds like something we'd hear from the Slow Food movement today, but it came from an editorial written for the *New England Kitchen Magazine* in 1895, the year Fig Newtons® turned three. By that time, the biscuit business was generating tens of million of dollars annually and bakeries had begun coalescing into regional alliances.[6]

Frank Kennedy cast his lot with the New York Biscuit Company, the largest of America's three major baking associations. In 1898, the hundred and twenty eight individual bakeries comprising those three groups teamed up to form the National Biscuit Company. Nabisco carried Frank's dainty goods into the twentieth century, introducing nationwide marketing strategies, stay-fresh packaging, and prices low enough to discourage baking at home.

Following this trail of corporate cookie crumbs, we can track America's transition from hand-made to brand-made and see how one bakery came to shape the sweet tooth of an entire nation.

VANILLA WAFERS

Vanilla wafers were among the first "dainty goods" introduced when biscuit companies expanded their offerings after the Civil War. They didn't require any fancy new equipment or unusual ingredients, and the lightly sweetened dough behaved much like that of a simple cracker.

The Scotch Bakery on Fulton Street advertised vanilla wafers in the *Brooklyn Daily Eagle* as early as 1871,[1] but before the turn of the century they were as common to commercial bakeries as they are today.[2] The increasing availability of this simple but dainty snack coincided with the rise of drugstore soda shops and ice cream parlors (see page 332), which counted vanilla wafers among their most essential elements of service. Pharmacy trade journals in the 1890s advised shopkeepers to include a dish of vanilla wafers as part of their daily *mise en place*, and to send a few out with every order of hot chocolate. They were the foundation of our earliest ice cream sandwiches, and a crunchy garnish for our first sundaes.

While any bakery could have supplied these wafers, the odds favored America's largest manufacturer—the National Biscuit Company. Nabisco set its vanilla wafers apart from other brands by packaging them in patented "In-er-seal" wrappers, stiff waxed paper that lined the interior of each box. But it wasn't the box we know today. Old-fashioned vanilla wafers were paper thin and nearly three inches across (perfect for layering with DIY Banana Pudding, page 258); Nabisco didn't introduce the now-familiar coin-sized variety until 1926.

Like graham crackers or chocolate chip cookies, "vanilla wafers" didn't enjoy any sort of legal protection. At any given grocery in the 1950s, you might find Keebler Vanilla Wafers, Sunshine Vanilla Wafers, Burry's Vanilla Wafers, Stauffer's Vanilla Wafers, and Mother's Vanilla Wafers, not to mention off-brand wafers from every grocery's private label.[3]

Having enjoyed tremendous success by rebranding their chocolate chip cookies as Chips Ahoy® in 1965, Nabisco gave it a go with vanilla wafers by shortening their name to *NILLA*® in 1968.[4] It sounded more like a nickname than a brand name, evoking homespun charm with the tagline "simple goodness."

Nabisco once advertised vanilla wafers made with "creamery butter," but that's the kind of ingredient you'll only find in homemade versions today.[5] Or, at least, that's how my Homemade Nilla® Wafers start. My recipe's inspired by the vanilla wafers in the *Melrose Household Treasure*, a Boston cookbook published in 1877.[6] It's a simple dough made from five ounces of butter, a cup of sugar, one egg, a quarter cup of milk, and "only enough flour to roll out."

The only difference is that my recipe requires less flour, resulting in a batter-like consistency that I can pipe from a pastry bag lickety-split. That saves me the work of having to roll and cut a million tiny cookies, and it creates perfectly domed little wafers just like the ones in that big yellow box.

HOMEMADE NILLA® WAFERS

Flavored with butter and vanilla alone, these simple wafers get back to the basics. They're light and tender but crisp, and sturdy enough to retain a gentle crunch whether buried in DIY Banana Pudding (page 258) or dunked in hot tea. Don't panic over the hundred-wafer yield—you can pipe fifty-four onto a single baking sheet and hold a dozen in the palm of one hand. Resist the temptation to make them bigger, as thick wafers won't soften as they should in your favorite recipes.

YIELD: about one hundred 1-inch wafers | **ACTIVE TIME:** 20 minutes

1¾ cups | 8 ounces all-purpose flour

¾ cup | 5¼ ounces sugar

1 stick | 4 ounces unsalted butter, soft but cool—about 65°F

1½ teaspoons baking powder

½ teaspoon Diamond Crystal kosher salt (half as much if iodized)

1 tablespoon vanilla extract

1 large egg, brought to about 70°F

¼ cup | 2 ounces heavy cream, brought to about 70°F

Adjust oven rack to middle position and preheat to 350°F. Sift flour (if using cup measures, spoon into the cups and level with a knife before sifting).

Combine sugar, butter, baking powder, salt, and vanilla extract in the bowl of a stand mixer fitted with a paddle attachment. Mix on low speed to moisten, then increase to medium and beat until light and fluffy, about 5 minutes. Meanwhile, beat together the egg and cream. With the mixer running, add the egg mixture in 5 or 6 additions, allowing each one to incorporate before adding the next. Reduce speed to low, sprinkle in the flour and mix until smooth, like a very stiff cake batter.

Transfer to a sturdy piping bag fitted with a ½-inch plain tip.

Line two aluminum baking sheets with parchment. Hold the piping bag perpendicular to the baking sheet, with the tip almost touching the parchment. As you squeeze, this position will force the batter to spread out into a thin disc, about 1-inch wide and ⅜-inch thick; a standard baking sheet will hold nine rows of six.

Bake until the wafers are golden brown around the edges but pale overall, about 20 minutes. Cool completely on the baking sheets. Store in a gallon zip-top bag for up to 2 months at room temperature.

→ *Mix it up!*

DOUBLE VANILLA: Along with the vanilla extract, add the seeds from 1 vanilla bean. This double dose of vanilla is lost when the wafers are used as an ingredient in other recipes, but it's my favorite way to enjoy them for snacking.

EGG WHITE: After making yolky custard or ice cream, use up those leftover whites with this delicate variation. Simply replace the egg with 2 ounces (¼ cup) egg whites and proceed as directed.

GLUTEN-FREE: Replace the cake flour with 8 ounces (2 cups) tapioca flour or arrowroot, 3 ounces (⅔ cup) white rice flour, and 1 ounce (¼ cup) coconut flour.

ANIMAL CRACKERS

Loaded with sugar, sometimes covered in pink and white frosting, bedazzled with sprinkles, or half-dipped in chocolate, today's animal crackers are a far cry from the ones that first appeared a hundred and twenty-five years ago. In those days, professional bakers just needed a way to make biscuits more fun than functional. The originals didn't have the appeal of sugar or butter, only the affordably adorable allure of an animal-shaped cracker.[1]

In the 1880s, *Good Housekeeping* declared them a must-have pantry staple, an easy way mothers could encourage picky eaters to finish their tomato soup— one kangaroo at a time.[2] The low price made them a hit with teachers too, the basis for edible lessons on counting and sorting.[3]

Until the debut of Barnum's Animals® Crackers in 1902, we're told England was America's sole source for animal crackers. Which leaves me wondering . . . in what universe do educators blow their budgets on British imports for teaching tiny tots to tally tigers? Then as now, teachers often paid for classroom expenses out of pocket, and animal crackers wound up in our magazines and kindergarten curriculums precisely because they were affordable, reflecting widespread domestic production.[4]

It's not sheer conjecture. Trade journals, newspaper advertisements, and government records point to dozens of large-scale American bakeries manufacturing animal crackers in the 1800s.[5] In Indiana, Parrott, Nickum & Company sold its cracker "menageries" by the barrel,[6] the Walter G. Wilson Cracker Company advertised animal biscuits "for family use,"[7] and the Boston Bakery packaged its Biscuit Animals inside little Noah's Arks.[8]

When the National Biscuit Company formed in 1898, it inherited a motley crew of lions, tigers, and bears from every bakery it absorbed. To streamline cracker production a few years later, the company chose one recipe, one package, and one name: Barnum's Animals Crackers.

Short histories of the animal cracker almost universally mistake that rebranding effort for a product launch, popularizing the notion that animal crackers were something new. Typically these stories also accuse Nabisco of cashing in on P. T. Barnum's popularity without ever paying the man a cent, but I'm sure he didn't mind. When Nabisco introduced Barnum's Animals, he'd been dead for over ten years.[9]

I was bonkers about Barnum's Animals Crackers as a kid, from the cardboard boxcar to the crinkly wax paper bag inside to the simple design stamped onto each and every cracker. As an adult, I was surprised to find that they're made with cornflour—an industrial product distinct from both cornmeal and cornstarch. It's impossible to buy online, which is shocking in and of itself, but easy to make at home. All you need is freeze-dried corn, which can easily be ground to a fine powder. It gives my Animal Crackers a flavor like kids' cereal, better replicating the taste of Barnum's than any other recipe I've tried.

ANIMAL CRACKERS

If you grew up loving cereal like Corn Pops and Kix, you don't need me to tell you that corn can be deliciously sweet. It's the secret ingredient in animal crackers too, that familiar flavor you can't quite put your finger on. Unlike cornmeal, which is gritty and coarse, freeze-dried corn grinds into a fine yellow powder. Along with malted milk powder, it gives these "crackers" the same warm and cozy flavor I loved as a kid. *See photo on page 192.*

YIELD: about seventy-five 2-inch cookies | **ACTIVE TIME:** 30 minutes

1⅓ cups | 6 ounces all-purpose flour, such as Gold Medal, plus more for dusting

¾ cup | 1½ ounces freeze-dried corn

⅔ cup | 4½ ounces sugar

¼ cup | 1 ounce malted milk powder

¼ teaspoon baking soda

¼ teaspoon Diamond Crystal kosher salt (half as much if iodized)

1 stick | 4 ounces cold unsalted butter, cut into ½-inch cubes

2 large egg yolks (2 tablespoons | 1½ ounces)

1 tablespoon vanilla extract

Make the dough:

Sift flour into the bowl of a food processor (if using cup measures, spoon into the cups and level with a knife before sifting). Add freeze-dried corn. Cover the bowl with plastic to contain the fine dust and grind until homogenous, about 2 minutes. Add sugar, malted milk powder, baking soda, salt, and cubed butter, pulsing to form a fine meal. Add egg yolks and vanilla and process until the dough balls up around the blade.

Turn the dough out onto a clean work surface and knead until smooth. Divide in half and flatten into discs. Use immediately, or wrap in plastic and refrigerate for up to 1 week; soften for 30 minutes at room temperature, then knead on a bare work surface until pliable and smooth.

Roll and cut the cookies:

Adjust oven rack to middle position and preheat to 350°F. On a lightly floured work surface, roll the dough into a 6-inch square. Sprinkle both sides with flour, then roll until 10 inches across and just over ⅛ inch thick. Slide an offset spatula under the dough to loosen and brush off excess flour.

With cookie cutters or plungers no larger than 2 inches across (larger crackers will burn around the edges before the centers fully crisp), stamp out lions, tigers, and bears, or the occasional T. rex, and arrange on a parchment-lined aluminum baking sheet, leaving ¼ inch between them. Gather scraps, knead briefly, re-roll, and cut again. Repeat with remaining dough.

Bake until the crackers are firm and just beginning to brown around the edges, about 12 minutes. Cool completely on the baking sheets. Enjoy out of hand, or store for up to 1 month in an airtight container at room temperature.

GRAHAM CRACKERS

From the late 1820s to his death in 1851, a Connecticut man named Sylvester Graham led a wild and crazy group of pro-fiber anti-sex crusaders known as the Grahamites. While lacking any sort of medical background, this Presbyterian minister made a career of dispensing advice on diet and nutrition. Sy Graham had quite the knack for baking, pioneering his own special brand of flour and writing a book on bread, but he would have despised everything about today's graham crackers.

His 1837 *Treatise on Bread and Bread Making* categorically condemned commercial crackers, as well as any whole wheat flour that was finely milled.[1] His lectures blamed overly processed flour for all manner of bodily frustrations, namely sexual desire and constipation. In an effort to, uh, relieve those issues, Graham urged his followers to abandon such "wanton" luxuries.

He considered white flour "contrary to both nature and reason," and whole wheat not whole (or holy) enough. In those days, commercial bolting could remove up to eighty percent of a flour's bran and still pass for "whole wheat." Graham equated the practice with nutritional divorce, a clear violation of the Biblical mandate, "What God had joined together, let no man put asunder."

Graham taught his followers to grow their own wheat, or else purchase it direct from the farmer, and to triple-wash the grains by hand. Dirt would dissolve, stray pebbles and debris would sink, while loose bran would float to the top and be saved. After thorough drying, the wheat and bran were cellared together and ground when needed—preferably with a hand mill and as coarse as possible.

There's absolutely no doubt that even the best whole wheat flour on the market today would have been an abomination to Graham, and I can't even dream up a hyperbole extreme enough to sum up his probable reaction to graham crackers—massproduced cookies chock-full of sugar, fat, white flour, superfine whole wheat flour, and chemical leavening.

It's almost as if graham crackers were designed to violate every principle that Graham stood for . . . and perhaps they were. See, American bakers had a bone to pick with Graham. His 1837 *Treatise* had claimed that no professional baker could be trusted to appreciate the importance of wholesome bread, and that manufactured goods were "immediately and universally injurious to the health."[2]

The book went on to single out the bakers and flour merchants of New York and Boston (where his book was published), claiming that their trade centered on spoiled and inferior wheat. Central to Graham's premise was that the "art and duty" of bread making belonged to "she who loves her husband and her children as women ought to love."

So when the reverend scheduled a series of women's lectures at Amory Hall in Boston the same year his book was published, we don't need a transcript to get the gist of his message. Graham apparently rained down enough hellfire and brimstone that riots broke out around Amory Hall, forcing the owners to cancel the remaining series for fear of their lives.[3] Graham made arrangements to resume his class at the Marlborough Hotel, but the mayor of Boston, unable (or unwilling) to provide constables for his protection, urged him to withdraw. The reverend refused, but the unrest was such that he wound up barricading himself inside the hotel while his followers shoveled slaked lime onto the protesting bakers below (for the uninitiated, being engulfed in a cloud of calcium hydroxide is a surefire recipe for chemical burns, blindness, and lung damage).

History doesn't tell us who these bakers were, but it doesn't have to. Crackers were one of Boston's most important exports, and by 1837 its bakers had already formed a coalition that would one day become the National Biscuit Company—Nabisco.

With a history like that, I think it was a form of silent protest that led New England bakers to start making cracker-shaped cookies called *grahams*.

And cookies they were! While it's often said that nineteenth-century graham crackers were a portrait of dietary restraint, contemporary sources prove otherwise. *The Complete Bread, Cake and Cracker Baker*, a handbook published mere decades after the Boston riots, includes a handful of indulgent formulas: one made with white flour and sugar, another from equal parts molasses and lard, and a third with butter, sugar, and milk.[4]

Even if those grahams weren't baked as a form of sweet revenge, the National Biscuit Company seemed to harbor some lingering resentment even in 1905, when their Graham Cracker advertisements declared Graham's original work "so tasteless and uninviting that it almost required a prescription."[5] Ultimately, these corporate grahams made a far more lasting impression than Graham himself, whose sanctimonious approach faded away, leaving only a vaguely heathy aura to his name. Again, it was Nabisco who advanced the cause of graham crackers, even acquiring the Honey Maid brand in 1925 to expand their offerings.

To prevent graham cracker sales from crashing with the stock market during the Great Depression, Nabisco rolled out a series of newspaper ads disguised as editorials for a "new science" they called "Cracker Cookery."[6] While not exactly molecular gastronomy,

this new approach turned the crackers into the basis of a cheap and easy pie crust that could be made without flour, sugar, or a rolling pin, prompting bakers from Florida to Manhattan to retrofit old-school recipes like Key Lime Pie (page 171) and New York Cheesecake (page 78) with graham cracker crusts.[7]

It was the culmination of everything Graham had ever preached against—not only were mass-produced crackers replacing the made-from-scratch originals, the packaged crackers were becoming ingredients of their own, with his very name at the center of it all. Perhaps the whole thing's just dramatic irony, but in my heart of hearts, I'll always believe those maligned Boston bakers set out to serve Graham his just desserts.

While I have little appreciation for the reverend's austerity, he was a passionate (if draconian) advocate for homemade, and there's no arguing with his love for whole grains. Compared to plain white flour, whole wheat makes a more fantastically crisp and flavorful graham, with a nutty flavor all its own. You don't even need to hunt down special graham flour, since the FDA considers the term merely a synonym for whole wheat. Despite that whole-grain foundation, I've no doubt ol' Sylvester would hate everything about my buttery sweet grahams, and I wouldn't have it any other way.

Vintage advertisements portrayed graham crackers as a health food, while companies laded the recipe with sugar and fat.

CRISPY WHOLE WHEAT GRAHAM CRACKERS

My homemade grahams are buttery and crisp, with an incredible depth of flavor thanks to earthy whole wheat flour and the mellow maltiness of golden syrup—a type of light molasses. For simplicity's sake, the dough is rolled and baked in sheets, then quickly snipped into pieces with a pizza wheel. Just don't forget to save the scraps, which make, of course, fantastic graham cracker crumbs.

YIELD: twenty-four 2¼-by-4¾-inch crackers, plus 8 ounces (2 cups) crumbs | **ACTIVE TIME:** about 45 minutes

¾ cup | 5½ ounces sugar

1½ teaspoons baking soda

½ teaspoon Diamond Crystal kosher salt (half as much if iodized)

¼ teaspoon ground cinnamon

1 tablespoon vanilla extract

¼ cup | 3 ounces golden syrup, such as Lyle's, sorghum, unsulfured molasses (not blackstrap), or honey

1½ sticks | 6 ounces unsalted butter, solid but creamy—about 70°F

2½ cups | 12 ounces whole wheat flour (not stone-ground or white whole wheat), plus more for dusting

Make the dough:
Combine sugar, baking soda, salt, cinnamon, vanilla, golden syrup, and butter in the bowl of a stand mixer fitted with a paddle attachment. Mix on low speed to moisten, then increase to medium and beat until somewhat light, about 3 minutes. Reduce speed to low, add whole wheat flour, and mix to form a soft dough.

Scrape dough onto a work surface and knead gently to form a ball. Divide in half. Use immediately or wrap in plastic and refrigerate for up to 1 week; soften for 30 minutes at room temperature, then knead on a bare work surface until pliable and smooth.

Roll and bake the dough:
Adjust oven rack to middle position and preheat to 350°F. Generously flour a large sheet of parchment and place one portion of dough in the center. Pat into a 5-by-6-inch rectangle, sprinkle with flour, flip, and dust again. Working from the center out and adding more flour as needed, roll the dough until roughly 15-by-11 inches and very thin. Slide onto an aluminum baking sheet and brush away excess flour. Repeat with remaining dough.

For grocery store look-alikes, score each sheet of dough into twelve 2¼-by-4¾-inch rectangles and dock with a bamboo skewer or the narrow end of a chopstick (a strictly cosmetic procedure). Otherwise, leave the dough uncut.

Bake until crackers are tawny brown and firm, though your fingertip may leave a faint indentation, about 20 minutes. *Immediately* cut along the prescored lines with a knife, or cut into free-form shapes using a pizza wheel. Cool to room temperature directly on the baking sheets. Enjoy scrap pieces as a snack, or pulverize into crumbs. The grahams can be stored in an airtight container for up to 3 weeks at room temperature or frozen for up to 3 months.

continued ↓

Graham is simply another word for whole wheat, which makes these crackers rich and crisp.

TROUBLESHOOTING

If the graham crackers seem anything less than earth-shattering crisp after baking, they were probably too thick. To revive soft crackers, simply return to a 350°F oven until fragrant and slightly darkened, about 10 minutes.

Although honey, molasses, and sorghum are all fine for this recipe, graham crackers cannot be made with maple syrup, due to its unique water content and pH.

→ *Mix it up!*

CHOCOLATE: My mom used to sandwich chocolate graham crackers with peanut butter for an after-school snack, a combo I re-create by reducing the whole wheat flour to 10 ounces (2¼ cups), sifted with 1 ounce (⅓ cup) natural or Dutch-process cocoa powder. To retain their deep cocoa color, roll the dough in sifted cocoa powder. Serve with generous smears of peanut butter and a tall glass of milk.

CINNAMON SUGAR: We rarely had sugar-coated grahams in our pantry when I was a kid, but they were always at my best friend's house, and seemed all the more special for their rarity. For the dough, increase the cinnamon to ½ teaspoon. Before docking, dust each sheet of dough with a half batch of Cinnamon Sugar (page 44), or any Sugar Sprinkle (page 46). Otherwise, dock and bake as directed. After the crackers cool, gently tap each against the baking sheet to knock off any excess sugar.

COCONUT (VEGAN): Replace the butter with 5½ ounces (¾ cup) virgin coconut oil (solid but creamy—about 70°F) and add 1 teaspoon pure coconut extract along with the vanilla.

GINGERBREAD: This variation has all the spicy complexity of a Christmas cookie, with the unique flavor and crunch of a classic graham. Make the dough with sorghum or unsulfured molasses (not blackstrap) and increase the cinnamon to 1 teaspoon. Along with the sugar, add 1 tablespoon orange zest, 2 teaspoons ground ginger, ⅛ teaspoon ground cloves, and a few cracks of black pepper.

GRAHAM CRACKER CRUMB CRUST: Combine 9 ounces (2 cups) finely ground graham cracker crumbs with 2 ounces (4 tablespoons) melted unsalted butter. Scatter into a 9-by-1¼-inch glass or ceramic pie plate and press into an even layer over the bottom and up the sides. Bake at 350°F until firm, about 18 minutes. Cool to room temperature for immediate use in your favorite recipe, or wrap tightly in plastic and refrigerate for up to 1 week.

GLUTEN-FREE: Replace the whole wheat flour with 6 ounces (1¼ cups) white rice flour, 4 ounces (1 cup plus 2 tablespoons) oat flour, and ½ ounce (1 tablespoon) kinako.

FIG NEWTONS®

In 1889, Joseph Pulitzer commissioned the tallest sky-scraper in the world, a towering feat of modern engineering that would become headquarters for the *New York World*. Meanwhile, an engineer named James Henry Mitchell was busy constructing a different sort of monument, made with bricks of flour and sugar.

JH made himself a fixture in reports of the U.S. Patent Office in the late nineteenth century, with inventions ranging from dough sheeters to production molds.[1] Surviving personal correspondence from 1881 shows that he was fascinated with the idea of developing a machine that could simultaneously extrude a dough and filling, and in 1892 he did just that.[2]

Culinary historians who bother to mention JH today reduce his crowning achievement to nothing more than a "fancy funnel," a blithe mischaracterization that ignores the importance of the man and his work. Aside from straight-up mechanical genius, JH's inventions suggest a deep understanding of food chemistry and the complexities of baking on an industrial scale. His designs required such specific parts that he eventually established his own foundry in 1897.[3]

His ingenuity brought JH to the attention of Kennedy Biscuit, a precursor to Nabisco.[4] We don't know the details of their partnership, only that Frank Kennedy would one day credit JH first and foremost among those responsible for the success of the entire industry, "taking part in the invention and development of the mechanical processes [behind an] endless variety of cakes and biscuits."[5]

Perhaps contemporary engineers would scoff at the notion of devoting one's career to something as impermanent as a cookie, but we've long since razed the Pulitzer Building, erasing its memory from the New York skyline. Yet every American knows the curving lines of JH Mitchell's timeless design, the Fig Newton.[6]

The simple "fruit biscuit" he patented in 1892 has remained in continuous production ever since, but neither he nor Frank Kennedy invented the flavor.[7] The cookie itself likely took inspiration from nineteenth-century "Fig Cakes," spiced with cinnamon and layered with thick fig jam.[8] Or they may have originated as a figgy twist on the "Rue Newton," an orange-scented butter cake mixed with dried currants that was popular in the 1880s.[9]

My own recipe draws from these sources, using a hint of cinnamon and orange to flavor the dough. It's loaded with brown sugar, honey, and egg yolks—ingredients that keep it pliable even straight from the fridge; an important trick, because it takes a wet and sticky dough for the cookies to bake up as cakey as they should.

I make the filling from dried figs, which can be quickly pureed into a faux jam (no cooking required). Not only does that make Homemade Fig Newtons possible all year round, the dried figs provide a more concentrated flavor that tastes just like the original. It's wonderfully thick too, so the filling won't bubble out as the cookies bake.

HOMEMADE FIG NEWTONS®

As Nabisco likes to remind us, Fig Newtons aren't just cookies, they're fruit and cake. True to that legacy, my homemade version pairs an easy, no-cook fig preserve with a soft dough inspired by yellow cake. Since everything hinges on the concentrated jammy flavor of dried figs, it's vital that you love their taste straight from the bag, so look for brands that are plump, moist, and naturally sweet. I dig Trader Joe's, having found other national brands disappointingly bland. *See photo on page 208.*

YIELD: thirty-two 1½-by-1-inch bars | **ACTIVE TIME:** 1 hour |
DOWNTIME: 1-hour refrigeration, plus 6 hours to "steam" and cool

Cakey Cookie Dough:

- 2¼ cups | 10½ ounces all-purpose flour, such as Gold Medal, plus more for dusting

- 1¼ sticks | 5 ounces unsalted butter, soft but cool—about 65°F

- ½ cup packed | 4 ounces light brown sugar

- ½ plus ⅛ teaspoon baking soda

- ¼ teaspoon Diamond Crystal kosher salt (half as much if iodized)

- ¼ teaspoon ground cinnamon

- 2 tablespoons | 1 ounce honey

- 1 teaspoon orange zest

- 1 tablespoon | ½ ounce freshly squeezed orange juice

- 3 large egg yolks, straight from the fridge

No-Cook Fig Preserves:

- 2½ cups | 12 ounces plump, sticky dried Mission figs, stems trimmed

- ⅓ cup | 3½ ounces applesauce, sweetened if you like

- 2 tablespoons | 1 ounce freshly squeezed orange juice

Prepare the dough:

Sift flour (if using cup measures, spoon into the cups and level with a knife before sifting).

Combine butter, brown sugar, baking soda, salt, cinnamon, honey, and orange zest in the bowl of a stand mixer fitted with a paddle attachment. Mix on low speed to moisten, then increase to medium and cream until light and fluffy, about 5 minutes. Add orange juice, then add the egg yolks one at a time and continue beating until smooth. Reduce the speed to low and sprinkle in the flour, mixing until well combined.

Knead the dough against the sides of the bowl to form a smooth ball. Flatten into a disc and wrap in plastic. Refrigerate until cool and firm but not hard, about 1 hour. (The dough can be refrigerated for up to 1 week; soften for 30 minutes at room temperature.)

Prepare the preserves:

Cut the figs in half. Pulse with applesauce and orange juice in a food processor until roughly chopped, then process to a thick, smooth paste. Scrape the bowl and blade with a flexible spatula, then process a minute more to ensure absolutely no chunks remain. Transfer to a sturdy piping bag fitted with a ½-inch plain tip and set aside until needed, up to 24 hours. (The preserves can be refrigerated in an airtight container for up to 3 weeks; bring to room temperature before using.)

Make the cookies:

Adjust oven rack to middle position and preheat to 350°F. Knead the cool dough on a bare work surface until pliable and smooth, then dust with flour and roll into an 8-inch square. Sprinkle both sides with flour and roll into a 15-inch square. Slide an offset spatula under the dough to loosen it, brush off excess flour, and cut into four 3¼-inch-wide strips.

Holding the bag at a 90-degree angle just above the surface of the dough (this will force the preserves to flatten as they leave the bag), pipe a 1-inch-wide strip down the center of each portion. Fold a long flap of dough over each strip, brush away excess flour, and roll each bar over, seam side down. Gently flatten each bar with your fingertips, then transfer to a parchment-lined aluminum baking sheet (all four bars will fit on a single sheet).

Bake until the bars are puffed and firm, without any significant browning, about 18 minutes. *Immediately* cut into 1-inch pieces (I use a metal bench scraper and cut 2 strips at a time), then transfer to an airtight container, with a paper towel between each layer and on top. This will steam the cookies and retain moisture for them to reabsorb, creating a uniquely soft and cakey texture Cover and "mature" for at least 6 hours before serving; prior to that, the cookies will taste dry.

Store for up to 1 week at room temperature or up to a month in the fridge.

→ *Mix it up!*

APRICOT STRAWBERRY: After making Philadelphia-Style Strawberry Ice Cream (page 340), you'll have 5 ounces (a heaping ½ cup) leftover super-dry strawberry pulp. Combined with 12 ounces (2 cups) dried apricots, it makes a beautifully pink fruit filling—no applesauce required. Simply pulse the two together in a food processor and use as directed.

BLUEBERRY LIME: In the dead of winter, this bright and tangy variation is a burst of summer sunshine. Swap the orange zest and juice in the dough for 2 tablespoons lime zest (from about 4 small limes) and 1 tablespoon lime juice. For the filling, replace the figs with 6 ounces (2 cups gently packed) plump dried apples and 6 ounces (1 rounded cup) dried blueberries with additional lime juice as necessary to loosen the consistency of the preserves.

CHERRY BANANA: If you've got some spotty bananas to use up, forget about banana bread. This tart, aromatic variation is perfect any time of year. Instead of figs and applesauce, prepare the filling with 6 ounces (2 cups gently packed) plump dried apples, 6 ounces (1 cup) dried cherries, and 4 ounces (½ cup) mashed ripe banana—the blacker the better.

PIG "NEWTONS": However great the pun, the sweet and savory reality is even better. If you love nibbling on bacon between bites of toast and jam, this version's for you. Fry up 12 ounces bacon (1 package or 12 strips) on a griddle over low to medium-low heat until very crisp, about 10 minutes. Transfer to a bed of paper towels. Pour the bacon fat through a fine-mesh sieve into a bowl. Reduce the butter in the dough to 3 ounces (6 tablespoons) and add 2 ounces (¼ cup) cooled bacon fat; otherwise, proceed as directed. Prepare the filling according to the recipe; once smooth, crumble in the bacon and pulse to combine.

Cakey cookies stuffed with a quick and easy dried fig jam (see page 206).

OREO®

During the biscuit boom of the nineteenth century, brothers Jacob and Joseph Loose bought a controlling interest in a Missouri baking company.[1] Guided by Jacob's expansionist philosophy, Loose Brothers Manufacturing became a multimillion-dollar business within a few years. But Jacob didn't see the sense in competing with his fellow bakers in the Midwest when they could all benefit from joining forces as a corporation. So in 1890, he hired a big-city lawyer named Adolphus Green to oversee the negotiations and paperwork needed to wrangle everyone together. The moment the ink dried, the American Biscuit and Manufacturing Company became the second-largest corporate bakery in America. Naturally, Jacob named himself president, then appointed Joseph to the board of directors and Adolphus to general counsel.[2]

On the national stage, American Biscuit fell between the New York Biscuit Company (home of Kennedy Biscuit; see page 194) and the United States Baking Company.[3] For the next seven years, they duked it out in a competition so fierce reporters called it "the biscuit war."[4] The battle took its toll, and in 1897, poor health forced Jacob to step down as president.

That put Joseph in control, and he'd seen enough war. He decided to end the biscuit battle and make peace, or profit at least. With Adolphus Green's legal savvy, ABC entered into an agreement with NYBC and USBC. Jacob fiercely opposed the alphabet-soup merger from his sickbed, and he begged Joseph not to go through with it, but alas: His two most bitter enemies gobbled up American Biscuit, creating the super-giant National Biscuit Company. On its board of directors: three of Jacob's former board members, his former lawyer, his treasurer, and his own brother.[5]

So you'll understand that when Jacob recovered his health, he had something of an ax to grid. From his perspective, the National Biscuit Company was resting on *his* laurels. In 1902, he teamed up with John Wiles to form the Loose-Wiles Biscuit Company. Setting out to reclaim all that was lost, Jacob pushed his new company through a decade of exponential growth, until he had once again become one of the largest corporate bakeries in America, second only to Nabisco—but a distant second. In 1912, Nabisco made 45 million dollars to Loose-Wiles's 12. To make matters worse, his old pal Adolphus had worked his way up to president.[6]

Yet Jacob's success demanded attention. With headlines such as "Exchange National for Loose-Wiles?" suggesting the National Biscuit Company had already peaked on the New York Stock Exchange, shares of Loose-Wiles seemed to offer nothing but growth.[7] The popularity of Jacob's company hinged in no small part on one biscuit, a best seller so in demand that groceries bought it by the ton. A little something called Hydrox®.

Hydrox was an instant classic, a national favorite and an ice cream parlor staple, the original cookies and cream.[8] Bitter chocolate shortbread joined with sweet vanilla fondant gave Hydrox a mighty crunch that put Nabisco's dainty Sugar Wafers to shame. Loose-Wiles advertised Hydrox as "a dessert of itself," but it looked like a work of art.[9] Each wafer had a scalloped edge, a border of scrollwork, and six seven-petaled flowers chained together by leaves and stems, with a laurel wreath at their heart.

Whether through coincidence or spite, Nabisco unveiled the Oreo on Loose-Wiles's tenth anniversary.[10] The clone advertised "two chocolate-flavored wafers with a rich, creamy filling," competing directly against Hydrox's "two chocolate wafers filled with sweet vanilla cream."[11] Oreo couldn't match the detail of the Hydrox design, but it imitated what mattered most: the laurel wreath.

That swipe went deeper than copycat aesthetics, straight to the heart of Oreo's darkest mystery: its name. Nabisco has always shied away from explaining its origin, which inspired decades of speculation. The most common version asserts that Oreo derives from *or*, French for "gold" and supposedly the color of the original packaging. Others say it stands for *orexigenic*, a medical term for substances that stimulate the appetite (including cannabis). Another popular explanation proposes an elaborate symbolic scheme wherein the two Os in Oreo represent cookies sandwiching cREam in the middle, a theory that makes more sense if you put on a tinfoil hat.

But consider the roster of Nabisco's fancy biscuits in 1913: Avena, Lotus, Helicon, Zephyrette, Zaytona, Anola, Ramona, and Oreo.[12] It seems like a random collection of exotic names, but I noticed a pattern. *Avena* is Latin for "oats," and we all know the famous lotus blossom. Helicon comes from *Heliconia*, a genus of flower native to Florida. Zephyrette matches with *Zephyranthes*, the genus of the tropical lily. Zaytona is Arabic for "olive," Anola was shortened from canola (one of its defining ingredients), and Ramona is in the buttercup family (buttercups dotted each box).[13] Someone at Nabisco clearly had a thing for botany, and to understand Oreo, you don't have to look any farther than the mountain laurel on every Hydrox—*Oreodaphne*. It was a copycat in every way.

For a time Hydrox remained the "King of Biscuits," and one of the most widely consumed cookies in America.[14] Despite what you hear today, Oreo didn't have much initial success.[15] Groceries struggled to entice customers away from Hydrox, and advertisements tied Oreos to sales on other Nabisco products to help unload their inventory.[16] In 1914, one store found itself with a seven-hundred-tin stockpile that refused to budge, so they slashed the price and berated their customers: "Yesterday we advertised those splendid Oreos and they were a

great bargain. While we sold a few, they didn't move anything like we expected. It's simply a case of your not knowing what a fine biscuit delicacy they are."[17]

Meanwhile, Loose-Wiles took a more diplomatic approach. In 1924, the company partnered with the Union of Orthodox Jewish Congregations of America (OU) to create the country's first kosher-certification program. The OU seal fostered tremendous support for Hydrox within the Jewish community.[18] Twenty years later, Oreo didn't even make it onto a list of Nabisco's most popular products, much less one worth the expense of certification.[19]

Whatever success it amassed in those early years, though, it's hard see Hydrox as anything other than the *Titanic*. Despite its craftsmanship, beauty, and popular appeal, it harbored a fatal flaw. When Hydrox debuted in 1908, its pseudo-scientific name (hydrogen + oxygen) was common to all manner of goods, from Hydrox Aerated Table Water to Hydrox Ice Cream and Hydrox Ginger Ale.[20] Cashing in on the Hydrox fad gave Loose-Wiles a bit of street cred, but it later meant they couldn't defend their brand in court. Eventually the number of random Hydrox products on the market stained the word with an inescapably generic vibe, and an icky one at that, as chemical companies in particular took a shine to the term.

Loose-Wiles realized they had an image problem, but instead of renaming Hydrox, they renamed the company: Sunshine Biscuits. Admittedly Loose-Wiles sounds like

Hydrox: the original chocolate sandwich cookie, with a beautiful laurel wreath design.

the sort of insult parents throw at the cigarette-smoking neighbor kid ("In my day, we didn't tolerate those types of loose wiles!"), but Sunshine didn't put Hydrox in a more appetizing light.

A decent PR team could have turned things around, but Sunshine's advertisements took a weird, curmudgeonly tone. From 1915 to 1965, Hydrox seemed hell-bent on exposing Oreo as a impostor, even going so far as advertising a tiny bear cub literally crying over stolen cookies.[21] They relentlessly billed Hydrox as the "first," the "finest," the "original," the "only," and the "classic," shaking a finger at America: "Don't be fooled by look-alikes!"[22]

They might as well have told Oreos to get off their lawn. That cranky campaign did nothing to win anyone's heart. Consumers wanted a tasty treat, and Oreo offered exactly that, with happy, colorful advertisements about crisp, chocolatey sandwich cookies crammed with more filling than any other brand.[23] Nabisco had the stamina and financial resources to sell Oreos at a loss. In the mid-1950s, the rope-a-dope strategy paid off when Nabisco sprang into action with a completely redesigned cookie and a snazzy campaign for "new Oreos."[24] Simultaneously, they jacked up the price—reverse psychology at its finest. Americans didn't flock to the suddenly affordable Hydrox, they shunned it as *cheap* in every sense of the word—the kind of low-budget, fuddy-duddy knockoff favored by penny-pinching grandpas.

Classic Oreo® cookies, with a familiar laurel design.

Indeed, by the 1960s grandpas were just about the only ones who could remember the glory days of Hydrox.[25]

The lights went out at Sunshine shortly thereafter, and the Hydrox brand bounced around the industry like a third-string baseball player, first sold to the American Tobacco Company, then resold to G.F. Industries, Keebler, and later Kellogg's, which formally pulled the plug. In something straight out of a Greek tragedy, Kellogg's returned Hydrox to production for the sole purpose of crushing them into bits for the wholesale market, supplying manufacturers who can't afford a license from Oreo. With Hydrox dead and buried in off-brand ice cream, Oreo celebrated its hundredth birthday as the uncontested king of cookies.

If opposites attract, Oreos generate a force nothing short of gravitational. Black and white. Creamy and crunchy. Bitter and sweet. Chocolate and Vanilla. Recent years have sadly added "natural and artificial" to the list, but we can make like Jacob Loose and reclaim what's been lost by striking out on our own.

My homemade version of Oreo® is a remarkably simple recipe and you don't have to seek out any special sort of "black" cocoa to duplicate the Oreo's inky color. All you need is Dutch cocoa and baking soda, which create an alkaline dough that darkens to a gorgeous chocolate black in the oven. The wafers are crisp, intensely chocolate, and just a little bitter to balance the sweet and creamy filling inside.

HOMEMADE OREO® COOKIES

You don't have to hunt down specialty black cocoa to make my homemade take on classic Oreos—the only essentials are Dutch cocoa and a little baking soda to alkalize the dough. Together they make crispy wafers as inky and intense as the original, with a hint of bitterness to balance the sweet vanilla filling. Though it's not a make-or-break ingredient, I've found that a little coconut extract gives the cookies an even more authentic flavor, adding aromatic complexity to the earthy, dark wafers.

YIELD: forty-five 1¾-inch sandwich cookies | **ACTIVE TIME:** 40 minutes

Chocolate Wafers:

1 stick | 4 ounces unsalted butter, creamy and soft—about 68°F

½ cup | 3½ ounces sugar

3 tablespoons | 2 ounces golden syrup, such as Lyle's, or light corn syrup

½ teaspoon baking soda

¼ teaspoon Diamond Crystal kosher salt (half as much if iodized)

¼ teaspoon coconut extract (optional)

1¼ cups | 5¾ ounces all-purpose flour, such as Gold Medal

⅓ cup plus 1 tablespoon | 1¼ ounces Dutch-process cocoa powder, such as Cacao Barry Extra Brute, plus more for dusting

1 recipe Homemade Vanilla Oreo® Filling (page 215)

Prepare the dough:

Combine butter, sugar, golden syrup, baking soda, salt, and coconut extract, if using, in the bowl of a stand mixer fitted with a paddle attachment. Mix on low speed to moisten, then increase to medium and beat until fluffy and light, about 5 minutes, pausing to scrape the bowl and beater halfway through.

Sift flour and cocoa together (if using cup measures, spoon into cups and level with a knife before sifting). Sprinkle into the butter mixture while mixing on low; it will seem dry and mealy at first but soon form a stiff dough. Knead against the sides of the bowl to form a smooth ball, then divide in half and flatten into discs. Use immediately, or wrap in plastic and refrigerate for up to 1 week; soften cold dough for 30 minutes at room temperature, and knead on a bare surface until pliable before using.

Make the wafers:

Adjust oven rack to middle position and preheat to 350°F. On a cocoa-dusted surface, roll a portion of dough into a 7-inch square. Sprinkle both sides with cocoa and roll until ¼ inch thick. Generously dust with cocoa and pass an embossed rolling pin over the dough, thinning it to about ⅛ inch, or continue rolling to ⅛ inch with a plain pin. Slide an offset spatula under the dough to loosen, brush away excess cocoa, and stamp into 1½-inch rounds with a fluted cutter. Arrange on a parchment-lined aluminum baking sheet, leaving ¼ inch between them. Gather scraps, knead, re-roll, and cut as before. Repeat with remaining dough. Any remaining scraps can be discarded or baked to grind for crumbs.

Bake until wafers are firm and dry, about 15 minutes. Cool completely on the baking sheets.

continued ↓

Whether chocolate, vanilla, or strawberry, Homemade Oreo® Cookies are ready for you to dunk, twist, or bite.

Sandwich the cookies:
Turn half the wafers upside down and pipe a generous dollop of filling in the center of each (just shy of a tablespoon, or a little more than ¼ ounce). Top with remaining wafers and join them together with a gentle twist. Transfer to an airtight container and let stand at room temperature until filling has set, about 30 minutes. The cookies will keep for up to 1 week at room temperature, up to a month in the fridge, or 3 months frozen; serve at room temperature.

→ *Mix it up!*

COOKIE CRUMBS: Grind broken wafers and scraps in a food processor until fine. Freeze in a quart zip-top bag for up to 6 months. Use to replace the graham cracker crumbs in Souffléed Cheesecake (page 80), or bake into a crumb crust according to the directions on page 204.

MINT OR ORANGE CHOCOLATE: Add 2 teaspoons peppermint extract along with the coconut. Roll, shape, and cut the dough according to the directions for Homemade Thin Mints® on page 228. Or, if you're not crazy about mint, use an equal amount of orange extract instead.

GLUTEN-FREE: Replace the all-purpose flour with 3 ounces (¾ cup) teff flour, and 3 ounces (¾ cup) tapioca flour or arrowroot and proceed as directed.

Homemade Vanilla Oreo® Filling

Not only do Homemade Oreo® Cookies need a sturdy filling that won't squish out with every bite, they need one that won't soften the wafers over time. The trick is to simmer melted butter, driving off the water to create a foundation that's rich but low in moisture. By whipping it with organic, tapioca-based powdered sugar (which tastes less gritty than the traditional sort), I'm able to create a filling that's thick, silky, and perfect for twisting, licking, and dunking.

YIELD: 1⅓ cups (13 ounces); enough to fill forty-five 1½-inch sandwich cookies | **ACTIVE TIME:** 10 minutes

1½ sticks | 6 ounces unsalted butter

1 teaspoon vanilla extract

⅛ teaspoon of Diamond Crystal kosher salt (half as much if iodized)

2 cups | 8½ ounces organic powdered sugar, sifted

Before getting started, bake and cool the wafers; this filling cannot be prepared in advance.

In a 2-quart stainless steel saucier, melt the butter over medium-low heat, then simmer, stirring with a heat-resistant spatula, while the butter hisses and pops; if you notice brown bits forming along the edges, reduce heat to low. Continue cooking and stirring until the butter falls silent, then strain into the bowl of a stand mixer fitted with a paddle attachment.

Add vanilla and salt, followed by powdered sugar. Mix on low speed to moisten, then increase to medium. Beat until creamy and soft, about 5 minutes. Transfer to a pastry bag fitted with a ½-inch plain tip and use immediately.

→ *Mix it up!*

CHOCOLATE: Add ¼ ounce (1 tablespoon) Dutch-process cocoa powder along with the powdered sugar.

COCONUT: Replace the butter with 4 ounces (⅔ cup) virgin coconut oil; no need to melt it. Add ¼ teaspoon coconut extract along with the vanilla.

STRAWBERRY: Omit the vanilla extract. Increase the powdered sugar to 10 ounces (2½ cups) and combine with ½ ounce (¾ cup) freeze-dried strawberries in the bowl of a food processor. Cover with plastic wrap to contain the dust and process until powdery and fine. Proceed as directed. The frosting will seem loose after creaming, so take care when sandwiching the cookies; it will thicken and set as firmly as the original.

NUTTER BUTTER® COOKIES

The same economics that made peanut butter a popular ingredient for baking at home (see Peanut Butter Cookies, page 49) led the National Baking Company to advertise "NBC Peanut Butter Patties" as early as 1925.[1] They looked like big sheets of uncut ravioli, wafer dough sealed around individual bites of peanut butter and baked to a crisp.

Other biscuit companies were quick to introduce versions of their own, but in the 1950s Keebler skipped the peanut butter patty party in favor of Pitter Patters, embossed shortbread cookies sandwiched around a thick peanut butter filling.[2] This Oreo-esque approach must have caught Nabisco's attention, because they quickly replaced Peanut Butter Patties with Rockets.[3]

Perhaps America's only Space Race–themed snack, Rockets looked like blonde Oreos. Each wafer had a peanut stamped in the center, and star-spangled packaging featured an anthropomorphic peanut astronaut, complete with a space helmet and a rocket blasting through the galaxy. Despite Neil Armstrong one-small-stepping all over the moon, NBC discontinued Rockets in 1969—the same year another NBC would cancel its voyage to the final frontier.[4] While *Star Trek* would have to wait two decades for a reboot, Nabisco relaunched Rockets just a few months later under a new name: Nutter Butter Cookies.

Nutter Butter Cookies never achieved Oreo-level popularity, but their whimsical shape and satisfying flavor earned a devout following. Unfortunately, a recent redesign demoted them to simple sandwich rounds. I bring back their classic shape with a tool that sounds slightly scandalous: a bikini cutter. Although this cutter is meant to make sassy swimsuit-shaped cookies, my friend and fellow pastry chef Gail Dosik noticed that their shape looks remarkably like a peanut, especially when gently stretched to widen the middle. It's a cute option for the perfectionist, but with crispy peanut butter shortbread sandwiching whipped peanut creme, the peanut theme is loud and clear even without a specialty cutter.

HOMEMADE NUTTER BUTTER® COOKIES

Made from equal parts butter and peanut butter, these shortbread wafers are ultra-crunchy and salty-sweet—perfect for sandwiching with whipped peanut butter creme. They're best made with commercial peanut butter, which makes the dough and filling easy to handle. *See photo on page 218.*

YIELD: about thirty 3-inch peanut-shaped or thirty-five 2¼-inch round sandwich cookies
ACTIVE TIME: 1 hour | **DOWNTIME:** 30 minutes

Peanut Butter Wafers:

- 2 cups | 9 ounces all-purpose flour, such as Gold Medal, plus more for dusting
- 6 tablespoons | 3 ounces unsalted butter, creamy and soft—about 68°F
- ⅓ cup | 3 ounces creamy peanut butter, such as Skippy
- 1 cup | 7 ounces sugar
- ¼ teaspoon baking soda
- ¼ teaspoon Diamond Crystal kosher salt (half as much if iodized)
- 2 large egg whites (¼ cup | 2¼ ounces)

Peanut Butter Creme:

- 6 tablespoons | 3 ounces unsalted butter, creamy and soft—about 68°F
- ⅓ cup | 3 ounces creamy peanut butter, such as Skippy
- 1 tablespoon | ¾ ounce honey
- 1 teaspoon vanilla extract
- ¼ teaspoon Diamond Crystal kosher salt (half as much if iodized)
- 1 cup | 4 ounces organic powdered sugar, sifted

Prepare the dough:

Sift flour (if using a cup measure, spoon into the cup and level with a knife before sifting).

Combine butter, peanut butter, sugar, baking soda, and salt in the bowl of a stand mixer fitted with a paddle attachment. Mix on low speed to moisten, then increase to medium and cream until fluffy and light, about 5 minutes. Beat the whites with a fork until foamy and thin, then add to the butter and sugar in four additions, letting each incorporate before adding the next. Scrape the bowl and beater with a flexible spatula, then resume mixing on low. Sprinkle in the flour, and mix to form a soft dough.

Knead against the sides of the bowl to form a smooth ball, divide in half, and flatten into discs. Use immediately, or wrap in plastic and refrigerate for up to 1 week; soften for 30 minutes at room temperature, then knead on a bare work surface until pliable and smooth.

Make the wafers:

Adjust oven rack to middle position and preheat to 350°F. On a flour-dusted surface, roll the dough until ½ inch thick. Sprinkle with flour, flip, sprinkle again, and roll just shy of ⅛ inch. Slide an offset spatula under the dough to loosen. Cut into "peanuts" with a 3-inch bikini cookie cutter or into simple 2¼-inch rounds and arrange on a parchment-lined aluminum baking sheet, leaving ¼ inch between them. If you like, gently score the cutouts with a bench scraper to make a diamond pattern. Gather scraps, re-roll, and cut as before. The remaining scraps can also be baked, to grind for crumbs.

Bake until wafers are firm and dry, about 15 minutes. Cool completely on the baking sheet. Use immediately, or transfer to an airtight container and store for up to a week at room temperature or a month in the fridge.

continued ↓

Crisp peanut butter shortbread stuffed with whipped peanut butter cream.

Make the creme:
Combine butter, peanut butter, honey, vanilla, and salt in the bowl of a stand mixer fitted with a paddle attachment. Mix on low speed to moisten, then sprinkle in the powdered sugar a little at a time. Once fully incorporated, increase to medium and beat until the creme is soft and light, about 5 minutes, pausing to scrape the bowl and beater halfway through. Transfer to a pastry bag fitted with a ½-inch plain tip.

Sandwich the cookies:
Pipe ¼ ounce (2 teaspoons) creme into the center of half of the rounds or ⅛ ounce (1 teaspoon) into each "lobe" of a peanut. Sandwich with the remaining wafers; there are extras to account for breakage. Transfer to an airtight container and refrigerate until the filling has set, about 15 minutes. Store up to 1 week at room temperature or up to a month in the fridge; serve at room temperature.

→ *Mix it up!*

COOKIE CRUMBS: Grind broken wafers and scraps in a food processor until fine; freeze in a quart zip-top bag for up to 6 months. Use to replace the graham cracker crumbs in Souffléed Cheesecake (page 80), or bake into a crumb crust according to the directions on page 204.

STRAWBERRY CREME: If you love a good peanut butter and jelly sandwich, try trading the Peanut Butter Creme for the Strawberry variation of Homemade Oreo® Filling on page 215.

VEGAN: Replace the butter in the dough and filling with an equal amount of refined coconut oil and omit the egg whites in the dough. Refrigerate for 15 minutes before rolling the dough.

GLUTEN-FREE: Replace the all-purpose flour with 4 ounces (1¼ cups) oat flour, 3 ounces (⅔ cup) white rice flour, and 2 ounces (½ cup) coconut flour.

FUDGE STRIPES™ COOKIES, PECAN SANDIES®, AND MAGIC MIDDLES®

In 1857, John Ricketts owned one of the largest buildings in Philadelphia—a bakery.[1] If you're imagining some grandfatherly shopkeep in his flour-speckled apron, think again. John's thirteen-thousand-square-foot facility spanned four floors, with a forty-five-foot oven and a production line that plowed through two hundred barrels of flour a day.[2] That's forty thousand pounds of flour. *A day.*

John entrusted day-to-day operations to his foreman, Godfrey, a German immigrant who'd grown up in Pennsylvania.[3] He'd spent his life in Philadelphia bakeries, so he knew the ins and outs of bulk purchasing, mass production, management, and distribution.[4] Near the end of the Civil War, John passed away and the company restructured, giving Godfrey an opportunity to acquire sixteen thousand dollars' worth of equipment to establish a bakery in his own name: Keebler.[5]

At forty years of age, Godfrey Keebler was just getting started.[6] For the next twenty years, he endured the typical trials and tribulations of a nineteenth-century biscuit boss: lawsuits, mysterious factory fires, and the Knights-Templar.[7] He eventually took on a partner, and the bakery continued as Keebler-Weyl until his death in 1893.[8]

The company thrived in local markets for the next thirty years, despite Nabisco encroaching on their shelf space.[9] Seeking safety in numbers, Keebler-Weyl eventually joined the United Biscuit Company of America, a cooperative of Midwestern bakeries.[10] Individual members kept their names and recipe rosters, but they pooled resources to advertise nationally under the brand Kitchen Rich.[11]

The sweet idea went horribly wrong. When United sponsored *The Flintstones*, families across America watched Fred scarf down Kitchen Rich cookies, but no one had heard of any company or cookie known as Kitchen Rich. No one could wrap their mind around the idea of a brand for brands. Undaunted, UBC took out full-page ads in *Life*, mixed-up tableaus piled up with four different boxes of saltines, two types of graham crackers, and ten mentions of Kitchen Rich.[12] Inevitably, these ads left everyone wondering what Kitchen Rich was. To answer the question, United adopted a bizarrely subjective slogan: "Who are the Kitchen Rich people? _____, of course!"[13] In Michigan, Hekman bakery filled in the blanks, while Strietmann took Ohio, and Keebler covered Pennsylvania.[14] Some states didn't even have a United bakery, making the ads comically meaningless in many areas.

This fill-in-the-blanks strategy failed so spectacularly that students at Cambridge University studied it as a textbook example on the importance of "product differentiation."[15] After twenty years of below-average profits, United realized it had to truly unite its members to survive and compete with brands like Nabisco. In 1966, United chose to operate under Godfrey's legacy, and began consolidating recipes, production lines, packaging, and operations under the Keebler name.[16]

With a treeful of "uncommonly good" elves, they continued baking up traditional favorites like vanilla wafers, graham crackers, and animal cookies, as well nouveau-classics like Newton-esque fig bars, Oreo look-alikes called Keebies,[17] Magic Middles, and Danish Wedding Cookies too. Most important, Keebler distinguished itself by drawing on the quirky recipes of its founding bakeries, including two Heckman originals: Fudge Stripes Cookies and Pecan Sandies.[18]

HOMEMADE FUDGE STRIPES™ COOKIES

Underneath those famous fudge stripes, Keebler's most iconic cookie tastes like a cracker—crispy, crunchy, and a little more salty than sweet. To capture those qualities, I've built this recipe around the dough I use to make oyster crackers, easy enough to mix by hand. These "cookies" are basically glorified spoons for sweet and creamy milk chocolate, so it's worth splurging on something rich.

YIELD: about twenty-four 2¼-by-¼-inch rounds | **ACTIVE TIME:** about 40 minutes | **DOWNTIME:** 45 minutes

1 cup | 4½ ounces all-purpose flour, such as Gold Medal, plus more for dusting

2 teaspoons sugar

½ teaspoon Diamond Crystal kosher salt (half as much if iodized)

¼ teaspoon baking powder

¼ teaspoon baking soda

3 tablespoons | 1½ ounces cold, unsalted butter, cut into ¼-inch cubes

¼ cup | 2 ounces cultured low-fat buttermilk, cold

3 cups (finely chopped) | 15 ounces milk chocolate, such as Valrhona's 36% Caramelia

Adjust oven rack to lower-middle position and preheat to 350°F. Sift flour into the bowl of a food processor (for accurate cup measurements, spoon into cup measure and level with a knife), along with sugar, salt, baking powder, and baking soda. Pulse to combine, then add butter and process until it disappears into a powdery meal. Transfer to a medium bowl and stir in buttermilk with a flexible spatula. Turn the soft dough onto a lightly floured surface, sprinkle with flour, and knead briefly to form a smooth ball. Flatten into a disc, dust both sides with flour, and (using as much flour as needed) roll until just over ⅛-inch thick.

Gently lift the dough to loosen from the counter, then cut into 2¼-inch rounds. Transfer to a parchment-lined aluminum baking sheet, arranging them as closely as you like, they will not spread at all in the oven. Gather up the scraps, knead briefly, then roll and cut as before. With a small cookie cutter or the large end of a pastry tip, cut a ¾-inch hole from the center of each round, and place in the gaps between each cracker. Bake until pale gold, about 25 minutes, and cool completely on the baking sheet. Use immediately, or store in an airtight container up to 3 weeks at room temperature.

Finish the cookies:
Set up a dipping station with the crackers to the left, a space for tempered chocolate in the center, and two parchment-lined baking sheets on the right. You'll also need to make a few parchment cones (page 324).

Temper milk chocolate according to the directions on pages 292–93, dollop a teaspoon on the bottom of a cracker, then place chocolate-side down on the parchment, pressing gently until the chocolate peeks from the edges. Repeat with the remaining crackers, lining them up in rows. If needed, pause to stir and rewarm the chocolate. With a parchment cone, drizzle a fat stripe of chocolate across each row. Repeat until the cookies have five stripes, then refrigerate 15 minutes to harden the chocolate.

Peel up the cookies, break off any excess chocolate, and transfer to an airtight container with a sheet of wax paper between each layer. Store up to 2 weeks at room temperature, or about a month in the fridge. Serve at room temperature. Cookies coated in *untempered* chocolate must be stored and served cold.

Brown butter and pecans team up for a cookie that's rich, nutty, and crisp.

HOMEMADE PECAN SANDIES®

Crunchy cookie lovers, unite! These golden shortbread cookies are crispy to the core, from the sturdy *snap* of the first bite to the pop of toasted pecans. The initial crunch gives way to a shower of sandy crumbs, which get their melting richness from brown butter. I love these cookies dunked in milk or hot tea, but they're also incredible crumbled over ice cream.

YIELD: thirty 2-inch cookies | **ACTIVE TIME:** about 15 minutes | **DOWNTIME:** 30-minute chill

1 cup | 4½ ounces all-purpose flour, such as Gold Medal

¾ cup | 3 ounces pecan pieces, toasted

1½ sticks | 5 ounces unsalted butter

¾ cup plus 2 tablespoons | 6 ounces white sugar

¼ cup packed | 2 ounces light brown sugar

2 teaspoons vanilla extract

1 teaspoon Diamond Crystal kosher salt (half as much if iodized)

¼ teaspoon baking soda

1 large egg yolk, straight from the fridge

Adjust oven rack to middle position and preheat to 350°F. Sift flour into a bowl (if using a cup measure, spoon into the cup and level with a knife before sifting). Finely chop the pecans and toss with flour.

In a 1-quart stainless steel saucier, melt butter over medium-low heat. When it begins to bubble and hiss, stir with a heat-resistant spatula, scraping the edges of the pan as brown bits form. Continue cooking and stirring until the butter is silent and takes on a golden yellow hue. Immediately scrape the butter and toasty bits into a medium bowl. Cool until thick and opaque but still a little warm—about 75°F (1 hour at room temperature or 25 minutes in the fridge).

Stir white sugar, brown sugar, vanilla, salt, and baking soda into the cooled brown butter, then add yolk. Fold in pecan-flour to form a sandy dough.

Arrange 1-tablespoon (¾-ounce) portions on a parchment-lined aluminum baking sheet, leaving 2 inches between, and flatten into ¾-inch discs. Bake until sandy brown, about 15 minutes. Cool to room temperature on the baking sheet. Store in an airtight container for up to 3 weeks at room temperature.

→ Mix it up!

CASHEW SHORTBREAD: Despite their decidedly mellow flavor, cashews have a buttery richness that's phenomenal in shortbread. Replace the pecans with an equal amount of cashews.

VANILLA BEAN SHORTBREAD: My quintessential cookie jar cookie, plain and simple yet rich and fragrant. Split a vanilla bean lengthwise with a paring knife and run the flat of the blade down each half to scrape out the seeds; rub the seeds into the sugar. Omit the pecans, and proceed as directed.

GLUTEN-FREE: Replace the all-purpose flour with 3 ounces (⅔ cup) tapioca starch and 2½ ounces (⅔ cup) oat flour.

HOMEMADE MAGIC MIDDLES®

Magic Middles are a Keebler classic from the '90s, plain and unassuming until you break one open to discover its molten chocolate core. Fresh from the oven, it's the best kind of gooey mess, warm and wonderful and soft. Perhaps the real magic is that the "middles" are just as good cold, as the chocolate centers develop a wonderfully fudge-like consistency.

YIELD: eighteen 4-inch cookies | **ACTIVE TIME:** about 30 minutes

2½ cups | 11¼ ounces all-purpose flour, such as Gold Medal

1¼ sticks | 5 ounces unsalted butter, creamy and soft—about 68°F

1 cup | 7¼ ounces white sugar

¼ cup packed | 2 ounces light brown sugar

¾ teaspoon Diamond Crystal kosher salt (half as much if iodized)

½ teaspoon baking powder

½ teaspoon baking soda

1 tablespoon vanilla extract

1 large egg, straight from the fridge, well beaten

1⅔ cups | 10 ounces finely chopped dark chocolate, between 60 and 70%

Adjust oven rack to middle position and preheat to 350°F. Sift flour (if using cup measures, spoon into the cups and level with a knife before sifting).

Combine butter, white sugar, brown sugar, salt, baking powder, baking soda, and vanilla extract in the bowl of a stand mixer fitted with a paddle attachment. Mix on low speed to moisten, then increase to medium and beat until light and fluffy, about 3 minutes, pausing to scrape the bowl with a flexible spatula halfway through. With the mixer running, add the egg in two additions, beating until smooth. Reduce speed to low, add flour, and mix to form a soft dough.

Divide into eighteen 2-tablespoon (1½-ounce) portions. Roll each piece into a smooth ball and arrange on a lightly greased sheet of wax paper, leaving 3 inches between

them. Cover with a second sheet of greased wax paper and use the bottom of a measuring cup to flatten each portion into a 3-inch disc. Discard the top sheet of wax paper.

Gently peel up a round of dough and rest it in the palm of your hand. Place a shy tablespoon of chopped chocolate in the center, slowly gather the edges toward the middle (like a coin purse). Pinch them together, and place seam side down on a parchment-lined aluminum baking sheet. Repeat with remaining dough, leaving 3 inches between the cookies.

Bake until puffed and pale gold around the edges but still steamy in the middle, about 12 minutes. Cool on the baking sheet until the chocolate is no longer dangerously hot, about 10 minutes. Serve warm. Store in an airtight container for up to 2 days at room temperature.

→ *Mix it up!*

PEANUT BUTTER: Soft and squishy peanut butter is a trickier filling than chocolate, but well worth the effort once you've got the hang of shaping the basic cookies. Reduce the salt to ½ teaspoon, and prepare the dough as directed. Instead of chocolate, fill each cookie with 1 tablespoon (½ ounce) creamy or crunchy commercial peanut butter. Bake as directed.

HOMEMADE DANISH WEDDING COOKIES

If you've ever walked down the cookie aisle, you've likely spotted these tiny little treats from Keebler—the neon pink box is hard to miss. Like Russian Tea Cakes or Mexican Wedding Cookies, these little snowball cookies are drenched in powdered sugar; inside, they're something quite unique, flecked with oats, coconut, and chocolate. They're remarkably sophisticated for a grocery store treat, all the more so with real butter, vanilla, and your favorite chocolate.

YIELD: about twenty 2-inch cookies | **ACTIVE TIME:** 30 minutes

1 cup minus 1 tablespoon | 4 ounces all-purpose flour, such as Gold Medal

⅓ cup | 1½ ounces powdered sugar, plus more for dusting

¼ cup | 1¼ ounces sweetened coconut flakes

3 tablespoons | ¾ ounce old-fashioned rolled oats

⅛ teaspoon Diamond Crystal kosher salt (half as much if iodized)

1 teaspoon vanilla extract

¾ teaspoon coconut extract

1 stick | 4 ounces cold unsalted butter, cut into ½-inch cubes

2 tablespoons | ½ ounce finely chopped 72% dark chocolate

Adjust oven rack to middle position and preheat to 350°F. Combine flour, powdered sugar, coconut flakes, rolled oats, and salt in the bowl of a food processor. Process until the oats disappear, about 1 minute, then add vanilla, coconut extract, and butter. Pulse only until the dough comes together in a ball; excessive processing will make a sticky dough. Stir in chocolate with a flexible spatula.

Divide dough into forty ¼-ounce (1½-teaspoon) portions, and arrange on a plate dusted with powdered sugar. Tumble in powdered sugar until well coated, then roll each piece smooth and round. Transfer to a parchment-lined aluminum baking sheet, leaving an inch between.

Bake until firm and golden around the edges, about 18 minutes. Cool completely on the baking sheet. Sift powdered sugar over the cookies before serving, and store in an airtight container up to 1 week.

MAKE AHEAD

Refrigerate portioned dough on a parchment-lined cutting board until firm, about thirty minutes, then transfer to a heavy-duty zip-top bag. Refrigerate up to 1 week, or freeze 6 months. Stand at room temperature until soft but cool, about 65°F, and bake as directed.

→ *Mix it up!*

MEXICAN WEDDING COOKIES: Also known as Russian Tea Cakes, one of my favorite Christmas cookies. Omit coconut extract, increase salt to ¼ teaspoon, and replace coconut and oats with 2 ounces (½ cup) toasted pecans, but do not grind; simply pulse everything together to form a stiff dough. Omit the chocolate, and divide into eighteen ½ ounce (1 tablespoon) portions. Otherwise shape, bake, and serve as directed.

GIRL SCOUT COOKIES

Regardless of the temperature outside, mint chocolate desserts unleash an Arctic breeze. Fittingly, the duo started off chilled—in soda shops and ice cream saloons. A few drops of peppermint oil could disguise the flavor of mediocre shakes and sundaes, or boost the good stuff to the stratosphere.[1] Bearing in mind the boozy underbelly of ice cream culture (see page 332), pre-Prohibition cocktails like the "Cocoa-mint" helped popularize the pairing too.[2]

Mint chocolate gets its kick from a chemical quirk of menthol; merely inhaling the stuff triggers the cold receptors in our mouths. Once we actually take a bite, it goes into overdrive and our breath feels icy. Aside from the pure fun of the experience, mint works so well with chocolate because it opens our palates, giving the cocoa an herbal, aromatic depth.

Biscuit manufacturers didn't tap into that menthol mojo until the 1930s;[3] it may have had something to do with combating the summer slump, traditionally a slow time for cookies. Whatever the cause, mint chocolate hit it big. From nationwide giants like Nabisco to independent regional bakeries like Johnson Educator in Massachusetts, everybody put "chocolate mint cookies" on the menu.[4]

Leading up to that, Girl Scouts had spent a decade leveraging "National Cookie Day" from a casual bake sale into a legitimate vehicle for world domination.[5] The quaint tradition of "homemade" flew out the window when the little mercenaries in Oak Park, Illinois, hired out "the best cooky bakers" in town in order to dedicate more troops to the salesforce.[6] That sparked a chain reaction. Girl Scouts in Philadelphia put Keebler on the job, and Wisconsin Scouts enlisted Erickson Bakers, makers of Sunbeam Bread.[7]

At the height of the mint chocolate cookie craze in 1937, Scouts in Lowell, Massachusetts, partnered with Megowen Educator (formerly the above-mentioned Johnson Educator).[8] In addition to the usual Trefoils, they announced "a new kind is being introduced, a chocolate mint flavored cookie."[9] We don't have any record of their sales figures, but I suspect "Cooky-Mints" gave the Lowell Scouts a record-breaking season.[10]

That same year, a nineteen-year-old boy started his first day at the Megowen factory and wrote an essay about his ordeal: "I have experienced a day in a cookie factory, and in this story, I shall do my damnedest to show the readers what it is like to do such a day's work."[11] Despite the teenage swagger, it's a rare glimpse at the backbreaking work of an industrial bakery, and the ten-page account read like a chocolate-covered edition of *The Jungle*.

For his shift, the boy spent eight hours with a shovel. He'd hoist seventy-pound lumps of chocolate dough onto a conveyor belt, then tear them into smaller pieces by hand before they traveled out of reach. The dough was fed into a huge pair of steel rollers, and a ribbon of chocolate streamed out the other side. Another machine punched the dough into rounds and shot out the scraps like wood chips, which landed in the kid's bucket to be shoveled again. He decried the conditions of this "asylum," with its workers "dropping large beads of sweat into the dough." It physically sickened him; the smell, the work, the concept. He thought life tasted sweeter when people baked cookies as an act of love.

Reflecting on what cookies had become, he imagined his life the same way: devalued. As a courtesy to his fellow workmen, he determined to finish his shift, but then and there he decided, "I would write scenario for a living rather than shovel dough in a blasting-furnace factory." Fortunately for us all, young Jack Kerouac made good on that promise and his career as a baker was short-lived.

I'd like to think he'd appreciate the idea of baking Thin Mints from scratch, trading mass-produced cookies for those handmade with love. My recipe is inspired by Girl Scout advertisements from the 1940s, which advertised Cookie Mints "coated in pure chocolate."

HOMEMADE THIN MINTS®

Doctoring my Homemade Oreo® dough with peppermint provides an intensely chocolate wafer just as crisp and refreshing as a genuine Thin Mint. The real trick is choosing the right chocolate. Most milk chocolates are simply too sweet, while the darkest varieties taste too astringent. Look for something with a strong cocoa flavor that's not overly bitter, such as Valrhona's 55% Equatoriale or Callebaut's 54.6% Couverture.

YIELD: about forty-eight 1¾-inch cookies | **ACTIVE TIME:** about 1 hour

1 recipe Mint Chocolate Wafer dough (page 214)

⅓ cup | 1 ounce Dutch-process cocoa powder for dusting

4 heaping cups | 24 ounces finely chopped dark chocolate, about 55%

Key Point: You can skip the tempering process if you plan to snack on cookies straight from the freezer, but it's critical for those who want their cookies crisp and dry at room temperature.

Make the cookies:

Adjust oven rack to middle position and preheat to 375°F. On a cocoa-dusted surface, roll the dough into a 6-inch square. Sprinkle both sides with cocoa, then roll until ¼ inch thick. Slide an offset spatula under the dough to loosen and brush off the excess cocoa. Cut with a 2-inch fluted round cutter and arrange on a parchment-lined aluminum baking sheet, leaving ¼ inch between them. Gather the scraps, knead briefly, re-roll and cut out more cookies. If you like, the remaining scraps can be baked to grind for crumbs.

Bake until the wafers are firm and dry, about 20 minutes. Cool completely on the baking sheet. Use immediately, or transfer to an airtight container. Store for up to 2 weeks at room temperature or up to 2 months in the freezer.

Dip the cookies:

Set up a dipping station with the wafers on the left, a space for tempered chocolate in the center, and two parchment-lined aluminum baking sheets on the right.

Temper the chocolate according to the directions on pages 292–93. Drop each cookie into the chocolate, dunk it under with a fork, and fish it back out, then knock the fork against the bowl so the excess chocolate drips off. Transfer to one of the prepared baking sheets; if you like, bounce the tines of the fork across the cookie to create a wavy design. Repeat with the remaining wafers, pausing to stir and rewarm the chocolate as needed. Refrigerate for 15 minutes to harden the chocolate.

Peel up the cookies, break off any excess chocolate, and transfer to an airtight container with a sheet of wax paper between each layer. Store for up to 1 week at room temperature, up to a month in the fridge, or up to 6 months in the freezer. Cookies coated in *untempered* chocolate must be stored and served cold.

Serve these minty cookies straight from the freezer if you don't want to temper the chocolate.

HOMEMADE TREFOILS®

These buttery shortbread are elegant in their simplicity, delicately crisp and tender, with a mellow flavor that takes me back to my brief stint selling Girl Scout cookies as a kid. My folks bolstered sales by loading up on Trefoils, which seemed to occupy a permanent place in our pantry thereafter. Since the dough spreads ever so slightly in the oven, it's best cut into simple rounds.

YIELD: about fifty 2-inch cookies | **ACTIVE TIME:** 30 minutes

2⅓ cups | 10½ ounces all-purpose flour, such as Gold Medal

1 stick | 4 ounces unsalted butter, pliable but cool—about 60°F

½ cup | 3½ ounces refined coconut oil, solid but creamy—about 70°F

1 cup | 7 ounces sugar

1½ teaspoons vanilla extract

¾ teaspoons Diamond Crystal kosher salt (half as much if iodized)

¼ teaspoon baking soda

⅛ teaspoon freshly grated nutmeg

1 large egg, straight from the fridge

Preparing the dough:

Sift flour (for accurate cup measurements, spoon into the cup and level with a knife before sifting).

Combine butter, coconut oil, sugar, vanilla extract, salt, baking powder, and nutmeg in the bowl of a stand mixer fitted with a paddle attachment. Mix on low to moisten, then increase to medium and beat until light, about 5 minutes, pausing to scrape the bowl with a flexible spatula halfway through. Beat in the egg until smooth. Reduce speed to low, add flour, and mix to form a stiff dough. Knead on a lightly floured surface to form a smooth ball, then divide in half and flatten into discs. Use immediately, or wrap in plastic and refrigerate up to 1 week; knead cold dough on a bare surface until pliable and smooth before use.

Making the Trefoils:

Adjust oven rack to middle position and preheat to 350°F. On a generously floured surface, gently roll half the dough about ¼ inch thick. Slide an offset spatula underneath to loosen, brush away extra flour, and stamp into 2-inch rounds with a cookie cutter. Arrange on a parchment-lined aluminum baking sheet, leaving 1 inch between them. Gather scraps, knead, re-roll, and cut as before. Repeat with remaining dough. Bake until firm and just beginning to brown around the very edges, about 12 minutes. Cool to room temperature on the baking sheet until the cookies are crisp, as they will be pliable and soft while warm. Store up to three weeks in an airtight container at room temperature.

MAKE AHEAD

Divide portioned dough between several heavy-duty zip-top bags and refrigerate up to 1 week, or freeze 6 months. Stand at room temperature until about 70°F and bake as directed.

→ *Mix it up!*

HOMEMADE ROYAL DANSK®-STYLE COOKIES: These remind me of the crispy butter cookies in the blue tin that Dad used to buy around Christmas. Shape the dough with a cookie press, sprinkle with coarse sugar, and bake as directed. Makes about eighty-five 1½-inch spritz cookies.

VANILLA BEAN: Split a vanilla bean lengthwise with a paring knife and run the flat of the blade down each half to scrape out the seeds; reserve the empty pod for another project. Rub the seeds into the sugar. Otherwise proceed as directed.

LITTLE DEBBIE® OATMEAL CREME PIES

Billed as a "snack cake," Little Debbie Oatmeal Creme Pies involve neither cake, nor cream, nor pie. I'm willing to let it slide because these mixed-up little cookies come with a side of entrepreneurship, innovation, and avant-garde spelling in the name of plausible deniability. A culinary, financial, technological, and legal triumph all at once: the epitome of American dessert.

Though they didn't make their brand-name debut until 1960, Oatmeal Creme Pies have existed in some form since Oather Dorris and Ruth McKee bought their first bakery in 1934.[1] Neither had any experience in the industry, but OD was a born salesman and Ruth had a knack for numbers. They had a friend in Chattanooga looking for a way out after his wholesale bakery had gone deep into the red. Privately, OD laid the blame on his friend's mismanagement and pictured himself the kind of guy who could turn things around. Ruth had her doubts about investing in a failure, but she was determined to give it her best shot.

According to biographer Bill Oliphant, the couple scraped together every penny, even pawning their car, to buy Jack's Cookie Company, debts and all. The bakery was just a small shop with a small oven, five employees, and three products: oatmeal, raisin, and vanilla wafers. The crispy oatmeal and raisin wafers sold for a penny each, but the vanilla variety went for ten cents a dozen.

Because wholesale bakeries thrive on volume, those vanilla wafers turned a higher profit. OD needed a way to make those one-cent cookies work harder, so he asked the bakers to adjust the formula, softening the oatmeal and raisin cookies in order to sandwich them with a pseudo-cream filling. With this little makeover, the resulting "creme pies" could be sold for five cents each. Even today, a few extra pennies per sale can represent major increases in annual profit, but during the Great Depression, that kind of change could make it rain. In a few weeks, the McKees had bought back their car and paid off their debts.

However sweet and savvy, the filling itself wasn't all that innovative.[2] By the time the McKees got into the business, "creme" had become as commonplace in commercial kitchens as preservatives are today.[3] Recipes for marshmallow frosting first appeared in the late 1890s, made with a hot sugar syrup to melt store-bought marshmallows into a spreadable paste. Ready-made jars of the fluffy stuff hit store shelves in the early twentieth century, from brands such as Hip-o-lite Marshmallow Creme, Heide's Marshmallow Cake Filler, and Emma Curtis's Snowflake Creme.[4] The cutesy spelling let companies comply with "truth in advertising"–type regulations, despite the complete lack of cream in their creamy creme.

Professional bakers loved it. Rich, super-sweet creme cost almost nothing to make, but it gave desserts a supernatural shelf life, sans refrigeration. Commercial creme inspired a pantheon of treats: Twinkies, Hostess CupCakes, Devil Dogs, and Moon Pies too.[5] Perhaps in homage to those Moon Pies, which date back to 1917, marshmallow-filled cookies were often known as cream pies.[6]

Through all the ups and downs of the business, Oatmeal Creme Pies never failed. Some thirty years later, joined by their grown sons, the McKees once again thought of a way to make their cookies work harder. They decided to treat Oatmeal Creme Pies like vanilla wafers, boxing them up twelve at a time. To ensure that the last would taste as good as the first, each one was wrapped in cellophane.

With this new format, the McKees hoped their cookies would become a weekly routine rather than a once-in-a-while treat. We're so accustomed to boxes of single-serve snacks today it's hard to think of the idea as revolutionary, but Oatmeal Creme Pies started it all. To introduce these "family packs," OD designed a brand name and logo, which he found in an unexpected place: a pocket portrait of his three-year-old granddaughter, little Debbie.[7]

Oatmeal Creme Pies were one of my favorite lunch-box treats, and when I tasted them again, I was surprised by their depth of flavor—fruity brightness balanced by dark molasses, sweet nutmeg, and a chocolatey aftertaste. Before you think I've turned into some crazed snack sommelier, check the label. Somewhere between sorbitan monostearate and polysorbate, you'll find dried apples, molasses, spices, and cocoa. Given a chance to shine, ingredients like that can't help but make a phenomenal cookie. I made those four ingredients the foundation of my recipe, but it turns out that dried apples are the lynchpin. Ground into tiny bits, they give OCPs a mild fruit flavor and springy texture distinct from that of traditional oatmeal cookies. I've found golden syrup, a type of light molasses, essential in avoiding the sharpness of pure molasses, which can push the spices into gingerbread territory (though it will do in a pinch). The finishing touch is a "creme" filling made from fluffy homemade marshmallow creme to mimic the chewiness of an authentic Little Debbie Oatmeal Creme Pie.

Homemade Oatmeal Creme Pies (page 234), as soft and chewy as the ones I loved as a kid.

HOMEMADE OATMEAL CREME PIES

My version of Oatmeal Creme Pies combines the cozy flavors of apple, ginger, and cinnamon with chewy rolled oats and marshmallowy vanilla creme (the only thing that's missing is a cellophane bag). Whether you start a week or an hour in advance, make the filling first so you can assemble the cookies as soon as they've cooled. *See photo on page 233.*

YIELD: twenty-four 2½-inch sandwich cookies | **ACTIVE TIME:** 1 hour | **DOWNTIME:** 1-hour rest

2 cups | 9 ounces all-purpose flour, such as Gold Medal

1 heaping cup | 4 ounces old-fashioned rolled oats (not quick-cooking or instant)

2 tablespoons | ½ ounce Dutch-process cocoa powder

⅔ cup | 2 ounces plump, moist, dried apples

½ teaspoon Diamond Crystal kosher salt (half as much if iodized)

½ teaspoon grated nutmeg

¼ teaspoon ground ginger

¼ teaspoon ground cinnamon

1¼ sticks | 5 ounces unsalted butter, soft but cool—about 65°F

1 cup packed | 8 ounces light brown sugar

1½ teaspoons baking soda

½ teaspoon baking powder

¼ cup | 3 ounces golden syrup, sorghum, or unsulfured molasses (not blackstrap)

1 large egg, straight from the fridge, well beaten

¼ cup | 2 ounces milk (any percentage will do)

1 recipe Vanilla Marshmallow Creme (page 236)

Prepare the dry mix:
Sift flour into the bowl of a food processor (if using a cup measure, spoon into the cup and level with a knife before sifting). Add oats, cocoa, dried apples, salt, nutmeg, ginger, and cinnamon, cover with a sheet of plastic to contain the dust, and process until the oats and apple disappear, about 3 minutes. This mix will keep for up to 3 months in an airtight container at room temperature.

Make the cookies:
Adjust oven rack to middle position and preheat to 350°F. Combine butter, brown sugar, baking soda, baking powder, and golden syrup in the bowl of a stand mixer fitted with a paddle attachment. Mix on low speed to moisten, then increase to medium and beat until light and fluffy, about 5 minutes. With the mixer running, add the egg in two additions, mixing until each one is well incorporated. Reduce speed to low and sprinkle in the dry mix, then add the milk, mixing to form a sticky dough. With a flexible spatula, fold the dough once or twice from the bottom up to ensure no unmixed streaks remain.

Arrange forty-eight 1-tablespoon (¾-ounce) portions on two parchment-lined and lightly greased aluminum baking sheets, leaving 2½ inches between them. Bake until the cookies are puffed and soft but dry around the edges, about 12 minutes. They will look steamy and wet, a side effect of the molten syrup in the dough. If necessary, use the inner edge of a 3-inch round cookie cutter to gently nudge apart any cookies that have grown together. Cool on the baking sheet until their crumb is set, about 20 minutes.

Sandwich the cookies:
Stir Marshmallow Creme with a flexible spatula, then transfer to a pastry bag fitted with a ¼-inch plain tip. Turn half of the wafers upside down and pipe a shy tablespoon (roughly ¼ ounce) onto the center of each. Top with remaining cookies, pressing gently to join them together.

Store in an airtight container, with a piece of wax paper between each layer, for up to 5 days at room temperature, up to a month in the fridge, or 6 months in the freezer. Serve at room temperature.

→ Mix it up!

COCOA CREME PIES: Reduce the flour to 7½ ounces (1⅔ cups), increase the cocoa to 1½ ounces (½ cup), and add 3 ounces (½ cup) roughly chopped 72% dark chocolate to the dry ingredients before grinding as directed. Omit the spices to focus on chocolate, or keep them if you like. These bake up adorably thick and chubby.

LEMON CREAM PIES: Omit the cocoa powder and spices and increase the flour by 1 tablespoon. Add 2 tablespoons lemon zest and ½ teaspoon lemon extract along with the golden syrup and proceed as directed.

VEGAN: Replace the butter with refined coconut oil and trade the egg for 2 ounces (¼ cup) plain applesauce. For the filling, use your favorite vegan marshmallow creme.

GLUTEN-FREE: Replace the all-purpose flour with 4 ounces (1 cup) tapioca flour or arrowroot, 2 ounces (½ cup) coconut flour, and 2 ounces (½ cup) white rice flour.

Vanilla Marshmallow Creme

This Marshmallow Creme has a s'mores-like gooeyness perfect for piping into the hearts of Homemade Hostess®-Style Cupcakes (page 247) and Homemade Twinkies® (page 244), as well as for sandwiching into Homemade Oatmeal Creme Pies.

YIELD: 1 cup (10 ounces) | **ACTIVE TIME:** 30 minutes | **DOWNTIME:** 2-hour rest

1½ teaspoons unflavored gelatin powder

2 tablespoons | 1 ounce cool water to bloom the gelatin

1½ teaspoons vanilla extract and/or 1 vanilla bean

¼ cup | 2 ounces water for the sugar syrup

¼ cup | 2¾ ounces light corn syrup

¾ cup | 5 ounces sugar

¼ plus ⅛ teaspoon Diamond Crystal kosher salt (half as much if iodized)

1 stick | 4 ounces unsalted butter, creamy and soft—about 68°F

Temperature Note: Most marshmallow mishaps are temperature related. The filling will be thick and rubbery if cooked to above 250°F, soft and runny if not cooled to 212°F, or impossibly thick if the syrup drops below 205°F as it cooks. Avoid these problems with an accurate digital thermometer, which should register 212°F in a pot of boiling water.

In a small bowl, mix the gelatin with 2 tablespoons (1 ounce) cool water and vanilla extract, if using. Or split the vanilla bean lengthwise with a paring knife, run the flat of the blade down each half to scrape out the seeds, and add to the gelatin without stirring. (Reserve the pod for another project.)

Combine remaining ¼ cup (2 ounces) water, corn syrup, sugar, and salt in a 1-quart stainless steel pot over medium heat. Stir with a fork until the mixture is bubbling hard around the edges, about 3 minutes, then increase heat to medium-high. Clip on a digital thermometer and cook, *without stirring*, until the syrup registers 250°F, about 4 minutes.

Transfer thermometer to a large heat-safe bowl and pour in the hot syrup all at once, scraping the pot with a heat-resistant spatula. Cool to exactly 212°F, about 4 minutes. Add

gelatin and, with a hand mixer, whip on medium-high until thick, snowy white, and roughly tripled in volume, about 10 minutes.

Add the softened butter in 5 or 6 additions, letting each fully incorporate before adding the next. Scrape the bowl with a flexible spatula to ensure the butter is well combined and whip a few seconds more. Transfer to a lightly greased container, cover, and let stand at room temperature until stiff, about 2 hours. The creme can be made up to 1 week ahead; stir the creme well before using.

TROUBLESHOOTING
This recipe works best with a hand mixer, which is better able to whip the small quantity of syrup. If using a stand mixer, double the recipe.

→ *Mix it up!*

HOMEMADE COOL WHIP®: This variation whips into a dense, silky cream that's wonderfully stable, perfect for picnics or other occasions where you wouldn't trust plain whipped cream. Omit the butter, and whisk 2 ounces (¼ cup) milk, any percentage will do, with ¾ ounces (3 tablespoons) powdered milk in a small bowl. Add to the marshmallow mixture in place of butter, then transfer to a greased container and let stand as directed. Before use, transfer to the bowl of a stand mixer fitted with the whisk attachment, along with 12 ounces (1½ cups) heavy cream. Mix on medium-low to roughly combine, then increase to medium-high and whip until thick, stiff, and creamy, about 5 minutes. Makes about 4 heaping cups; refrigerate up to 3 weeks in an airtight container or freeze for 2 months.

WONDER® BREAD, TWINKIES®,
& HOSTESS® CUPCAKES

Emigrating to a war-torn country doesn't seem like a smart career move for anyone but an arms dealer, but the Civil War made America look pretty sweet to Old World bakers. Hungry troops needed rations, after all. Alexander Taggart grew up as the son of a baker, entered the trade at fifteen, and spent a decade apprenticing under his father.[1] He decided to trade a career on the Isle of Man for a shot at the isle of Manhattan.

Unfortunately, Alexander didn't arrive until 1865, which was without a doubt the worst time and place in history for a baker to get a foot in the door. So he hopped a train west and wound up in Indianapolis, a growing city that didn't have enough bakers in the first place, never mind a surplus. While East Coast biscuit companies spent the postwar years inventing "dainty goods" to pay off their equipment, folks in the Midwest simply needed bread. After working for a few years to get a feel for the American market, Alexander opened his own bakery in 1869.

His business grew with the city itself. With the aid of an investor, Taggart's expanded from daily bread to the full range of fancy biscuits so popular back East. Taggart's eventually became a subsidiary of the United States Baking Company, which merged into the National Biscuit Company in 1898 (see page 209).[2] Changes in ownership meant little to a baker like Alexander. As a regional director for Nabisco, he continued to oversee "his" bakery until he cashed out in 1904.

Not that he had any intention of puttering around in retirement. After his son Alex graduated from Princeton, the two opened a new bakery in 1905.[3] Built on the reputation of its predecessor, Taggart's 2.0 eclipsed the original in every way, unseating Nabisco in local markets. A team of salesmen established wholesale accounts with groceries, restaurants, and retail bakeries, and a fleet of branded automobiles delivered fresh milk-bread, graham crackers, animal cookies, and other treats daily.[4] Taggart's even took on contract work with Continental, another conglomerate.[5]

Experience with those megabakeries gave a family-owned business like Taggart's insight into corporate strategy. While other mom-and-pop shops futzed around with homespun ads, Taggart's established a marketing department of its own, with Princeton grad Elmer Cline at the helm.[6] Elmer's signature move was the blind advertisement, an anonymous ad designed to generate buzz before a second wave of ads delivered the details. With this clever one-two punch, he turned two fledgling brands into American icons.

The first began as a series of personal ads in the classified section of local papers in the early 1920s. "The cake of your heart's desire," seeking "housewives."[7] Then came a door-to-door campaign for "Miss Hostess." After a few days, the next round debuted Taggart's line of boxed Hostess Cakes. These frosted layer cakes and cupcakes promised easy entertaining and "freedom from baking."[8]

Next Elmer commissioned a series of cryptic ads in the *Indianapolis Star*. He kept the ads stark, chunks of white space drawing the eye to a single question: "Wonder what?" The ads continued throughout the spring of 1921, hinting at "something out of the ordinary." Finally, Taggart's announced their splendid new product, Wonder Bread.[9]

Advertisements dedicated "to the boys and girls of Indianapolis" explained that "WONDER BREAD is made from milk, and plenty of it," a nourishing loaf for growing children. Each loaf came sealed in a novel wax-and-cellophane wrapper, made even more memorable by Elmer's decision to decorate it like a birthday present, spotted all over with red, yellow, and blue balloons.[10]

The enormous success of Wonder Bread prompted Continental to want more than contract work from

Taggart, and by December 1924, the two companies had merged.[11] As part of the buyout, Alex became Continental's vice president and Elmer its director of sales and advertising.[12] With an outsized budget and more than a hundred licensed Continental baking facilities, the two men put Wonder Bread and Hostess Cake in grocery stores across the country.

Continental would later expand the Hostess line with Dessert Fingers, first advertised in the spring of 1931.[13] With a filling of fluffy cream baked right into the middle, they were the basis of a five-minute strawberry shortcake. Just add fruit![14] Packaged in pairs, the chubby cakes looked like Twinkies, the Kewpie doll look-alike twin mascots for a Buster Brown shoe of the same name.[15] By September, Continental was ready to admit that "cream-filled Twinkies" were a dessert of their own—no strawberries required.[16]

This line of two-for-one snack cakes would be complemented by "Hostess CupCakes" after the war, a miniaturized version of Taggart's full-sized Devil's Food "Hostess Cake."[17]

Though Hostess CupCakes were an official sponsor of Howdy Doody, topped with kid-friendly loop-de-loop icing, their advertisements clearly targeted Mom and Dad, promising a "secret blend of chocolate from the African Gold Coast and the blue-green jungles of Brazil."[18] (Which is to say: the major chocolate-producing regions of the era.)

With that trio of products, Wonder® Bread, Twinkies®, and Hostess® CupCakes, Continental became an iconic part of the American lunch box, from sandwiches to snacks. Given their rollercoaster of on-again, off-again production, why not make my versions of them yourself?

WHITE BREAD

When I started culinary school, I gave up on white bread. Not because I didn't love it, but because I thought I wasn't supposed to. A chef-in-training should like tangy sourdough, dark rye, and crusty baguette. White bread came with an arsenal of preservatives and commercial baggage that made it easy to feel like I had the high ground. In truth, I was looking down on my own white-bread Kentucky roots.

A few years after graduation, I moved to Japan to learn the language before ostensibly worming my way into some kitchen, where I hoped to expand my knowledge of baking beyond a strictly Western perspective. By the time I landed in Tokyo, I hadn't had a slice of white bread in years and thought for sure it was something I'd left far behind.

But at a little bakery near the school where I spent upwards of ten hours a day, I discovered *shokupan*—the whitest white bread in the world. It was sold in perfectly cubical loaves, each about the size and weight of a tissue box, pre-sliced in outrageously thick, Texas-toast style proportions. With my first bite, I found myself floating on a cloud of impossible fluffiness, like bread-flavored cotton candy or an edible snowdrift—everything Wonder® Bread should be but isn't: wonderful.

Shokupan means "food bread," but practically speaking, it's the platonic ideal of a white sandwich loaf. Puffy and soft, with a golden brown crust and creamy interior as tender as brioche, but lean. Because it's made from milk, each slice turns to gold in the toaster, fantastic with nothing more than a smear of butter, but sturdy enough to handle hearty sandwiches too.

Years later, I learned how to make *shokupan* while working in a Japanese bakery (ironically, as a translator in Kentucky). While some bakers handle it like a French *pain de mie*, Chef Noura made it with *yukone*, an unfermented starter. This hot water roux delivered a payload of water bound by pre-gelatinized flour, adding moisture without turning the dough into a soupy mess. In the oven, that extra water turns to steam, so the bread bakes up billowy and light.

Soft and fluffy Homemade Wonder®
Bread (page 242), perfect for a sweet
and simple sandwich.

HOMEMADE WONDER® BREAD

America's favorite white bread doesn't require a slow rise because its simple flavor depends on milk and barley malt, so with those two ingredients this copycat recipe comes together in four hours flat (including the time it takes to cool the loaf). It's impossibly fluffy, tender, and gleaming white—perfect for anything from PB&J to grilled cheese. *See photo on page 241.*

YIELD: one 9-by-5-inch loaf | **ACTIVE TIME:** 1 hour | **DOWNTIME:** 2-hour rise

Hot Water Roux:

⅓ cup | 1½ ounces all-purpose flour, such as Gold Medal

¾ cup | 6 ounces milk (any percentage)

Dough:

3⅓ cups | 15 ounces all-purpose flour, such as Gold Medal

¼ cup | 2 ounces sugar

⅓ cup | 1½ ounces malted milk powder

2 teaspoons instant dry yeast (not rapid-rise)

1½ teaspoons Diamond Crystal kosher salt (half as much if iodized)

¾ cup | 6 ounces whole milk

¼ cup | 1½ ounces refined or virgin coconut oil, solid but creamy—about 70°F

Bubble-Gum-Test: Chop off a walnut-sized lump of dough and roll it into a ball. With both hands, slowly stretch and rotate the dough in all directions, pulling it into a translucent sheet. Keep stretching! If the dough tears in half, return it to the bowl, knead 5 minutes more, and test again. If the dough forms an irregularly shaped hole, knead 3 minutes more and test again. If it stretches like bubble gum and "pops" a round hole, it's ready.

Make the roux:
Sift flour into a 2-quart stainless steel saucier (if using cup measures, spoon into the cup and level with a knife before sifting). Add milk, stirring with a flexible spatula until smooth, and cook over medium heat, stirring, to form a thick mashed potato–like paste, about 2 minutes. Set aside and cool to 120°F, about 15 minutes.

Make the dough:
Sift flour into the bowl of a stand mixer (if using a cup measure, spoon into the cup and level with a knife before sifting). Add sugar, malted milk powder, yeast, salt, milk, coconut oil, and roux. Stir to combine, then knead on low with the dough hook until the dough can pass the bubble-gum test, about 12 minutes. Remove dough hook and cover with plastic, and prepare a warm place for the dough to rise. I like to microwave a mug of water until boiling-hot, then push it to the back of the microwave so it continues to radiate heat and steam. Let the dough rise inside until

puffy and light, though not doubled, about 30 minutes.

With a flour-dusted fingertip, gently press the dough. If it springs back, let rise 15 minutes more. If it feels firm but retains a shallow impression, it's ready to shape.

Shape and bake the loaf:
Adjust oven rack to lower-middle position and preheat to 350°F. Lightly grease an 8-by-5-by-2¾-inch metal loaf pan.

Turn the dough onto a lightly floured surface and pat into an 8-inch square. Fold into thirds, as you would a business letter (a very thick and chubby business letter), then fold lengthwise to create a narrow log, pinching the dough along its seam. Nestle it into the pan, seam side down, and loosely cover with plastic.

Warm the microwave as before and let the dough rise until it crowns the pan, about 25 minutes. Use your fingertip to test it again, and let the dough continue rising only if it springs back when you poke it. If it retains a shallow impression, it's ready.

Bake the loaf until the crust is nutty brown, about 45 minutes, or 200°F. Carefully tip the bread onto a wire rack and remove the pan. Turn it upright and let cool for at least 1 hour before you even dream about slicing it; this loaf will *severely* deform if cut too soon.

The loaf will be extraordinarily soft on the first day, but after 24 hours, it can be easily cut into thin slices with a serrated knife. Store in an airtight container for up to 1 week at room temperature or up to 2 weeks in the fridge.

TROUBLESHOOTING

The exact timing for each rise depends on the temperature of the dough, determined by the ingredients and proofing area. The times listed are based on using a warm seed and milk straight from the fridge in a roughly 70°F kitchen.

→ *Mix it up!*

DINNER ROLLS OR HAMBURGER BUNS: Divide dough into twelve 3-ounce pieces. Round each into a ball and arrange on a parchment-lined aluminum baking sheet. Cover with plastic. Place a second baking sheet on top (this forces the dough to rise out instead of up). Proof and test as instructed, then uncover and bake until golden brown, about 25 minutes. Serve rolls immediately, but transfer warm hamburger buns to a gallon zip-top bag so the steam can soften the crust.

VEGAN: Reduce the sugar to 1 ounce (2 tablespoons) and replace the malted milk powder with 1 tablespoon (¾ ounce) barley malt syrup. Replace the milk with 6 ounces (¾ cup) soy or almond milk cut with 1 ounce (2 tablespoons) water.

WHOLE WHEAT: Reduce the all-purpose flour in the dough to 6 ounces (1⅓ cups), and sift it together with 6¾ ounces (1½ cups) whole wheat flour (not stone-ground) and 2½ ounces (⅔ cup) oat flour. Replace the sugar with 2 ounces (¼ cup) honey and increase the milk to 8 ounces (1 cup). Knead for approximately 18 minutes.

HOMEMADE TWINKIES®

Club soda is the surprising trick to Homemade Twinkies as cotton-soft as real Twinkies from the store. It releases a steady stream of bubbles that provide the baking powder with plenty of air cells to expand. Nailing the flavor depends on cake flour, made from mild, soft white wheat, and plenty of egg yolks. Generally I'm an advocate of organic, but in this case I've found conventional eggs offer a mellow flavor more in line with the original.

To make these, you'll need a canoe pan from brands such as Hostess or Norpro, found online or in baking supply stores; the unusual cakes will stick viciously to traditional cupcake pans and papers. Otherwise, try my Homemade "Twinkie" Torte variation.

YIELD: eight 4-inch-long cakes | **ACTIVE TIME:** about 30 minutes

---

1 cup | 4 ounces bleached cake flour, such as Swans Down

¾ teaspoon baking powder

6 large egg yolks (⅓ cup | 3½ ounces)

½ cup | 3½ ounces sugar

⅛ teaspoon Diamond Crystal kosher salt (half as much if iodized)

1 teaspoon vanilla extract

2 tablespoons | ¾ ounce safflower oil, or another neutral oil

½ cup | 4 ounces club soda, still fizzy

½ recipe (2 cups | 12 ounces) Homemade Cool Whip® (page 237)

★

Key Point: The high pH and starch content of unbleached cake flour will cause these cakes to collapse, as will the relatively high protein content of all-purpose flour. No substitutions!

Make the cakes:
Adjust oven rack to middle position and preheat to 350°F. Sift flour into a medium bowl (if using a cup measure, spoon into the cup and level with a knife before sifting). Whisk in baking powder.

Combine egg yolks, sugar, salt, and vanilla in the bowl of a stand mixer fitted with the whisk attachment. Mix on low speed to moisten, then pause to scrape the bowl. Increase to medium-high and whip until thick and roughly doubled in volume, with a clear vortex pattern left by the whisk, about 5 minutes. Do not overbeat, as this will destabilize the foam.

Reduce speed to medium-low and drizzle in oil, followed by club soda. As soon as you've added the last drop, shut off the mixer and remove the bowl. The batter will look thin and foamy. Add cake flour and gently combine with a balloon whisk. Use a flexible spatula to fold the thin batter once or twice from the bottom up.

Lightly grease a nonstick canoe pan (see headnote) with pan spray— do not do this in advance—and fill each mold three-quarters full (about 1¾ ounces). Bake until cakes have domed above the pan and spring back to the touch, though your fingertip will leave a light impression in the pale crust, about 12 minutes. Cool 10 minutes, then pry the cakes from the pan while still warm and flexible. Store in an airtight container at room temperature for up to 24 hours.

Fill the cakes:
Transfer Homemade Cool Whip® to a piping bag fitted with a ¼-inch plain tip. Poke the piping tip into a cake from the bottom, about 1 inch from one end, and give the bag a gentle squeeze. Wait a second for the filling to settle, then repeat on the other side. Repeat with remaining cakes and filling. Serve immediately. Store leftovers in an airtight container for up 2 days at room temperature or up to a week in the fridge.

Club soda, seltzer water, and sparkling water can all be used here, but the variable sodium content of mineral water makes it a bad choice for this recipe, as does the bitter quinine in tonic water.

This batter cannot be made in advance.

→ *Mix it up!*

"TWINKIE" TORTE: Don't have a canoe pan? No problem, just serve your Homemade Twinkies by the slice. Pour the batter into a greased and parchment-lined 8-by-2-inch aluminum cake pan. Bake until the cake is pale gold and firm, about 25 minutes. Loosen with a knife and invert onto a wire rack. Peel off the parchment and reinvert onto a serving plate. Once cool, top with Homemade Cool Whip® (page 237) and serve in wedges. Wrapped tightly in plastic, leftovers will keep for up to 2 days at room temperature.

GLUTEN-FREE: Replace the cake flour with 1¼ ounces (¼ cup) white rice flour, 1 ounce (¼ cup) tapioca flour or arrowroot, 1½ ounces (⅓ cup) cornstarch, and ½ ounce (2 tablespoons) oat flour. Bake about 5 minutes longer.

"Twinkie" Tres Leches

Torta de tres leches is arguably Mexico's most famous dessert, a thick layer of sponge cake soaked with evaporated and condensed milk, then topped with whipped cream. Served cold, it's both rich and refreshing in summer, a feat few cakes can manage. When baked as a single layer, my club soda–fueled Homemade Twinkie batter is perfect for the task—absorbent enough to soak up plenty of dairy, yet sturdy enough to retain its fluffy crumb. Homemade condensed milk gives this cake a freshness like no other, whether you keep things plain and simple or opt for one of the variations on page 170.

YIELD: one 8-inch cake; 8 servings │ **ACTIVE TIME:** 20 minutes │ **DOWNTIME:** 3-hour refrigeration

1 "Twinkie" Torte (page 245)

½ recipe (1 cup | 9 ounces) Quick Condensed Milk (page 169), or any variation

⅛ teaspoon Diamond Crystal kosher salt (half as much if iodized)

½ recipe (2 cups | 8 ounces) Make-Ahead Whipped Cream (page 89), or any variation

Bake the "Twinkie" Torte as directed. After inverting onto a serving plate, pierce the hot cake about 75 times with a bamboo skewer.

Microwave the Quick Condensed Milk until bubbling hot, about 30 seconds, and stir in the salt. Spoon over the cake, allowing each addition to soak in before adding the next (this will take a few minutes). Cover with plastic and refrigerate until cold, about 3 hours.

Top with Make-Ahead Whipped Cream, using the back of a spoon to sculpt it into swoops and swirls. Cut into wedges with a chef's knife, or cover and refrigerate for up to 24 hours before serving.

→ *Mix it up!*

BLUEBERRY LAVENDER: A colorful, aromatic twist that's perfect for spring. Prepare the Quick Condensed Milk according to the Lavender variation on page 170, and top with the Blueberry variation of Make-Ahead Whipped Cream (page 89).

MALTED SPICE: In cooler months, there's something undeniably comforting about this spicy, butterscotchy variation. Prepare the Quick Condensed Milk according to the Chai Spice variation on page 170, and top the torte with Butterscotch Chantilly (page 352).

HOMEMADE HOSTESS®-STYLE CUPCAKES

To re-create the preternatural "freshness" of a packaged chocolate cake, my Homemade Hostess®-Style Cupcakes start with safflower oil, which does a particularly good job evoking the flavor of the original. Combining Dutch cocoa with baking soda matches the inky darkness too, so accept no substitutions! I like to make the filling a day in advance, which lets me bake and assemble the cupcakes without any fuss. *See photo on page 249.*

YIELD: 24 cupcakes | **ACTIVE TIME:** about 1½ hours

Chocolate Cupcakes:

1⅓ cups | 6 ounces all-purpose flour, such as Gold Medal

1⅓ cups | 4 ounces Dutch-process cocoa powder, such as Cacao Barry Extra Brute

1¼ cups | 8½ ounces sugar

1 teaspoon baking soda

½ teaspoon Diamond Crystal kosher salt (half as much if iodized)

1¼ cups | 10 ounces cultured low-fat buttermilk

4 large eggs, straight from the fridge

1 tablespoon vanilla extract

1½ cups | 10½ ounces refined or virgin coconut oil, melted and still warm

Chocolate Topping:

½ cup | 4½ ounces heavy cream

1 cup | 6½ ounces finely chopped dark chocolate, about 60%

1 tablespoon | ½ ounce corn syrup

½ recipe (2 cups | 12 ounces) Homemade Cool Whip® (page 237)

Decorative Icing:

1 cup | 4 ounces powdered sugar

2 tablespoons | 1 ounce heavy cream, or as needed

Make the cupcakes:

Adjust an oven rack to the middle position and preheat to 350°F. Sift the flour and cocoa together into a medium bowl (if using cup measures, spoon into the cups and level with a knife before sifting). Whisk in the sugar, baking soda, and salt, followed by the buttermilk, eggs, vanilla, and coconut oil, mixing until smooth. Divide batter between two paper-lined cupcake pans, filling each cavity about two-thirds full (just shy of 2 ounces).

Bake until the cupcakes are domed and firm but still a touch steamy and soft at the very top, about 16 minutes. A toothpick inserted into the center of a cupcake will emerge with a few crumbs attached. Cool the cupcakes completely in their pans.

Make the topping:

Meanwhile, bring the cream to a simmer in a 2-quart stainless steel saucier over medium heat. Remove from the heat and whisk in the chocolate, followed by the corn syrup. Set aside until thick and warm, about 20 minutes (roughly 90°F); stir well before using.

Assemble the cupcakes:

Gently work a 1⅛-inch round cookie cutter through the upper crust of a cupcake (leave the cupcakes in the pans), pushing through to the center but stopping short of the bottom. Angle the cutter slightly as you pull it out, leveraging it to "grab" the core of cake inside. Plunge the cake core onto a plate (you'll need it later), and repeat with the remaining cupcakes.

With the handle of a wooden spoon, roughly compress the cake layer at the bottom of each cavity to make room for more filling. Transfer Homemade Cool Whip to a piping bag fitted with a ¼-inch round tip and fill each cupcake, stopping just shy of the top. Tear the crust layer off *each* cupcake core and use *them* to plug the holes. Dollop a shy tablespoon (⅜ ounce) of the topping over each cupcake, smoothing it into an even layer with the back of a spoon. Refrigerate until firm, about 20 minutes.

continued ↓

Finish the cupcakes:

Sift powdered sugar into a medium bowl. Stir in cream with a flexible spatula, scraping and stirring until perfectly smooth but stiff, like peanut butter. If too stiff to pipe, add a few drops of additional cream, but take care not to overdo it, or the icing will lose its shape after piping. This recipe makes more than strictly needed, to allow for some practice piping.

Divide between two parchment cones (see page 324). Snip ⅛ inch from the tip of one cone, and gently squeeze over a sheet of foil until the icing hangs down like a piece of string. Squeeze until the strand of icing touches the foil, then move the bag so it lays down a series of loop-de-loops. Once you've got the hang of it, move on to the cupcakes. I find it easiest to pipe across each row, including the gaps between,

rather than starting and stopping for each one. Set aside at room temperature until the icing dries, about 10 minutes.

Store leftovers in an airtight container for up to 2 days at room temperature or for up to a week in the fridge; let refrigerated cupcakes stand at room temperature for 3 hours before serving.

→ *Mix it up!*

BUTTERSCOTCH: If you're not married to nostalgia, this malty variation is an excellent change of pace. For the cake batter, replace white sugar with an equal amount of brown sugar. For the filling, use a batch of Butterscotch Chantilly (page 352). In place of the Chocolate Topping, prepare a batch of Caramelized White Chocolate Ganache (page 60). Serve at room temperature, and refrigerate up to 3 days in an airtight container.

CHOCOLATE-COVERED STRAWBERRY: This variation adds tangy fruit flavor and a bright pop of color to the heart of every chocolate cupcake. Replace Homemade Cool Whip® with a batch of Make-Ahead Whipped Cream, prepared according to the strawberry variation on page 89. Serve at room temperature, and refrigerate up to 3 days in an airtight container.

GLUTEN-FREE: Replace the all-purpose flour with 2 ounces (½ cup) teff flour, 2 ounces (½ cup) tapioca flour or arrowroot, 1 ounce (¼ cup) coconut flour, and 1 ounce (¼ cup) white rice flour.

Dark chocolate cupcakes with marshmallowy vanilla cream.

These cookies are for your inner child; adults need not apply.

HOMEMADE LOFTHOUSE®-STYLE COOKIES

Honestly, it's not even fair to call these cookies. They're like muffin tops made from vanilla cupcakes: buttery, soft, and sweet with a light and creamy frosting. Even the dough starts off more like a batter, so treat it a little more delicately than you would a batch of chocolate chip. Your reward will be something pillowy and tender, perfect for serving with tea, coffee, or a tall glass of milk.

MAKES: twenty-eight 3-inch cookies | **ACTIVE TIME:** 20 minutes | **DOWNTIME:** 20 minutes

For the Frosting:

10 ounces | 3½ cups powdered sugar

¼ teaspoon Diamond Crystal kosher salt (half as much if iodized)

Shy ⅓ cup | 2½ ounces heavy cream, cold

1 teaspoon vanilla extract

For the Cookies:

2 sticks | 8 ounces unsalted butter, cut into ¼-inch pieces; firm but pliable—about 60°F

1 cup | 7 ounces sugar

2 teaspoons baking powder

1¼ teaspoons Diamond Crystal kosher salt (half as much if iodized)

2 large egg whites (¼ cup | 2 ounces)

2 tablespoons | 1 ounce heavy cream

1 tablespoon vanilla extract

2⅔ cup | 11 ounces bleached cake flour, such as Swans Down

Rainbow Sprinkles (page 325; optional)

Make the frosting:
Combine powdered sugar, salt, cream, and vanilla in the bowl of a stand mixer fitted with a paddle attachment. Mix on low to moisten, increase to medium, then beat until airy and smooth, about 3 minutes. Transfer to a zip-top bag, scraping the bowl as cleanly as you can. Wipe any excess frosting from the bowl and beater with a paper towel.

Make the cookies:
Adjust oven rack to middle position, preheat to 350°F, and line two aluminum baking sheets with parchment. Combine butter, sugar, baking powder, and salt in the prepared bowl. Mix on low with the paddle attachment, then increase to medium and beat until creamy, about 5 minutes.

Meanwhile, whisk egg whites, cream, and vanilla together in a glass measuring cup; add to butter in four or five additions and beat until

smooth. Scrape bowl and beater with a flexible spatula, then resume on low. Sprinkle in cake flour, mixing to form a soft dough. Fold once or twice from the bottom up to ensure it's well mixed, then transfer to a piping bag fitted with a ½-inch plain tip.

Pipe twelve 1¼-ounce portions onto each baking sheet, leaving 2½ inches between them. Bake until puffed and pale gold around the edges, about 15 minutes, and cool until no trace of warmth remains, at least 20 minutes. Snip off a corner of the frosting bag; working two or three at a time, squeeze a tablespoon of frosting over each cookie and spread into an even layer with a knife. Top with sprinkles, if you like, and devour immediately. Wrapped in plastic, leftovers will keep 3 days at room temperature.

→ Mix it up!

GLUTEN FREE: Replace all-purpose flour with 4½ ounces (1¼ cups) tapioca flour, 2½ ounces (½ cup) cornstarch, 2 ounces (½ cup) coconut flour, and 1½ ounces (⅓ cup) white rice flour. Cookies will be hyper-fragile while warm, but firm when cool.

Most thrilling of all pie fillings
—new Jell-O Chiffon

Make it in 4 minutes. All you do is add water and sugar to Lemon Jell-O Chiffon Pie Filling. And beat.

No cooking! No mistakes possible. Thousands of tests in the General Foods Kitchens prove you can't make a mistake if you try!

Costs pennies! At your grocer's now. Enjoy Jell-O Chiffon Pie in all three happy flavors: Lemon, Strawberry, Chocolate.

Jell-O is a registered trademark of General Foods Corporation

In the 1930s, America got its first taste of a brand-new sort of pie: chiffon (see pages 259–60)

Chapter 6

PUDDINGS

Americans have a particular fondness for creamy, stovetop desserts. Served as simple vanilla pudding, whipped into an airy chiffon pie, or topped with meringue and baked like banana pudding, these recipes are as comforting as they are simple to prepare.

AMERICANS HAD a rather mixed-up notion of pudding in the nineteenth century, which *Webster's American Dictionary of the English Language* defined as a "species of food of a soft or moderately hard consistence, variously made, but usually a compound of flour, or meal of maize, with milk and eggs, sometimes enriched with raisins."[1]

Browse through a few old-timey cookbooks and you'll find this species ranged from steamed gingerbread to soufflé, yet it didn't include simple custards.[2] Just as we wouldn't classify whipped cream a legit dessert today, stovetop custards didn't count as proper dessert. They were considered a component in more complex "puddings" like trifle or cream pie. There was even a type of frosting called "Mock Cream," made from custard whipped with butter.[3]

America didn't develop its laser-specific definition of pudding until 1936, when we learned to spell it J-E-L-L-O.[4] Jell-O had already made a name for itself with jiggly congealed salads and fruity gelatin desserts, but its cooked custards had come on (and off) the market with varying degrees of success. The company made another push in 1936, advertising their custard as more than a quick and easy cake or pie filling, but a full-fledged "pudding" on its own. Jell-O instant custard effectively gave folks permission to skip time-consuming elements like cake layers and pie crust in favor of a simple dish of pudding.

It's no coincidence that Americans slowly stopped thinking of pudding as a spectrum of dessert and instead as a specific style of stovetop custard. Jell-O advertisements in the early 1940s portrayed old-fashioned pudding as a daunting thirteen-step endeavor, whereas eight-minute instant custard tasted "like Grandma's—only more so."[5]

Jell-O's promise became a self-fulfilling prophecy, and as a child of the '80s, I can attest to that firsthand; I'd never tasted homemade pudding until my first bite of pastry cream in culinary school. Truth be told, I wasn't much impressed. It seemed gloppy and thick, totally unlike the creamy vanilla Jell-O® my grandmother used to make.

I loved everything about it, from the cloud of vanilla that puffed from the packet when she tore it open to the clatter of her whisk as she poured in the milk. She had sparkling coupe glasses just like the one on the box, and a way of piling the custard on top of itself in wobbly, concentric rings. I'd clink my spoon down to the bottom and scoop up the uncomplicated sweetness of warm vanilla pudding, something I still crave whenever I start to miss my grandmother.

Like so many other midcentury Americans who embraced the innovations of instant-this and canned-that, she didn't leave any recipes behind, only boxes of pudding that didn't taste like what I remembered. I've made a thousand delicious failures in search of one that will remind me of an afternoon at her house, but they were all too eggy.

I started making puddings thickened with cornstarch alone, but they were too thin—until one day it occurred to me that I could simply ditch the yolks. Of course, when we think of custard, we think of egg yolks, but their flavor was all wrong when it came to replicating the taste and texture of instant pudding. With my experiment, I discovered that egg whites will thicken a pudding just as well, exorcising its custardy flavor.

The result is a pudding that tastes like nothing but fresh milk, cream, and Tahitian vanilla. I know that sounds ridiculously highbrow for something as trashy as a Jell-O pudding knockoff, but it plays a crucial role. Compared to Madagascar vanilla, what's most commonly used in home kitchens, Tahitian vanilla has a much higher concentration of *piperonal*, the essential oil that artificial vanillin is meant to copy. Because mass-produced snacks almost universally rely on synthetic vanilla, Tahitian vanilla is my favorite in copycat recipes, a bit of life imitating art imitating life.

Since my recipe is formulated to mimic the wonderfully thick and creamy flavor of stovetop Jell-O vanilla pudding, it's best served warm. Once cold, it's a fantastic filling for Boston Cream Pie (page 105). Lightened with whipped cream, it becomes a sophisticated mousse (see page 256) that can be spooned into a graham cracker crust for Icebox Chiffon Pie (page 260) or paired with Homemade Nilla® Wafers (page 197) for DIY Banana Pudding (page 258).

TAHITIAN VANILLA PUDDING

This light and creamy pudding is best served warm, especially in winter, when the comforting simplicity of vanilla offers a reprieve from a barrage of holiday spices. It owes its unusual silkiness to egg whites, for a creamy pudding that's not too thick—like the softly set vanilla Jell-O® my grandmother used to make.

YIELD: six ½-cup servings | **ACTIVE TIME:** about 20 minutes | **DOWNTIME:** 30-minute steep

1½ cups | 12 ounces milk (any percentage will do)

1 cup | 8 ounces heavy cream

1 vanilla bean, preferably Tahitian

1 cup | 7 ounces sugar

Shy ½ teaspoon Diamond Crystal kosher salt (half as much if iodized)

¼ cup | 1¼ ounces cornstarch

4 large egg whites (½ cup | 4 ounces)

2 tablespoons | 1 ounce unsalted butter

1 teaspoon vanilla extract

⅛ teaspoon almond extract (optional)

Steep the dairy:
In a 3-quart stainless steel saucier, bring milk and cream to a simmer over medium heat. Split vanilla bean lengthwise with a paring knife and scrape the seeds from each half; add the empty pod to dairy, and rub the seeds into the sugar. Once the dairy begins to bubble, turn off the heat, cover to prevent evaporation, and steep 30 minutes. Alternatively, cool to room temperature and refrigerate for up to 24 hours.

Make the pudding:
Whisk vanilla-sugar, salt, and cornstarch together in a medium bowl, followed by the egg whites. Return dairy to a simmer, fish out the vanilla pod, and scrape its flavorful pulp back into the pot. Ladle ½ cup of hot dairy into the egg white mixture, whisking to combine. Repeat with a second and third ladleful, then add warmed whites to the pot, along with butter.

Cook over medium heat, whisking constantly but not vigorously, until custard begins to thicken and bubble, about 3 minutes. Set a timer and continue whisking for *1 full minute more*. This ensures that the custard gels without a starchy mouthfeel, but excessive cooking can result in a grainy texture. Strain through a fine-mesh sieve into a bowl and stir in the vanilla and almond extract, if using. Allow the steam to subside, about 5 minutes.

Spoon into dishes and serve warm. Alternatively, pudding can be refrigerated for up to 1 week in an airtight container for use in another recipe.

continued ↓

→ Mix it up!

BROWN SUGAR CINNAMON: Along with the vanilla bean, steep the dairy with a 3-inch cinnamon stick (preferably overnight). Replace white sugar with 8 ounces (1 cup) light brown sugar, but otherwise proceed as directed.

GOAT'S-MILK: This variation is more easily digested by those with lactose intolerance, but it has a rich flavor (like cultured yogurt) that almost anyone will love. Simply swap the milk and cream for 20 ounces (2½ cups) goat's milk, and omit butter or replace with an equal amount of goat butter.

SNOW WHITE VANILLA MOUSSE: Prepare the pudding as directed and refrigerate in an airtight container until cold, at least 4 hours. In the bowl of a stand mixer fitted with the whisk attachment, whip 6 ounces (¾ cup) heavy cream on medium-high speed until thick and stiff, about 5 minutes. Meanwhile, stir the chilled pudding until smooth, then gently fold into the whipped cream until well combined. Refrigerate until firm, about an hour, or, tightly covered, up to 1 week.

To serve, spoon mousse into serving dishes, layered with fresh fruit, toasted nuts, or whatever you like—even Homemade Oreo® crumbs (page 214) for a cookies 'n' cream parfait! Makes about nine 4-ounce (½-cup) servings.

BANANA PUDDING

For all that banana pudding is hailed as a southern specialty today, the oldest recipe I could find dates back to the 1887 publication of *The White House Cookbook* by Fanny Lemira Gillette.[1] Born in Wisconsin, she relocated to Chicago just before the Civil War and then after the Great Chicago Fire, moved on to New York. Despite having no ties to the South (or the White House), she developed a recipe for "Banana Pudding" that all others would follow: sliced sponge cake, bananas, and soft custard layered in a glass dish with meringue heaped on top.

With several million copies of her cookbook in print at the turn of the twentieth century, her recipe was no secret, but southerners had better access to bananas than most—more bananas entered the country through New Orleans than through any other port. When railroads took their cargo east, they unloaded overripe fruit on the cheap at every stop along the way. As Atlanta was the intersection of several major railways, ultraripe bananas had a way of piling

In-store displays, like this one in a Texas supermarket, helped popularize Banana Pudding nationwide.

up there, making it a veritable "dumping ground," according to banana historian John Soluri.

Those same railways brought the National Biscuit Company to Atlanta, where it established a branch office in 1901. With Nabisco came an influx of Vanilla Wafers, a staple of commercial bakeries since the 1870s. Though perfectly tasty as a dainty snack, the little cookies were a popular stand-in for sponge cake in European desserts like Charlotte Russe, Tipsy Pudding, and Trifle.

While Nabisco installed a two-story railroad distribution hub in Atlanta in 1914, they didn't do any actual baking in the city—which is perhaps the reason Georgians preferred vanilla wafers made by the Frank E. Block Company, fresh baked and delivered twice a week to all the local groceries. In 1921, Block's Bakery sponsored the *Atlanta Woman's Club Cookbook*, so it's only appropriate that their recipe for banana pudding included two whole boxes of vanilla wafers.[2]

This Atlanta tradition graduated to the national stage when Nabisco took ownership of Block's in 1927. After discovering that their Atlanta sales outstripped those of any other locale, Nabisco began printing the recipe for Banana Pudding on every large box of Vanilla Wafers. Following World War II, they persuaded supermarkets to move Vanilla Wafers out of the cookie aisle and into the produce department, where bright yellow boxes and bunches of ripe bananas advertised "The All-American Dessert, Nabisco Banana Pudding."[3]

Although she grew up on an Appalachia farm, where her family survived by making everything from clothing to cheese from scratch, my grandmother embraced every semi-homemade trick known to man, always making her banana pudding with Nabisco Nilla® wafers and Jell-O® vanilla pudding. She'd probably shake her head at the very notion of making my own version at home ("Sugar, I don't know why you work so hard"), but the combination is incredibly delicious. The milky custard is aerated with whipped cream, so it's silky soft even straight from the fridge, and thanks to a no-weep Marshmallow Meringue, you can keep it there for a week. Hypothetically, anyway—in my experience, Banana Pudding never lasts longer than a day.

DIY BANANA PUDDING

Banana Pudding is pure bliss. Creamy vanilla pudding, slices of ripe banana, the soft crunch of Homemade Nilla® Wafers and toasted meringue. It's all the more satisfying when those wafers are your own, loaded with real butter and vanilla. Since even homemade wafers will keep for a month on the shelf, and the mousse can be made a week in advance, this recipe needn't be any more difficult to assemble than the one printed on the back of the yellow box.

YIELD: twelve ¾-cup servings | **ACTIVE TIME:** 20 minutes

1 recipe Homemade Nilla® Wafers (page 197)

1 recipe Snow White Vanilla Mousse (page 256)

8 medium bananas (about 40 ounces unpeeled), fully ripe and speckled brown

½ recipe Marshmallow Meringue (page 156)

Assemble the pudding:
Cover the bottom of a 7-by-11-inch glass or ceramic baking dish with Homemade Nilla Wafers. Add half the Vanilla Mousse and spread into an even layer with the back of a spoon. Slice half the bananas into ¼-inch pieces and tile over the top. Repeat with another layer of wafers, then mousse and bananas. Cover with plastic and refrigerate until needed, or up to 24 hours. (The top layer of bananas may turn brown, but they will be covered by meringue.)

Toast the meringue and serve:
Adjust oven rack to lower-middle position and preheat to 375°F.

Top pudding with Marshmallow Meringue, spreading so that it touches the baking dish all the way around. Sculpt into swoops and swirls with the back of a spoon, and place on a wire rack nested in a baking sheet. Bake until meringue is well browned all over, with slightly darker caps here and there, about 15 minutes. Cool one hour at room temperature, then wrap loosely in plastic and refrigerate until cold, about an hour more, or 50°F on a digital thermometer. Dish up each portion with a large spoon and serve with a few extra wafers on the side for crunch. Tightly covered, leftovers will keep up to a week in the fridge.

→ *Mix it up!*

MALTED BUTTERSCOTCH: For this version, you'll need a batch of Malted Butterscotch (page 352), cooled to room temperature. Drizzle 3½ ounces (⅓ cup) over each pudding layer before topping with bananas, but otherwise assemble, bake, and serve as directed.

CHIFFON PIE

The earliest recipes for Chiffon Pie are simple meringue pies disguised with a euphemism, but the idea took an intriguing turn in 1929. That October, New York's *Kingston Daily Freeman* introduced a Lemon Chiffon Pie "different than lemon pie, for a change from the ordinary."[1] While the ingredients were perfectly ordinary in every way, the directions were truly remarkable. Instead of piling the meringue on top, the recipe had it folded into the lemon custard to create something like a mousse.

By 1930, newspaper recipe columns had adapted coconut, chocolate, and even pumpkin pies to the technique. The trend coincided with the rise of Nabisco's "Cracker Cookery" campaign (see page 201), which earned chiffon pie a graham cracker crust. While the results were deliciously light, they were no doubt fragile. As early as 1931, some recipes began adding a packet of gelatin for stability, giving bakers a chance to take things up a notch with flavored options like lemon, lime, orange, strawberry, raspberry, and cherry.[2]

In 1941, Jane Knox (of Knox Gelatin, go figure) appeared in a series of newspaper advertisements disguised as editorials, declaring chiffon "the newest addition to the pie family, [with] a permanent place in our culinary affections."[3] Just a few years later, Vanilla Chiffon Pie would win first place in the pie division of the first annual Pillsbury Bake-Off, and recipe advertisements kept it in the public eye throughout 1949.

With all due respect to Knox, my recipe is based on Jell-O–style vanilla pudding lightened with whipped cream for a wonderfully mousse-like filling that's rich but light, and dead easy to make. Its creamy sweetness is balanced by the earthy crunch of my Whole Wheat Graham Cracker Crumb Crust. Dress it up with a handful of fresh raspberries, and it's a perfect summer dessert.

ICEBOX CHIFFON PIE WITH FRESH RASPBERRIES

Thanks to homemade graham crackers and airy vanilla mousse, this Chiffon Pie is a study in contrast—equal parts creamy and crunchy, earthy and ethereal. I love it with nothing more than a handful of red raspberries for garnish, which add a burst of color and tart flavor. It's a lovely make-ahead dessert that can be kept in the fridge for days.

YIELD: one 9-inch pie; 12 servings | **ACTIVE TIME:** 5 minutes | **DOWNTIME:** 3-hour refrigeration

1 recipe Snow White Vanilla Mousse (page 256)

1 fully baked Graham Cracker Crumb Crust (page 204), or any variation

2 cups | 12 ounces fresh raspberries

Scrape the mousse into the prepared crust, sculpting gentle swoops and swirls with the back of a spoon. Cover loosely with plastic and refrigerate until firm, at least 3 hours. The pie can be refrigerated for up to 2 days.

Just before serving, heap the fresh berries on top. Cut into wedges with a chef's knife, wiping the blade clean between slices. Cover any leftovers with plastic and refrigerate for up to 2 days more.

SILKY CHOCOLATE PUDDING

If you didn't grow up licking chocolate pudding off the foil lid of a plastic cup, imagine a rich and wobbly custard like panna cotta but even softer and more silky. Brown sugar rounds out the deep, dark flavor of Dutched cocoa with a hint of butterscotch for a simple yet satisfying chocolate pudding. There's a bit of downtime while the gelatin works its magic, but with only five minutes of actual effort, this recipe's fast enough to knock out on a weekday morning. After dinner, all you need to do is give your homemade "snack pack®" a stir.

This pudding is also the base for the Whipped Chocolate Crémeux (page 263).

YIELD: four ½-cup servings | **ACTIVE TIME:** 5 minutes | **DOWNTIME:** 3-hour refrigeration

1 envelope (2¼ teaspoons | ¼ ounce) unflavored gelatin powder

2 tablespoons | 1 ounce milk (any percentage will do) to bloom the gelatin

2 teaspoons vanilla extract

⅔ cup gently packed | 5 ounces light brown sugar

½ cup | 1½ ounces Dutch-process cocoa powder, such as Cacao Barry Extra Brute

¼ teaspoon Diamond Crystal kosher salt (half as much if iodized)

1½ cups | 12 ounces milk (any percentage will do) to make the pudding

★ ······

Key Point: This pudding's deep chocolate flavor depends on the alkalinity of Dutch-process cocoa, so even the best natural cocoas (acidic by nature) will make it tangy and thin. For this simple recipe, it's well worth splurging on full-fat, high-quality cocoa over a grocery store brand.

Mix gelatin, 1 ounce (2 tablespoons) milk, and vanilla together with a fork in a small ramekin.

Combine brown sugar, cocoa powder, and salt in a 2-quart stainless steel saucier, rubbing the ingredients together with a flexible spatula to break up any lumps. Add the 1½ cups (12 ounces) milk and warm over medium heat, stirring gently until steaming hot—no more than 5 minutes (or 200°F) or the milk will curdle. Remove from heat, add gelatin, and stir until fully melted. Pour into a 4-cup container and cool for 5 minutes, then cover and refrigerate until firm, at least 3 hours, or up to 1 week.

Scrape pudding into the bowl of a stand mixer fitted with a paddle attachment and beat on medium speed until creamy, about 1 minute. It will start out lumpy like cottage cheese but smooth out as it's beaten. Scrape the bowl and beater with a flexible spatula, then beat for a moment more to ensure no lumps remain.

Spoon into serving dishes and enjoy immediately. Leftovers can be refrigerated up to 2 weeks in an airtight container; rewhip before serving.

continued ↓

→ Mix it up!

BUTTERSCOTCH: This variation tastes like a butterscotch milkshake, especially when whipped as a crémeux (page 263). Instead of light brown sugar, use dark brown sugar and replace the cocoa with 1¾ ounces (shy ½ cup) Carnation instant nonfat dry milk (other brands will differ in volume and dissolve less readily). It will take an extra minute to beat out the lumps; if you like, pass the beaten pudding through a fine-mesh sieve for especially silky results.

COCONUT: Replace the milk throughout the recipe with unsweetened coconut milk (full-fat or lite). If you'd like, add ½ teaspoon coconut extract along with the vanilla to coax out a more intense flavor.

WHIPPED CHOCOLATE CRÉMEUX

Crémeux simply means "creamy" in French, but pastry chefs often use the term for any concoction lighter than a pudding but less airy than a mousse. It seems like the perfect description for this recipe, which uses whipped cream to aerate Silky Chocolate Pudding into something like pots de crème crossed with milk chocolate mousse. Or maybe a little bit better, since this eggless crémeux is easier than both and more chocolatey too.

YIELD: eight ½-cup servings | **ACTIVE TIME:** about 10 minutes | **DOWNTIME:** 30-minute refrigeration

1 recipe Silky Chocolate Pudding (page 261), or any variation, chilled

1 cup | 8 ounces heavy cream

Cocoa Nib Crunch (page 321; optional)

Scrape the pudding into the bowl of a stand mixer fitted with a paddle attachment. Mix on low speed for a few seconds, then slowly increase to medium-high. At first the cold pudding will look something like cottage cheese, but continue beating and it will smooth out in a minute. Return to its original container and pour the cream into the empty mixer bowl.

With the whisk attachment, whip on medium until the stiff cream begins to ball up inside the whisk, about 4 minutes. Gently fold in the pudding, cover, and refrigerate for 30 minutes, or up to 5 days.

To serve, spoon the chilled crémeux into parfait dishes and, if you like, top each with a tablespoon of Cocoa Nib Crunch.

My secret weapon on Christmas morning: soft and puffy cinnamon rolls (page 268) pulled from the freezer the night before.

Chapter 7

BREAKFAST TREATS

Whether it's a hot and flaky McDonald's®-style apple turnover or a yeasty sticky bun dripping with butter and honey, there's no denying the uniquely American indulgence of a freshly baked breakfast treat.

PILLSBURY CINNAMON ROLLS

It's not the idea of a dough twirled up with cinnamon sugar that's so American, it's the execution. European versions use a yeasted Danish dough or a flaky pastry base. While the details vary from country to country—some spice the filling with cardamom or finish things with an apricot glaze—they're all pastries meant to be eaten out of hand. Our thick-cut cinnamon rolls are doughy and soft, with gooey cinnamon filling, often stuffed with pecans, and usually dripping with vanilla frosting or sticky caramel. In any case, you need a fork to dig in and a shower to clean up.

In a roundabout way, the story of these rolls begins in France. According to Jessup Whitehead's 1898 essay, "Hotel French Rolls—An Inquiry into Their Origin," hotel magnate Paran Stevens traveled to Europe and became enamored with some type of French bread.[1] He didn't know the name or the recipe, but on his return to Boston, he worked with his bakers at the Tremont House to replicate it. Paran had presumably fallen in love with brioche, because the "French Rolls" that baker Charles Wood put on the menu in 1868 were downy soft and tender. When a competing hotel put the same soft rolls on their menu as well, they gained their American identity as Parker House Rolls.

The story's a little suspect, as milky soft French Rolls had been turning up in American cookbooks since the 1840s, but there's no denying the success they gained at the Parker House. Milwaukee's *Semi-Weekly Wisconsin* printed the earliest known recipe in 1869, "Good Rolls—The Famous Parker House Rolls."[2] While not exactly eggy brioche, the rolls were distinctly rich and a little sweet: one part butter, two parts milk, four parts flour, and a handful of sugar for a thrice-risen dough (after mixing, after kneading, and after shaping).

Parker House Rolls appeared in seemingly every magazine, newspaper, and cookbook of the 1870s, with recipes introducing the unique shape of the roll.[3] After the second rise, the dough was rolled thin, cut into rounds, then brushed with butter and folded in half like a pocketbook. They were set aside to rise for up to eight hours more. Timing that reflected the rhythms of a hotel kitchen, where shifts of bakers could babysit multiple batches of dough to ensure waves of hot bread coming out of the oven for every meal.

Cooking schools from Chicago to Boston incorporated the recipe into their curriculum, establishing Parker House as the definitive American dinner roll for a generation of professional bakers.[4] Although anyone could tackle the simple recipe at home, the timing made it tricky. With some twelve to fifteen hours of total downtime, the rolls would finish up in either the middle of the night or the wee hours of the morning.

May Perrin Goff, editor of the *Detroit Free Press*, turned this problem into an asset in 1881, with "Cinnamon Rolls" tacked onto the Parker House recipe in her cookbook *The Household*.[5] This variation added an egg to the basic dough which was rolled up with butter, cinnamon, and sugar. It was sliced into pinwheels, then left to rise and bake. With this format, the timing didn't matter; cinnamon rolls tasted equally delicious whether served as a midday snack, late-night dessert, or an early morning breakfast. The convenience of an overnight rise, however, favored breakfast.

Of course cinnamon rolls were nothing new, but made with scraps of biscuit or pie dough, they turned out flaky and crisp. As an addendum to Parker House Rolls, they became something tender and soft. Piggybacking on the popularity of Parker House Rolls, this type of cinnamon roll rode a wave of popularity into the twentieth century, where they met a drizzle of white icing à la hot cross buns.[6]

Thanks to those explosive tubes of refrigerated dough introduced in the 1950s, we're more likely to think of Pillsbury when it comes to cinnamon rolls today,[7] or perhaps an oversized Cinnabon from the food court, but my recipe goes back to the "brand" first associated with cinnamon rolls, the Parker House. It calls for the same ratio of ingredients found in "the Famous Parker House Rolls" of 1869, but with only two rises (one overnight) and the egg of Mary Goff's recipe. I've also replaced half the milk with Greek yogurt to thicken the dough so it's a bit easier to handle. When I want to change things up, I trade that for creamy purees like banana or sweet potato to flavor the dough.

HOMEMADE CINNAMON ROLLS

Cinnamon Rolls are the harbinger of a lazy morning, filling the kitchen with the aroma of butter, cinnamon, and freshly baked bread. With each puffy swirl of dough dripping with cream cheese frosting, every bite is tangy and sweet. This recipe's my secret weapon around the holidays, because it's an all-in-one method that only takes one bowl for the filling, frosting, and dough. The rolls can even be made in advance to bake and frost without any fuss. *See photos on pages 264 and 270.*

YIELD: twelve 3½-inch rolls | **ACTIVE TIME:** about 45 minutes | **DOWNTIME:** 45-minute initial rise, 8-hour second rise

Frosting:

½ cup | 4 ounces full-fat cream cheese, very soft—about 70°F

2 teaspoons vanilla extract

1¼ cups | 5 ounces powdered sugar

Cinnamon Filling:

1 stick | 4 ounces unsalted butter, creamy and soft—about 70°F

¾ cup packed | 6 ounces light brown sugar

2 tablespoons | ½ ounce ground cinnamon

½ teaspoon grated nutmeg

¼ teaspoon Diamond Crystal kosher salt (half as much if iodized)

Dough:

3½ cups | 16 ounces all-purpose flour, such as Gold Medal, plus more for rolling

½ cup | 3½ ounces sugar

2 teaspoons instant dry yeast (not rapid-rise)

1¾ teaspoons Diamond Crystal kosher salt (half as much if iodized)

¼ teaspoon baking soda

1 stick | 4 ounces unsalted butter

½ cup | 4 ounces milk (any percentage)

1 cup | 8 ounces plain Greek yogurt (any percentage)

1 cup | 4 ounces pecans, toasted

Prepare frosting, filling, and dough:
Combine cream cheese and vanilla with half the powdered sugar in the bowl of a stand mixer fitted with a paddle attachment. Mix on low to moisten (it may look curdled), then sprinkle in the rest of the sugar a little at a time. Once incorporated, increase speed to medium and beat until pale ivory, about 5 minutes. Transfer to a zip-top bag and set aside until needed, up to 24 hours at room temperature.

Prepare filling in the same bowl, mixing butter, brown sugar, cinnamon, nutmeg, and salt with the paddle on low speed until moistened. Increase to medium and beat until the dark paste is creamy, light, and very soft, about 5 minutes. Transfer to a zip-top bag and set aside until needed, up to 24 hours at room temperature.

Wipe the bowl with a paper towel, then stir together flour, sugar, yeast, salt, and baking soda until thoroughly combined.

Melt butter in a 2-quart saucier over low heat, then stir in milk and yogurt and warm to about 80°F. Add to flour and stir with a flexible spatula to form a very dry, shaggy dough. With the dough hook, knead on low speed until silky smooth and elastic, about 20 minutes; you should be able to gently stretch it into a thin but rough sheet without tearing.

Proof and shape the dough:
Cover with plastic and proof until the dough is puffy, light, and doubled in bulk, about 90 minutes at roughly 70°F. If the dough feels dense, firm, or overly resilient, proof 15 minutes longer and test again (this is more likely in chilly months).

Turn the dough out onto a lightly floured surface, dust with flour, and roll into a 13-inch square. Briefly microwave cinnamon filling if firm, snip a corner from the bag, and squeeze over the dough; spread into an even layer with an offset spatula.

Sprinkle nuts on top and roll into a log, ending seam side down.

Slide an 8-inch strand of thread or unflavored dental floss under the dough until you reach the middle. Cross the ends over the top and pull tight to divide the log in two. Cut each half into 6 slices and arrange in a parchment-lined 9-by-13-by-2-inch aluminum baking pan (or two 8-by-3-inch round cake pans). Cover with foil and refrigerate overnight, or for up to 48 hours.

Bake and serve:
Adjust oven rack to middle position and preheat to 350°F. Let the cinnamon rolls stand at room temperature until the oven is hot.

Bake the rolls (covered) until puffed and firm but pale, about 45 minutes. Remove the foil and continue baking until lightly browned, about 15 minutes more (or 205°F).

Snip a corner from the bag of vanilla frosting and squeeze over the rolls; spread into an even layer. Serve immediately, and leave no survivors; life's too short for day-old cinnamon rolls.

TROUBLESHOOTING
Don't rush the kneading process, which is longer than usual in order to develop gluten in the soft, rich dough.

In this recipe, baking soda isn't meant to provide leavening to the dough, but to regulate its pH, allowing the rolls to brown more easily in the oven.

MAKE AHEAD
The bag of frosting and the pan(s) of Cinnamon Rolls can be frozen for up to 3 months. Thaw both overnight (about 8 hours) at cool room temperature (no warmer than 70°F). In the morning, bake in a *fully preheated* oven for 45 minutes. Remove and discard the foil and continue baking until golden, about 5 minutes (or 205°F).

→ *Mix it up!*

APPLE CINNAMON: Prepare the frosting with 2 ounces (4 tablespoons) unsalted butter instead of the cream cheese; prepare the filling and dough according to the recipe. During the first rise, dice a medium (6-ounce) Granny Smith apple into ¼-inch chunks, and scatter over the filling in place of, or in addition to, the pecans.

BANANA: A fantastic change of pace from ordinary banana bread, this variation will help you use up overripe bananas to make a wonderfully aromatic cinnamon roll. Reduce the milk in the dough to 2 ounces (¼ cup)

and replace the Greek yogurt with an equal amount of ripe mashed bananas (from 3 to 4 large bananas).

BROWN BUTTER SWEET POTATO: This sweet, nutty, and vibrant ochre dough is perfect for chilly autumn mornings. Prepare frosting and filling as directed. For the dough, melt butter in a 1-quart saucier and continue cooking until golden brown, then cool to roughly 115°F. Replace yogurt with an equal amount of cold mashed sweet potato.

continued ↓

Though thick to start, this tangy frosting quickly melts from the heat of fresh-baked cinnamon rolls.

DOUBLE CHOCOLATE: After the powdered sugar, gradually add ¾ ounce (¼ cup) Dutch process cocoa to the frosting. For the filling, add 1 ounce (⅓ cup) Dutch process cocoa and 1 tablespoon vanilla extract; omit the spices if you like, or leave them in for a Mexican chocolate vibe. Instead of (or in addition to) pecans, sprinkle the dough with 3 ounces (½ cup, roughly chopped) 72% dark chocolate just before rolling up.

HONEY BUNS: Convenience stores sell these sticky snacks with and without frosting, so make it or skip it as you prefer. For the filling, replace brown sugar with 5¼ ounces (¾ cup) white sugar, reduce cinnamon to 1 teaspoon, and add 1 tablespoon vanilla extract. Otherwise, prepare the cinnamon rolls as directed. During the first rise, cream 4 ounces (1 stick) soft unsalted butter with 8 ounces (¾ cup) clover honey and ¼ teaspoon kosher salt (half as much if iodized). Spread into an even layer in the baking pan(s), and arrange sliced Cinnamon Rolls on top; otherwise refrigerate and bake as directed. After baking, loosen the rolls from the pan with a knife and invert onto a serving platter.

PUMPKIN SPICE: For the filling, add 2 teaspoons ground ginger and ⅛ teaspoon ground cloves along with the other spices; after creaming the butter, fold in 6 ounces (¾ cup) canned pumpkin puree. For the dough, replace the Greek yogurt with an equal amount of canned pumpkin puree.

STICKY BUNS: During the first rise, put 12 ounces (1½ cups gently packed) light or dark brown sugar into the baking pan(s). Drizzle with 3 ounces (⅓ cup) heavy cream, sprinkle with ¼ teaspoon kosher salt (half as much if iodized), and mash into an even layer with a fork. Arranged the sliced Cinnamon Rolls on top and proceed as directed. After baking, loosen the rolls from the pan with a knife and invert onto a serving platter.

If you don't like the original, these Homemade Pop-Tarts® (page 274) may not be your cup of tea. A sweet butter crust stuffed with dried apples and strawberries, then frosted with vanilla.

POP-TARTS®

Toasters don't seem to require any major feats of engineering. Drop a slice of bread into a slot lined with heating coils, let it brown, and then lift it out. However intuitive toasters are today, America's early versions took a more awkward approach. "Tipper" models had side-loading mechanisms for tipping several slices in the way you'd feed coins into a parking meter. "Floppers" held the bread against an exposed heating element with hinged plates that flopped open like the tailgate of a pickup truck. Extra-tall "Droppers" released the toast through a trap door at the bottom.[1]

Luckily we didn't get saddled with Tip-Tarts, Flop-Tarts, or Drop-Tarts. Kellogg's didn't debut toaster pastries until 1964, well into the era of spring-loaded "pop-ups." Junk food historians call Pop-Tarts a cheeky reference to the Pop Art movement, but their name was a calculated nod to the new breakfast market that popped up around toasters.

Since introducing Corn Flakes in 1906, Kellogg's had dominated at breakfast. They maintained their position for half a century, with a steady stream of new cereals: All-Bran (1916), Shredded Wheat and Rice Krispies (1927), Raisin Bran (1942), Corn Pops (1950), Smacks (1953), Cocoa Krispies (1958), and Fruit Loops (1963). The evolution from stodgy flakes of nutrition to sugared cereal shapes reflected Kellogg's understanding of their real customer base: kids.

The original toasters didn't pose a threat to Kellogg's kid-friendly angle. Tippers, floppers, and droppers all involved manually turning slices of bread to toast both sides—way more work than a bowl of cereal, with the added risk of burned fingers (a genuine problem with older models). And any concerns Kellogg had ended with World War II, when toaster factories turned from browning bread to building bombs.

After the war, production resumed, prices dropped, and chrome-plated pop-up toasters became a mid-century icon. Their prevalence inspired an industry of ready-to-heat "pop-up" breakfast treats. Snowcrop Frozen waffles led the way, with the motto "pop-up, they're done!"[2] Downyflake advertised "No batter! No bother!" waffles to "pop in the toaster,"[3] and Pepperidge Farm marketed frozen turnovers in apple, strawberry, and cherry.[4] Schulze and Burch introduced "Flavor Kist Apple Turnovers" in snack packs and family-sized boxes,[5] and on the savory side, Taylor Ham sold "Pork Roll Pop Ups" in toaster-safe aluminum pouches.[6]

Suddenly toasters had become a threat. Kellogg's wanted into the market but couldn't exactly turn Frosted Flake factories into frozen waffle plants, which needed specialized equipment. Meanwhile, their archnemesis, General Foods (makers of Grape-Nuts, Alpha-Bits, and Sugar Crisp), was facing the same problem. In 1962, they approached the experts at Schulze and Burch to see about commissioning a new line of pop-ups similar to Flavor Kist turnovers.[7] To Kellogg's dismay, General Foods unveiled Country Squares Strawberry Pop-Ups to test markets in 1963, with a national debut slated for the following year.[8]

With pop-ups eating at cereal sales and their biggest rival already ahead of the game, Kellogg's had to act fast. In September 1963, they contacted the manager of a nearby Keebler plant to see if they had any interest in teaming up to create a new breakfast pop-up.[9] With a Fig Newtons knockoff already in production, Keebler knew a thing or two about fruit-filled pastries.[10] Six months and a few MacGyver–like modifications later, Keebler delivered a top notch pop-up and Kellogg's landed on the perfect name: Pop-Tarts.

"Country Squares" never stood a chance. Under the conventions of 1960s slang, the name pretty much translated to "Redneck Dorks," and their commercials inexplicably depicted people doing household chores, like Mom and Dad hanging new drapes or washing the dog. Pop-Tarts may have arrived late to the party, but their undeniable cool made up for a lot.[11]

Kellogg's commercials featured Pop-Tarts vaulting out of toasters and into all sorts of fun (if not entirely relevant) situations: roller-coaster rides, darkened movie theaters, and coed dance parties. By the time General Foods had the wherewithal to restyle Country Squares as the slightly more hip Toast'em Pop-Ups, Pop-Tarts had already moved on to frosting—an irresistibly sweet idea from Keebler.[12]

HOMEMADE POP-TARTS®

Like a gingerbread house, Homemade Pop-Tarts are more like an arts-and-crafts project than a traditional recipe, but the results are freakishly authentic. From their size and shape to the shellacking of vanilla glaze and the crumbly sweet dough, my Homemade Pop-Tarts taste exactly like the original. They even have what it takes to survive the wrath of a toaster: a thick strawberry filling that won't bubble or drip. *See photo on page 272.*

YIELD: twelve 3¼-by-4¼-inch pastries | **ACTIVE TIME:** about 1½ hours | **DOWNTIME:** 2½-hour refrigeration

Filling:

1½ cups | 1¼ ounces freeze-dried strawberries

4 cups | 12 ounces dried apples, still soft and moist

2 tablespoons | 1 ounce applesauce, sweetened if you like

Dough:

3¼ cups | 14½ ounces all-purpose flour, such as Gold Medal, plus more for dusting

1 teaspoon baking powder

¼ teaspoon Diamond Crystal kosher salt (half as much if iodized)

¼ cup | 1¾ ounces sugar

2 sticks | 8 ounces cold unsalted butter, cut into ½-inch cubes

½ cup | 6 ounces light corn syrup

Glaze:

1¾ cups | 7 ounces organic powdered sugar, sifted

3 tablespoons | 1½ ounces whole milk or lightly beaten egg whites

⅛ teaspoon Diamond Crystal kosher salt (half as much if iodized)

1 teaspoon vanilla extract

Rainbow Sprinkles (page 325)

Prepare the filling:
Place freeze-dried strawberries in the bowl of a food processor. Cover with a sheet of plastic to contain the dust and grind until powdery and fine. Discard the plastic, add the apples, and pulse until the mixture forms a ball, about 2 minutes. Add applesauce and process for a minute more, pausing halfway through to scrape the bowl and blade with a flexible spatula.

Place a large piece of parchment (not wax!) paper on the counter, secure with tape, and grease lightly. Scrape the fruit paste in the center and shape into a 5-inch square. Top with a second sheet of lightly greased parchment and roll into an 11-inch square. Peel off the top sheet and slide onto a cutting board.

Sprinkle the paste with a little water to prevent sticking. Use a ruler and pizza wheel to cut it into four 2½-inch-wide strips, then cut each into three 3½-inch-long rectangles, pressing firmly with the knife to cut through the parchment as well. Refrigerate, uncovered, for an hour

to dry the paste. Use immediately, or stack the pieces, still on the paper, in a zip-top bag, and refrigerate for up to 1 month.

Make the dough:
Sift flour into the bowl of a stand mixer fitted with a paddle attachment (if using cup measures, spoon into the cups and level with a knife before sifting). Add baking powder, salt, sugar, and butter and mix on low until the butter disappears. Add corn syrup and continue mixing to form a stiff dough.

Knead against the sides of the bowl to form a smooth ball, then divide in half and flatten into discs. Use immediately, or wrap in plastic and refrigerate for up to 1 week; soften chilled dough for 30 minutes at room temperature before using.

Roll and assemble the tarts:
Knead one piece of dough on a bare work surface until pliable and smooth. On a well-floured work surface, roll into an 8-inch square. Sprinkle both sides with flour and roll into a 15-inch square, no more than ⅛-inch thick. Slide an offset

spatula under the dough to loosen it and brush off excess flour.

Cut into four 3¼-inch-wide strips, then then cut each into three 4¼-inch-long rectangles. Arrange on a parchment-lined aluminum baking sheet. Top each with a piece of chilled filling, peel off the parchment backing, and refrigerate.

Roll and cut the remaining dough as before. Place each piece over the chilled filling and lightly "squeegee" the dough with your index finger to expel any air pockets. Press gently to mold it against the filling and dough (the pieces will meld together as they bake). Pierce each tart 8 times with the narrow end of a chopstick or bamboo skewer, pressing until you hit the baking sheet. Cover with plastic and refrigerate for 30 minutes, or up to 3 days.

Bake and glaze the tarts:
Adjust oven rack to middle position and preheat to 350°F. Bake the chilled tarts until firm and dry but still very pale, about 16 minutes. If you like, use a pizza wheel to "sharpen" the edges of each tart. Cool to room temperature on the baking sheet.

Meanwhile, combine powdered sugar, milk, salt, and vanilla in the bowl of a stand mixer fitted with a paddle attachment. Mix on low speed to moisten, then increase to medium and beat for 5 minutes to dissolve the powdered sugar; the glaze will be quite thin.

Dust tarts with a paper towel to remove any stray crumbs and arrange on a wire rack. Use a pastry brush to swipe glaze down the length of each tart, going over the bottom edge, repeating as needed for even coverage. Clean up stray dribbles with a paper towel, then top with sprinkles and let the glaze harden, about 30 minutes.

Enjoy at room temperature or toasted. In an airtight container with a sheet of parchment between each layer, Homemade Pop-Tarts® will keep for up to 2 weeks at room temperature.

→ *Mix it up!*

BROWN SUGAR CINNAMON: Omit the freeze-dried fruit and process apples with 6 ounces (¾ cup packed) dark brown sugar instead. Along with the applesauce, add 1½ tablespoons ground cinnamon and ⅛ teaspoon kosher salt (half as much if iodized), then proceed as directed. If you like, flavor the glaze with 1 tablespoon ground cinnamon.

No-Knead English Muffins (page 278).

ENGLISH MUFFINS

"Every stranger from the country, who comes to the city, is astonished at the variety of noises which assail his ears on every side . . . the constant rumbling of heavy drays, carts, and carriages over the pavement, and the bawling cries of all sorts of petty traders." So begins *The City Cries of Philadelphia*, a tourist's handbook from 1850.[1]

It profiles the noisiest citizens of Philadelphia with remarkable tenderness, lingering on small details like the scuffle of the Muffin Man's shoes down a quiet alley. This fellow roamed the neighborhood streets every afternoon, with an apron around his waist and a basket of English muffins crooked under his elbow. Not that anyone called them *English* muffins, mind you. There simply wasn't any other kind.

Muffins started with a dough of milk, yeast, eggs, and flour set to rise while the Muffin Man went about town. When he came home, he'd portion the dough into small metal hoops or improvised molds pressed in trays of flour.[2] After an overnight rise, the muffins went on a hot griddle to sizzle in a slick of lard until golden on either side.

Though universally beloved, the Muffin Man had become something of an endangered species even before the Civil War. The anonymous author of *City Cries* lamented, "His visits are not nearly so frequent as they used to be in old times. People are growing rich so fast. . . ." With that affluence, American households gained the oven, and a means for *baking* muffins of their own. The baked muffins didn't have the same crispy crust, but split and toasted with butter, they tasted almost as good. Hardware stores even sold special muffin pans, making a griddle on the hearth (and the cry of the Muffin Man) obsolete.

At the same time, moisture-resistant packaging, improved formulation, and larger production facilities improved the quality of America's baking soda and baking powder. Brands like Arm & Hammer and Rumford raised the profile of these chemical leavenings in the 1860s, giving rise to "quick breads" free from the demanding timetable of yeast.

As yeasted muffins fell out of favor, muffin pans became home to little cornbreads or blueberry teacakes. By virtue of the pan's name, these treats became muffins too,[3] while the term *English* came to indicate muffins made with yeast and a griddle.[4] Across the pond, crumpet lovers saw things the other way around. Nineteenth-century editions of *Cassell's Dictionary of Cookery*, published in London, defined the "American Muffin" as a "yeast-raised griddle bread."[5]

Even so, an Englishman living in New York embraced the Yankee distinction when he established a wholesale bakery in the 1880s. Nearly a century after his death, Samuel Thomas' English Muffins still have the market cornered (or at least nooked and crannied), cementing the concept of English muffins as yeasty, in contrast to cakey, oven-baked American muffins.

I've always had a soft spot for Thomas' English Muffins, but I wanted a recipe that would follow in the Philadelphia Muffin Man's footsteps, with milk, eggs, and a long, slow rise. Although nineteenth-century recipes are notoriously vague, those for English muffins took that ambiguity to the extreme. Typical recipes spent more time providing instructions on the muffins' extended double rise than petty details such as specific quantities of flour.

By adding as much flour as I reckoned might make a suitable dough, I inevitably wound up with overproofed hamburger buns. My luck changed with an issue of *Everyday Housekeeping* from 1901 that described English muffin dough as "almost too stiff to stir and altogether too soft to knead."[6] Suddenly I realized where I'd gone wrong. I'd been using enough flour to form a kneadable dough, but this was America's first no-knead bread!

Through an ultra-long rise, wet doughs can effectively knead themselves through the slow action of yeast and gas working the gluten into shape.[7] It made perfect sense for a recipe developed by Muffin Men, bakers who spent more time on the streets than in the kitchen. So I slashed my flour estimate by half and tried again, without kneading. Bingo! The muffins griddled up chewy but tender, and far more flavorful than anything from the store.

NO-KNEAD ENGLISH MUFFINS

These chewy, yeasty muffins involve a lot of downtime but next to no effort. Stir the ingredients together after breakfast, then scoop out the portions before bed—no kneading, no rolling, no cutting. Refrigerate overnight, fry up some bacon in the morning, and slip the muffins into the shimmering fat. Or just stick with butter. Either way, they'll cook up golden and crisp on both sides, with nooks and crannies in between. *See additional photo on page 276.*

YIELD: twelve 3½-inch muffins | **ACTIVE TIME:** 30 minutes | **DOWNTIME:** 10-hour initial rise, a 10- to 24-hour second rise

3⅔ cups | 16 ounces unbleached bread flour, such as King Arthur

2 tablespoons | 1 ounce sugar

2 teaspoons Diamond Crystal kosher salt (half as much if iodized)

1¼ teaspoons instant dry yeast (not rapid-rise)

2 cups | 16 ounces milk (any percentage will do)

4 tablespoons | 2 ounces unsalted butter, melted

½ cup | 2 ounces stone-ground cornmeal, polenta, or grits

2 tablespoons | 1 ounce butter or bacon fat at room temperature, or a neutral oil such as safflower.

Key Point: In summer, the dough will need to be kept cool—try proofing in the fridge.

Make the dough:
Sift flour into a large bowl (if using cup measures, spoon into the cups and level with a knife before sifting). Stir in sugar, salt, and yeast with a flexible spatula, followed by milk and melted butter. Cover with plastic and let stand at cool room temperature (60° to 70°F) until spongy and roughly tripled in volume, 10 to 12 hours.

Shape and second rise:
Without stirring the spongy dough, dollop twelve ⅓-cup (2¾-ounce) portions onto a cornmeal-covered baking sheet. Pinch with damp fingers to tidy their shape, then sprinkle with cornmeal, cover loosely with plastic, and refrigerate for 10 to 24 hours.

Finish the muffins:
Set the tray of dough out at room temperature, and preheat an electric griddle to 350°F or heat a cast-iron skillet over medium heat. Brush the hot griddle with butter. Transfer the puffy dough portions to the hot surface, gently stretching the dough to widen each muffin to 3½ inches. Cook until the muffins are golden brown on the bottom, about 8 minutes. Dab the tops with melted bacon fat, flip with a spatula, and griddle as before.

Cool on a wire rack for about 10 minutes to set the crumb, then split by hand to create those coveted nooks and crannies (a knife will destroy their texture). Instead of trying to peel each muffin open like a book, work a little at a time and rotate as you go.

Toast fresh muffins before serving—they will be quite steamy and moist. Store in an airtight container for up to 1 week at room temperature or up to a month in the fridge.

→ *Mix it up!*

WHOLE WHEAT: For something a little heartier, reduce the bread flour to 10 ounces (2¼ cups) and sift it with 6 ounces (1⅓ cups) whole wheat flour (not stone-ground). Serve with a generous smear of old-fashioned apple butter.

*Griddled and toasted English Muffins,
with butter and apricot preserves.*

AMERICAN MUFFINS

In 1944, Betty Crocker's popular radio show, *Cooking School of the Air*, introduced listeners to layer cakes and muffins made with the "Double-Quick" method.[1] Instead of beating butter and sugar into a fluffy paste, these recipes incorporated the butter into all the dry ingredients, flour included. After the milk and eggs were added, the powdery mix transformed into a cake batter like any other.

In retrospect, the Double-Quick method was a savvy precursor to boxed cake and muffins mixes. By downplaying the benefits of traditional creaming, General Mills acclimatized folks to a style of baking that made mixes feel intuitive—just the dry ingredients you'd assemble yourself! We can thank those mixes for the popularity of muffins today. While cold cereal undermined the tradition of hot breakfast in the 1950s, Betty Crocker kept warm muffins on the American table. Bakeries followed the trend, offering an array of muffins alongside classic breakfast pastries—and by the 1980s, Betty Crocker ads promised muffins to "give your local bakery a run for its money."[2]

Profiling "Muffins on the Rise" in 1987, *New York Magazine* traced their popularity to convenience.[3] Companies like Entenmann's, Sara Lee, and Dunkin' Donuts sold ready-to-eat muffins, while Betty Crocker, Duncan Hines, and Pillsbury refined their game at home. Between Dunkin' and Duncan, fewer than forty-five percent of Americans reported making muffins from scratch. In the escalating competition among manufacturers, industrial formulas made muffins sweeter and richer through the preservative qualities of sugar and fat.

My mom made muffins at least twice a week when I was a kid. She'd tear open a packet, stir in the milk and eggs, and have the batter scooped before our oven even finished preheating; no banging around the pantry for ingredients, no noisy mixer. Those memories govern my concept of muffins today, a weekday breakfast that I can throw together in five minutes flat.

The first step was puzzling out a homemade muffin mix that would be stable on the shelf, a surprisingly easy task with coconut oil, which is virtually immune to rancidity (most manufacturers suggest a shelf life of between two and three years). It's actually richer than butter, so it makes the muffins particularly moist.

With my recipe, you can trade the all-purpose flour in the basic mix for a blend of whole wheat, cornmeal, or oat bran, or even go gluten-free, then add your favorite extras, like poppy seeds, orange zest, toasted pecans, or chocolate chips.

Just stir in some milk and eggs, then bake. That's it!

Five-Minute Muffins (page 282), using the butter variation of my Top-Shelf Muffin Mix (page 284), with fresh blueberries and sparkling sugar.

FIVE-MINUTE MUFFINS

These muffins are fluffy and light, but not so rich you can't enjoy them with a pat of butter. How do they taste? Well, that's up to you—Top-Shelf Muffin Mix can be prepared with a plain and simple base, or customized with toasted pecans and whole wheat, zesty lemon and cornmeal, or dried cranberries and oat flour. Along with the milk and eggs, you can stir in all kinds of last-minute additions like banana or pumpkin puree, even fresh blueberries or diced peaches. With so many different combinations, this recipe is a springboard for your cravings, whatever they may be. *See photo on page 281.*

YIELD: 12 muffins | **ACTIVE TIME:** about 5 minutes

1 bag Top-Shelf Muffin Mix (page 284)

½ cup | 4 ounces milk (any percentage will do)

2 large eggs, straight from the fridge

1 tablespoon | ½ ounce vanilla extract or ½ teaspoon other extract (optional)

Adjust oven rack to middle position and preheat to 350°F.

Combine muffin mix with milk, eggs, and extract, if using, in a medium bowl, stirring with a flexible spatula to form a thick, dough-like batter. Divide evenly among paper-lined muffin cups. Bake until the muffins are domed and firm but still pale, about 18 minutes for the basic mix, 22 minutes for the variations below. Serve immediately. Store leftovers for up to 3 days in an airtight container at room temperature.

→ *Mix it up!*

BANANA BREAD: Along with the milk and eggs, stir in 12 ounces (1⅔ cups) mashed bananas from 4 medium bananas. Fantastic with an oat-based mix with cinnamon and pecans.

BRAN: In a medium bowl, combine 2 ounces (1 cup) wheat bran with 8 ounces (1 cup) boiling water. Cool 5 minutes, then mix in 4 ounces (½ cup) plain, nonfat Greek yogurt instead of milk. Add to the Muffin Mix along with the eggs and bake as directed; works well with the whole wheat mix.

CLASSIC BLUEBERRY: Prepare the batter as directed, and drop a heaping spoonful into each paper-lined cup (this "cushion" prevents the fruit from sinking to the bottom). Fold 10 ounces (1¾ cups) blueberries into the remaining batter; it will be super-thick and chunky. Divide evenly among the muffin cups, piling the batter high; if you like, top each with a tablespoon of sparkling sugar. This variation works well with blackberries, pitted cherries, or diced fruits like apples, peaches, or pears.

COCONUT: Replace the milk with an equal amount of unsweetened coconut milk (full-fat or light) and 1 teaspoon coconut extract.

PUMPKIN OR BUTTERNUT SQUASH: For this variation, replace milk with an equal amount of plain, nonfat Greek yogurt, mixed with the eggs and up to 8 ounces (1 cup) pumpkin, butternut squash, or sweet potato puree. Especially good with the Snickerstreusel topping below.

SNICKERSTREUSEL: Instantly upgrade any muffin into a bakery-style luxury by sprinkling ¾ cup (3 ounces) frozen Snickerstreusel (page 48) over the muffins before baking.

STRAWBERRY: Along with the milk and eggs, stir in 5 ounces (½ cup) super-dry strawberry pulp, left over from making Philadelphia-Style Strawberry Ice Cream (page 340). Do not use fresh strawberry puree. I love this variation with a lemon poppy seed mix.

ZUCCHINI: Gently fold 12 ounces (3 cups) shredded zucchini into the finished batter. Try a whole wheat mix that includes cinnamon and chocolate chunks.

Top-Shelf Muffin Mix

The secret to homemade muffin mix is coconut oil, which behaves just like butter except that it's richer, making dry muffins a thing of the past. Even better, it's nonperishable, which means I can stock my pantry with bags of muffin mix for dreary mornings when I'm craving something warm for breakfast. The basic recipe is perfect for classic blueberry or pumpkin muffins, but with the chart opposite, you can quickly customize the ingredients for anything from lemon–poppy seed and oat bran to vanilla-pecan.

YIELD: enough to make 12 muffins (volume and weight will vary by flavor) | **ACTIVE TIME:** 10 minutes

2⅔ cups | 12 ounces all-purpose flour, such as Gold Medal

¾ cup | 5¼ ounces sugar

2 teaspoons baking powder

¾ teaspoon Diamond Crystal kosher salt (half as much if iodized)

¼ teaspoon baking soda

⅛ teaspoon grated nutmeg

¾ cup | 5¼ ounces virgin or refined coconut oil, soft but cool—about 68°F

Sift flour into the bowl of a stand mixer (if using cup measures, spoon into the cups and level with a knife before sifting). Add sugar, baking powder, salt, baking soda, nutmeg, and coconut oil. Mix on low with a paddle attachment until coconut oil disappears in a mealy powder, about 2 minutes. Store in a zip-top bag at room temperature (65° to 74°F), up until the date stamped on the jar of oil; do not refrigerate, or the mix will not behave as it should.

Use according to the recipe or variations on pages 282–83.

→ *Mix it up!*

ALL BUTTER: Replace coconut oil with 6 ounces (1½ sticks) unsalted butter, creamy and soft—about 68°F. Prepare mix as instructed and use *immediately* according to the recipe or variations on pages 282–83. This variation can be held a few hours at room temperature, no longer; refrigeration will change how the mix behaves.

Use these suggestions to customize your Top-Shelf Muffin Mix every step of the way, from a simple whole wheat mix laced with cinnamon and pecans for banana bread to a gluten-free blend mixed with dark chocolate for zucchini muffins. Remember to check the date on your package of almonds or poppy seeds and adjust the expected shelf life of your mix.

Step 1: Flour. Choose a blend to replace the all-purpose flour.	3½ ounces (⅔ cup) yellow cornmeal, 9 ounces (2 cups) all-purpose flour
	6½ ounces (1½ cups) whole wheat flour, 5½ ounces (1¼ cups) all-purpose flour
	3 ounces (¾ cup) oat flour, 9 ounces (2 cups) all-purpose flour
	Gluten-Free: 4 ounces (1 cup) tapioca flour or arrowroot, 4 ounces (¾ cup) cornstarch, 2 ounces (½ cup) white rice flour, and 2 ounces (½ cup) oat flour
Step 2: Flavor. Add up to 3 of the following ingredients before mixing.	1 tablespoon ground cinnamon
	2 teaspoons ground ginger
	1 tablespoon lemon, lime, orange, or grapefruit zest
	4 teaspoons matcha powder (not bagged or loose green tea)
	2 teaspoons poppy seeds
	Seeds from 1 vanilla bean
	½ teaspoon ground coriander—excellent for blueberry muffins
Step 3: Texture. Choose one ingredient to fold into the finished mix. Or, if you can't resist adding two, use half as much of each; otherwise, the overloaded muffins may crumble.	1 cup roughly chopped (4 ounces) toasted pecan pieces, almond slivers, or other chopped nuts
	1 cup (1 ounce) freeze-dried fruit, such as blueberries, cherries, or peaches
	¾ cup (4 ounces) dried fruit, such as raisins, cranberries, or apricot chunks
	½ cup (3 ounces) dark, milk, or white chocolate chips or roughly chopped chunks

McDONALD'S®-STYLE APPLE TURNOVERS

I've been known to snub apple pie as the least American dessert of all, a European import that fails to distinguish itself from the other apple pastries of the world. Double-crust, apples, sugar, and spice—it's all the same! But what could be more American than a mass-produced apple turnover, packaged in a cardboard sleeve and sold from a drive-through window for breakfast? At McDonald's, we finally find a true original.

I'll forgive you for mistaking that for sarcasm, but I mean it. McDonald's actually brings something unique to apple pie, blending fresh apples with dehydrated apple powder. It sounds like industrial shenanigans, but it's a brilliant idea. Apples contain loads of water, forcing recipes to either cook it out or soak it up.

The first option is tasty but time consuming, while the second is flavorless but fast. Apple powder offers a third option, the best of both worlds. It's a quick and delicious way to thicken small pastries by soaking up whatever juices fresh apples release. Binding with that extra water keeps the crust flaky and crisp while doubling down on apple flavor.

To take advantage of this nifty trick, pick up a bag of freeze-dried apples. You can find them in markets like Whole Foods and Trader Joe's or online. Different brands sell freeze-dried apples in 1¼- or 1½-ounce packages, a subtle variation that won't make any difference in this at all.

Flaky and crisp, with a filling twice as thick 'n apple-y as any pie (see recipe page 288).

HOMEMADE McDONALD'S®-STYLE BAKED APPLE TURNOVERS

These hand pies start with my super-flaky All-Butter Pastry Crust, and a sweet-tart filling puts apples front and center. I like using a variety of fresh apples to diversify the taste and texture of the filling, but tart Granny Smith matches the tang of the McDonald's original. Take your time cutting the apples small and cube-like, to maximize the amount of filling you can cram into each pie while keeping air pockets to a minimum. *See photo on page 287.*

YIELD: ten 5-inch turnovers | **ACTIVE TIME:** 1 hour | **DOWNTIME:** 2¾-hour refrigeration

1 recipe No-Stress All-Butter Pastry Crust (page 150), divided

Apple Filling:

1½ cups | 1½ ounces freeze-dried apples

½ cup | 3½ ounces sugar

2 teaspoons ground cinnamon

⅛ teaspoon Diamond Crystal kosher salt (half as much if iodized)

3 medium apples (about 20 ounces), such as Braeburn, Granny Smith, and/or Honey Crisp

4 tablespoons | 2 ounces unsalted butter, melted

2 tablespoons | 1½ ounces unsulfured molasses (not blackstrap) or sorghum

1 tablespoon | ½ ounce freshly squeezed lemon juice

Cinnamon Sugar:

¼ cup | 2 ounces sugar

1 teaspoon ground cinnamon

Roll and cut the dough:

Roll each portion of dough into an 11-by-13-inch rectangle, using as much flour as needed to prevent sticking. Stack on a parchment-lined cutting board or baking sheet, with a sheet of parchment between them, cover with plastic and refrigerate at least 2 hours, or up to 24.

Cut each chilled sheet into four 5-by-6-inch rectangles. Gather scraps, knead briefly, roll into a 6-by-13-inch strip, and cut 2 additional pieces. Arrange on two parchment-lined baking sheets and refrigerate while you prepare the filling.

Fill the turnovers:

Combine freeze-dried apples, sugar, cinnamon, and salt in the bowl of a food processor. Cover with a sheet of plastic to contain the dust, and grind until powdery and fine, about 1 minute. (This mixture will keep for up to a month in an airtight container, at room temperature.)

Peel, core, and dice the apples into ¼-inch cubes. Measure exactly 12 ounces (3 level cups) into a large bowl, and set scraps aside for snacking. Even if it's a very small amount, *do not add any extra apples to the filling!* Toss apples and apple-cinnamon powder together with a flexible spatula, then add melted butter, molasses, and lemon juice (this cannot be done in advance).

Imagine each portion of dough as an open book: lightly brush the edges of the "right page" with water, then place 2 tablespoons filling inside that boundary. Close the "book" and crimp the short sides with a fork, leaving the long side open, like a pita pocket. Repeat with remaining dough. To finish, pick up each pastry and spoon in another tablespoon of filling, letting gravity help you work it into the corners. Return to the baking sheet and crimp with a fork to seal.

Refrigerate turnovers until firm, about 45 minutes, or up to 4 hours.

Bake the turnovers:

Adjust oven racks to the upper- and lower-middle positions and preheat to 400°F. Mix sugar and cinnamon together in a small bowl.

Lightly brush turnovers with water and sprinkle generously with cinnamon sugar. Snip a few decorative slits across each with a pair of scissors.

Bake until the turnovers are puffed, crisp, and golden brown, about 30 minutes. Transfer to a wire rack and cool for 10 minutes before serving.

To keep the pastry crisp, store leftover turnovers at room temperature under a cake dome or upturned bowl, and rewarm in a hot oven before serving.

TROUBLESHOOTING

In an especially hot and humid summer kitchen, periodically refrigerate the dough to keep it cool and firm.

Homemade Reese's® Peanut
Butter Cups (page 299).

Chapter 8

CANDIES & CANDY BARS

This chapter is a celebration of America's penchant for confections of every type, from fluffy nougat dunked in milk chocolate to caramel-glazed popcorn, and crispy rice coated in marshmallow creme. When made from scratch, these classic candies become so much more.

DON'T LOSE YOUR TEMPER
How to Handle Chocolate Like a Pro

Chocolatiers describe tempering in terms of Roman numerals (Form IV Crystals), Greek letters (beta double prime), scientific lingo (polymorphous crystallization), and jargony advice (agitation promotes crystallization) that make little sense to those on the outside. Our brains skip over the parts we don't understand, leaving what sounds like the hokey pokey: You put expensive chocolate in, then you melt it out, you put more chocolate in, and you stir it all about. . . .

Tempering doesn't have to be a confusing song and dance. Just think of a stick of butter. Straight from the fridge, it's hard, but it softens into something creamy at room temperature and melts into a clear liquid when hot. You can go back and forth between cold and soft, popping the stick of butter in and out of the fridge every morning with your toast, but it's not so flexible once you melt it. The lovely golden liquid gives way to milky layers of fat and water as it cools, and there's no going back. It's a stubborn mess even if you stir it up.

Chocolate faces the same problem, only at a much lower point of no return: just 92°F. That means it's almost impossible to melt it in a microwave (or over a water bath) without throwing things out of whack. It may melt into something beautifully thick and glossy, but overheated chocolate turns mealy and soft as it cools, swirled with streaks of gray. Like the milk solids that float to the top of melted butter, cocoa butter rises to the surface of melted chocolate, a phenomenon so unattractive it's often mistaken for mold.

Tempering is any process that protects melted chocolate from overheating, ensuring that it stays crisp and glossy after it cools. There are pros and cons to every technique, but my favorite option for tempering at home is the "seeding" method. It doesn't require any special equipment like a marble slab or sous vide machine, or the hard-won skill of being able to judge a chocolate's temper by sight—only patience and a digital thermometer.

It starts with chocolate that's in good temper, and barring some sort of accident in shipping or storage, that's how any top-notch chocolate is sold. I prefer Valrhona simply because my local co-op sells it by the pound, but any reputable brand will do. Whether in bars, discs, or callets, look for chocolate that's made with cocoa butter, not vegetable oil, and free from stabilizers.

Terms like "dark" and "bittersweet" are unregulated, so pay attention to the cocoa percentage instead—even with milk and white chocolates. For example, Republica del Cacao's 31% white chocolate, Endangered Species' 48% milk chocolate, and El Rey's 60.5% Cariaco among others. Whatever you do, steer clear of grocery-store baking chocolate and bags of chocolate chips, which are specially formulated for high-heat applications and fussy (if not impossible) to temper.

The actual tempering process is remarkably simple. You first warm a big batch of chopped chocolate 92°F to break its temper, then vigorously stir in a smaller portion of finely chopped chocolate. These "seeds" help the melted chocolate return to good temper and then disappear as they melt from the residual warmth. The result is fluid chocolate that's able to return to its former state, coating cookies and candies in a crisp and glossy shell.

In order to provide a wide margin of error and a minimum depth for dipping, most of my recipes call for tempering two pounds of chocolate. Leftover chocolate can be cooled and stored at room temperature, then used as an ingredient in any recipe that calls for chopped or melted chocolate. Because dipping may leave trace amounts of butter or sugar, leftovers should not be reused for tempering.

TEMPERING CHOCOLATE

ACTIVE TIME: about 30 minutes

2 pounds dark, milk, or white chocolate

Get ready

Roughly chop two-thirds of the chocolate (about 20 ounces | ⅓ cup) into ¼-inch chunks and put in the bowl of a stand mixer or a similarly shaped stainless steel bowl; do not use glass, ceramic, or other heat-retaining bowls. Finely chop the remaining chocolate and place in a small bowl; reserve a handful, roughly 2 ounces (¼ cup) of this chocolate in a ramekin for emergency use.

Melt the chocolate

Fill a 3-quart pot with ½-inch of water and place over medium-low heat; if too wide to cradle the large bowl of chocolate, make a "booster seat" with a long strip of foil crumpled into a ring. Place the bowl over the steamy water and adjust the heat to maintain a steady supply of steam without letting it simmer. Stir with a flexible spatula, keeping the chocolate in motion so that it will not overheat along the bottom, until it is fully melted, 8 to 10 minutes; when semi-melted, begin monitoring the chocolate with a digital thermometer, removing the bowl and stirring off heat if necessary to prevent dark chocolate from exceeding 115°F (105°F for milk or white). Remove from the heat when the chocolate is completely melted and a few degrees shy of its maximum working temperature.

Seed the chocolate

Set the bowl of melted chocolate on a dry towel, then add half the "seed" chocolate and stir until fully melted, about 3 minutes. Add the remaining seed and stir for another 3 minutes, scraping the bowl all around to ensure an even mix. The goal of the seed is to cool the hot melted chocolate to about 90°F for dark or 86°F for milk/white. If the chocolate cools too quickly and the seed does not melt, place the bowl over the water bath for 5 seconds, then stir vigorously off heat. Repeat as needed to melt the seed without overheating.

When the chocolate is smooth and glossy, smear a small spoonful across a piece of wax paper and refrigerate for 2 minutes—if it still feels tacky, stir the chocolate for another 2 minutes and test again. If the chocolate is streaked or swirled, scrape the bowl and *stir, stir, stir*. If the chocolate is firmly set and glossy, *ta-da!* It's tempered.

Scrape the bowl with a flexible spatula and use the chocolate according to the recipe. When the chocolate becomes too thick or difficult to use, carefully rewarm it as before. To keep the chocolate in temper, it's extremely important not to exceed 90°F for dark (or 86°F for milk or white). If it is accidentally overheated during this rewarming phase, add half of the "emergency chocolate" and stir like crazy.

STORING

Scrape leftover chocolate onto a sheet of parchment paper and spread into a ½-inch-thick layer. Refrigerate until hard, then chop into ¼-inch pieces and store in a zip-top bag for up to 3 months at room temperature. You may notice a few dusty polka dots of cocoa butter bloom along its surface after a few days; this cosmetic defect will not affect its shelf life or quality as an ingredient in recipes that call for chopped or melted chocolate.

TROUBLESHOOTING

Tempering requires a fast and accurate digital thermometer; it should register 212°F within seconds of touching boiling water.

Chocolate that is dull, cloudy, or gray is out of temper and cannot be used as the seed in this method.

CRUNCH BARS

In the throes of the Great Depression, Americans discovered a sort of loaves-and-fishes miracle for the cash-strapped sweet tooth. A handful of crushed soda crackers or saltines could transform a measly square of melted chocolate into a big, crispy candy bar.

It's likely to have originated in mom-and-pop candy shops during the 1920s, but recipes for salty-sweet "Chocolate Crunch" bars spread through newspaper kitchen columns in the 1930s.[1] The idea went pro when Nestlé whipped up a Crunch bar of its own in 1938, swiftly followed by Hershey's Krackel (the perpetually distant runner-up).[2]

Instead of purchasing a million truckloads of saltine crackers, both companies opted for inexpensive puffed rice. These so-called "bubble grains" were more delicately crisp than any cracker, and puffy enough to inflate the volume of chocolate by fifty percent. It was ridiculously cost effective, allowing manufacturers to sell more chocolate bars at a lower price while turning a higher profit.

Crunch bars have been with us ever since, and they're so simple to make you'll wonder why you've never tried it before. The trick is a bit of malt, in the form of malted milk powder, which mimics the malt syrup manufacturers use to flavor and sweeten puffed rice. Aside from that, it's simply a matter of choosing a top-notch milk chocolate, which has the creamy consistency of the original, a texture dark chocolate can't match.

Unleash your inner Willy Wonka with crispy rice, creamy chocolate, and malted milk (see recipe page 296).

HOMEMADE CRUNCH BARS

The crispy bits of rice in a Nestlé Crunch® bar are flavored with barley malt, a sticky syrup that coats every grain with a hint of butterscotch. I've found that malted milk powder is less messy to work with at home, adding a toasty sweetness that blends perfectly with mellow milk chocolate. In this recipe, the dairy richness of Callebaut's 33% gives my candy bars a flavor and texture much like the famous brand, only better. *See photo on page 295.*

YIELD: ten 2-by-5¼-inch candy bars | **ACTIVE TIME:** 20 minutes | **DOWNTIME:** 20-minute refrigeration

3 heaping cups | 18 ounces finely chopped 33% milk chocolate, such as Callebaut

1½ cups | 1½ ounces Rice Krispies® cereal

2 tablespoons | ½ ounce malted milk powder (omit for gluten-free/vegan)

Temper chocolate according to the directions on pages 292–93. Stir in cereal and malted milk powder with a flexible spatula, then scrape onto a parchment-lined cutting board. Spread into an 11-inch square with an offset spatula and refrigerate until the chocolate loses its sheen, about 3 minutes.

While the chocolate is still soft, use a pizza wheel to lightly score ten 5¼-by-2-inch bars. Refrigerate until the chocolate hardens, another 15 minutes.

Cut into bars along the scored lines, and wrap in foil. Store in an airtight container for up to 1 month at room temperature, up to 2 months in the fridge, or up to 6 months in the freezer; serve at room temperature.

→ Mix it up!

HOMEMADE NESTLÉ BUNCHA CRUNCH®: When I was a kid, these popcorn-sized bites were one of my favorite movie theater treats because they seemed even more chocolatey than the original. Reduce Rice Krispies to 1 ounce (1 cup), and prepare the Crunch mixture as directed. Scoop into ¾-inch clusters with two small spoons and drop onto parchment-lined baking sheets. Refrigerate until firm, then transfer to an airtight container and store as above.

PEANUT BUTTER CUPS

America's salty-sweet snacks have relied on peanuts for over two hundred years, from peanut brittle and peanut butter cookies to Cracker Jacks and Nutter Butter Cookies. But none can compare to the twentieth-century union of peanut butter and chocolate.[1]

Like puffed rice, cheap and crunchy peanuts helped bakers and confectioners offset the expense of chocolate in a fun and tasty way. In 1914, fifty percent of the American peanut crop reportedly wound up in some sort of candy, primarily as peanut butter fondant centers for chocolate bars and "buttercups."[2] Ever-increasing production drove prices down, a worrisome development so far as George Washington Carver was concerned. He feared that African-American farmers wouldn't be able to earn a living wage, and so he focused his efforts on expanding the market. By lecturing industry professionals about the "possibilities of the peanut,"[3] and providing confectioners with well-tested recipes for peanut fudge and chocolate peanut caramels,[4] he succeeded in making peanut-centric candies the backbone of small-town confectionery shops.

Fast forward to 1928. When the Blue Bird Candy Shop in Harrisburg, Pennsylvania, ran out of "buttercups," owner John Armour asked one of his chocolate suppliers, a friendly guy known as HB, for help.[5] HB had always aspired to graduate from work as a "jobber" to become a full-fledged candy man, but as a newcomer to the industry he didn't have a recipe. Even so, he told John he'd come up with something, and a few months later he delivered a batch of peanut butter truffles. To keep costs down, he roasted peanuts to make his own peanut butter and bought milk chocolate wholesale from his friend Milton Hershey, just down the road.

Eventually HB invested in a special machine for piping and slicing the filling into discs, eliminating the time-consuming process of hand-rolling each piece. Workers dipped these in tempered chocolate, then nestled each into a paper cup sent down a small conveyor belt to be hand packaged with HB's own name: Reese.

Their low-tech origins make Reese's® Peanut Butter cups easy to replicate at home with little more than cupcake papers and a food processor. Plus peanuts. Lots and lots of peanuts, in the form of peanut brittle and peanut butter, which combine to give the filling just the right sweetness and a subtle crispiness that can't be beat.

There's no wrong way to eat them.

HOMEMADE REESE'S® PEANUT BUTTER CUPS

Creamy peanut butter is too soft and smooth to mimic the cookie dough–like filling of a Reese's® Peanut Butter Cup, but blended with finely ground peanut brittle, it thickens into a lightly sweetened paste with hints of caramel and vanilla. Encased in mellow milk chocolate and molded in crinkled cupcake liners, this look-alike is everything you need.

YIELD: twenty-four 2-inch cups | **ACTIVE TIME:** about 45 minutes | **DOWNTIME:** 30-minute refrigeration

½ recipe (twelve 2-inch pieces | 9 ounces) Caramel-Vanilla Peanut Brittle (page 69), roughly chopped

¾ cup | 7 ounces creamy peanut butter, such as Skippy

2 teaspoons vanilla extract

¼ teaspoon Diamond Crystal kosher salt (half as much if iodized)

5 cups | 30 ounces finely chopped milk chocolate, such as Callebaut's 33.6%

Prepare the filling:

Pulse peanut brittle in a food processor until powdery and dry. Add peanut butter, vanilla, and salt and grind to a smooth paste, about 2 minutes. Transfer to a piping bag fitted with a ½-inch plain tip, or refrigerate in an airtight container for up to 1 month (bring to room temperature before use).

Assemble the peanut butter cups:

Line two muffin pans with fluted cupcake papers. Temper chocolate according to the directions on pages 292–93. Dollop a shy tablespoon (½ ounce) chocolate into 12 of the papers. Holding the piping bag at a 90-degree angle just above the chocolate, pipe a tablespoon (½ ounce) filling into the center of each cup (this will force the chocolate up the sides of the paper). Top each with another shy tablespoon (½ ounce) chocolate, and rap the pan against the counter until the tops are smooth. Repeat with the remaining pan. Refrigerate until the chocolate is set, about 30 minutes, and bring to room temperature before serving.

Store in an airtight container for up to 1 week at room temperature, a month in the fridge, or 6 months in the freezer. Candies coated in *untempered* chocolate must be kept and served cold.

→ *Mix it up!*

PEANUT BUTTER SLABS: This rustic alternative delivers all the flavor and texture in about half the time. Spread half the tempered chocolate over a parchment-lined baking sheet and refrigerate until hard. Spread the filling on top, then cover with the remaining chocolate and refrigerate until hard. Cut into candy bar–sized slabs for snacking, or chop into bite-sized chunks to stir into a batch of freshly churned Honey-Vanilla Ice Cream (page 336).

PEANUT BUTTER SPREAD: On its own, the lightly sweetened filling is a crispy, crunchy spread you can use like Nutella®—enjoy it smeared across a thick slice of Homemade Wonder® Bread (page 242), spread over Chocolate Graham Crackers (page 204), or layered into DIY Banana Pudding (page 258).

MARS® BARS

During World War I, special taxes on soft drinks and even carbonation put the brakes on traditional soda fountain formulas.[1] But dairy dodged a bullet, allowing druggists to formulate new recipes based on milk, nonhomogenized in those days so it frothed up remarkably well in a cocktail shaker with shaved ice.[2] These foamy "milk shakes" caught on, and by the summer of 1920, Minnesota dairymen had nicknamed St. Paul's business district "The Milky Way."[3]

That wasn't the only change war forced upon the industry; a steep tax on sugar forced pharmacists to use malt syrup instead.[4] Its nutty roasted flavor became an instant hit in "milk shakes," especially with powerhouse combos like butterscotch and chocolate.[5]

At the intersection of malt and The Milky Way stood Frank Mars, Twin Cities confectioner. He owned the Nougat House, where he made small batches of fresh candy every day.[6] It was an honest living, but a modest one; unlike Hershey's sprawling chocolate factory, the Nougat House was home to more than a candy kitchen—Frank's wife and daughter lived upstairs.

In the summer of 1923, Frank got an unexpected call from his estranged son, Forrest. History doesn't tell us how he wound up in jail, only that Frank went to bail him out and then took him to a five-and-dime for an awkward heart to heart. Frank and his son had never

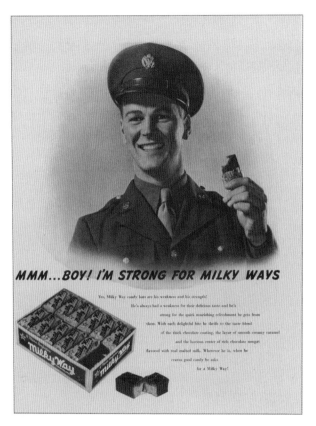

During World War II, advertisements like this one helped widen the market for candy bars, once aimed at children alone.

quite seen eye to eye. Forrest thought small batches of boring nougat kept Dad's business in Shmuckville, USA. He told his old man to think big, dream up something new that would take the industry by storm, like the malted milkshakes they were sipping.[7] Frank took the suggestion quite literally, developing a soft nougat that tasted like those very shakes.[8]

In honor of the local soda fountains that inspired it, he called his candy bar the Milky Way. It defined the notion of overnight success, earning more than a quarter million dollars in 1924 (roughly eleven million dollars today).[9] Fluffy nougat made Milky Ways chubby and thick, which looked mighty impressive compared to a slim Hershey's bar.

By the end of the decade, the Nougat House was Mars, Inc., with a proper factory in Chicago that tripled their earlier profits.[10] Frank developed a caramel-peanut nougat bar in 1930 (named after his racehorse, Snickers),[11] and two years later he introduced easy-to-share three-packs of chocolate, vanilla, and strawberry nougat mini bars sold as 3 Musketeers®.

Producing that much nougat meant cracking a million local eggs each week,[12] endearing Mars to the poultry industry and distinguishing his nougat from that of his competitors. We tend to imagine everything "back then" as fresh and local by default, but manufacturers in the 1930s typically relied on albumen powder imported from China. Being able to advertise something as "wholesome" as fresh eggs allowed Mars to market Milky Way as a nourishing snack for children and adults. In fact, at the onset of World War II, Mars heavily advertised its chocolate as a source of energy, and the company sent crates of Milky Way, Snickers, and 3 Musketeers bars overseas to support the troops. That resulted in a surprising shift in the public's perception of candy bars, once considered nothing more than a childish indulgence. Advertisements featuring soldiers in smartly pressed uniforms, candy bar in hand, transformed Mars bars into the official snack of American heroes. Candy bars don't enjoy a reputation quite that illustrious today, but I've discovered that sharing a batch of my Homemade Milky Way®, Homemade Snickers®, or Homemade 3 Musketeers® bars will make you a hero among friends.

For my take on these classic candy bars, you'll have to follow in Frank's footsteps and establish a Nougat House of your own. Fortunately, it's not half as tricky as a traditional recipe would suggest. Nougats typically involve two boiling sugar syrups beaten into a meringue at different stages. The first merely warms and stabilizes the whites so they whip up fluffy and light, while the second determines the final texture of the candy. As if wrangling two messy pots of hot syrup weren't bad enough, such recipes require you to time things just right on both occasions or risk ruining it all.

I take a simplified approach to nougat with Swiss meringue, warmed over a water bath. It eliminates the second pot of syrup and the need for precise timing in one fell swoop, as Swiss meringue is stable enough to whip continuously until the hot sugar syrup is ready. The result is a light and airy nougat that can be flavored with cocoa, peanut butter, or malt to re-create America's favorite candy bars.

Fluffy Cocoa Nougat

My Fluffy Cocoa Nougat is a dead ringer for the mellow milk chocolate inside a 3 Musketeers® bar, but with each variation it can become the malted core of the Homemade Milky Way® bar, or the honeyed heart of a Homemade Snickers® bar. This recipe makes a little more than strictly necessary, so you don't have to worry about "losing" nougat or fighting to scrape the bowl if it hardens too soon. Before jumping in, be sure to read through the directions to familiarize yourself with my unconventional technique.

YIELD: one 8-inch square pan | **ACTIVE TIME:** 45 minutes | **DOWNTIME:** 1-hour rest

Meringue:

3 large egg whites (⅓ cup | 3 ounces) straight from the fridge

½ cup | 3 ounces sugar

¾ teaspoon Diamond Crystal kosher salt (half as much if iodized)

Nougat:

⅔ cup | 5 ounces water

1 cup | 12½ ounces light corn syrup

1¼ cups | 11 ounces sugar

Shy ½ cup | 2 ounces Carnation instant nonfat dry milk

½ cup plus 2 tablespoons | 1¾ ounces Dutch-process cocoa powder, such as Cacao Barry Extra Brute

Powdered sugar for dusting

Get ready:

Line an 8-by-2-inch square baking pan with two 8-by-15-inch strips of parchment (not wax paper or foil), creasing the corners so they lie flush against the pan, and lightly grease. Fill a 3-quart pot with an inch of water and place over medium-low heat with a "booster seat" made from a long strip of foil crumpled into a ring. Off heat, stir egg whites, sugar, and salt in the bowl of a stand mixer.

Make the nougat:

Combine water, corn syrup, and sugar in a 2-quart stainless steel saucier set over medium heat. Stir with a fork from time to time until it comes to a roiling boil, about 6 minutes; it will foam considerably at first but will not overflow a 2-quart saucier. Clip on a digital thermometer and cook, *without stirring*, until the clear syrup registers 250°F, about 8 minutes.

As soon as the thermometer is in place, set egg whites over the "preheated" water and stir with a flexible spatula until steaming hot and the sugar has completely dissolved, about 2 minutes. Transfer to the mixer stand fitted with the whisk attachment, and whip on medium-high speed until the syrup is ready, about 6 minutes (there is no risk of overbeating even after another 5 minutes, so don't stress about the timing).

Warm a pint-sized Pyrex measuring cup with hot water. When the syrup hits 250°F, empty the measuring cup and *very slowly* pour in the bubbling syrup, pausing to let the foam subside as needed; scrape the pot with a heat-resistant spatula. With the mixer running, rest the measuring spout against the edge of the bowl and add the hot syrup in a steady stream, letting it dribble down the side of the bowl to avoid the whisk (don't fuss with scraping the cup, just add what you can). The meringue will roughly triple in volume during this time; continue whipping until glossy, thick, and beginning to ball up inside the whisk, about 3 minutes.

Reduce speed to low and sprinkle in the milk powder, followed by the cocoa, then increase speed to medium for a few seconds to roughly combine. Fold the nougat once or twice with a flexible spatula and scrape into the prepared pan. With powdered sugar-dusted fingers, press into an even layer. Cover with foil and "ripen" at room temperature between 24 and 48 hours; prior to that, the nougat's texture may be too firm or gooey to slice.

A note on cleanup: Hardened candy syrup makes dishes difficult to scrub, and few dishwashers have the power to blast it away, but it will soak off easily in a sinkful of hot soapy water.

TROUBLESHOOTING

Nougat depends on an accurate digital thermometer; if things go wrong, you can bet the readings were off. If the boiling syrup does not reach 250°F, the nougat will be gummy and soft; cooked more, and it will be dense and tough. An accurate digital thermometer should register 212°F in a pot of boiling water.

This recipe absolutely *cannot* be made with a hand mixer.

→ *Mix it up!*

HOMEMADE MILKY WAY MIDNIGHT® NOUGAT: Omit the cocoa. Split a vanilla bean lengthwise with a paring knife and run the flat of the blade down each half to scrape out the seeds; reserve empty pod for another project. Add seeds to the syrup along with the salt.

HOMEMADE MILKY WAY® NOUGAT: Reduce kosher salt to ½ teaspoon (half as much if iodized) and replace the powdered milk with an equal amount of malted milk powder. *This version is not gluten-free.*

HOMEMADE SNICKERS® NOUGAT: Reduce corn syrup to 9 ounces (¾ cup) and add 3 ounces (¼ cup) clover honey. Use a 5-quart pot to accommodate the foaming syrup. Omit the cocoa and flavor nougat with 5 ounces (½ cup) crunchy peanut butter.

HOMEMADE 3 MUSKETEERS® BARS

If you've never tasted fresh nougat, prepare to fall in love with candy bars all over again. It's wonderfully airy and light, but a little chewy too, then creamy as it melts. This one has a deep cocoa flavor that's not too sweet, perfect for pairing with milk chocolate. The combination tastes just like a real 3 Musketeers bar, but far more satisfying, thanks to genuine cocoa butter in every bite.

YIELD: twenty-four 2-by-1½-by-1-inch candy bars | **ACTIVE TIME:** 1 hour

5½ cups | 32 ounces roughly chopped milk chocolate, such as Callebaut's 33%

1 recipe Fluffy Cocoa Nougat, (page 302), aged for 24 hours

Precoat and slice the nougat:
Carefully melt 4 ounces (⅔ cup) of the chocolate; there's no need to temper (although you can if you prefer), but take care not to let it scorch. Coat the top of the nougat with melted chocolate and refrigerate until hardened, about 5 minutes.

Lift chilled nougat from the pan, peel away the parchment, and place chocolate side down on a cutting board. Cut into four 4-inch squares with an oiled knife, rinsing the blade under hot running water, drying, and reoiling after each slice. However time-consuming, this is the only way to ensure clean cuts of the soft, sticky candy. Slice the squares into three 1⅜-inch bars, cleaning the knife as before, and cut into 2-inch lengths. Cover with plastic and refrigerate until needed, up to 8 hours.

Finish the candy bars:
Set up a dipping station with the candy bars on the left, a space for tempered chocolate in the middle, and a foil-lined cutting board on the right (opposite for lefties).

Temper chocolate according to the directions on pages 292–93. Drop a chilled candy bar into the chocolate, nougat side down, flip it over with a fork to coat, and fish it back out. Knock the fork against the bowl so the excess chocolate can drip off, then swipe an index finger across the top to leave only a thin layer behind (scrape your finger against the edge of the bowl to de-chocolify). Drag the bottom of the fork against the edge of the bowl, place the candy bar on the prepared cutting board, and bounce the tines across the top to create a wavy design. Repeat with remaining bars, pausing to stir and warm the chocolate as needed (no warmer than 86°F). If necessary, pause to wash up about halfway through. Once the bars are coated, let stand until the chocolate is shiny and hard, or refrigerate to speed things along.

Store in an airtight container for up to a week at room temperature or a month in the fridge.

HOMEMADE MILKY WAY® BARS

Milky Way's blend of chewy caramel and malted nougat changed everything America knew about candy bars. Without artificial flavorings or hydrogenated oils, the homemade version will change everything for you as well.

YIELD: twenty-four 2-by-1½-by-1-inch candy bars | **ACTIVE TIME:** 1 hour | **DOWNTIME:** 24- to 48-hour refrigeration

1 recipe Chewy Caramel (page 306)

1 recipe Homemade Milky Way® Nougat (page 303)

5½ cups | 32 ounces roughly chopped milk chocolate, such as Callebaut's 33%

Layer the candy:
Prepare the Chewy Caramel according to the directions on page 306, then make the nougat and press it into the pan. Cover with foil and "ripen" for 24 to 48 hours at room temperature. Refrigerate for at least 2 hours to harden the caramel before cutting.

Cut the bars:
Lift chilled nougat from the pan, peel away the parchment, and place caramel side down on a cutting board. Cut into four 4-inch squares with an oiled knife, rinsing the blade under hot running water, drying, and re-oiling it after each slice. However time-consuming, this is the only way to ensure clean cuts of the soft, sticky candy. Slice the squares into three 1⅜-inch bars, cleaning the knife as before, and cut into 2-inch lengths. Cover with plastic and refrigerate until needed, up to 8 hours.

Finish the candy bars:
Set up a dipping station with the candy bars on the left, a space for tempered chocolate in the middle, and a foil-lined cutting board on the right (opposite for lefties).

Temper chocolate according to the directions on pages 292–93. Drop a chilled candy bar into the chocolate, caramel side down, flip it over with a fork to coat, and fish it back out. Knock the fork against the bowl so the excess chocolate can drip off, then swipe an index finger across the top to leave only a thin layer behind (scrape your finger against the edge of the bowl to dechocolify). Drag the bottom of the fork against the edge of the bowl, place candy bar on the prepared cutting board, and bounce the tines across the top to create a wavy design. Repeat with remaining bars, pausing to stir and warm the chocolate as needed (no warmer than 86°F). If necessary, pause to wash up about halfway through. Once the bars are coated, let stand until the chocolate is shiny and hard, or refrigerate to speed things along.

Store in an airtight container for up to a week at room temperature or a month in the fridge.

→ *Mix it up!*

HOMEMADE MILKY WAY MIDNIGHT®: Replace the Homemade Milky Way® Nougat with Homemade Milky Way Midnight® Nougat (page 303) and finish the bars with dark chocolate instead of milk.

GLUTEN-FREE: Replace the Homemade Milky Way® Nougat with Fluffy Cocoa Nougat (page 302), or any other variation (malt powder contains gluten).

Chewy Caramel

As a candy and not a sauce, caramel is creamy, gooey, chewy, salty, stretchy, wow. It's the salty-sweet ribbon running through the center of a Homemade Snickers® Bar (page 308), but it's also tasty enough to stand on its own. With a little less cooking, it can also be spooned over cheesecake or whipped into cream.

You may have heard horror stories about pots of caramel bubbling over, but there's no risk of that here; I shock the caramel into submission by adding the cream *cold*, which halts caramelization so you can rest assured it'll never taste bitter or burned. Just be sure to measure the cream in advance—you won't have a moment to spare when the time comes.

YIELD: 12 ounces (enough to make 24 bars) | **ACTIVE TIME:** 30 minutes

1 vanilla bean

1¼ cups | 8½ ounces sugar

½ cup | 4 ounces water

¾ teaspoon Diamond Crystal kosher salt

1 cup | 8 ounces heavy cream

★

Key Point: Iodized salt, or kosher salt that includes yellow prussiate of soda, may give the caramel a grainy texture. Diamond Crystal kosher salt is free from such additives, making it perfect for candies.

Line an 8-by-2-inch square baking pan with two 8-by-15-inch strips of parchment (not wax paper or foil), creasing the corners so they lie flush against the pan, and lightly grease. Split the vanilla bean lengthwise with a paring knife and scrape the seeds from each half; rub the seeds into the sugar and reserve the empty pod for another use.

Combine sugar, water, and salt in a 3-quart stainless steel saucier and set over medium heat. Stir occasionally with a fork until the sugar dissolves and the clear syrup is bubbling hard around the edges, about 4 minutes. Simmer, without stirring, until the syrup begins to turn pale gold, roughly 8 minutes more. Shake and swirl the pan to encourage even caramelization as the color deepens to light amber, another 30 seconds or so. *Immediately* add the cold cream and reduce heat to medium-low. Cook, stirring with a heat-resistant spatula, until caramel is homogenous but foamy, just over a minute. Clip on a digital thermometer and continue cooking, stirring occasionally, until foam subsides and the caramel reaches 250°F, about 9 minutes.

Immediately scrape into the prepared pan. Cover with foil and set aside until needed, up to 3 days at room temperature.

→ *Mix it up!*

CARAMEL SAUCE: Cook the caramel for only 6 minutes after adding the cream, or until it reaches 225°F. Use while warm and runny, or pour into a wide-mouth pint jar and refrigerate up to 2 months. Makes just over 13 ounces (1⅓ cups).

CARAMEL WHIPPED CREAM: In the bowl of a stand mixer fitted with the whisk attachment, combine 5 ounces (⅔ cup) heavy cream with 5½ ounces (½ cup) *chilled* Caramel Sauce. Mix on low speed to combine, then increase to medium-high and whip until thick and stiff, about 5 minutes. Use immediately, or cover and refrigerate for up to 1 week. Thanks to the thickening power of caramel, it will not need to be rewhipped. Makes 10 ounces (2 cups).

COCONUT (VEGAN): Replace the cream with unsweetened full-fat coconut milk.

HOMEMADE MILK DUDS®: Cook caramel to 260°F. Once cool, transfer to a cutting board and cut in a 7-by-7 grid, making forty-nine ¼-ounce squares. Shape into roundish blobs, transfer to an airtight container with a sheet of wax paper between each layer, and refrigerate until hard (up to 1 week). To coat, temper 8 ounces (1⅓ cups) finely chopped 33% milk chocolate such as Callebaut, according to the directions on pages 292–93. Gently fold in the caramel drops with a flexible spatula to coat, then scrape onto a parchment-lined baking sheet. Transfer the candy to a second parchment-lined baking sheet, separating the caramels to harden individually (this delightfully messy work is infinitely faster than hand-dipping each piece). When the chocolate has set, transfer to an airtight container and store for up to 2 weeks at room temperature or up to 1 month in the fridge.

HOMEMADE SNICKERS®: Follow the recipe as directed, but when the caramel reaches 250°F, stir in 5 ounces (1 cup) roughly chopped dry-roasted peanuts and pour into the prepared pan.

HOMEMADE SNICKERS® BARS

The salty-sweet combination of fluffy peanut butter nougat, chewy caramel, crunchy peanuts, and creamy milk chocolate makes Snickers my favorite candy bar of all. Follow the recipe as is for a classic Snickers clone, or use different types of chocolate, nougat, and nuts to make your own custom creation.

YIELD: twenty-four 2-by-1½-by-1-inch candy bars │ **ACTIVE TIME:** 1 hour │ **DOWNTIME:** 24- to 48-hour refrigeration

1 recipe Chewy Caramel (Homemade Snickers® variation, page 307)

1 recipe Homemade Snickers® Nougat (page 303)

5½ cups | 32 ounces roughly chopped milk chocolate, such as Callebaut's 33%

Layer the candy:
Prepare the pan of caramel according to the directions on page 306, then make the nougat and press it into the pan. Cover with foil and "ripen" for 24 to 48 hours at room temperature. Refrigerate for at least 2 hours to harden the caramel before cutting.

Cut the bars:
Lift chilled nougat from the pan, peel away the parchment, and place caramel side down on a cutting board. Cut into four 4-inch squares with an oiled knife, rinsing the blade under hot running water, drying, and re-oiling it after each slice. However time-consuming, this is the only way to ensure clean cuts of the soft, sticky candy. Slice the squares into three 1⅜-inch bars, cleaning the knife as before, and cut into 2-inch lengths. Cover with plastic and refrigerate until needed, up to 8 hours.

Finish the candy bars:
Set up a dipping station with the candy bars on the left, a space for the tempered chocolate in the middle, and a foil-lined cutting board to the right (opposite for lefties).

Temper chocolate according to the directions on pages 292–93. Drop a chilled candy bar into the chocolate, caramel side down, flip it over with a fork to coat, and fish it back out. Knock the fork against the bowl so the excess chocolate can drip off, then swipe an index finger across the top to leave only a thin layer behind (scrape your finger against the edge of the bowl to de-chocolify). Drag the bottom of the fork against the edge of the bowl, place candy bar on the prepared cutting board, and bounce the tines of the fork across the top to create a wavy design. Repeat with remaining bars, pausing to stir and warm the chocolate as needed (no warmer than 86°F). If necessary, pause to wash up about halfway through. Once the bars are coated, let stand until the chocolate is shiny and hard, or refrigerate to speed things along.

Store in an airtight container for up to a week at room temperature or a month in the fridge.

CRACKER JACK®

There once lived a toffee named taffy—Butterscotch Taffy (see page 318). Butterscotch Taffy fell in love with Peanuts, and Peanut Brittle was born (see page 67). Years later, Peanut Brittle met Popcorn, bringing crispy-crunchy Cracker Jack into the world, though it didn't start out with that kind of brand-name recognition.

In the earliest recipe I could find, dating back to 1861, caramel corn didn't even have a name.[1] It was nothing more than a footnote, a poor-man's Peanut Brittle.[2] A concession. Quite literally, in fact, as street vendors could make it on the cheap without any special equipment. It was light and fluffy enough that every ounce seemed like a lot, with a sprinkling of peanuts to justify the markup at carnivals and baseball games. Children couldn't seem to get enough, and by the 1890s, commercial caramel corn was definitively associated with prizes, and balls of caramel corn with trinkets tucked inside seemed to be a popular home-spun party favor.[3]

Sweet, sweet popcorn was big business in the late nineteenth century, with seemingly shady corporations like Popcorn Crispettes promising investors "more money than you ever dreamed of!"[4] Patents for candied popcorn were filed as early as 1884,[5] and export records show the Goodwin Brothers tried to send a shipment of sugar-coated popcorn from Philadelphia to London in 1887 (spoiler alert: It turned to mush).[6] A few years later, the U.S. government issued patents to a Utah inventor who'd developed "an apparatus for [candy] coating pop-corn" in 1892.[7]

All of that is to say, it's sheer *poppycock* that anyone would could think Americans were introduced to caramel corn by a pair of German confectioners at the 1893 Chicago World's Fair. At that point, our nation had already crunched and munched its way through thirty years of candy-coated popcorn, complete with peanuts and prizes. So far as I'm concerned, the very notion that the Rueckheim Brothers sold Cracker Jack at the Fair is pure fiddle-faddle.[8]

Not only are the Rueckheims nowhere to be found in *The Official Directory of the World's Columbian Exposition*,[9] the Fair's *Official Guide* included a subclause titled, no joke, "the Pop Corn Privilege." It declared in no uncertain terms that "the exclusive privilege of selling pop corn within the Exposition went to Messrs. Nichols and Martin."[10] A privilege that required a ten-thousand-dollar deposit, no less,[11] casting doubt on the notion Nichols and Martin might have turned a blind eye to competition.

Which isn't to say the inventors of Cracker Jack didn't play an important role in the evolution of caramel corn. Prior to Cracker Jack's official debut in 1896, caramel corn had always been sold fresh. As the Goodwin Brothers discovered, any trace of moisture or humidity turns popcorn into a soggy mess. But the Rueckheim brothers invested heavily in manufacturing equipment and advanced triple-seal packaging, efforts that turned a common candy into something truly crackerjack.[12]

As the name suggests, my caramel corn has a deep caramel flavor that's better off without molasses (which will smoke and burn at high temperatures). Aside from its rich golden hue and bittersweet flavor, true caramel drives off more water, for a super-crispy candy shell.

Sweet and salty caramel corn with peanuts and a prize.

HOMEMADE CRACKER JACK®

It may not come with a decoder ring, but homemade caramel corn is a crackerjack prize of its own: crispy popcorn and crunchy peanuts coated in a crackly caramel shell. It's real caramel, too, salty sweet and just a little buttery. I use only a handful of peanuts so each one's a happy discovery, but the amount can be doubled if you prefer.

YIELD: nine 1-cup servings │ **ACTIVE TIME:** 30 minutes │ **DOWNTIME:** 45 minutes

2 tablespoons | ¾ ounce refined coconut oil or other neutral popping oil

¼ cup | 2 ounces yellow popcorn kernels

⅓ cup | 2½ ounces water

⅓ cup | 4 ounces light corn syrup

3 tablespoons | 1½ ounces unsalted butter or refined coconut oil

1¼ cups | 9 ounces sugar

1 teaspoon Diamond Crystal kosher salt

¾ teaspoon baking soda

¾ cup | 4 ounces salted dry-roasted peanuts

Temperature Note: This recipe depends on an accurate digital thermometer, and if things go wrong you can bet the readings were off. Check your thermometer by making sure it reads 212°F in a pot of boiling water.

Key Point: Because of their unique pH, honey, sorghum, and molasses cannot be used in this recipe.

Pop the corn:
Put oil in a 5-quart stainless steel pot over medium heat. Add 4 corn kernels and wait until they pop, about 3 minutes, then remove. Add remaining kernels, cover the pot, and shake to coat with oil. Continue cooking and shaking until the noise dies down and corn has fully popped, 2 to 3 minutes. Remove from heat and let stand, uncovered, until the steam subsides, about 5 minutes.

Measure 1¾ ounces (7 rounded cups) popcorn into a gallon zip-top bag, and reserve extras for snacking. Wipe the pot clean with a paper towel; it's now a perfectly greased container for candy making! Return portioned popcorn to the pot, but keep the bag for later. Adjust oven rack to lower-middle position, heat to 170°F, and place popcorn inside to keep warm; this will ensure a thin, even candy coating.

Make the candy coating:
Combine water, corn syrup, butter, and sugar in a 3-quart stainless steel saucier over medium heat, and stir

with a fork until bubbling, about 4 minutes. Increase to medium-high, clip on a digital thermometer, and cook, *without stirring,* until the clear syrup develops a toffee color and registers 345°F, about 10 minutes.

Meanwhile, lightly grease an aluminum baking sheet. Measure salt and baking soda into one ramekin and peanuts in another. When the syrup comes to temperature, remove from heat, set thermometer aside, and stir in salt/baking soda with a heat-resistant spatula. Once the syrup begins to foam, add peanuts and stir until well coated.

Immediately pour over warm popcorn and fold until well coated. Scrape onto the prepared baking sheet, pulling chunks of popcorn into bite-sized clusters with a pair of forks. Cool until the candy shell is hard and crisp, about 45 minutes.

Transfer popcorn to the zip-top bag and store for up to 2 weeks at room temperature.

continued ↓

→ *Mix it up!*

BUTTERED PECAN: Replace peanuts with a half batch (heaping ½ cup, 3 ounces) of Brown Butter Pecans, prepared according to the recipe on page 345.

LITTLE PIGGY POPCORN: I'm allergic to pork, but I'll risk it once a year for a handful of this sweet-savory popcorn. Replace the oil and butter with an equal amount of bacon drippings and proceed as directed. In addition to the peanuts, stir in 3 ounces (1 cup) crumbled bacon.

MAPLE CINNAMON: This version isn't as delicately crisp, as maple syrup is prone to crystallization—but in a good way, delivering some big-time crunch. After measuring the freshly popped corn, toss with 1 teaspoon ground cinnamon. Replace the corn syrup with an equal amount of grade B maple syrup, but otherwise proceed as directed. The syrup will foam more than the basic recipe, but will not overflow a 3-quart pot.

WHITE CHOCOLATE BUTTERSCOTCH: This rich, mellow variation has a pronounced vanilla aroma that reminds me of butterscotch. Omit the butter. While the syrup simmers, melt 3 ounces (½ cup) finely chopped 30% white chocolate. Stir in just before the baking soda and salt.

RICE KRISPIES TREATS®

You can tell a lot about the history of a dessert from its ingredients. Some recipes require a technological breakthrough (the invention of cocoa powder, or refrigeration), but others seem almost inevitable—like replacing peanuts with popcorn in brittle (page 67) or stirring chopped chocolate into a dough (page 30). Desserts like caramel corn and chocolate chip cookies inspire my inner Indiana Jones, sending me to the library for clues to prove they're older than corporate propaganda would suggest. But certain snacks are so obviously modern their pedigrees seem undeniably cut-and-dried. Rice Krispies Treats, for example.

Their thoroughly documented existence traces directly back to Kellogg's Battle Creek test kitchen, where home economics guru/marshmallow savant Mildred Day developed the recipe in 1939. Who else would have been motivated to experiment with breakfast cereal as an ingredient in an outrageously sugary dessert? Boom! Case closed.

But as Doctor Jones would remind his students, "X never, ever marks the spot." If you dust off your fedora and dig a little deeper, there's an entire branch of American candy making forgotten by history: puffed rice confectionery. But first, a little background.

When commercial cereals debuted in the early twentieth century, a bowl of grain with cold milk was hardly an alluring breakfast compared to warm biscuits and jam, bacon and eggs, steaming pancakes topped with butter, and other hot and hearty meals. The trick was to even get consumers to try them at all. Back in 1915, Quaker Oats advertised Corn Puffs as a sprinkle for ice cream.[1] "In candy," another Quaker advertisement suggested, "use Puffed Rice in place of nuts."[2]

Perhaps because it tasted milder than "bubble grains" like puffed wheat or corn, rice became a particular favorite. In *My Candy Secrets*, author Mary Evans suggested puffed rice in recipes for children, including "Rice Crackle" and "Honey Krisp Roll."[3] Professionals took a shine to the cheap cereal as well, and by 1919, the Interstate Commerce Commission distinguished puffed rice confectionery as a category of its own.[4]

That popularity was likely driven by snowy "Puffed Rice Balls" in a crisp molasses candy modeled after caramel corn.[5] But a new variety appeared in 1921 in the thirteenth edition of *Rigby's Reliable Candy Teacher*, the professional's definitive guide. Based on corn syrup and cooked to only 242°F, Rigby's recipe would have produced a soft and sticky vanilla candy. Rigby's tome went through countless printings and nine subsequent editions before the decade was through, making it familiar to anyone working toward a bachelor's degree in a field as narrow as home

One of the very first advertisements for Rice Krispies Marshmallow Squares, printed in 1941.

economics. Like, say . . . Mildred Day, who graduated from Iowa State University in 1928.

Even if she wasn't familiar with old man Rigby, she certainly would have been familiar with the crispy rice treats made by tens of thousands of American confectioners. What made Mildred's recipe so remarkable was that it produced the same chewy/crispy results with only three ingredients: marshmallows, cereal, and butter. By pressing the candy into a pan so it could be cut with a knife, Mildred also skipped the messy process of forming the puffed rice balls by hand.

Mildred's awkwardly named "Rice Krispies Marshmallow Squares" debuted in 1939 at a Kellogg's-sponsored bake sale for the Campfire Girls,[6] pint-sized patrons of the marshmallow arts. Kellogg's ran the recipe in Battle Creek area newspapers the following year, and it must have been a hit.[7] In 1941, the company began printing the recipe right on the cereal box.

While I've yet to crack the code for puffed rice at home, jet-puffed marshmallows are easily replaced. With made-from-scratch marshmallow creme, Homemade Rice Krispies Treats® have a far more mellow sweetness, and an all-natural vanilla flavor that can't be beat.

Treat yourself to the creamiest,
chewiest, gooiest treats in town
(see recipe page 316).

HOMEMADE RICE KRISPIES TREATS®

With DIY marshmallow creme, my Homemade Rice Krispies Treats are truly made from scratch, with a balanced flavor that's rich and intensely vanilla. They're buttery, crisp, and chewy, everything I loved about the childhood classic, but fresh in a way bagged marshmallows can never capture. Homemade creme allows more opportunities for customization too; be sure to check out the variations. *See photo on page 315.*

YIELD: twelve 3-inch squares | **ACTIVE TIME:** 30 minutes | **DOWNTIME:** 1-hour rest

11 cups | 11 ounces Rice Krispies® cereal

2 envelopes (4½ teaspoons | ½ ounce) unflavored gelatin powder

¼ cup | 2 ounces cool water to bloom the gelatin

1 tablespoon vanilla extract

½ cup | 4 ounces water for the sugar syrup

1 cup | 12 ounces light corn syrup

2¼ cups | 16 ounces sugar

1 teaspoon Diamond Crystal kosher salt (half as much if iodized)

1 stick | 4 ounces unsalted butter, melted

Temperature Note: The creme will be thick and tough when cooked above 250°F, sticky and gooey if not cooled to 212°F, or obnoxiously thick if cooled below 205°F. Avoid these problems with an accurate digital thermometer, which should register 212°F in a pot of boiling water.

Key Point: In winter months, the hot syrup may harden in the bottom of a chilly mixing bowl. Warm the bowl in hot water to avoid this problem, and dry well before use.

Adjust oven rack to lower-middle position and preheat to 175°F. Generously grease a 5-quart bowl, pot, or roasting pan, add cereal, and place in the oven to keep warm.

In a small bowl, mix gelatin, 2 ounces (¼ cup) cool water, and vanilla with a fork. Combine remaining 4 ounces (½ cup) water, corn syrup, sugar, and salt in a 3-quart stainless steel pot over medium heat. Stir with a fork until bubbling, about 8 minutes, then increase to medium-high. Clip on a digital thermometer and cook *without stirring* until the clear syrup registers 250°F, about 6 minutes.

Transfer thermometer to the bowl of a stand mixer and pour in the hot syrup all at once, scraping the pot with a heat-resistant spatula. Cool to exactly 212°F, about 8 minutes, then add gelatin. With the whisk attachment, mix on low speed to combine, then increase to medium-high

and whip until syrup is thick, snowy white, roughly tripled in volume, and beginning to ball up around the whisk, about 5 minutes. Meanwhile, grease a 9-by-13-inch aluminum baking pan.

When the creme is thick, reduce speed to low, add melted butter, and return to medium-high for a few seconds more. Scrape the creamy mixture over the warm cereal and fold with a greased spatula to coat. Transfer to the prepared pan and gently press into an even layer, taking care not to crush the cereal. Cover with foil and let stand at room temperature until firm, about 1 hour.

To serve, cut only as many portions as needed (each cut opens countless grains of rice, speeding the staling process). Store leftovers tightly wrapped in plastic for up to 3 days at room temperature or for up to a week in the fridge.

→ *Mix it up!*

APPLE PIE: With warm spices to offset the tart flavor of fresh apple cider, this variation is perfect for fall. Toss the cereal with 2 teaspoons ground ginger, 4 teaspoons cinnamon, 1 teaspoon grated nutmeg, and ½ teaspoon ground cloves. Instead of water, bloom the gelatin in 2 ounces (¼ cup) unsweetened apple cider. Prepare the syrup in a 5-quart pot with 12 ounces (1½ cups) cider in place of the water, but otherwise proceed as directed.

BROWN BUTTER: Increase the butter to 8 ounces (2 sticks) and melt in a 2-quart stainless steel saucier over medium-low heat. Increase to medium and simmer, stirring with a heat-resistant spatula while the butter hisses and pops. Continue cooking and stirring, scraping up any brown bits that form in the bottom of the pan, until the butter is golden yellow and perfectly silent. Pour into a Pyrex measuring cup, along with all the toasty brown bits, and drizzle into the marshmallow creme in place of plain butter.

COCONUT: Lightly caramelized coconut milk gives this variation a uniquely toasty, tropical flare. Toss the cereal with 4 ounces (1 cup) shredded unsweetened coconut. Replace the water throughout the recipe with unsweetened full-fat coconut milk, and prepare the syrup in a 5-quart pot to allow for foaming. To amp up the coconut flavor, add 1 teaspoon coconut extract along with the vanilla.

MALTED MILK: Reduce the corn syrup to 6 ounces (½ cup) and combine with 6 ounces (½ cup) barley malt syrup in a 5-quart pot. Decrease the kosher salt to ¾ teaspoon, and toss 4 ounces (1 cup) malted milk powder with the cereal at the last minute, just before adding the marshmallow creme. *This version is not gluten-free.*

PEANUT BUTTER HONEY: Reduce corn syrup to 8 ounces (⅔ cup), combined with 4 ounces (⅓ cup) honey in a 5-quart pot. Omit the butter, replacing it with up to 8 ounces (1 cup) creamy peanut butter.

ULTIMATE CHOCOLATE: Add chocolate every step of the way, or pick and choose which options work for you. First, toss the dry cereal with 1 ounce (⅓ cup) Dutch-process cocoa powder, such as Cacao Barry Extra Brute. Second, bloom the gelatin in an equal amount of crème de cacao. Third, melt 2 ounces (⅓ cup) finely chopped 72% dark chocolate with the butter. Finally, sprinkle 1 ounce (shy ¼ cup) cocoa nibs over the treats before covering with foil.

HEATH® TOFFEE

America's favorite toffee has a name that evokes the British countryside and a package proclaiming "Finest Quality English Toffee." The jolly good vibe rolling off one Heath advertisement in 1935 virtually demanded that readers imagine the cultured voice of an English butler. "I say there, have you tried our new, delicious English Toffee Ice Cream?"[1]

For nearly a hundred years, that Anglo aura has obscured the decidedly Midwestern heritage of a candy company founded in Robison, Illinois. The Heath brothers, Bayard and Everett, came by their family name honestly enough, and in 1914 their business was as all-American as they come—a small soda fountain and candy parlor.

How they got into the toffee business, and why it had to be "English," is the legacy of a candy parlor that had opened in Halifax some twenty-five years earlier. In 1890, Violet Taylor was a confectioner's apprentice engaged to John Mackintosh, who worked at a cotton mill.[2] Days after their wedding, the two opened a toffee shop together.[3] At the time, toffee was little more than boiled molasses, very hard and crunchy—hence the name (pronounced "toughy" by the Brits[4]). Violet's toffee was unusual, rich with butter in the American style, which made it more tender.[5] John saw to it that the neighborhood was plastered with advertisements, which gave his competitors a chuckle; toffee was small potatoes compared to the more lavish confections of the day.

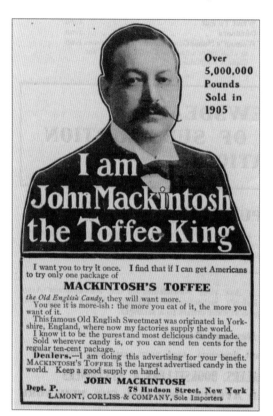

Over 5,000,000 Pounds Sold in 1905

I am John Mackintosh the Toffee King

I want you to try it once.   I find that if I can get Americans to try only one package of

MACKINTOSH'S TOFFEE

the Old English Candy, they will want more.
You see it is more-ish: the more you eat of it, the more you want of it.
This famous Old English Sweetmeat was originated in Yorkshire, England, where now my factories supply the world.
I know it to be the purest and most delicious candy made.
Sold wherever candy is, or you can send ten cents for the regular ten-cent package.
Dealers.—I am doing this advertising for your benefit. MACKINTOSH'S TOFFEE is the largest advertised candy in the world. Keep a good supply on hand.

JOHN MACKINTOSH
Dept. P.   78 Hudson Street, New York
LAMONT, CORLISS & COMPANY, Sole Importers

Though called butterscotch in America, toffee became the term of choice thanks to the influence of English candy makers.

But the combination of persistent marketing and a truly top-notch toffee paid off; in four years, the company had moved to a manufacturing warehouse, and then to a proper factory five years after that. In 1904, John traveled to America to further the business of "Mackintosh Toffee" overseas.[6] He landed in New York with a stiff upper lip, playing the stereotypical Englishman shtick hard, donning an ascot and all but twirling his mustache in advertisements styled as "royal decrees" from the King of Toffee.[7] Thing was, his would-be subjects had no idea what he was talking about. In a classic case of tomato/tomahto, our Yankee twang had morphed toffee to *taffy*.[8]

Adding to the confusion, American confectioners sold two different sorts: pulled taffy and butterscotch taffy.[9] The former was soft and chewy, what's known as saltwater taffy today, and the latter was rich and tender-crisp—what we'd consider toffee. Butterscotch "taffy" generally started with white sugar and butter, boiled to about 300°F, the poured onto a slab and "scotched" into pieces[10]—hence the name (the 1857 edition of *Webster's Dictionary* defines *scotch* as a "shallow cut or incision"[11]). That meant butterscotch taffy stopped cooking some forty-five degrees before the sugar could even start to caramelize, so its flavor and golden color essentially came from brown butter.

Instead of explaining what "English toffee" actually was (butterscotch taffy made with molasses),

Mackintosh advertisements dealt in the abstract. They called toffee an "Olde English" tradition, a restorative fuel, a nourishment as "wholesome as bread" and "as pure as the crystal spring." In some markets, the confusion was so great that folks thought it must be *coffee* and tried dissolving it in hot water.[12]

So despite tremendous financial investment, outlets in most major cities, lavish advertising, and a candy well suited to American tastes, toffee tanked. John Mackintosh shuttered his New Jersey factory less than four years after it opened, cutting his losses and returning to his business with Violet in England. It wasn't that Mackintosh Toffee failed to pique interest, only that in the days before television and radio, it was a very slow burn.[13] After five years spent priming the market, the Toffee King simply relinquished his crown too soon. That left American confectioners scrambling to fill a vacuum of power in the candy kingdom, with consumer interest in English toffee at an all-time high.[14]

All across America, butterscotch taffy was being abandoned in favor of English toffee—in name, at least. In 1910, the Wieda Bakery in Hutchinson, Kansas, advertised "Butterscotch—the real thing." But they'd completely changed their tune by 1912, proclaiming, "The English beat us a mile on Toffees. Try them and be convinced. We make them the old English way!"[15] Butterscotch taffy was out, and English toffee was in. Or, as Peggy Pan's candy shop put it in 1920, "English Toffee—ten times better than butterscotch."[16]

Which brings us back to the Brothers Heath.[17] Their business had grown from an ice cream and candy parlor to include a small dairy to supply their needs. Soon they were churning their own butter, and by 1921, they were operating a full-fledged ice cream factory too.[18] With the market for English toffee still booming, the brothers put their dapper name to good use as a brand: "Heath English Toffee."[19]

Some of my earliest food memories revolve around English toffee, which was the secret ingredient in my grandmother's everything-but-the-kitchen-sink oatmeal–chocolate chip cookies. Mine too, until I noticed the all-caps declaration on the bag: ARTIFICIALLY FLAVORED. Fortunately, toffee is incredibly easy to make at home, particularly if you replace the butter with cream. Traditional recipes call for equal parts sugar and butter, which separates into layers of water and fat. That can be a real problem for toffee—if the water's simmered off too quickly, the emulsion of sugar and fat will break. Worst-case scenario, you'll wind up with a lump of toffee swimming in a lake of clarified butter. More commonly, this manifests itself in slabs of toffee coated with a greasy film.

But cream is homogenized, producing a more stable emulsion. Even better, it contains a higher percentage of lactose, resulting in a deeper "butterscotch" flavor via Maillard browning. By that same token, a higher percentage of milk solids makes the toffee itself more stable, helping it retain its shape in the oven. Did somebody say toffee chip cookies?

HOMEMADE HEATH® TOFFEE BITS

Historically, butterscotch was simply the American name for toffee—the crunchy "English" candy made famous by Heath. Its toasty flavor came from brown butter, or more specifically, the browning of its lactose (a type of milk sugar). As it turns out, cream is a far richer source of lactose, making it a more flavorful foundation for this classic candy.

YIELD: 13 ounces (about 2¼ cups) | **ACTIVE TIME:** about 20 minutes | **DOWNTIME:** 45 minutes to cool

1 vanilla bean

1 cup | 7 ounces sugar

1⅓ cups | 11 ounces heavy cream

½ teaspoon Diamond Crystal kosher salt

Temperature Note: If cooked below 290°F, the toffee will not crisp as it should. With experience, toffee is easily judged by color alone, but first timers will appreciate the accuracy of a digital thermometer.

Key Point: Some brands of kosher salt include an anticaking agent called yellow prussiate of soda, aka sodium ferrocyanide, that interferes with crystallization, causing the toffee to crumble apart. Before getting started, be sure your salt is pure!

Lightly grease an aluminum baking sheet.

Split the vanilla bean lengthwise with a paring knife, scrape the seeds from each half, and blend into the sugar (reserve pod for another project). Combine vanilla-sugar, cream, and salt in a 3-quart stainless steel saucier over medium heat and stir with a fork until foamy, about 6 minutes.

Discard the fork, which may harbor sugar crystals, and stir with a heat-resistant spatula until the airy foam reduces to a thick ivory syrup, about 8 minutes. Continue stirring, scraping all along the edges, until the molten candy is light brown, another 5 minutes, or roughly 295°F. A digital thermometer is useful only to spot-check the toffee, as clip-on thermometers make scraping a chore.

Immediately pour onto the prepared baking sheet and spread into a ¼-inch layer. Cool until no trace of warmth remains, then break or chop into bite-sized pieces. Store in an airtight container for up to 6 months at room temperature; with a packet of food-grade desiccant (available online), the toffee will keep for up to a year.

→ Mix it up!

BACON TOFFEE: Reduce the cream to 8 ounces (1 cup) and add 1 ounce (2 tablespoons) bacon fat.

BUTTERSCOTCH SAUCE: Prepare the syrup as directed, but add 8 ounces (1 cup) cold water when it hits 285°F. The toffee will seize into a hard lump, but continue cooking and stirring until smooth, about 220°F. Pour the sauce into a wide-mouth pint jar, seal, and refrigerate until lusciously thick, at least 4 hours, or up to 2 months. Makes 1⅔ cups, about 16 ounces.

CHOCOLATE-COVERED TOFFEE BARS: Make a double batch of toffee in a 4-quart pot according to the directions, and spread over a greased baking sheet in the same way. While it cools, temper 12 ounces (2 cups roughly chopped) dark or milk chocolate according to the directions on page 293. Spread half the tempered chocolate over the toffee and refrigerate until hard; about 2 minutes. Flip the toffee and coat the other side. If you like, scatter 4 ounces (¾ cup roughly chopped) toasted pecans or other nuts on top. Refrigerate until hard, then break into pieces for snacking. Store in an airtight container up to 3 months in the fridge; serve at room temperature.

COCOA NIB CRUNCH: I don't know what's so addictive about the combination, but I'm inclined to sprinkle this mix of toasty-sweet toffee, bitter cocoa nibs, and crunchy graham crackers over just about every dessert. Combine 5½ ounces (1 cup) finely crushed Butterscotch Toffee, 4½ ounces (1 cup) Crispy Whole Wheat Graham Cracker crumbs (page 202), and 1¼ ounces (¼ cup) cocoa nibs in a wide-mouth quart jar and shake to mix. Store in the refrigerator for up to 3 months.

VEGAN TOFFEE: In place of the cream, use one 13.5-ounce can unsweetened full-fat coconut milk, and cook the toffee a few minutes longer, to about 340°F.

SPRINKLES

Despite what Mary Poppins would have you believe, a spoonful of sugar does not, in fact, make the medicine go down in the most delightful way. Its finely granulated crystals coat the tongue, sucking up every trace of moisture and making it more difficult to swallow. So when pharmacists in the early nineteenth century needed to help patients with difficult medicines, they sprang for the good stuff, a specialized grade of sugar called *nonpareil*.[1]

These tiny beads of sugar let pharmacists stretch a single drop of dangerously potent medicine (think opium or heroin) into a week's supply, allowing customers to safely administer the medicine at home.[2] Yes, one spoonful at a time. And nonpareils, as any sprinkle lover knows, are absolutely delightful by the spoonful.

Only certain types of confectioners could manufacture nonpareils,[3] which required specialized equipment for "pan work," tumbling sugar crystals with glucose in big steam-heated drums.[4] Like concrete mixers, these kept the sugar in constant motion, polishing each crystal into a tiny sphere that slowly grew in size with every addition of glucose.

Nonpareils turned out so itty bitty that pharmacists measured them by the *grain*, a unit of sixty-four milligrams.[5] Common one-grain nonpareils measured 437 per ounce, while an ounce of sixteenth-grain nonpareils might contain as many as seven thousand individual spheres.[6] With continued dredging, confectioners could eventually produced big five-grain *dragées*.[7]

Pastry chefs paid a premium for dragées coated in gold or silver, but pharmacists preferred their nonpareils by the "100s and 1000s," as the smaller sizes were known.[8] Some confectioners manufactured these nonpareils exclusively for the "drug trade,"[9] while others sold them in bulk for resale as a private-label candy,[10] which folks purchased to decorate birthday cakes and other festive desserts.[11]

As sugar pellets fell out of favor with modern medicine in the late 1800s,[12] confectionery firms that had once relied on pharmaceutical sales entered the mainstream candy market in force,[13] resulting in a profusion of whimsical names: cachous, comfits, mites, pellets, shot goods, rifle balls, sweetmeats, and sugar plums (maddeningly, many of these names also applied to older, more traditional candies).[14]

The widespread availability of such festive candies made them a popular ingredient in American kitchens and cookbooks at the turn of the twentieth century.[15] To avoid confusion, recipes abandoned capricious names in favor of hyperspecific descriptions: "sugar pellets the size of poppy seeds," "the tiny colored candies that you put on birthday cakes," or "those tiny colored candies so dear to the heart of a child."[16]

Popular authors like Janet McKenzie Hill fell back on the pharmaceutical term 100s and 1000s,[17] but the very act of *sprinkling* would ultimately unify the mishmash of terms. Throughout the 1920s and '30s, sprinkles embellished cakes and cookies galore.[18] Rationing during World War II sidelined pure-sugar sprinkles,[19] but when the war was over, rainbow-colored sugar burst back onto the scene like a flurry of celebratory confetti.[20]

Because the hot "pan work" needed for nonpareils would have melted cocoa butter, food historians say chocolate sprinkles didn't come along until Dutch manufacturer Venz introduced *hagelslag* in 1936.[21] But according to my research, the first chocolate sprinkles were actually manufactured in Brooklyn around 1915, when Rockwood & Company began advertising "Vanilla Chocolate Decorettes."[22] These came in gorgeous blue tins illustrated with a dish of ice cream covered in chocolate sprinkles, short and slender little batons exactly like the chocolate sprinkles we know today.

Whether rainbow or chocolate, homemade sprinkles have a power like no other. I've heard grown men gasp at the sight of them, totally gobsmacked that anything so utterly commercial could be made by hand. My friends, who should be numbed to the variety of things I'm willing to make by hand, still flip out whenever I present them a besprinkled birthday cake—even when they've seen my "100s and 1000s" a hundred and thousand times before.

Homemade sprinkles are all the more magical because they taste as good as they look. Chocolate sprinkles taste like real chocolate, and rainbow sprinkles can be doctored with any sort of extract, giving desserts a burst of cherry, blueberry, coconut, lemon, lime, or any other rainbow of flavors. They're a little time-consuming, but well worth the effort—a single batch will last the whole year through.

CHOCOLATE SPRINKLES

The jagged spikes and shards of these earthy cocoa sprinkles have an undeniably rustic charm, adding whimsy and crunch to any dessert. They have a deeper chocolate flavor than the waxy "jimmies" sold in stores, so while two cups should technically be a lifetime supply, you may find yourself sprinkling more often.

YIELD: 2 cups | **ACTIVE TIME:** 1 hour | **DOWNTIME:** 36-hour rest

1¾ cups | 7 ounces organic powdered sugar, sifted

½ cup | 1½ ounces Dutch-process cocoa powder, such as Cacao Barry Extra Brute

3 tablespoons | 1½ ounces crème de cacao or water

2 teaspoons vanilla extract

¼ teaspoon espresso powder, such as Medaglia d'Oro

⅛ teaspoon Diamond Crystal kosher salt (half as much if iodized)

½ teaspoon ground spices or 1 teaspoon of your favorite extract (optional)

½ teaspoon water if needed

Make the parchment cones:
Fold two 15-inch squares of parchment in half on the diagonal, then cut along the crease to make 4 triangles. Form a cone with one triangle by curling the short side toward the center, wrapping the long side around, and sliding the paper until it rolls tight. Tuck the remaining parchment "tail" into the cone, folding to secure. Repeat with the remaining parchment, and stand each cone upright in a small drinking glass.

Make the Sprinkles:
Sift powdered sugar and cocoa into the bowl of a stand mixer fitted with a paddle attachment (if using cup measures, spoon the sugar and cocoa into the cups and level with a knife before sifting). Add crème de cacao, vanilla, espresso powder, and salt, plus any additional flavoring, and mix on low speed to moisten. Increase to medium and beat until the thick paste is creamy and smooth like peanut butter, about 5 minutes. Halfway through, pause to scrape the bowl and beater with a flexible spatula. If the paste seems too thick, beat in the water.

Divide the paste among the parchment cones and fold the top edges down to secure. Snip ⅛ inch from the tip of one cone and squeeze from the top to pipe thin, tight rows of chocolate down the length of a parchment-lined baking sheet (do not use wax paper). Repeat with the remaining cones, pausing whenever you like; the paste will keep for up to 4 hours in the parchment. Dry the sprinkles at room temperature until firm and crisp, about 36 hours.

Gather the "sticks" into bundles and roughly chop. Store for up to a year in an airtight container at room temperature.

RAINBOW SPRINKLES

Sprinkles don't just look like confetti, they *are* confetti, the colorful *confections* originally thrown at parades. Fortunately, homemade sprinkles don't taste like paper. Hop online and you'll find an endless array of gel paste colors and all sorts of potent extracts. My favorite source is Silver Cloud Estate, which offers everything from Key lime to banana and acai, allowing me to blend up a jubilant rainbow of tutti-frutti sprinkles. *See photo on page 326.*

YIELD: 1½ cups (10 ounces) | **ACTIVE TIME:** 1 hour | **DOWNTIME:** 36-hour rest

2¼ cups | 9 ounces organic powdered sugar, sifted

½ teaspoon Diamond Crystal kosher salt (half as much if iodized)

1 large egg white (about 1¼ ounces)

1 teaspoon vanilla extract

1 teaspoon water

Assorted food colorings, preferably gel paste

Assorted extracts

Make the paste:

Fill a 3-quart pot with 1 inch of water and place over medium heat; if the pot is too wide to cradle the bowl of a stand mixer, make a "booster seat" with a long strip of foil crumpled into a ring. In the mixer bowl, combine 8 ounces (2 cups) powdered sugar with egg white, salt, and vanilla, stirring to form a smooth paste. Place over the steamy water, and stir constantly with a flexible spatula until hot, 150°F on a digital thermometer.

Transfer to the mixer stand and beat on medium-low speed with a paddle attachment, adding the remaining 1 ounce (¼ cup) powdered sugar a little at a time. Continue mixing until the paste is fluffy and smooth, about 3 minutes. If necessary, add a few drops of water, until the paste has a soft, pipeable consistency, like peanut butter.

Flavor and form the sprinkles:

Divide the paste among as many bowls as you'd like colors/flavors, covering each tightly with plastic. One by one, stir a few drops of gel paste and extract into each, then transfer to a parchment cone (see page 324), folding the top edge down to secure.

Snip ⅛ inch from the tip of one cone, and squeeze from the top to pipe thin, tight rows of sugar-paste down the length of a parchment-lined baking sheet (do not use wax paper). Repeat with the remaining cones, pausing whenever you like; the paste will keep for up to 4 hours in the parchment cones. Dry the sprinkles at room temperature until firm and crisp, up to 36 hours.

Gather the "sticks" into bundles and roughly chop. Store for up to a year in an airtight container at room temperature.

continued ↓

Taste the rainbow: cherry, orange, banana, vanilla, key lime, strawberry, and blueberry sprinkles (recipe page 325).

→ *Mix it up!*

CONFETTI CAKE: Quite possibly the most joyful child's birthday cake imaginable. Gently fold 1½ ounces (⅓ heaping cup) Rainbow Sprinkles into a batch of White Mountain Layer Cake batter (page 110). Bake and cool as directed. This is especially pretty when frosted with Cherry Almond Buttercream (page 115).

VANILLA MINT: Split and scrape a vanilla bean and add the seeds to the powdered sugar along with ¼ teaspoon peppermint extract.

Part III

Classic American Ice Cream

RAINBO
SPRANK

*Philadelphia-Style Strawberry
(page 340), Devil's Food
Chocolate (page 338), and
Double-Vanilla (page 334) ice
creams, with homemade Rainbow
Sprinkles (page 325).*

Chapter 9

SCOOPS & FOUNTAIN SPECIALS

Though perhaps considered a retro throwback today, ice cream sodas, floats, and sundaes were remarkably modern inventions. These fizzy, festive frozen treats are among my favorites to make at home because they're so hard to procure anywhere else.

ICE CREAM SALOONS

SODA SHOP CLASSICS like ice cream floats and hot fudge sundaes call to mind twirling poodle skirts and doo-wop on the jukebox, but scenes like that marked the end of an era that had begun before the Civil War. You'd need an entire book to tell the tale, but the abridged edition starts in a saloon. Not the seedy world of gunslingers, whiskey, and raucous card games, but the elegant parlors within a nineteenth-century fruit and ice cream saloon.

Eighteen-year-old Sam Clemens moved to New York City in 1853, where he briefly worked as a printer.[1] In a letter to Mom, he described a trip to "one of the finest fruit saloons in the world," a "glittering hall" filled with countless delicacies. It was by no means his first time in a saloon; George Murray had established an ice cream saloon in his hometown of Hannibal, Missouri, back in 1847.[2] Nor would it be his last; as Mark Twain, Sam would later frequent (and fictionalize) a San Francisco saloon famous for its strawberries and champagne.

My point isn't Mark Twain's fondness for saloons, but their prevalence in nineteenth-century life. Whether on the East or West Coast or some tiny town in between, you could count on a nearby saloon for novelties like a fresh mango or scoop of chocolate ice cream. These treats weren't meant to be eaten on the go, but savored, and saloons offered an environment befitting the luxury: sparkling cut-glass parfait dishes, long silver spoons, and marble tabletops.

Before the convenience of electric refrigeration,[3] saloons relied on ice cream cabinets to keep things cold.[4] These handsome wooden chests, which held canisters of ice cream and tubs of fruit packed in salt and ice, required constant attention.[5] Clerks had to drain off the melted water, chip in fresh ice, adjust the salt levels, scrub mold from the interior panels, and wash away any crusty buildup that might fall into the ice cream pails.

Considering the financial investment and daily upkeep, to say nothing of hand-churning the ice cream itself, nobody could afford to keep oddball options on ice when chocolate, strawberry, and vanilla were guaranteed to sell. These are still three of America's favorite flavors, and I can't imagine a summer without them.

Most ice cream recipes require you to chill the custard base overnight, but I've discovered this precaution doesn't make a difference with my formulas. While it's true the base will thicken more if "aged" overnight, skipping that step only affects the ice cream's potential volume by a subtle degree. So long as the base is nice and cold, it churns up just as creamy and smooth as one that's been chilled overnight.

Truth be told, nineteenth-century ice creams weren't very fluffy or light. That style of American ice cream wouldn't take hold until the twentieth century, when manufacturers began pumping their ice creams full of air. While I'm actually quite fond of that aerated texture, it's nearly impossible to achieve at home, so my ice creams tend to be a little more like gelato, creamy and thick.

My approach to flavor is decidedly modern, with an intensity not found in the more subtle flavors of the past. For vanilla, I double up with beans and extract, resulting in a flavor that's both aromatic and deep. With chocolate, I use fewer eggs to offset the richness of cocoa butter, and a higher ratio of sugar to keep it creamy and soft, despite a whopping six ounces of chocolate and cocoa. Finally, my strawberry ice cream is made without any eggs at all, thickened with nothing but a homemade strawberry reduction for a taste like pure berries and cream.

ALL ABOUT DAIRY

You've no doubt heard the debate over conventional versus organic ingredients, whether at the grocery store or the farmers' market, but you probably haven't heard anything about what these labels mean in terms of ice cream (every good debate should first be framed in terms of ice cream). Back in the nineteenth century, American farmers didn't have pesticides, growth hormones, antibiotics, or the equipment necessary for pasteurization and homogenization. You and I have to make a special effort to buy milk, cream, and eggs produced under such conditions today, but what we call "organic" was once the only option.

Organic milk and cream have a robust flavor that varies over the course of the year, as the cow's diet shifts from grass to corn and hay, depending on the season. Without the heat of pasteurization or pressurized homogenization (techniques introduced at the turn of the twentieth century), milk retained these delicate flavors after bottling, and the cream rose to the top. And chickens (allowed to feed on bugs, grass, leaves, fallen apples, and whatever else they might scavenge) laid flavorful eggs with vibrantly yellow yolks.

That meant nineteenth-century ice cream, vanilla in particular, had a stronger custard flavor and a rich, golden hue, as well as a subtle aroma of corn or grass from the milk. Because it was nonhomogenized, the natural dairy fat froze into larger ice crystals that felt slightly grainy on the tongue; on the flip side, they melted more slowly for a longer-lasting finish. These factors added complexity to ice cream, which we can re-create with low-temperature-pasteurized, nonhomogenized, organic dairy, and free-range eggs.

While pasteurization was a boon for food safety in the twentieth century, the extremely high temperatures obliterated dairy's natural flavor and seasonal variation. By blasting milk through a pressurized chamber, homogenization forced the dairy fat into suspension, not only preventing the cream from rising to the top but also improving the milk's shelf life. Caged, feed-raised chickens allowed for mass production and lower pricing, but their strict diet resulted in egg yolks with less flavor and color.

Conventional milk, cream, and eggs bring little flavor of their own to ice cream, emphasizing the other ingredients—vanilla feels more intense, strawberry seems fruity and fresh, chocolate tastes pure. Homogenized dairy makes for silkier ice cream, as the crystals of frozen fat are too small to detect, melting instantaneously on the tongue. Some experience this as refreshing, while others miss the tongue-coating richness.

Instead of considering ice cream made with organic or conventional ingredients in terms of "good" and "bad," I find it more useful to consider how these ingredients can help or hinder certain flavors. Think of organic as the embodiment of French vanilla ice cream: eggy, rich, and complex. Think of conventional like soft serve: creamy, light, and simple. I find that organic ingredients add depth to earthy flavors like cinnamon and pecan but distract from the refreshing qualities of orange and mint. Likewise, conventional ingredients allow delicate ice creams like lavender or lemongrass to shine but don't add enough *oomph* when paired with butterscotch or malt.

You may reach a different set of conclusions after experimenting for yourself, but being aware of potential differences will help you choose the right ingredients for whatever ice cream you have in mind.

DOUBLE-VANILLA ICE CREAM

Whether atop a warm brownie or in a dish on its own, nothing compares to a scoop of pure vanilla ice cream. My version is rich but light, as a slightly higher proportion of cream allows it to gain more air as it churns. Typically vanilla beans and extract are an either/or proposition, but working in tandem, they deliver an earthy yet aromatic flavor. All the more so when you choose a vanilla bean from Mexico, Tahiti, or Tonga to complement the distinctive taste of classic (Madagascar) vanilla extract. *See photo on page 330.*

YIELD: about 1 quart | **ACTIVE TIME:** about 30 minutes | **DOWNTIME:** 30-minute steep, plus 4-hour refrigeration

1¼ cups | 10 ounces heavy cream

1 cup | 8 ounces whole milk

1 vanilla bean

¾ cup plus 2 tablespoon | 6 ounces sugar

7 large egg yolks (shy ½ cup | 4½ ounces)

½ teaspoon Diamond Crystal kosher salt (half as much if iodized)

1 tablespoon vanilla extract, bourbon, or rum

Is this safe for kids? Given that vanilla extract itself is 70 proof, replacing a single tablespoon with an equal amount of rum or Triple Sec won't turn your ice cream into a Happy Hour special. Even if you grab a high-proof whiskey, 1/2 ounce divided among eight servings leaves mere drops to contend with. If you abstain from alcohol, simply omit the vanilla and/or liquor and let your ice cream stand for a few minutes at room temperature before scooping.

Steep the dairy:
In a 3-quart stainless steel saucier, bring cream and milk to a simmer over medium heat. Split the vanilla bean lengthwise with a paring knife and add to dairy. When it begins to bubble, turn off the heat and cover tightly. Steep 30 minutes, or cool to room temperature and refrigerate for up to 24 hours.

Make the ice cream base:
Whisk sugar, yolks, and salt in a medium bowl. Return dairy to a simmer; remove the vanilla pod and reserve. Ladle ½ cup of hot dairy into the yolks, whisk to combine, then repeat with a second and third ladleful. Pour warmed eggs into the pot and cook over medium-low heat, stirring constantly with a flexible spatula until steaming hot. Strain through a fine-mesh sieve into a large bowl. Stir in the vanilla extract and add vanilla bean. Cool to room temperature (using an ice bath, if you prefer) and refrigerate until very cold, at least 4 hours, or up to one week.

Finish the ice cream:
Scrape the flavorful pulp inside the vanilla pod back into the ice cream base and discard the pod. Churn according to the manufacturer's directions until fluffy and light; if your machine has an open top, cover with an inverted cake pan to keep it cold as it churns. Meanwhile, place a flexible spatula and quart container (an empty yogurt tub works great) in the freezer.

Enjoy freshly churned ice cream as "soft serve," or scrape it into the chilled container. Press a sheet of plastic against the ice cream to minimize risk of freezer burn, and seal the container. Freeze until firm enough to scoop, about 12 hours, or up to 3 weeks.

TROUBLESHOOTING
When ice cream fails to churn up light, the most likely culprits are an insufficiently chilled canister or imbalanced ingredients from simple mismeasurement, substitution, or mathematical errors when halving or doubling a recipe.

MAKE BEN & JERRY® JEALOUS

Both dark chocolate and fresh strawberry ice cream warrant recipes of their own, but I consider almost everything else a variation on classic vanilla. By steeping the milk and cream with toasted nuts, swapping a portion of the sugar for molasses, replacing vanilla extract with a flavorful liquor, you can transform Double-Vanilla Ice Cream (page 334) into anything from Bourbon Pecan to Malted Banana.

Simply adjust the ingredients according to any of the suggestions below and proceed as directed. Especially when doubling up on variations, I recommend jotting down the "new" recipe to avoid any mix-ups.

Vanilla Variations

Vanilla extract complements everything from nuts and spices to fresh herbs and fruit, but sometimes it's fun to reach for flavored liquors instead—like the malty aroma of bourbon to play up brown sugar, or rum to coax out the tropical notes in banana.

To that end, most of the variations include the option of replacing the vanilla extract with an equal amount of liquor. Bear in mind these are just suggestions, so let your creativity (or liquor cabinet) decide what works best. If a pairing piques your interest, souvenir-sized bottles are a great way to test-drive unfamiliar liquors. When in doubt, stick with vanilla extract or vodka to keep things neutral.

Banana. Slice 1 pound (3 large) overripe bananas into ½-inch pieces (10 ounces | 2 cups sliced fruit) and steep with the vanilla bean. Once the dairy begins to simmer, turn off the heat, cover, and refrigerate overnight.

Return the dairy to a simmer, stirring occasionally to prevent scorching, and strain though a fine-mesh sieve into a medium bowl. Gently mash the bananas to release as much liquid as possible, but discard the pulp. Whisk the sugar, egg yolks, and salt together in the empty pot, then slowly whisk in the flavored dairy. Proceed as directed. *Vanilla Variation:* Bols banana liquor, bourbon, rum.

Black Tea. This works well with straight Ceylon or Assam, as well as Irish Breakfast or flavored blends like Earl Grey or Chai. After returning the vanilla-dairy to a simmer, add 3 tablespoon loose black tea. Steep off the heat for exactly 5 minutes, then strain through a fine-mesh sieve lined with cheesecloth into a medium bowl. Whisk the sugar, egg yolks, and salt together in the empty pot, then slowly whisk in the flavored dairy. Proceed as directed. *Vanilla Variation:* Madeira.

Caramelized White Chocolate. Reduce sugar to 5¼ ounces (¾ cup). Reserve 2 ounces (¼ cup) heavy cream and make a ganache. Bring it to a boil in a 1-quart stainless steel saucier, then whisk in 4 ounces (⅔ cup) finely chopped Caramelized White Chocolate (page 60). Prepare the custard as directed and whisk in the ganache just before straining. *Vanilla Variation:* Scotch.

Cinnamon. Use the overnight steeping technique described for Banana (above) with four 2¾-inch cinnamon sticks (¾ ounce). The type of cinnamon will dramatically affect the final flavor—papery sticks of Ceylon have a delicate, floral aroma, while sturdy strips of cassia pack a sharp, spicy heat. *Vanilla Variation:* Spiced rum.

Coffee. Use the overnight steeping technique described for Banana (above), with 4 ounces (½ cup) whole coffee beans, preferably dark or espresso roast. *Vanilla Variation:* Tía Maria, Kahlúa.

Corn Cob. Use the overnight steeping technique described for Banana (above) with 2 large corn cobs (reserve the kernels for another use) sliced into ½-inch rounds. *Vanilla Variation:* Cachaça, bourbon, or white whiskey.

Eggnog. Roughly chop a 2-inch piece of fresh ginger, quarter 4 whole nutmegs with a sharp chef's knife, and break a 4-inch cinnamon stick in half. Add with the vanilla bean. Once the dairy begins to simmer, turn off the heat, cover, and steep for 1 to 6 hours, or until the mix is just a little spicier than you'd typically prefer (the intensity will be diluted by sugar later on). Strain through a fine-mesh sieve and proceed as directed. Finish with ¼ teaspoon grated nutmeg. *Vanilla Variation:* Bourbon, brandy, Triple Sec.

continued ↓

Fresh Ginger. Use the overnight steeping technique described for Banana (page 335) with 1½ ounces (⅓ cup) diced peeled ginger. *Vanilla Variation:* Domaine de Canton ginger liqueur.

Gingerbread. Reduce sugar to 4½ ounces (⅔ cup). Whisk into the yolks along with 2 ounces (2½ tablespoons) molasses, 1 tablespoon ground ginger, 2 teaspoons ground cinnamon, ½ teaspoon grated nutmeg, ¼ teaspoon ground cloves, and ¼ teaspoon cracked black pepper. *Vanilla Variation:* Art in the Age SNAP.

Honey. Reduce sugar to 4½ ounces (⅔ cup). Whisk into the egg yolks along with 2 ounces (3 tablespoons) honey. *Vanilla Variation:* Bourbon, Koval Chrysanthemum.

Lemongrass. Omit the vanilla bean. Trim the root tips from 2 large stalks (4 ounces) lemongrass and discard any outer layers that feel loose or dry. Split the stalks lengthwise, chop into ¼-inch pieces, and pulse in a food processor to bruise them. Add to the dairy and steep as directed (the minced lemongrass will be strained later). *Vanilla Variation:* St-Germain.

Malt. Reduce sugar to 4½ ounces (⅔ cup). Whisk into the egg yolks along with 2 ounces (3 tablespoons) barley malt syrup and 2 ounces (½ cup) malted milk powder. *Vanilla Variation:* Bourbon, rum, Scotch.

Matcha (Green Tea). Whisk 4 teaspoons matcha into the sugar and proceed as directed. No other sort of green tea can be used. *Vanilla Variation:* Maraschino, Żubrówka.

Milk Chocolate. Reserve 3 ounces (⅓ cup) heavy cream and bring to a boil in a 1-quart stainless steel saucier, then whisk in 4 ounces (½ cup) finely chopped milk chocolate, such as Endangered Species 48%. Prepare the custard as directed and whisk in the ganache just before straining. *Vanilla Variation:* Crème de cacao.

Mint or Basil. Grind sugar with 3 ounces (3 cups loosely packed) fresh mint or basil leaves in a food processor until damp and green, like pesto (the leaves will be strained out later). *Vanilla Variation:* Crème de menthe, or for basil, gin.

It may seem like an astronomical quantity of fresh herbs, but my method keeps the flavor clean by eliminating the steeping period, which can produce a stale or dull flavor. As a bonus, this technique produces a vibrant Oscar-the-Grouch green without a drop of dye.

Orange Blossom. Omit the vanilla bean to focus on pure orange, or leave it for a Creamsicle-like flavor. In either case, whisk 1 tablespoon packed, orange zest into the egg yolks. After straining the custard, stir in ¼ teaspoon orange flower water and ¼ teaspoon orange extract. *Vanilla Variation:* Patrón Citrónge, Curaçao.

Peach Pit. Use the overnight steeping technique described for Banana (page 335) with 10 whole peach pits for a summery peach/almond flavor. *Vanilla Variation:* Amaretto, Maraschino.

Pistachio, Peanut, Pecan, Hazelnut, Black Walnut, Cashew . . . you get the idea. Use the overnight steeping technique described for Banana (page 335) with an additional 6 ounces (¾ cup) whole milk to account for what the nuts will absorb. Toast 8 ounces (2 cups) chopped nuts in a 350°F oven until fragrant but pale, about 5 minutes. *Vanilla Variation:* Rum, Dumante Verdenoce (pistachio), Praline Pecan, Frangelico (hazelnut), nocino (walnut).

Rooibos. Use the steeping technique described for Black Tea (page 335) with ¾ ounce (¼ cup) loose-leaf rooibos, steeping the dairy for 8 to 10 minutes. *Vanilla Variation:* Rum.

Star Anise. Use the overnight steeping technique described for Banana (page 335) with 8 whole star anise. *Vanilla Variation:* Jägermeister, Pernod, Art in the Age, ROOT.

Thyme Lemon. Omit the vanilla bean. Add five 6-inch sprigs of thyme and 1 tablespoon packed lemon zest to the dairy and steep as directed (the herbs and zest will be strained out later) *Vanilla Variation:* Gin, Chartreuse, Koval, Chrysanthemum, limoncello.

Toasted Rice. In a 3-quart stainless steel saucier, toast 2 ounces (¼ cup) brown Basmati rice over medium-low heat, shaking and swirling the pan to prevent the rice from burning, until the grains are fragrant and crackling hot, about 9 minutes. Add 4 ounces (½ cup) whole milk to cool the rice and account for what it will absorb. Otherwise, add the milk, cream, and vanilla bean and steep 1 hour as directed (the rice will be strained out at the end). *Vanilla Variation:* rye.

Tonka. Along with the vanilla bean, steep the dairy with a single tonka bean, finely chopped—not grated! Strain the finished ice cream base through a double-mesh sieve to remove the tonka pieces. *Vanilla Variation:* Żubrówka, cachaça.

Tonka has an elusive aromatic quality something like vanilla, but with a unique minerality. It can stand as a flavor of its own, but it pairs especially well with anything fruity or floral. Like nutmeg, tonka beans should never be consumed whole.

White Chocolate. Reduce sugar to 5¼ ounces (¾ cup). Reserve 2 ounces (¼ cup) heavy cream and bring it to a boil in a 1-quart stainless steel saucier, then whisk in 3½ ounces (⅔ cup) finely chopped white chocolate, such as Valrhona 35% Ivoire. Prepare the custard as directed and whisk in the ganache just before straining. *Vanilla Variation:* Frangelico.

DEVIL'S FOOD CHOCOLATE ICE CREAM

To give this jet-black ice cream the most intense chocolate flavor, I've taken a page from the devil's food playbook (see page 122) by splitting the recipe into a "yellow" custard base and a boiled chocolate paste. That lets me incorporate more chocolate and cocoa than the low cooking temperature of a custard could normally dissolve. A generous splash of crème de cacao thwarts chocolate's tendency to freeze like a rock, for an intensely flavored ice cream that's creamy and soft.

YIELD: about 1 quart | **ACTIVE TIME:** 45 minutes | **DOWNTIME:** 4-hour refrigeration

Ice Cream Base:

5 large egg yolks (⅓ cup | 3 ounces)

¼ cup | 2 ounces sugar

¼ teaspoon Diamond Crystal kosher salt (half as much if iodized)

1 cup | 8 ounces whole milk

Chocolate Paste:

¾ cup | 5½ ounces sugar

1 cup | 3 ounces Dutch-process cocoa powder, such as Cacao Barry Extra Brute

½ cup | 3 ounces roughly chopped 72% dark chocolate

1½ cups | 12 ounces heavy cream

1 tablespoon vanilla extract

2 tablespoons | 1 ounce crème de cacao

Make the ice cream base:
Whisk egg yolks, sugar, salt, and milk in a 3-quart stainless steel saucier over low heat and stir gently until warm, about 5 minutes. Increase to medium-low and stir until custard is slightly thickened and steaming hot, about 5 minutes more. Strain through a fine-mesh sieve into a large bowl, scraping the pot as best you can (leave the sieve in place).

To make the chocolate paste, whisk sugar and cocoa together in the same pot, then add chopped chocolate and cream. Bring to a boil over medium heat, whisking constantly until the sugar has fully dissolved and the mixture is bubbling hot. Strain into the custard, then stir in vanilla extract and crème de cacao. Cool to room temperature (using an ice bath, if you prefer) and refrigerate until cold and thick, at least 4 hours, or up to 1 week.

Finish the ice cream:
Churn according to the manufacturer's directions until the ice cream is creamy and thick. If your machine has an open top, cover with an inverted cake pan to keep it cold as it churns. Meanwhile, place a flexible spatula and quart container (an empty yogurt tub works great) in the freezer.

Enjoy freshly churned ice cream as "soft serve," or scrape it into the chilled container. Press a sheet of plastic against the ice cream to minimize risk of freezer burn, and seal the container. Freeze until firm enough to scoop, about 12 hours, or up to 3 weeks.

TROUBLESHOOTING

If you don't have crème de cacao, use neutral vodka or add a complementary note of flavor with bourbon, Triple Sec, crème de menthe, or another liqueur. Omitting the alcohol altogether will cause the ice cream to freeze more quickly, so it won't churn up to its full potential. Aside from being more dense, it will also be harder to scoop.

*As black as sin, but twice as sweet—
made from both dark chocolate and
Dutch-process cocoa powder.*

PHILADELPHIA-STYLE STRAWBERRY ICE CREAM

With this recipe, I'm able to cram two pounds of strawberries into a quart of ice cream. The trick is to toss the berries and sugar into a hot oven to rapidly extract their juice, then simmer it down into a ruby red syrup. This one-two method is faster than roasting or simmering alone, so it helps keep the flavor fresh. It also concentrates the strawberry essence by eliminating excess (icy, tasteless) water. The result is a silky, pale pink ice cream that tastes like pure strawberries and cream. *See photos on pages 330 and 342.*

YIELD: about 1 quart | **ACTIVE TIME:** 1 hour | **DOWNTIME:** 4-hour refrigeration

7 cups | 32 ounces whole strawberries, washed and drained

¾ cup | 5¼ ounces sugar

⅛ teaspoon Diamond Crystal kosher salt (half as much if iodized)

1¾ cups | 14 ounces cold heavy cream

1 tablespoon freshly squeezed lemon juice

¼ teaspoon rose water

2 teaspoons Fragoli, framboise, St-Germain, or vodka

Key Point: The strawberry syrup may bubble out of a baking dish smaller than 7-by-11 inches or roast too quickly in one that is larger than 9-by-13 inches or made of metal.

Roast and concentrate the fruit:
Adjust oven rack to middle position and preheat to 375°F. Slice off the strawberries' leafy caps, removing as little fruit as possible. Halve the berries, place in a 9-by-13-inch glass or ceramic baking dish, then stir in sugar and salt.

Roast, stirring once or twice along the way, until the berries are fork-tender and swimming in bright red juice, about 35 minutes. Strain through a double-mesh sieve into a 3-quart stainless steel saucier, gently mashing the berries with a flexible spatula until only ½ cup (5 ounces) dry pulp remains; discard. Refrigerate for up to a week and use to flavor Five-Minute Muffins (page 282) or Homemade Fig Newtons®, (page 206).

Simmer strawberry juice over medium heat, scraping the pot with a heat-resistant spatula until thick, syrupy, and reduced to 1⅔ cups (16 ounces), about 15 minutes. Whisk in cream, lemon juice, rose water, and liqueur. Cover and refrigerate until very cold, at least 4 hours, or up to 1 week.

Finish the ice cream:
Churn according to the manufacturer's directions until the ice cream is fluffy and light. If your machine has an open top, cover with an inverted cake pan to keep it cold as it churns. Meanwhile, place a flexible spatula and quart container (an empty yogurt tub works great) in the freezer.

Enjoy freshly churned ice cream as "soft serve," or scrape it into the chilled container. Press a sheet of plastic against the ice cream to minimize risk of freezer burn and seal. Freeze until firm enough to scoop, about 12 hours, or up to 3 weeks.

→ *Mix it up!*

BLACKBERRY ICE CREAM: When blackberries are in season, tart but not bitter in the least, this brightly colored variation is as refreshing as sorbet. Start with 40 ounces (8 cups) fresh blackberries; roast and strain as directed, discarding 10 ounces (1 heaping cup) seedy pulp. Simmer as directed, allowing an extra 5 minutes for the syrup to reduce, and omit the lemon juice.

FROZEN YOGURT: For a bright and tangy variation, omit the lemon juice and replace the cream with 14 ounces (1¾ cups) plain full-fat, unsweetened Greek yogurt.

PEACH: Wash 38 ounces (about 6 medium or 4 large) ripe yellow peaches, but do not peel. Pit the peaches and cut into 1-inch chunks. Roast, strain, and simmer as directed, allowing an extra 10 minutes for the syrup to cook down. Reduce the cream to 1½ cups (12 ounces), and pair with a peach liqueur such as Mathilde Peche.

STRAWBERRY OR PEACH SODA: Prepare the fruit syrup as directed but omit the cream. Transfer the syrup to a wide-mouth jar and refrigerate for up to 3 months. For a single serving, whisk 2 ounces (3 tablespoons) cold syrup with 1 tablespoon fresh lemon juice. Pour over ice, or a scoop of ice cream, and top with 4 ounces (½ cup) club soda.

Scoops of Philadelphia-Style Strawberry (page 340) and Cream Cheese Ice Cream (page 343), with Homemade Nilla® Wafers (page 197).

CREAM CHEESE ICE CREAM

Cream cheese gives this ice cream a lingering richness, not unlike a bite of New York cheesecake—fresh, tangy, and none too sweet. I love serving scoops over warm Blueberry Cobbler (page 181), because the only thing more beautiful than that sweet/tart combination is the melting ice cream and fruit juices swirling together in the bottom of the bowl.

YIELD: about 1 quart | **ACTIVE TIME:** 30 minutes | **DOWNTIME:** 4-hour refrigeration

1 cup | 8 ounces full-fat cream cheese, softened to about 75°F

⅓ cup | 3 ounces egg yolks, from about 5 large eggs

½ cup | 4 ounces sugar

⅛ teaspoon Diamond Crystal kosher salt, or more to taste (half as much if iodized)

1 cup | 8 ounces whole milk

½ cup | 4 ounces heavy cream

1 tablespoon vanilla extract

1 tablespoon freshly squeezed lemon juice, from half a lemon

Make the ice cream base:

In the bowl of a stand mixer fitted with a paddle attachment, beat cream cheese on medium speed until soft and smooth; scrape the beater as best you can, then set aside. In a 3-quart stainless steel saucier, whisk together egg yolks, sugar, and salt, followed by milk and cream. Cook over medium-low heat, stirring constantly with a flexible spatula until the custard is steaming hot, about 8 minutes.

Strain into the bowl of cream cheese through a fine-mesh sieve, then stir in vanilla and lemon juice. The custard may seem curdled in winter months; it will still churn up a-okay. Cool to room temperature (in an ice bath if you want to speed things along), and refrigerate until cold and thick, at least 4 hours or up to 1 week.

Finish the ice cream:

Churn according to the manufacturer's directions, or until fluffy and light. If you have a freestanding machine with an open top, help keep it cool by covering with an inverted 8-inch cake pan while the ice cream churns. Meanwhile, chill an airtight container in the freezer (I save empty quart-sized yogurt containers for this very purpose) along with a flexible spatula.

Enjoy freshly churned ice cream as "soft serve," or scrape into the chilled container to freeze until firm enough to scoop, about 12 hours. Before closing the lid, press a sheet of plastic against the ice cream to minimize the risk of freezer burn. Freeze up to 3 weeks.

continued ↓

→ *Mix it up!*

FROZEN CHEESECAKE PIE: Transfer the freshly churned ice cream to a chilled Graham Cracker Crumb Crust (page 204), and cover tightly with plastic. Freeze until firm enough to slice, about 6 hours, and cut with a chef's knife dipped in hot water. Serve with Sliced Summer Strawberries (page 88), briefly warmed on the stove.

RED VELVET ICE CREAM: Next time you make a Red (Wine) Velvet Cake (page 130), save the scraps leftover from leveling the cakes. Freeze in a zip-top bag until the day you churn up a batch of Cream Cheese Ice Cream, then fold them in at the last minute, right before you transfer the ice cream to a new container. Outstanding with scraps of Brown Butter Carrot Cake too (page 138).

BROWN BUTTER PECANS

Butter Pecan dates back to the early days of ice cream saloons, one of the most popular flavors after the Big Three. Not only does butter taste amazing, it changes the texture of frozen pecans, giving them an unusual, toffee-like crunch. Instead of simply melting the butter, I brown it in a skillet on the stove, driving off the water for especially rich and nutty pecans.

YIELD: 1¼ cups (6 ounces) | **ACTIVE TIME:** 5 minutes | **DOWNTIME:** 1 hour

3 tablespoons | 1½ ounces unsalted butter

1¼ cups | 5 ounces pecan pieces

⅛ teaspoon Diamond Crystal kosher salt (half as much if iodized)

Adjust oven rack to lower-middle position and preheat oven to 350°F. Melt butter in an 8-inch stainless steel skillet over medium-low heat. Increase to medium and stir with a heat resistant spatula while the butter simmers noisily. Soon you'll notice brown bits beginning to form around the edges; continue cooking and scraping until the butter is golden brown. Remove from heat, stir in pecans, and sprinkle with salt.

Let stand 15 minutes, then bake until fragrant and golden brown, about 10 minutes.

Cool to room temperature, then use a metal spatula to transfer pecans to a pint-sized zip-top bag. Freeze until cold, about 30 minutes, or up to 3 months. Stir into a quart of freshly churned Double-Vanilla Ice Cream (page 334).

→ *Let's get crazy!*

BACON PECAN: if you're the sort of person who keeps a dish of bacon fat on the stove, make use of your stash by replacing the butter with an equal amount of bacon fat. Since it won't brown, simply warm until shimmering and hot before adding the pecans, then shut off the heat and proceed as directed.

COOKIE DOUGH NUGGETS

When Ben Cohen and Jerry Greenfield introduced cookie dough ice cream in 1984, newspapers reviewed it with thinly veiled disdain. In less than a decade, it would ascend to the pantheon of classic American ice creams, second only to chocolate.[1] While such a recipe may seem straightforward, you'd chip a tooth eating real cookie dough straight from the freezer. Keeping it soft, chewy, and flavorful involves a nontraditional approach, but the result is a cookie dough that freezes into the smooth and creamy nuggets I loved hunting for in ice cream as a kid.

YIELD: about 2 cups, enough for 1 quart of ice cream | **ACTIVE TIME:** 20 minutes | **DOWNTIME:** 1-hour freeze

2 tablespoons | 1 ounce unsalted butter, softened to about 70°F

¼ cup | 2 ounces light brown sugar

2 teaspoons vanilla extract

¼ teaspoon Diamond Crystal kosher salt (half as much if iodized)

3 tablespoons | 2¼ ounces golden syrup, or light corn syrup, divided

¼ cup | 1 ounce all-purpose flour

3 tablespoons | 1½ ounces finely chopped chocolate, about 60%

Combine butter, brown sugar, vanilla, and salt in the bowl of a stand mixer fitted with a paddle attachment. Mix on low speed to moisten, then increase to medium and beat about 5 minutes to help the sugar dissolve. Pause to scrape the bowl and beater, then beat in the golden syrup one spoonful at a time. Reduce speed to low and sprinkle in the flour, followed by the chocolate.

Drop the dough in ¼-teaspoon nuggets on a parchment-lined cutting board. Your inner child may scream for bigger chunks, but in a spoonful of ice cream I promise those pieces will seem huge. Cover with plastic and freeze until the nuggets are firm, about 1 hour. Stir into a quart of freshly churned ice cream, or freeze up to 6 months in a zip-top bag.

→ *Let's get crazy!*

OATMEAL RAISIN: Along with salt, season the dough with ⅛ teaspoon cinnamon and a pinch of grated nutmeg. Reduce all-purpose flour to ½ ounce (2 tablespoons), mixed with ½ ounce (2 tablespoons) rolled oats. Replace chocolate with ½ ounce (1 tablespoon) toasted pecan pieces and 1½ ounces (¼ cup) golden raisins, roughly chopped.

PEANUT BUTTER: Replace butter with an equal amount of creamy peanut butter.

GLUTEN FREE: Replace all-purpose flour with an equal amount of white rice flour.

ICE CREAM SODAS AND FLOATS

Aside from visiting a saloon, the best way to get a scoop of ice cream in the nineteenth century may or may not have required a prescription. In those days, the pharmaceutical industry wasn't exactly raking in hundreds of billions of dollars each year. Pharmacists filled so few genuine prescriptions they had to sell ice cream on the side.[1] They quickly realized that while aches and pains will heal, the sweet tooth requires a daily fix.

Inspired by their success with ice cream, pharmacists began to concoct new "treatments." First came ice cream soda, a literalist combination of ice, cream, and soda.[2] People drank plain soda water as a curative, or as a tonic with quinine, but combined with cream, it was said to soothe sour stomachs with the nourishment of a full meal. Back in 1867, Dow's Drug Store in Boston advertised itself as a "depot for herbs and botanic medicines [with] ice cream soda and mineral water always on draught."[3]

A Philadelphia man named Robert Green is widely credited with the radical innovation of replacing ice and cream with *ice cream* in 1874, but Sheldon's Drug Store in Providence actually beat his claim by more than a decade.[4] In 1863, schoolteachers in Rhode Island took to their official newsletter, inviting all citizens to visit Sheldon's for "a glass of his Ice Cream Soda, and see if all ideas of soda water and ice cream are not concentrated in one fairy-like mixture."

The first and best review of an ice cream soda ever written. Period.

Sheldon's dessert evolved into a drugstore staple, served in two styles: sodas and floats. Ice cream sodas put ice cream at the bottom of the glass, with flavored syrup and soda poured on top. The churning foam rapidly dissolved the ice cream into a cream soda. Floats did the opposite, mixing the syrup and soda alone, then "floating" the ice cream on top.[5] Done right, the scoop caught on the lip of the glass so that it slowly dissolved from the bottom up, allowing for alternate bites of ice cream and sips of soda.

We can't go back in time to put Sheldon to the test, but we can come close with a bottle of club soda, a jar of Mexican Vanilla Syrup, and a batch of Double-Vanilla Ice Cream. However it's assembled, there's definitely something fairy-like about the frothy concoction of swirling bubbles and cream, with flecks of vanilla drifting through the white soda like a snow globe in reverse.

Sodas and floats are kid-friendly treats today, but they were once a sophisticated and decidedly adult indulgence.

ICE CREAM SODAS OR FLOATS

With the bold flavor and gentle fizz of homemade Mexican Vanilla Soda, ice cream sodas and floats are truly remarkable—an-ever evolving mix of ethereal foam and melting ice cream, layers of creamy richness and refreshing sparkle that require a spoon and straw in turns. Everything depends on how quickly the ice cream dissolves, which comes down to placement: straight into the glass for a creamy soda, or perched on the rim for a fizzy float.

YIELD: one 10-ounce serving | **ACTIVE TIME:** about 5 minutes

½ cup | 4 ounces Double-Vanilla Ice Cream (page 334) or any variation

3 tablespoons | 2 ounces chilled Mexican Vanilla Syrup or any variation (page 349)

½ to ¾ cup | 4 to 6 ounces very cold club soda

Chill large parfait or pilsner glass in the freezer until frosty cold, at least 15 minutes.

For an ice cream soda: Drop ice cream into the chilled glass, top with syrup, and add club soda to taste. **For an ice cream float:** Gently stir syrup and club soda in the chilled glass, then top with ice cream, anchoring the scoop against the rim of the glass to keep it afloat.

Serve with a spoon and straw.

TROUBLESHOOTING

Club soda, seltzer water, and sparkling water can be used interchangeably, but avoid tonic water, which is flavored with bitter quinine.

→ *Mix it up!*

CHEESECAKE: This rich and tangy dessert starts with Cream Cheese Ice Cream (page 343), paired with strawberry soda syrup (see Philadelphia-Style Strawberry Ice Cream, page 340) to create beautiful swirls of pink and white. If you like, serve with a side of Crispy Whole Wheat Graham Crackers (page 202).

PEACHES 'N' CREAM: Made with eggless Philadelphia-Style Peach Ice Cream (page 341), this variation is particularly refreshing. If you like, prepare the syrup with a Tahitian vanilla bean, which will lend a floral note that plays up the peachy aroma.

Mexican Vanilla Syrup

Handcrafted soda doesn't have to involve any special equipment, only chilled syrup and club soda. Compared to "simple" syrup, made from equal parts sugar and water, this "rich" syrup has a higher proportion of sugar, to account for dilution. Plus, I've added a generous squeeze of lemon juice to encourage extra fizz. I love the bold flavor of Mexican vanilla beans, which taste more refreshing in soda than a heavy alcohol-based extract.

YIELD: 1 cup (10 ounces); enough for 5 sodas | **ACTIVE TIME:** about 10 minutes

1 vanilla bean, preferably Mexican

1 cup | 7 ounces sugar or Roasted Sugar (page 102)

⅓ cup plus 1 tablespoon | 5 ounces water

⅛ teaspoon Diamond Crystal kosher salt (half as much if iodized)

1½ teaspoons | ¼ ounce freshly squeezed lemon juice

Split the vanilla bean lengthwise with a paring knife and scrape the seeds from each half. Rub the seeds into the sugar (reserve the pod for another project). Combine sugar, water, and salt in a 2-quart stainless steel saucier and set over medium heat. When bubbling hot, stir in the lemon juice. Pour syrup into a wide-mouth pint jar, seal to prevent evaporation, and cool to room temperature. The syrup can be refrigerated for up to 3 months.

→ Mix it up!

BLUEBERRY: Replace the water with pure unsweetened blueberry juice and trade the lemon juice for lime.

COCONUT: Replace the water with pure unsweetened coconut water (available in stores or online) and trade the lemon juice for lime.

GINGER ALE: Replace the vanilla bean with 2½ ounces (½ cup) peeled diced ginger (from a roughly 4-inch finger). After simmering the syrup, cover and steep for 20 minutes off heat, then strain. Trade the lemon juice for lime.

HIBISCUS ROSE: Replace the vanilla bean with ½ ounce (⅓ cup) loose dried hibiscus petals. After simmering the syrup, cover and steep for 1 hour off heat. Strain and mix with the lemon juice, along with ¼ teaspoon rose water.

ICE CREAM SUNDAES

By understanding the construction of an ice cream soda (ice cream, flavored syrup, soda water) a chef can see the ice cream sundae as a streamlined version (ice cream, flavored syrup). But the name itself isn't quite as intuitive without a grasp of nineteenth-century blue laws—regulations that forced ice cream saloons to close on Sunday. Saloons had to comply or face steep fines, so officially they closed their doors. But *wink-wink, nudge-nudge* sales happened all the time via, I kid you not, ice cream bootleggers. Historians have always known that the illegal sale of ice cream on Sunday inspired the name but lacked a definitive "first case," despite claims from dozens of parlors across America.[1] The general consensus points to an advertisement for fruit "Sundays" at a New York pharmacy in 1892, but George Payson's 1854 novel *Totemwell* may include an earlier allusion.[2]

In the story, our hero slips down to the ice cream saloon one blistering Sunday for an illicit pint of the good stuff. While fetching spoons from the kitchen, his sweetheart teased, "How could you be so wicked as to buy ice cream Sunday?" Despite the awkward phrasing and lack of toppings, it was the first time the phrase "ice cream Sunday" ever described a sneaky Sabbath snack.

In an *actual* incident correlating blue laws and ice cream, the state of Pennsylvania sued WC Burry in 1888 for operating a secret Sunday saloon, hidden behind his bakeshop, as well as for selling ice cream "delivered to the customer in a paper package" (no mention as to whether or not he requested payment in unmarked bills).[3] Burry appealed the verdict on the grounds that a bakery license exempted him from the ban, but the court tossed out his case.

While saloons shut down or went underground, pharmacists flaunted their free reign to sell ice cream on Sunday[4]—soda water technically functioned as a medicinal tonic, ice cream could be prescribed to treat gastric ulcers, and chocolate syrup was a vehicle for many medicines, while lime and mint syrups were said to cure nausea.[5] So indignant hellfire and brimstone types put new *blues* in effect, such as the 1888 "Sunday Soda Water" ban in Pennsylvania.[6]

Drugstores complied to the letter of the law with glasses of ice cream drenched in flavored syrup, sans soda, with whipped cream to simulate the foamy head.[7] Or so the story goes; actual recipes wouldn't appear until a 1900 issue of *The Spatula Soda Water Guide* described "Sunday's or Sundae" as a parfait dish of ice cream covered with chocolate syrup or crushed fruit.[8]

Hot fudge sundaes became a particular favorite at the turn of the twentieth century, as did butterscotch sundaes a decade later. While we think of butterscotch as a sauce today, it was once known only as a hard candy (see Homemade Heath® Toffee Bits, page 320). In 1912, the Cedar Rapids Candy Company popularized a liquid form, advertised in *The American Druggist* as "a new syrup made up to an old and well known flavor."[9] The company offered to send a free Joy Jar of butterscotch to anyone who asked, putting their "Original Butterscotch Sundae" on soda shop menus across the country.

AUTHENTIC HOT FUDGE SUNDAE

Hot fudge wasn't originally a type of sauce, but rather a molten confection. Poured over ice cream, melted fudge crystallized with the abrupt change of temperature, creating a thick, warm candy shell with a creamy, melt-in-your-mouth consistency. You can't go wrong with hot fudge and classic vanilla ice cream, but I love how tart strawberry (page 340) and bitter coffee ice cream (page 335) offset its sweetness.

YIELD: 4 servings | **ACTIVE TIME:** about 5 minutes

1¼ cups | 6 ounces Baltimore Fudge (page 74)

About 2 cups Double-Vanilla Ice Cream (page 334) or any variation (see pages 335–37)

Chill four parfait glasses in the freezer until frosty cold, at least 15 minutes. Meanwhile, crumble fudge into a microwave-safe bowl.

Divide the ice cream among the parfait glasses. Melt fudge in a few 15-second bursts on normal power, pausing to stir briefly after each round, until melted and gooey but still thick; stir only enough to prevent scorching, as excessive stirring will thicken the fudge.

Spoon molten fudge over the ice cream and allow it to set, about 30 seconds. Serve immediately.

MALTED BUTTERSCOTCH SAUCE

Butterscotch, like revenge, is a dish best served cold. Straight from the fridge it's as gooey as the caramel heart of a Milky Way bar, clinging to ice cream in chewy ropes. Unlike authentic butterscotch toffee (see pages 318–19), made from browned butter, this sauce mimics the sweet and simple butterscotch found in ice cream parlors across America today. Its toasty flavor and amber hue come from barley malt, though sorghum will do in a pinch if you need to go gluten-free.

YIELD: 2 cups (18 ounces) | **ACTIVE TIME:** about 15 minutes

½ cup | 4 ounces water

1¼ cups | 9 ounces sugar

¾ teaspoon Diamond Crystal kosher salt, or more to taste (half as much if iodized)

1 scraped vanilla bean pod (reserved from another project; optional)

¾ cup | 6 ounces heavy cream

6 tablespoons | 3 ounces unsalted butter

1 tablespoon | ¾ ounce barley malt syrup

1½ teaspoons vanilla extract

Combine water, sugar, salt, and vanilla bean, if using, in a 2-quart stainless steel saucier set over medium heat. Stir with a fork until bubbling hard around the edges, about 4 minutes. Increase to medium-high and cook, *without stirring*, until the clear syrup takes on the faintest hint of gold, even if only in one spot, about 8 minutes.

Immediately add cream and butter, then reduce heat to medium-low; the syrup will bubble and steam but not overflow a 2-quart pot. Stir with a heat-resistant spatula until the bubbles subside. Add barley malt syrup and vanilla extract off heat. Set a spoonful aside to cool, then taste and adjust with more salt if desired.

Pour the runny sauce into a wide-mouth pint jar, seal to prevent evaporation and cool to room temperature. Refrigerate up to 2 months.

Serve cold, drizzled over scoops of ice cream or slices of cake.

→ *Mix it up!*

BUTTERSCOTCH CHANTILLY: In the bowl of a stand mixer fitted with the whisk attachment, combine 5 ounces (⅔ cup) heavy cream with 5½ ounces (½ cup) chilled Butterscotch Sauce and mix on low for a minute, then increase to medium-high and whip until thick and stiff, about 5 minutes. Use immediately, or cover and refrigerate for up to 1 week. Makes 10½ ounces (2¼ cups), enough to garnish about 12 desserts.

SORGHUM SYRUP (GLUTEN-FREE): Replacing the barley malt with an equal amount of unsulfured sorghum molasses creates a similar but unique syrup that's fantastic drizzled over waffles, pancakes, and even Buttermilk Biscuits (page 85).

CHOCOLATE SYRUP

Long before the economy forced pharmacists to dispense prescriptions à la mode (see page 332), nineteenth-century drugstores relied on "syrup of chocolate" to make repulsive remedies like cod liver oil or bitter quinine a bit easier to choke down.[1] From the 1860s until just past the turn of the century, you could count on a recipe for chocolate syrup in just about any given pharmaceutical journal.[2]

With eight times more sugar than chocolate, those formulas were super sweet; then again, they had to be, lest the taste of something fishy slip through. As drugstores morphed into soda fountains, that same intensity allowed pharmacists to doctor sundaes, sodas, and floats. Perhaps that's why Milton Hershey's 1896 cocoa advertisements appealed to clinical rather than culinary sensibilities: WARRANTED ABSOLUTELY PURE.[3]

This targeted approach encouraged pharmacists to advertise their cocoa purchases in turn, lending brand-name recognition to their tried-and-true recipes with *Hershey's* chocolate in their syrup. It'd be another thirty years before Hershey itself manufactured any

such thing. While by no means the first commercial chocolate syrup, it was certainly the cheapest, sold for as as little as eight cents per sixteen-ounce can (Hershey's cocoa itself cost fifteen cents a pound).[4]

When I was growing up, that little can with the yellow lid had a permanent place in our refrigerator door. It never had to be warmed or stirred, it never spoiled, it never crystallized, it never clumped. My brother and I stirred up chocolate milk after school, Dad poured an unspeakable amount into the chocolate milkshakes he made for us, and Mom always drizzled it over a few peanut butter–smeared graham crackers (still one of my favorite snacks).

You won't see that yellow lid in my fridge today, but you can count on a jar of homemade chocolate syrup. I've based my recipe on the basic formula laid out in nineteenth-century pharmaceutical journals—cocoa, sugar, and water—but with a few small tweaks.[5] In addition to cocoa, a small amount of chocolate adds thickness and body, and the acidity of coffee and brown sugar helps keep the syrup smooth.

HOMEMADE HERSHEY'S®-STYLE SYRUP

This inky chocolate syrup tastes just like that childhood classic, mellow and sweet, with the heady aroma of vanilla. Lots of vanilla. If you happen to have an empty pod left over from another project, toss it on in! That seemingly over-the-top potency means its flavor won't be lost when stirred into a tall glass of milk or cut with ice cream for a chocolate shake.

YIELD: about 2 cups (18 ounces) | **ACTIVE TIME:** 10 minutes

1 cup | 8 ounces hot black coffee or tea, such as Assam

⅔ cup | 2 ounces Dutch-process cocoa powder, such as Cacao Barry Extra Brute

3 tablespoons | 1 ounce roughly chopped 72% dark chocolate

1 cup gently packed | 8 ounces light brown sugar

¼ teaspoon Diamond Crystal kosher salt (half as much if iodized)

1 vanilla bean pod, reserved from another project (optional)

1 tablespoon vanilla extract

Whisk coffee and cocoa in a 2-quart stainless steel saucier set over medium heat until thick and bubbly. Add chocolate, brown sugar, and salt, along with the vanilla pod, if using, and continue whisking until syrupy and smooth. Stir in the vanilla extract.

Pour the runny syrup into a wide-mouth quart jar, and seal to prevent evaporation. Cool to room temperature, then refrigerate until cold and thick, about 4 hours. Store up to 2 months.

→ *Mix it up!*

BLACK CHERRY: For a chocolate cherry vibe, replace the coffee with sweetened tart cherry juice and use 1 ounce (2 tablespoons) kirsch in place of vanilla.

DARK MINT CHOCOLATE: This variation tastes like liquefied Thin Mints®, perfect for topping scoops of chocolate or vanilla ice cream (my mom stirs it into her afternoon coffee). Use a dark mint chocolate such as Endangered Species 72% Rainforest, and substitute white sugar for brown. Replace the vanilla extract with crème de menthe, adding more to taste.

HOMEMADE MAGIC SHELL®

Melted chocolate quickly hardens over ice cream, so hard it sits on your tongue like a waxy lump, refusing to melt—an easy problem to avoid with a few spoonfuls of coconut oil to raise the chocolate's melting point. Whether you opt for refined coconut oil, or virgin for a hint of chocolate flair, make certain you choose a chocolate you love eating out of hand, be it dark, milk, or white; you can even use Caramelized White Chocolate (page 60), for a butterscotch-like twist.

YIELD: ½ cup (5 ounces); enough to top eight servings of ice cream | **ACTIVE TIME:** about 5 minutes

⅔ cup | 4 ounces dark, milk, or white chocolate, finely chopped

3 tablespoons | 1 ounce refined coconut oil

Microwave chocolate in a small bowl with a few 30-second bursts, stirring every 20 seconds to prevent scorching. Stir in coconut oil and cool for just a minute. Drizzle over scoops of ice cream, allowing 30 seconds for the shell to harden. Store leftovers in an airtight container for 1 week at room temperature, or 6 months in the fridge. Rewarm before using.

→ *Mix it up!*

TO MAKE CHIPS FOR ICE CREAM: After adding coconut oil, spread half the mixture over a piece of parchment. Freeze until solid, about 15 minutes, then crumple the paper to break chocolate into pieces. Stir into a quart of freshly churned ice cream or transfer to a zip-top bag and freeze up to 6 months.

BUTTERSCOTCH: In place of white chocolate, use Caramelized White Chocolate (page 60).

ICE CREAM SANDWICHES

There have always been various ways to eat ice cream out of hand, and recipes for dainty frozen "sandwiches" weren't at all uncommon in the late nineteenth century.[1] But these were rarely more than awkward servings of cake à la mode. A truly handheld version wouldn't get legs until 1900, when the *American Kitchen Magazine* reported "a new fad" in the Big Apple: ice cream sandwiches sold from pushcarts down on the Bowery.[2]

The author was absolutely enthralled at the novelty, if not the seedy location ("the idea is worthy of a better field"), and described the setup in great detail: "the thin wafers which go to make up the sandwich help to modify the coolness of the ice-cream, so that it can be eaten more readily." Sold for a penny apiece, these sandwiches were a low-budget knockoff of a spiffier version made by the Brooklyn Ice Cream Company.[3]

Or maybe vice versa— it's hard to say. According to a 1910 profile in the *Ice Cream Trade Journal*, owner William Woodruff "introduced ice cream sandwiches into this country" at the turn of the century.[4] By the time of the article, William's Brooklyn factory housed two industrial ice cream freezers, a ten-ton ice machine, ice chippers, ice cream wagons, and a stable full of horsepower. His wagons brought ice cream sandwiches to

BROWNIE wafers used in this sandwich are made by National Biscuit Company with flour, sugar, shortening, cocoa, corn syrup, salt, leavening, and synthetic vanillin flavors.

BROWNIE ICE CREAM SANDWICH

You'll say they're great!

Mass-produced wrappers let business owners market ice cream sandwiches with two nationally known brands: Nabisco wafers and the Brownies from Palmer Cox.

every corner of New York, yet it was those Bowery pushcarts that set the market price. Fed up with razor-thin profit margins, William auctioned off the business in 1910, complaining to the *Journal* that "when you're putting out a product that cells for a cent, and that won't sell for two cents, you can't transfer the burden of increased cost onto the customer."

With business so tough that the father of the industry had given up, surviving dealers cut corners recklessly, eliminating unnecessary expenses like, you know, *packaging*. So ice cream sandwich men would tend their horses, load their carts, drive around the city, handle money, and then serve unwrapped ice cream sandwiches with their bare hands.

We tend to laugh off that sort of old-fashioned obliviousness and remind ourselves, "They survived," but many did not. Between 1911 and 1913, there was a wave of deaths directly connected to ice cream sandwiches and "ptomaine poisoning," an outdated term to describe the misunderstood circumstances of food-borne illness. A highly publicized rash of "poisonings" in Yonkers culminated with the death of a two-year-old girl, and a similar outbreak in Pennsylvania made headlines after killing a little boy.[5]

Public outrage led to new regulations on street vendors, requiring ice cream sandwiches with dirt-proof packaging.[6] But individually wrapped sandwiches proved too time-consuming and costly for a penny-novelty, so ice cream pushcarts and wagons went the way of William Woodruff. This vacuum spawned a whole industry of "sandwich machine" manufacturers with hygenic-sounding names like Sanesco or Sanitary. "*Sanitary*" seems like the lowest bar a company could set for itself, yet in that climate, it was exactly what the public needed to hear. Sanitary advertisements in the 1920s promised ice cream sandwiches that would "never come in contact with human hands until you buy them yourself."[7] Others offered tepid reassurance, "You needn't be afraid to let children have them."[8]

Ice cream sandwich machines had compartments for a full sleeve of packaged wafers and a standard "brick" of ice cream. With the turn of a crank, a blade sliced off a chunk of ice cream and pushed it between two wafers that could be snatched from the machine with a square of waxed paper. These bulky contraptions took frozen sandwiches off the street and back into drugstores, a reassuring environment in the wake of so much sickness and death.

Pharmacists loved the machines because they made a predictable profit. Rather than an unpredictable number of hand-scooped portions from each brick, machines divvied up ten 3.2-ounce slices every time—and established the exact size and shape of the ice cream sandwiches we buy today.

In the 1930s, Nabisco introduced "Brownie Thins" for professional use. These tasted like Oreos, with a brownie-like texture that cut down on crumbs while ensuring each bite applied less pressure to the ice cream (anti-squish physics, if you will). Of course, slapping Nabisco's name on the serving wrapper further assured customers of the sandwich's quality, but it also provided pharmacists with a ready-made mascot: Palmer Cox's Brownies (see page 53).

Ice cream sandwiches have returned to the realm of street vendors today, but they're incredibly fun to make at home. Inspired by Brownie Thins, my recipe starts with two inky-black chocolate wafers that are soft and pliable. They're sandwiched with a quart of homemade ice cream in an eight-inch cake pan, then easily cut into a dozen pieces. While I'm fond of classic vanilla, the sandwich is particularly good with chocolate or strawberry ice cream as well (or any of the Vanilla Variations on pages 335–37).

ICE CREAM SANDWICHES

These chocolatey wafers have the taste and texture of an Oreo®/Brownie hybrid, intensely dark and bitter but soft, perfect for preventing the ice cream from squishing out with every bite. Keep things traditional with Double-Vanilla Ice Cream, or go for broke with a batch of creamy Devil's Food Chocolate.

YIELD: twelve 4-by-1⅓-by-¾-inch sandwiches | **ACTIVE TIME:** about an hour | **DOWNTIME:** 12-hour freeze

Soft Chocolate Wafers:

½ cup | 2¼ ounces all-purpose flour, such as Gold Medal

¾ cup | 2¼ ounces Dutch-process cocoa powder, such as Cacao Barry Extra Brute

4 tablespoons | 2 ounces unsalted butter, creamy and soft—about 68°F

⅔ cup gently packed | 3 ounces light brown sugar

¼ teaspoon Diamond Crystal kosher salt (half as much if iodized)

¼ teaspoon baking soda

2 large egg yolks

⅓ cup plus 1 tablespoon | 3 ounces boiling water (hot coffee or black tea will also work)

1 recipe liquid ice cream base: Double-Vanilla (page 334), Devil's Food Chocolate (page 338), Philadelphia-Style Strawberry (page 340), Cream Cheese (page 343), or any Vanilla Variation (pages 335–37)

Make the wafers:

Adjust oven rack to middle position and preheat to 350°F. Trace a 9-by-17-inch rectangle on a sheet of parchment paper (not wax) and place ink side down on a lightly greased aluminum baking sheet. Smooth out any pockets of air.

Sift flour and cocoa together (if using cup measures, spoon into the cups and level with a knife before sifting).

Combine butter, brown sugar, salt, and baking soda in the bowl of a stand mixer fitted with a paddle attachment. Mix on low speed to moisten, then increase to medium and beat until fluffy and light, about 5 minutes. With the mixer running, add yolks one at a time, letting each incorporate before adding the next. Scrape the bowl and beater with a flexible spatula, then resume mixing on low. Sprinkle in the flour/cocoa, followed by hot water, mixing to form a smooth paste. If any lumps remain, increase speed to medium and beat a few seconds more.

Scrape onto the prepared baking sheet, using an offset spatula to spread the stiff batter just beyond the borders of the outline. It will be quite thin! Bake until the cake is puffed and dry but still soft to the touch, about 6 minutes. Cool to room temperature on the baking sheet, then cover tightly with foil and refrigerate until needed, up to 1 week.

Prepare the pan:

Line an 8-by-2-inch square aluminum baking pan with two 8-by-15-inch strips of parchment paper, creasing it along the edges so it is flush against the bottom and sides.

With the pan as a guideline, use a knife to cut the wafer into two 8-inch squares, pressing hard along the center line to cut through the parchment below. Reserve the scraps.

Holding onto the parchment, lay one wafer upside down in the bottom of the pan. Carefully peel away the parchment and patch any cracks or tears with reserved scraps, pressing firmly to mold the pieces together. Cover pan with foil and place the remaining wafer on top, leaving the parchment in place. Wrap in plastic and freeze until needed, up to 1 month.

Assemble the sandwiches:
Churn the ice cream according to its recipe. When ready, grab the frozen pan of wafers from the fridge and set aside the topmost wafer.

With a flexible spatula, scrape ice cream into the pan and smooth into an even layer. Top with the second wafer, shiny side up, and press firmly to secure. Cover with foil and freeze until hard, at least 12 hours, or overnight.

To serve, gently tug on the parchment flaps until the ice cream sandwich can be lifted from the pan, then transfer to a cutting board. Cut into quarters with a chef's knife, then cut each square into three 1½-inch bars. Serve immediately, or tuck into sandwich bags and freeze in an airtight container up to 1 month.

→ Mix it up!

GLUTEN-FREE: Replace the all-purpose flour with white rice flour.

ACKNOWLEDGMENTS

IT'S NO EXAGGERATION TO SAY this book would not exist without my friend and mentor Ed Levine, who first convinced me that becoming an author needn't be some farfetched dream. Your confidence and relentless support made my fear of failure seem small, and I am stronger for it. Thank you.

To my agent, Vicky Bijur, who slays dragons. Thank you for holding my hand every step of the way, for all the coffee and bialys and guidance that shaped my rambling proposal into the kernel of a full-fledged book. I could not have done this without you, nor would I want to.

Thank you to my editor, Maria Guarnaschelli, you are a force of nature and I am indebted to your expertise. You shaped this book, and my life, in ways I never expected. I've learned so much from our time together; thank you most of all for your patience, and not rushing my book out the door. To Nathaniel Dennett, for keeping me in the loop and on task through that final year of production. My thanks to Judith Sutton for wrangling every footnote and misplaced modifier back into place, and to the extraordinary efforts of proofreader Robert Byrne. Sincere thanks to Elizabeth Parson for creating such a thoughtful and comprehensive index, one that will certainly help readers navigate the many recipe variations that might otherwise be lost. To director of marketing Meredith McGinnis and publicist Will Scarlett, for giving more folks an excuse to bake. My thanks to everyone at W. W. Norton & Company: Louise Mattarelliano, Anna Oler, Nancy Palmquist, and Susan Sanfrey in particular—I can't fathom navigating the chaos of this book without your attention to detail. And I'd especially like to thank Laura Goldin.

My heartfelt thanks to designer Toni Tajima, for turning a pile of text into a beautiful book. Your style and grace brings clarity to each recipe, and I'm so happy your fingerprints are on every page.

This book has been immeasurably improved by Christine Burns and Carolyn Malcoun. Their individual efforts opened my eyes to the art and science of professional recipe testing. Thank you for putting these recipes through the paces, asking the right questions, and guiding me toward the safest answers.

To Penny De Los Santos, babe. Thanks for taking a chance on me before we'd ever met. Your photography is compelling and honest and true, just how I envision American dessert. To Stephanie Munguia, I'm so thankful for your technical prowess and mastery of wayward crumbs. My thanks to Kaitlyn Du Ross Walker: collector of beautiful things. Thank you for every sparkling glass and smoking candle, and to Sophia Pappas, for all that you did behind the scenes. To John Bjostad and Jan Fort: what an incredible team. Thank you for planning and plotting everything from the start, for stocking an empty kitchen with all the equipment and ingredients I could ever need, and joining me for a marathon week of baking in the midst of a heat wave. The champagne was a classy touch.

To my family at Serious Eats, past and present, sweet mother of mercy: thank you. Your patience, support, and enthusiasm kept me afloat during the most difficult year of my life. In particular, I want to thank The Food Lab, aka J. Kenji López-Alt, who first welcomed me to Serious Eats when I was still a stranger in some restaurant far, far away. You ask smarter questions, provide better answers, work longer hours, and have more fun while you're at it. Thank you for challenging me to do the same.

To Sarah Jane Sanders: I don't even know where to begin. I'm so proud of everything we achieved together, and all the memories and photographs made along the way, and all the things I can't put into words. Thank you.

To Rosco Webber: thank you for everything. For convincing me to start a blog. For pouring your time and creativity into it so generously, and for all the remarkable photography that put our little blog on the map.

To those who've been with BraveTart from the beginning, my friends, and family, and strangers around the world. To old-school Serious Eaters, and all the new folks I've met along the way. Thank you for commenting, and emailing, and tweeting, and reaching out across the void; you've made the many long years of this project less lonely, and I'm more grateful than you'll ever know.

NOTES ON SOURCES

TO PARAPHRASE ONE OF MY CHILDHOOD HEROES, the imitable Dr. James McCoy, "Damn it, Jim! I'm a pastry chef, not a journalist." Yet to tell the tale of American dessert, I believed delving into historical archives would prove far more valuable than simply repeating the tales so often told (and retold) in modern sources. I spent five years digging through libraries, newspaper archives, antique shops, used book stores, and online catalogues of vintage advertisements. Through eBay, I amassed stacks of paper ephemera: nineteenth-century biscuit factory receipts, employee training manuals, yellowed photographs, trade journals, personal letters, and pages torn from obscure community cookbooks. Digital collections from the likes of Cornell University, the New York Public Library, and even Google allowed me to explore nineteenth-century magazines and menus online, while print-on-demand services like Abe Books delivered physical copies of long-forgotten tomes.

I looked to these texts not as a scholar, but as a pastry chef seeking to evolve our simplistic understanding of American desserts and cultivate a greater appreciation for our sweet history, culture, and heritage. In no way is this work meant to be definitive; as long as we continue to pull dusty cookbooks from the attic, discover lost manuscripts, and digitize yellowing stacks of newspapers, it's a story that will never be complete.

It's not possible to mention every book, newspaper, and magazine that shaped my understanding of dessert through the years, so this bibliography aims to support each story with a few key references rather than provide an exhaustive list.

Chocolate Chip Cookies

1 "Chocolate Jumbles," *Osage County Chronicle* (Burlingame, KS), August 16, 1877.

2 Warner, W. A., "Chocolate Jumbles," *Kings Highway Cookbook* (Bridgeport: Park Street Congregational Church, 1894), 47. Markham, Loena G., "Chocolate Cookies," *The Ann Arbor Cookbook*. (Ann Arbor: Ladies' Aid Society, 1899), 192. "Recipes and Replies," *Good Housekeeping* 8, no. 5 (January 1889): 117.

3 R. W. Keys., Advertisement. *Oshkosh Daily Northwestern*, August 17, 1928.

4 Buy Rite. Advertisement. *Davenport Democrat and Leader*, March 8, 1929. Kroger. Advertisement. *Jackson Daily Journal*, November 2, 1934. Kroger. Advertisement. *Sandusky Star Journal*, October 28, 1935. Smith's Model Grocery and Market. Advertisement. *Daily Chronicle*, March 15, 1935.

5 *Publishers Weekly*, 137 (1940): 1913.

6 Nestlé. Advertisement. *Fitchburg Sentinel*, December 21, 1939. Nestlé. Advertisement. *Racine Journal Times*, May 3, 1940. Toll House Tried and True Recipes. Advertisement. *Syracuse Herald Journal*, May 24, 1940.

Oatmeal Cookies

1 *Official Gazette of the U.S. Patent Office* (September 1877): 397.

2 "Quaker Oats Special," *Cedar Rapids Evening Gazette*, April 6, 1892. "Quaker Oats Special." *Waterloo Courier*, April 13, 1892.

3 *The Official Railway Equipment Register* (New York: Railway and Equipment Publishing Company, 1897), 241.

4 *Railway Conductor* 16, no. 3 (March 1899): 245.

5 *The Ann Arbor Cookbook* (Ann Arbor: Ladies' Aid Society, 1899), 121, 193, 249.

6 *San Antonio Gazette*, May 4, 1907.

7 *Souvenir California Raisin Recipe Book* (Fresno: California Associated Raisin Producers, 1915), 10.

8 "Big Possibilities Seen on Coast," *Fourth Estate*, no. 1170 (July 1916): 20. Cruikshank, Jeffrey L., and Schultz, Arthur W. *The Man Who Sold America: The Amazing (but True!) Story of Albert D. Lasker* (Boston: Harvard Business Press, 2010), 103–104.

9 Iten Biscuit Company. Advertisement. *Lincoln Star*, February 11, 1918. *Denton Record-Chronicle*, August 12, 1938.

Snickerdoodles

1 "Queer Little Cakes," *Frederick (MD) News*, January 18, 1908.

2 "Culinary Oddities," *Philadelphia Times*, April 15, 1902.

3 "Snip Doodles," *Melrose Household Treasure* (Boston: T. W. Ripley, 1877), 9.

4 J. C. Lins. *Common Sense Pennsylvania German Dictionary* (Reading, PA: J. C. Lins, 1895).

5 "Serve Them Hot," *Zanesville Signal*, December 30, 1932.

6 "Snickerdoodles," *Home Maker* (April 1889): 58.

7 "Points for the House-Keeper," *Idaho Statesman*, October 20, 1901.

8 "Serve Them Hot," *Zanesville Signal*, December 30, 1932.

9 "Snickerdoodles," *American Notes & Queries* (June 1941): 39.

10 "Snickerdoodles," *The A. A. Cook Book: Containing Three Hundred Tested Recipes* (Springfield, MA: Atwood Print, 1895), 28; Ogle, George. Mrs., *The New Century Cook Book* (Chicago: Wesley Hospital Bazaar, 1899), 185. "Snip Doodles," *Fitchburg Sentinel*, March 14, 1928. Leonard, H. O.,

"Snip Doodle," *Vermont Cookery* (Montpelier: Argus and Patriot Press, 1899), 102.

11 *Kokomo Tribune*, December 9, 1932.

12 "Serve Snickerdoodles for Supper," *Pantagraph* (Bloomington, IL), January 15, 1941. "Snickerdoodles," *El Paso Herald-Post*, July 31, 1952. "Tasty Morsels," *Salt Lake Tribune*, September 13, 1949.

13 Cleveland Baking Powder. Advertisement. *Poughkeepsie Eagle-News*, August 20, 1891.

Peanut Butter Cookies

1 Piers, Ada Maye, "Peanuts in Many Dishes," *New York Observer* 76, no. 28 (July 1898): 57. "Peanut Cookies," *Forest Republican*, November 4, 1896.

2 "Peanut Cookies," *Times (Philadelphia)*, February 5, 1895.

3 Ray, Grove. "Peanut Cookies," *The Ann Arbor Cookbook*, 2nd ed. (Ann Arbor: Ladies' Aid Society, 1904), 338. "A Unique Luncheon," *Battle Creek Idea* 4, no. 25 (May 1911): 4.

4 Simpson Crawford. Advertisement. *New York Times*, December 6, 1903.

5 "Peanut Cookies," *Indianapolis Star*, November 28, 1909.

6 "Special Information Service of the U.S. Department of Agriculture," *Casa Grande Dispatch*, December 20, 1918.

7 "Conservation Recipes," *Brooklyn Daily Eagle*, June 12, 1918.

8 "Peanut Butter Cookies," *Manitowoc Herald-Times*, December 21, 1931.

9 *Berkeley Daily Gazette*, January 10, 1936.

Brownies and Blondies

1 Wells, Lillian E., "A Brown Dinner and a Chocolate Tea," *Ladies'*

Home Journal 5, no. 11 (October 1888): 4.

2 Dodge, Mary Mapes, ed., "The Letter Box," *St. Nicholas* 24, no. 2 (October 1897): 877.

3 Candee, Isabella Laning, "A Brown Sociable," *Good Housekeeping* 5, no. 9 (July 1889): 103.

4 Hutto, Lawrence, "The Brownies at Home," *The Book Buyers Guide* 10 (February 1893–January 1894): 491–492.

5 Bates, Clara Doty, "The Children's Building of the Columbian Exposition" and "Saint Nicholas at the Fair," *St. Nicholas* 20 (November 1892–April 1893): 715, 792. "The Children's Library," *The Publishers' and Other Book Exhibits at the World's Columbian Exposition* (New York: Publishers Weekly, 1893), 69.

6 "Brownies in the Sky," *Chicago Daily Tribune*, July 4, 1893.

7 "Mrs. Palmer's Message to the Board of Lady Managers," *Woman's Column* 5, no. 5 (November 1892): 4.

8 "Brownie Cake," *Our Horticultural Visitor* 5, no. 7 (July 1899): 2. Owens, Frances E., "Chocolate Cake," *Mrs. Owens' New Cook Book and Complete Household Manual* (Chicago: Owens Publishing, 1899), 463.

9 *The Service Club Cook Book* (Chicago: Service Club, 1904).

10 Hibbard, Laura B., and Vaughn, Mary Alice, "Brownies," *Home Cookery* (Laconia, NH: Laconia Press Association, 1904), 132.

11 Quinby, Henry Cole, *Genealogical History of the Quinby (Quimby) Family in England and America* (New York: New England Historical-Genealogical Society, 1915).

12 "The Laconia Woman's Club," *Granite Monthly* 38, no. 1 (January–December, 1906): 103–108.

S'mores

1 "Afternoon Teas and Tea Cakes," *Good Housekeeping* 51, no. 4 (October 1910): 482.

2 Miller, Eva Alice, "Marshmallow Mixtures," *Table Talk* 28, no. 1 (January 1913): 93.

3 *Tramping and Trailing with the Girl Scouts*, rev. ed. (New York: Girl Scouts, Inc., 1930), 71–72.

Peanut Brittle

1 Fisher, Deborah. Advertisement. *Philadelphia Public Ledger*, December 23, 1843.

2 Leslie, Eliza. "Molasses Candy," *Directions for Cookery in Its Various Branches* (Philadelphia: Carey & Hart, 1844), 365.

3 Rutledge, Sarah. *House and Home, or The Carolina Housewife* (Charleston: John Russell, 1855), 139–140.

4 "Molasses Candy," *The Art of Confectionery.* (Boston: J. E. Tilton, 1865), 55.

Fudge

1 Sunday June 12th and Monday June 13th, 1664, *The Diary of Samuel Pepys*, rev. ed. (New York: Modern Library, 2003.)

2 "The Origin of Fudge," *New York Times*, October 7, 1883.

3 Scribner, Annie Nyan, *Alpha Phi Annual* 9, no. 3 (May 1897): 125, 147.

4 Firkins, Ina, ed., *Anchora Delta Gamma* (Minneapolis: Hall, Black, 1892). "The Wegg-Smith Nuptials," *Milwaukee Journal*, August 28, 1891.

5 The Women's Guild of St. Mark's Church, *Clever Cooking*, recipe contributed by Mrs. Winifield R. Smith (Seattle: Metropolitan Printing & Binding, 1896).

6 Allen, Mrs. Willis, ed., and Smith, Grace Content (recipe contributor), *Machias Cook Book* (Machias,

ME: C.O. Furbish, 1899), 76. Chandler, Julia Davis. "Up to Date Fudge," *Boston Cooking School Magazine* 9, no. 5 (December 1904): 273–274.

7 Harkness, Mary Leal. "The College Course for Women," *Independent*, July 4, 1912.

8 Church of the Holy Comforter, *The Favorite Receipt Book* (Baltimore: Trade Press, 1884).

9 "Chocolate Caramel," *Burlington Daily Hawk Eye*, September 11, 1880.

10 "Domestic Economy," *Cultivator & Country Gentleman* 39 (March 1874): 151.

11 "Domestic Economy," *Cultivator & Country Gentleman* 41 (1879): 159.

12 From a personal letter of Emelyn Hartridge, courtesy of Vassar College.

Cheesecake

1 Brown, Simon, ed., *The New England Farmer* (Boston: Reynolds and Nourse, 1852), 293.

2 Leslie, Eliza, *Miss Leslie's New Cookery Book* (Philadelphia: T. B. Peterson and Brothers, 1857), 481.

3 De Voe, Thomas F., "Cream Cheese," *Market Assistant* (New York: Hurd and Houghton, 1867): 404.

4 *Report of the Pennsylvania State Dairymen's Association*, no. 4 (1879): 13.

5 "The Cheese Brand—Relation to Skim Cheese—The General Interest," *Fifth Annual Report of the New York State Dairy Commissioner* (Albany: Troy Press Company, 1889), 359–361.

6 *Portrait and Biographical Record of Orange County, New York* (New York: Chapman Publishing, 1895), 793. "International Cheese Co. vs Phenix Cheese Co.," *New York Supplement* 103 (April–May 1907): 362–363.

7 *Fourth Annual Report of the State Board Health of New York* (Albany: Reed, Parsons, 1884), 266–267.

8 "Phenix Cheese Co. vs Ridgeway Kennedy," *Trade-Mark Reporter* 7 (1917): 537. "International Cheese Co. vs Phenix Cheese Co.," *New York Supplement* 103 (1907): 362. "Lawrence vs P.E. Sharpless," *Trade-Mark Reporter* 3 (1917): 211–220.

9 *Perry Daily Chief*, April 9, 1909.

10 *New York Times*, February 2, 1909.

11 *Sheboygan Daily Press*, February 28, 1910.

Strawberry Shortcake

1 Randall, Willard Sterne, *Thomas Jefferson: A Life* (New York: Harper Perennial Modern Classics, 2014).

2 "News Items," *Baltimore Sun*, May 23, 1843.

3 Fletcher, S.W., *The Strawberry in North America.* (New York: MacMillan, 1917.)

4 "New Strawberries," *Vick's Illustrated Magazine* (April 1878): 106. Pardee, Richard Gay, *A Complete Manual for the Cultivation of Strawberries* (New York: C.M. Saxton, 1854).

5 "Strawberry Festival," *What to Eat* 22, no. 4 (April 1907): 137. *Annual Report of the Children's Aid Society* (New York: Wynkoop and Hallenbeck, 1873), 15.

6 Ellison, Betty Boles, *The True Mary Todd Lincoln: A Biography* (Jefferson, NC: McFarland, 2014), 87.

7 Garfield, Charles W., *Eighth Annual Report of the Secretary of the Michigan State Pomological Society* (Lansing: W. S. George, 1879), 90.

8 Gill, J. Thompson, *The Complete Bread and Cracker Baker* (Chicago: Confectioner and Baker Publishing, 1881), 190. "Strawberry Shortcake," *Good Housekeeping* 21, no. 1 (July 1895): 38.

Pineapple Upside-Down Cake

1 Kramer, Bertha F., *Aunt Babette's Cook Book* (New York: Blogh, 1914), 314.

2 "Dashes Here and There," *Saint Louis Dispatch*, November 10, 1876.

3 "Pine-Apple Cake," *Weekly Wisconsin*, May 4, 1889.

4 "Southern Correspondence," *Vermont Watchman and State Journal*, June 11, 1890. "Pineapple Cake," *Good Housekeeping* 25, no. 5 (November 1897): 225.

5 Heenan, David Jr., "The Hawaiian Pineapple," *Canning Age* (May 1922): 5–16.

6 "Widened Market for the Pineapple Sought by Advertising," *Printers' Ink* 116 (July 1921): 10–12.

7 "Advertising Drive on Pineapple," *Weekly Commercial News* 64, no. 19 (May 1922): 5. Association of Hawaiian Pineapple Canners. Advertisement. *Western Canner and Packer* 14, no. 1 (May 1922): 17.

8 "Ninety-nine Tempting Pineapple Treats," *Western Canner and Packer* 14, no. 4 (August 1922): 61.

9 The Association of Hawaiian Pineapple Packers. Advertisement. *Good Housekeeping* 78, no. 1 (January 1924): 116.

10 The Association of Hawaiian Pineapple Packers. *Good Housekeeping*, 78, no. 2 (February 1924): 211.

11 *Huntingdon Daily News*, September 17, 1925.

12 *Middlesboro Daily News*, May 22, 1925

13 *Sandusky Star Journal*, April 16, 1925.

14 "Pineapple Upside-Down Cake," *Lincoln Evening Journal*, April 7, 1928.

Angel's Food Cake

1 Latham, A. W., ed., "Food Preparations," *Annual Report of the Minnesota State Horticultural Society* 19 (1891): 227.

2 Bryan, Lettice, *The Kentucky Housewife* (Cincinnati: Shepard and Sterns, 1839), 283; facsimile (Bedford, MA: Applewood Books, 2001).

3 Robinson, Helen, "White Sponge," *The Practical Cook Book* (New York: Abbey and Barrett, 1864), 78.

4 "White Sponge Cake or Snow Cake," *The Home Cook Book: Tried and True Recipes* (Toledo: T. J. Brown, Eager, 1876), 215. Assorted recipes, *Housekeeping in the Blue Grass* (Cincinnati: George E. Stevens, 1875), 96–97.

5 "White Sponge," *Melrose Household Treasure* (Boston: T. W. Ripley, 1877), 9.

6 Frost, Annie. "Angel's Food—A New Dish," *The Godey's Lady's Book Receipts* (Philadelphia: Evans, Stoddart, 1870), 263. A Practical Housekeeper (pseud.), *Cookery as It Should Be* (Philadelphia: Willis P. Hazard, 1856), 310. "Honey and Cream—Angel's Food," *Cultivator & Country Gentleman* 35, no. 908 (June 1870): 375.

7 Stewart, Isabella, Sill, Sally, and Duffield, Mary, comps, "Angel's Food," *The Home Messenger Book of Tested Recipes* (Detroit: E. B. Smith, 1878), 169.

8 "10 Recipes for Angel's Cake," *My Favorite Receipt* (New York: Royal Baking Powder, 1898), 54.

Boston Cream Pie

1 *Metal Worker* (August 1874): 7.

2 Blog of the Omni Hotel (accessed September 2013).

3 Adams, George, *The Boston Directory for the Year 1852* (Boston: George Adams, 1852), 13.

4 Young, David, *The Methodist Almanac* (New York: Carleton and Lanahan, 1872), 57.

5 *Three Rivers Cookbook* (Three Rivers, MI: King's Daughter's Society, 1876), 70–71. *Durham Herald*, March 22, 1876.

6 Frazer, Mary Harris, *Kentucky Receipt Book* (Louisville: Bradley and Gilbert, 1903), 211. Richards, Paul, "Boston Cream Pie," *The Lunch Room* (Chicago: Hotel Monthly, 1911), 31. Gillette, F. L., and Ziemann, Hugo, *The White House Cook Book* (New York: Saafield, Publishing, 1913), 331. *Boston Cooking School Magazine* 17, no. 9 (April 1913): 712. Weaver, Louise Bennett, and Le Cron, Helen Cowles, *A Thousand Ways to Please a Husband with Bettina's Best Recipes* (New York: Britton Publishing, 1917), 384–385. "Boston Cream Pie," *American Cookery* 26 (June–July 1921): 38. Barr Hotel Pastry Shop. Advertisement. *Lima News*, November 3, 1930. Mother's Cakes. Advertisement for Boston Cream Pie. *Bakersfield Californian*, April 23, 1930.

7 Glaus Pastry Shop. Advertisement. *Salt Lake Tribune*, March 18, 1933.

8 Pillsbury's Best. Advertisement. Vintage paper.

9 *Harrison Daily News Record*, March 14, 1940.

10 "Housewives' Question Box," *Sandusky Register*, July 11, 1935.

11 Bender's Foods. Advertisement. *Oakparker*, December 4, 1936.

12 *Llano News*, September 30, 1937. Softasilk. Advertisement. *San Antonio Light*, August 26, 1945. *Charleston Gazette*, October 6, 1949.

White Layer Cake

1 Scott, Marion L., *The Practical Housekeeper* (Toledo, OH: Blade Steam Printing, 1855), 16–53

2 Mann, Mary, *Christianity in the Kitchen: A Physiological Cook Book* (Boston: Ticknor and Fields, 1858), 87.

3 Elliot, Sarah, *Mrs. Elliot's Housewife* (New York: Hurd and Houghton, 1870), 239–246.

4 "Boiled Icing," *Good Housekeeping* (May 1888): 12.

5 "Query No. 27," *Boston Cooking School Magazine* (1896): 207.

6 "Marshmallow Frosting," *Wichita Eagle*, October 31, 1902.

7 "Home Lessons by an Expert in Pastry Cooking," *Chicago Daily Tribune*, December 13, 1908. "Birthday Cake," *Springfield Missouri Republican*, September 4, 1920.

8 Crisco. Advertisement. *Evening Review*, September 24, 1911. Crisco. Advertisement. *Pittston Gazette*, January 7, 2930.

9 "Wedding Cake," *The Successful Housekeeper* (Detroit: M. W. Ellsworth 1884), 71–74.

10 "Another Mountain Cake," *American Agriculturalist* 17, no. 6 (May 1858): 152.

Yellow Layer Cake with Fudge Frosting

1 Mrs. Bliss (pseud.), "Gold Cake," *The Practical Cook Book* (Philadelphia: Lippincott, Grambo, 1850), 178. Harris, S. D., "Yellow Cake," *Ohio Cultivator* 16, no. 4 (February 1860): 63. Lyman, Joseph and Laura, "Gold Cake," *The Philosophy of Housekeeping* (Hartford: S. M. Betts, 1869), 497.

2 Scott, Marion L., *The Practical Housekeeper* (Toledo, OH: Blade Steam Printing, 1855), 16–53.

3 "Domestic Recipes," *Edgefield Advertiser*, October 28, 1857.

4 "Chocolate Cake," *Chicago Daily Tribune*, October 21, 1876.

5 Daskam, Josephine Dodge, *Smith College Stories* (New York: Charles Scribner's Sons, 1900), 237.

6 Scott, Marion L., *The Practical Housekeeper* (Toledo, OH: Blade Steam Printing, 1855), 16–53.

Devil's Food Cake

1 Leslie, Eliza, *New Receipts for Cooking* (Philadelphia: T. B. Peterson, 1852), 201.

2 *Cocoa and Chocolate* (Boston: Walter Baker Chocolate Company, 1886), 116. "Home and Farm," *Belvidere Standard*, January 10, 1882.

3 "Chocolate Cake," *Highland Weekly News*, September 9, 1869.

4 Youman, A. E., "Chocolate Paste Cake," *A Dictionary of Everyday Wants* (New York: Frank M. Reed, 1872), 47.

5 "Home Interests," *Reading Times*, December 21, 1876. "Home Interests," *Wyandotte Gazette*, November 9, 1877.

6 "Chocolate Jelly Cake," *Bangor Daily Whig and Courier*, April 27, 1880. "Chocolate Jelly Cake," *Holton Recorder*, April 29, 1880.

7 Smith, Andrew, and Kraig, Bruce, eds., *The Oxford Encyclopedia of Food and Drink in America* (New York: Oxford University Press, 2013), 622.

8 "Chocolate Jelly Cake," *Indiana Herald*, December 20, 1871. *Melrose Household Treasure* (Boston: T. W. Ripley, 1877), 56.

9 "Devil's Cake," *Table Talk* 8, no. 4 (April 1893): 139–140.

10 Kramer, Bertha F., "Chocolate (Iced) Cake," *Aunt Babette's Cook Book* (New York: Blogh Publishing, 1914), 313.

11 *Daily News* (Frederick, MD), January 20, 1894.

12 "Devil's Food," *Table Talk* 10, no. 10 (October 1895): 335. The Ladies of the First Baptist Church, *The Howell Cook Book* (Howell, MI: Republican Printing House, 1896), 90. "Devil Cake," *Clever Cooking* (Seattle: Metropolitan Printing and Binding, 1896), 221. *The Florida Agriculturalist* 25, no. 26 (June 1898): 310. Ogle, George. Mrs. *The New Century Cook Book* (Chicago: Wesley Hospital Bazaar,

1899), 161–162. Crittenden, S. S., *The Greenville Century Book* (Greenville: Press of Greenville News, 1903), 156.

Red Velvet Cake

1 Chase, Alvin Wood, "Velvet Cake," *Dr. Chase's Family Physician, Farrier, Bee-Keeper, and Second Receipt Book* (Ann Arbor: Ann Arbor Printing and Publishing, 1873), 215.

2 "Velvet Cocoa Cake," *Chronicle-Telegram*, November 20, 1911.

3 *Logansport Pharos Reporter*, December 8, 1914. *Janesville (WI) Daily Gazette*. November 10, 1914. *Pittsburgh Press*, November 25, 1914.

4 "Red Chocolate Cake," *Sandusky Register*, May 17, 1923. "Red Devil's Food Cake," *Alton Democrat*, December 17, 1926. "Red Devil's Food Cake," *Iola (KS) Register*, April 26, 1928.

5 *Evening Huronite* (SD), October 30, 1931.

6 *Sumner Gazette*, May 18, 1933. *Llano News*, June 9, 1938. Baker's Chocolate. Advertisement. *Life* (February 1940): 85. "Red Devil's Food," *Mexico (MI) Evening Ledger*, February 5, 1948.

7 *Roland Record*, February 15, 1933.

8 Swans Down. Advertisement. *Good Housekeeping* (February 1931). *Miami Daily News Record*, March 25, 1932.

9 "Household Hints by Lynn Chambers," *Boyden Reporter*, March 19, 1942.

10 *Ruthven Free Press*, March 18, 1942. *Iowa City Press Citizen*, September 28, 1948. *Evening Independent*, January 1, 1940. "Use Coloring," *Marysville Tribune*, May 4, 1944.

11 *San Antonio Light*, March 23, 1951. *Santa Cruz Sentinel*, August 23, 1951.

12 *Van Nuys News*, December 1, 1959. *Joplin Globe*, August 19, 1960. *Petersburg Progress Index*, August 2, 1960. *Hays Daily News*, February 17, 1961. *Times* (San Mateo), February 12, 1964. *Emporia Gazette*, October 26, 1967. *Hays Daily News*, May 25, 1964.

13 *Arizona Republic*, January 14, 1970.

The Legend of Devil's Food and Red Velvet at the Waldorf-Astoria

1 "$100 Cake Recipe," *Express*, August 27, 1949.

2 Sutton, Horace, *Confessions of a Grand Hotel: The Waldorf-Astoria* (New York: Henry Holt, 1951), 154.

3 Sutton, *Confessions*.

4 *Charleston Gazette*, August 13, 1954.

5 *San Antonio Light*, March 23, 1951. *Quitman Wood County Democrat*, June 15, 1950. Advertisement (insert torn from unnamed newspaper), April 4, 1951. *Atchison Daily Globe*, January 31, 1954. *Zanesville Signal*, September 18, 1959.

6 *San Mateo Times*, April 3, 1963.

7 *Amarillo Globe Times*, June 27, 1960.

Carrot Cake

1 Ministry of Food. *War Cookery Leaflet*, no. 4 (London: July, 1943).

2 British Food in America, interview with Jane Fearnley-Whittingstall. "British wartime cooks seem not to have known about carrot cake." Website accessed January 2016.

3 Burnett's Vanilla. Advertisement. *Good Housekeeping* (May 1918): 123.

4 *Twentieth Century Club War Time Cook Book* (Pittsburgh: Pierpont, Siviter, 1918), 84.

5 Jane Eddington, "Currant Cake," *Chicago Tribune*, December 16, 1921. "Currant Cake," *Cincinnati Enquirer*, December 10, 1920.

6 *Oakland Tribune*, December 21, 1928. *Oshkosh Daily Northwestern*, December 3, 1932. *Lincoln Star*, November 11, 1938. *Wisconsin Rapids Daily Tribune*, August 15, 1940.

7 "Carrot Cake," *Brooklyn Daily Eagle*, January 20, 1921.

8 *Racine Journal Times*, July 14, 1940. *Woodland Daily Democrat*, September 1, 1936. *Middletown Times Herald*, May 31, 1933.

9 *Lemars Semi-Weekly Sentinel*, September 21, 1935. Campbell's Soup. Advertisement. *Greenly Daily Tribune*, February 19, 1932.

10 *Oak Park Oak Leaves*, April 6, 1939. *Hutchison News Herald*, September 27, 1942. *Denton Record Chronicle*, June 16, 1960.

11 *Oshkosh Daily Northwestern*, August 1, 1935.

12 Campbell's. Advertisement. *Life* (November 1950): 39. Philadelphia Cream Cheese. Advertisement. *San Antonio Light*, February 14, 1937.

13 *San Antonio Light*, January 22, 1933. *Piqua Daily Call*, May 4, 1932. *Pampa Daily News*, November 20, 1934. "Norwegian Tomato Soup Cake," *Altoona Mirror*, November 18, 1946. *Stevens Point Daily Journal*, September 10, 1934. *Middlesboro Daily News*, October 15, 1938.

14 "Vegetable Desserts," *Erie County Independent*, March 26, 1942.

15 *Altoona Mirror*, December 5, 1946.

All-American Pies

1 Whitehead, Jessup, *The Steward's Handbook and Guide to Party Catering* (Chicago: John Anderson, 1889), 400–401.

2 Hale, Sarah Josepha, *The Ladies' New Book of Cookery* (New York: H. Long and Brother, 1852), 260.

3 *The Cook's Own Book* (Boston: Munroe and Francis, 1842), 135. "Home Life and Character," *Arthur's Home Magazine* 43, no. 9 (September 1875): 613. Owens, Frances, *Mrs. Owens' Cookbook* (Chicago: Owens Publishing, 1884), 175.

Lemon Meringue Pie

1 *Tables of the Revenue, Population, Commerce, etc., of the United Kingdom* (London: W. Clowes and Sons, 1843), 94–95.

2 "Lemon Pie," *Godey's Ladies' Book* (March 1858): 272. Lupton, Frank, *The National Farmer's and Housekeeper's Cyclopaedia* (New York: F. M. Lupton, 1888), 400.

3 "Lemon Pie," *Harris Telegraph*, December 18, 1867.

4 Durrenberger, Robert W., "The Evolution of the American Lemon-Growing Industry," *California Geographer* 8 (1967): 103. Seelig, R.A., Sunkist Growers, Inc., *Fruit & Vegetable Facts & Pointers: Lemons* (Washington, DC: United Fresh Fruit & Vegetable Association, 1974).

Coconut Cream Pie

1 Ellis, Sarah. *Mrs. Ellis's Housekeeping Made Easy* (New York: Burgess and Stringer, 1843), 49.

2 "Manufacture of Desiccated Cocoa-nut," *Annual Report of the Commissioner of the Patents* (Washington, DC: Government Printing Office, 1870), 226.

3 Gillette, F. L., and Ziemann, Hugo, *The White House Cook Book* (New York: Saafield Publishing, 1897), 291. *The American Housewife and Kitchen Dictionary* (New York: Dick and Fitzgerald, 1869), 87.

4 Bakers Cocoanut. Advertisement. *Confectioners' and Bakers' Gazette* 28, no. 303 (December 1906): 10.

5 FranklinBaker.com (accessed September 2013).

6 "Grocery Specialty Revived When Form of Product Is Changed," *Printers Ink*, no. 4 (July 1917): 28–32.

7 "Familiar Fruits—The Cocoanut," *Fruit Trade Journal* 1, no. 6 (June 1890): 172.

8 Johnson, Samuel, "Cocoa," *A Dictionary of the English Language* (London: T. T. and J. Tegg, 1776 and 1833 editions referenced).

9 "Spell It Coconut" (an open letter from Franklin Baker Jr.), *Coffee and Tea Industries and the Flavor Field* 38, no. 8 (August 1915): 890. Bakers Coconut. Advertisement. *American Cookery* 24, no. 8/9 (March 1920): 631, 697. Bakers Coconut. Advertisement. *Journal of Home Economics* 12, no. 12 (December 1920): 9.

10 Bakers. Advertisement. *Morning Tulsa Daily World*, July 28, 1920.

Pumpkin Pie

1 "Pumpkin-pie and Corn-cake," *Arthur's Home Magazine* 49 (Philadelphia: T. S. Arthur & Son, 1881): 128.

2 Leland, E. H., *Farm Homes In-Doors and Out-Doors* (New York: Orange Judd, 1890), 146.

3 Wilson, S. J., *Michigan Dairyman's Association* (Lansing: Wynkoop, Hallenbeck, Crawford, 1907), 206.

4 Libby's. Advertisement. *Century Illustrated Monthly Magazine* (November 1912): 161. Carnation. Advertisement. *Saturday Evening Post* 186, no. 4 (July 1913): 28.

5 "Meeting of the Pumpkin Section," *Canner's Convention* (January 1921): 150–151.

6 Davis-Hollander, Lawrence, "The Great Moschata," *Heirloom Gardener* (Fall 2012): 12–21.

Key Lime Pie

1 Williams, Joy. *The Florida Keys: a History & Guide* (New York: Random House, 1995), 209.

2 *Florida East Coast Homeseeker* 14, no. 1 (Jan–Dec 1912).

3 *The Florida Tropical Cook Book* (Miami: First Presbyterian Church, 1912), 20, 133, 203.

4 Borden's. Advertisement. *Bakersfield Californian*, March 22, 1932. Borden's. Advertisement. *Wyoming County (NY) Times*, August 27, 1936.

5 "Magic Lemon Cream Pie," *San Antonio Light*, September 22, 1931.

6 "Cooking School Packs House," *Casa Grande Dispatch*, February 25, 1932. "Sentinel's School for Cooks Drew Big Throng," *Lodi Sentinel*, May 19, 1932.

7 Borden's Eagle Brand. Advertisement. *Centralia Daily Chronicle*, April 1, 1932; *Titusville Herald*, May 19, 1933; *Oakland Tribune*, September 14, 1934; *Carbondale Free Press*, June 14, 1935.

8 Strause, Monroe Boston, "Florida Key Lime Pie," *School and College Cafeteria* 4, no. 9 (May 1941): 20, 21, 26, 27.

9 *Fort Pierce News Tribune*, January 7, 1952.

10 Claiborne, Craig, *Craig Claiborne's Southern Cooking* (New York: Times Books, 1987), 315.

Key Lime Primer

1 Hume, H. Harold, *Citrus Fruits and Their Culture* (Jacksonville: H. and W. B. Drew, 1904), 47.

2 Harcourt, Helen, *Florida Fruits and How to Raise Them* (Louisville: John P. Morton, 1886), 161–166. Norton, Charles, *Handbook of Florida* (New York: Longmans, Green, 1892), 24. Finck, Henry, *Nation*, no. 1266 (October 1889): 268.

3 "Some Tropical Fruits," *Florida Agriculturist* 19, no. 50 (December 1892): 792.

4 *Statistical Report of the California State Board of Agriculture* (Sacramento: California State Printing Office, 1918), 132.

5 Advertisement. *Panama City News Herald,* July 1, 1937.

6 "The Florida Key Lime," *Country Gentleman* 70, no. 2761 (December 1905): 1198.

7 *St. Petersburg Times,* January 6, 1950.

Chapter 4: Doughnuts

1 Beecher, Catharine, *Miss Beecher's Domestic Receipt Book* (New York: Harper & Brothers, 1848).

2 McKerrow, George, ed., *Wisconsin's Farmers' Institutes Handbook of Agriculture*, no. 10 (1896): 220.

3 *The Story of Crisco,* seventh ed. (Cincinnati: Proctor and Gable, 1914), 109. Crisco. Advertisement. *Woman's Home Companion* (October 1916): 4.

4 Crisco. Advertisement. *American Cookery* 19 (June–July 1914): 393. Crisco. Advertisement. *Saturday Evening Post* 187, no. 24 (December 1914): 52; Crisco. Advertisement. *Ladies' Home Journal* (October 1916): 50. Crisco. Advertisement. *Good Housekeeping* 69 (December 1919): 7.

5 U.S. Department of Agriculture, *Weekly News Letter* 4, no. 13 (November 1916): 6. *Weekly News Letter,* U.S. Department of Agriculture 5, no. 38 (April 1918): 6.

6 "The Salvation Army Drive," *American Hebrew* 110, no. 25 (May 1922): 693, 716.

7 *Annual Report of the Commissioner of Patents* (Washington, DC: Government Printing Office, 1920), 519.

8 Bake-Rite Mfg. Co. v. Tomlinson, 16 F.2d 556 (December 20, 1926). U.S. Court of Appeals for the Ninth Circuit, 16 F.2d 556 (1926).

9 Steinberg, Sally Levitt, *The Donut Book: The Whole Story in Words, Pictures & Outrageous Tales* (North Adams, MA: Storey Publishing, 2004).

10 Bakery System of Bakeries. Advertisement. *Oshkosh Daily Northwestern,* March 29, 1919.

11 "Doughnuts," *Paris News,* July 28, 1935.

12 "Maintain Concessions," *Billboard* 59, no. 34 (August 1947): 126. Fiene, F., and Blumenthal, Saul, *Handbook of Food Manufacture* (New York: Chemical Publishing, 1938), 350.

Chapter 5: Cookies & Snacks

1 Kennedy, Artemas, "Extract from the Renunciation of Artemas Kennedy," *Opinions on Speculative Masonry* (Boston: Perkins and Marvin, 1830), 226.

2 *An Abstract of the Proceedings of the Antimasonic State Convention of Massachusetts* (Boston: Boston Press, 1831), 9.

3 Letter from Samuel G. Anderson to the United States Anti-Masonic Delegates Assembled in Philadelphia dated August 20, 1930, sent from Boston.

4 Stabile, Donald R., "Bakery Products," *Handbook of American Business History: Manufacturing* (Westport CT: Greenwood Publishing, 1990), 43–51.

5 "The Cooky Jar," *New England Kitchen Magazine* (Boston: New England Kitchen Publishing Company, 1895), 196.

6 Wiley, H. W., "Biscuits or 'Crackers,'" *Foods and Food Adulterants* (Washington, DC: Government Printing Office, 1892), 1353.

Vanilla Wafers

1 Scotch Bakery. Advertisement. *Brooklyn Daily Eagle,* November 23, 1871.

2 Walter G. Wilson. Animal Biscuit advertisement, advertising booklet and almanac dated 1880.

3 Sunshine. Advertisement. *Zanesville Times Recorder,* January 31, 1968. Sunshine. Advertisement. *Gastonia Gazette,* December 29, 1955. Burry's. Advertisement. *Statesville Record and Landmark,* December 15, 1955.

4 Nabisco. Advertisement. *Life* (March 1968): 44–45. U.S. Patent and Trademark Office. "Nilla," registered November 1968.

5 Nabisco. Advertisement. *Lincoln Star,* February 27, 1931.

6 "Vanilla Wafers," *Melrose Household Treasure* (Boston: T. W. Ripley, 1877), 66.

Animal Crackers

1 Wiley, H. W., "Biscuits or 'Crackers,'" *Foods and Food Adulterants* (Washington, DC: Government Printing Office, 1892), 1353.

2 *Chariton Herald,* December 15, 1887. E. M., "The Animal Party," *Good Housekeeping* 37, no. 3 (September 1903): 222–223. Smith, Laura A., "Answers to Queries from Household Club Members," *What to Eat* 22, no. 4 (April 1907): 153.

3 "Number Work," *Clinical Reporter* 16, no. 1 (January 1903): 205.

4 *Twelfth Annual Report of the Golden Gate Kindergarten Association* (San Francisco: George Spaulding and Company, 1891), 124.

5 Tilton, E. Stephens, Stanton and Co. Advertisement of goods sold (Larabee Animal Biscuits). *Home Dissertations* (New York: Hunter and Beach, 1886). Grocery advertisement. *Concord Enterprise,* February 12, 1892. Wiley, H. W.,

"Biscuits or 'Crackers,'" *Foods and Food Adulterants* (Washington, DC: Government Printing Office, 1892), 1353. Kennedy Biscuit. Advertisement. *Boston Daily Globe*, August 18, 1895.

6 Voucher for "Assorted Menagerie" from Parrot, Nickum and Company, *Annual Report of the Board of Management and Superintendent of the Indiana Institution* (1879).

7 Walter G. Wilson. Animal Biscuit advertisement, advertising booklet and almanac dated 1880.

8 Boston Bakery. Advertisement. *Atlantic Monthly* 80 (1897).

9 Saxon, A. H., *P. T. Barnum: The Legend and the Man* (New York: Columbia University Press, 1989), 54.

Graham Crackers

1 Graham, Sylvester, *Treatise on Bread and Bread Making* (Boston: Light and Stearns, 1837).

2 Graham, Sylvester. *Treatise on Bread and Bread Making*.

3 *Harper's New Monthly Magazine* 60 (December 1879–May 1880): 190.

4 Gill, Thomson J., ed., *The Complete Bread, Cake and Cracker Baker* (Chicago: Confectioner and Baker Publishing, 1881), 98.

5 National Biscuit Company. Advertisement. *Outlook* 80 (May-August 1905): 987.

6 "Lemon Chiffon Pie," *Elyria Chronicle Telegram*, December 20, 1932. "Honeymaid Graham Cracker Sandwiches," *Independent Record*, April 13, 1937; *Reno Evening Gazette*, October 10, 1938. *Emporia Gazette*, September 15, 1932. *Spokane Daily Chronicle*, September 26, 1931. *San Antonio Light,* December 23, 1932.

7 *Bradford Era*, March 22, 1930.

Fig Newtons®

1 "Recent Patents," *Northwestern Miller* 43 (February 1897): 310. Mitchell, J. Henry, "Machine for Sheeting Dough," *Annual Report of the Commissioner of Patents* (1888): 222. Mitchell, J. Henry, "Cake Machine," *Annual Report of the Commissioner of Patents* (1888): 181 and 484.

2 A communication to William Robert Lakes from J. Henry Mitchell of Philadelphia, dated 14th January, 1881. James H. Mitchell, "Duplex Dough-Sheeting Machine," *Official Gazette of the U.S. Patent Office* 58 (January 1892): 177. Patent issued to J. H. Mitchell for "machines for making fruit biscuits," *Patents for Inventions* (London: Darling and Son, 1899), 28.

3 "Among the Foundries," *Foundry* 11, no. 61 (September 1897): 240.

4 Grocery advertisement. *Hutchinson News*. November 15, 1901. "Fig Newtons," *Official Gazette of the U.S. Patent Office* 201 (April 1914): 1205.

5 Kennedy, Frank, "The Biscuit Industry," in *1795–1895: One Hundred Years of American Commerce* (New York: D. O. Haynes, 1895), 446–450.

6 Grocery advertisement. *Boston Daily Globe,* November 11, 1902. Grocery advertisement. *Boston Daily Globe,* August 28, 1904.

7 Grocery advertisement. *Emmet County Republican*, May 11, 1899.

8 "Fig Cake," *Table Talk* 14, no. 11 (November 1899): 407. "Fig Cake," *My Favorite Receipt* (New York: Royal Baking Powder, 1898), 118. Owens, Frances E., "California Fig Cake," *Mrs. Owens' New Cook Book and Complete Household Manual* (Chicago: Owens Publishing, 1899), 513. Ogle, George. Mrs., "Fig Cake," *New Century Cook Book* (Chicago: Wesley Hospital Bazaar, 1898), 167. "Fig Cake," *The*

Successful Housekeeper (Detroit: M. W. Ellsworth, 1884), 55.

9 "Rue Newton," *Junction City Weekly Union*, April 17, 1880.

Oreo®

1 "Jacob L. Loose," in *Men and Women of America: A Biographical Dictionary of Contemporaries* (New York: L. R. Hamersly, 1910), 1047.

2 "American Biscuit and Manufacturing Company" (charter), *Chicago Securities* (Chicago: Chicago Directory, 1894), 115.

3 Coniff, John J., "United States Baking Company" (Permission to use railroad switch, filed 1892, signed S. S. Martin, President), *Laws and Ordinances for the Government of the City of Wheeling, West Virginia* (Wheeling: WV: Intelligencer Publishing, 1901), 635–637.

4 "The Biscuit War," *Dun's Review* 4, no. 186 (February 1897): 11.

5 Wallace, Henry E., ed., "National Biscuit Company Charter," *Manual of Statistics* 21 (1899): 332.

6 "Loose-Wiles Biscuit Co. Officers" and "Officers National Biscuit Co.," *The Miller's Almanack and Yearbook of the Trade* (Minneapolis: Miller Publishing, 1916), 70. Smith, Andrew F., "Nabisco," *Fast Food and Junk Food: An Encyclopedia of What We Love to Eat*, vol. 2 (Santa Barbara: ABC-CLIO, 2011), 493.

7 "Exchange National for Loose-Wiles?" *United States Investor* 23, no. 50 (December 1912): 2237.

8 "Hydrox," *The Dispenser's Formulary* (New York: D. O. Haynes, 1915), 108. "Chocolate Hydrox Special," *Southern Pharmaceutical Journal* (September 1913): 29.

9 Sunshine Biscuits. Advertisement. *Saturday Evening Post* (March 1917): 53. Loose-Wiles Biscuit Company. Advertisement. *Saturday Evening Post* (July 1911): 37.

10 "Oreo," *Official Gazette of the U.S. Patent Office* 192 (June 1913), 569.

11 Loose-Wiles Biscuit Company. Advertisement. *Good Housekeeping* (July 1910).

12 Nabisco. Advertisement (Lotus and Anola Biscuits). *Fame* (January 1917): 21. National Biscuit Company. Advertisement (Ramona and Athena Biscuits). *Life* (1901).

13 Nabisco. Advertisement (Anola, 1916) via PeriodPaper.com (accessed July 2016). "Clematis Ramona," *National Nurseryman* 1, no. 1 (February 1893): 94.

14 Hydrox. Advertisement. *Syracuse Herald*, December 16, 1913. "West Coast Reports," *Billboard* (May 1952): 88.

15 "Loose-Wiles Biscuit," *Financial World* 19, no. 5 (August 1912): 15.

16 Grocery store. Advertisement. *Lebanon Daily News*, August 28, 1921.

17 Grocery store. Advertisement. *Anaconda Standard*, January 21, 1914.

18 Burch, David, and Lawrence, Geoffrey, "Kosher Food in the US," *Supermarkets and Agri-food Supply Chains: Transformations in the Production and Consumption of Food* (Northhampton, MA: Edward Elgar Publishing Limited), 137.

19 "Nabisco," *Magazine of Wall Street and Business Analyst* 64 (1939): 30.

20 "Aerated Table Waters," *World's Work* 2 (May 1900–October 1901).

21 Sunshine Hydrox. Advertisement. *Life* (March 1951): 7.

22 Sunshine Hydrox. Advertisement. *Life* (May 1961): 118. Sunshine Hydrox. Advertisement. *Life* (October 1951): 164. Sunshine Hydrox. Advertisement. *Life* (September 1966): 14.

23 Oreo. Advertisement. *Life* (July 1961): 94.

24 Grocery advertisement. *Uniontown Evening Standard*, September 4, 1958.

25 Mueller, Dennis, *Profits in the Long Run* (New York: Cambridge University Press, 1986), 92–94.

Nutter Butter® Cookies

1 Nabisco. Advertisement. *Lebanon Daily News*, July 21, 1949. Nabisco. Advertisement. *Better Homes & Gardens* (September 1952). Brockelman's Market. Advertisement. *Fitchburg Sentinel*, May 8. 1925.

2 Keebler. Advertisement. *Progress*, December 27, 1956. Keebler. Advertisement. *Frederick News Post,* February 2, 1957. Keebler. Advertisement. *Coshocton Tribune,* March 13, 1968. "Grandma's Peanut Butter Patties," *Catalog of Copyright Entries* 38, no. 1 (1943): 150. Keebler. Advertisement. *Florence Morning News,* March 7, 1968. Keebler. Advertisement. *Lebanon Daily News,* July 35, 1957.

3 Nabisco. Advertisement. *Port Arthur News*, September 14, 1967. Nabisco. Advertisement. *Life* (March 1968): 44–45.

4 Wallace, Emily, "The Story of William A. Turnier, the Man Who Designed the Oreo Cookie," Indy Week, www.indyweek.com, August 24, 2011.

Fudge Stripes™ Cookies, Pecan Sandies®, and Magic Middles®

1 Winslow, Stephen N., "John T. Ricketts," *Biographies of Successful Philadelphia Merchants* (Philadelphia: James K. Simon, 1864), 111–113.

2 "The Baking Business in Philadelphia and Brooklyn," *Merchants Magazine and Commercial Review* 36 (January–June 1857): 258.

3 McMichael, Clayton, ed., "Keebler-Weyl Baking Company," *Philadelphia and Popular Philadelphians* (Philadelphia: American Printing House, 1891), 157.

4 *Keebler Company, A Historical Sketch* (Philadelphia: Keebler Company, 1966).

5 Winslow, Stephen N., "John T. Ricketts," *Biographies of Successful Philadelphia Merchants* (Philadelphia: James K Simon, 1864), 111–113.

6 Godfrey Keebler. Advertisement. *Burley's United States Centennial Gazetteer and Guide* (Philadelphia: S. W. Burley, 1876), 796.

7 *Annual Message of William S. Stokley, Mayor of the City of Philadelphia* (Philadelphia: E. Markley and Sons, 1879), 904. Schultz, Edward T., *History of Freemasonry in Maryland* (Baltimore: J. H. Medairy, 1888) 613.

8 Keebler and Weyl Baking Company. Advertisement. *Philadelphia Securities* (1892): 566. Crittend, J. P., and Helffrich, Charles. comps. "Keelber-Weyl Baking Company (charter)," *Philadelphia Securities: A Descriptive & Statistical Manual* (Philadelphia: Burk and McFetridge, 1892), 566. Obituary of Godfrey Keebler, *Public Ledger Almanac* (Philadelphia: George W. Childs, 1894).

9 Harvard Business School Baker Library online, Lehman Brothers Collection, "United Biscuit Company of America." Accessed January 2013.

10 Lee, Laura, *The Name's Familiar: Mr. Leotard, Barbie, and Chef Boyardee* (Gretna, LA: Pelican Publishing, 1999), 147. Reitz, Caroline, "Those Out-of-Town Owners," *Cincinnati Magazine* (September 1989): 101. Fuller, George, *Michigan: A Centennial History of the State and Its People* (Chicago: Lewis Publishing, 1939), 93.

11 Kitchen Rich. Advertisement. *Life* (March 1963): 85. Kitchen Rich/The Flintstones animated commercial.

http://www.youtube
.com/watch?v=0oMGm9NJ7oQ
(accessed July 2013).

12 Kitchen Rich. Advertisement. *Life* (May 1963): 67.

13 Kitchen Rich. Advertisement. *Hagerstown Daily Mail*, September 16, 1965. Strietmann/Kitchen Rich. Advertisement. *Life* (March 1965): 21.

14 Strietmann/Kitchen Rich. Advertisement. *Florence Morning News*, January 10, 1963. Keebler/Kitchen Rich. Advertisement. *Lebanon Daily News*, April 25, 1963.

15 Mueller, Dennis. *Profits in the Long Run* (New York: Cambridge University Press, 1986), 92–94.

16 Keebler Fudge Stripes™. Advertisement. *Lebanon Daily News*, October 26, 1966.

17 Keebler. Advertisement. *Arizona Republic*, May 4, 1969.

18 Hekman/Kitchen Rich. Advertisement. *Findlay Republican Courier*, October 15, 1944.

Girl Scout Cookies

1 Buzzell, Arthur, ed., *Bulletin of Pharmacy* (January–December 1918), throughout.

2 Hiscox, Gardner, ed., *Henley's Twentieth Century Formulas, Recipes and Processes* (New York: Norman W. Henley, 1919), 115.

3 Levy Brothers. Advertisement. *San Mateo Times*, September 5, 1933.

4 Nabisco. Advertisement. *Kalispell Daily Inter-Lake*, March 19, 1936. Joe's Store. Advertisement. *Blockton News*, December 23, 1937. Educator Cookies. Advertisement. *Fitchburg Sentinel*, August 7, 1936.

5 "Girl Scouts Cookie Day," *Portsmouth Herald*, November 5, 1923.

6 "Girl Scouts Cookie Week," *Oak Park Oakparker*, March 13, 1936. "Girl Scout Cookies," *Oak Park Oak Leaves*, March 25, 1922.

7 Girl Scout Cookies. Advertisement. *La Crosse Tribune and Leader Press*, March 27, 1936. Erickson Bakers. Advertisement. *La Crosse Tribune*, March 25, 1950.

8 "Scout Cookie Campaign On," *Lowell Sun*, April 22, 1937. "Greater Lowell Girl Scout Camp Reunion Saturday at Lowell High School," *Lowell Sun*, April 13, 1939. "Bridge Party Held by Girl Scout Leaders," *Lowell Sun*, March 23, 1939.

9 "Girl Scouts Ready to Start Sale of Cookies," *Lowell Sun*, March 25, 1941.

10 "Greater Lowell Girl Scout News," *Lowell Sun*, March 24, 1949.

11 Kupetz, Joshua, "Jack Kerouac," *The Cambridge Companion to American Novelists* (New York: Cambridge University Press, 2013), 224.

12 Kerouac, Jack, "The Birth of a Socialist," *Atop an Underwood* (New York: Viking Penguin, 1999).

13 *Gastonia Daily Gazette,* April 9, 1942.

Little Debbie® Oatmeal Creme Pies

1 House Joint Resolution 894, 6th Assembly of the State of Tennessee. (Accessed online July 2013).

2 "Mrs. Perkins' Marshmallow Cookies," *Kimball Class Cook Book* (Boston: Gage Printing, 1913), 28.

3 Wiley, Harvey W., "Snowflake Marshmallow Creme," *1001 Tests* (New York: Hearst's International Library, 1916), 258.

4 "Filling for Chocolate Roll Cake," *American Cookery* 21, no. 8 (March 1917): 553. Blackmore, M.O., "Desserts, Marshmallow Cremes, etc.," *Merchants Manual of Advertising* (Chicago: Merchants Manual of Advertising, 1921), 480. "Lowly Birth of a Successful Product," *Printers Ink* 117, no. 11 (December 1921): 41–42. Emma Curtis.

Advertisement. *American Cookery* 26, no. 6 (January 1922): 482.

5 The Merchants' Biscuit Company. Advertisement. *Colorado Manufacturer and Consumer* (1925): 12–13. "Devil Dogs," *Official Gazette of the U.S. Patent Office* 354 (January 1927): 731.

6 Marshmallow Pie. Advertisement. *Lowell Sun*, September 12, 1914. Grocery advertisement. *Lowell Sun*, May 19, 1916. Grocery advertisement. *Boston Daily Globe*, February 3, 1921.

7 Oliphant, C. A., *Sweet Success: O.D. Mckee, America's Snack Cake King* (Cleveland, TN: Sundial Press, 1994).

Twinkies® & Hostess® Cupcakes

1 Dunn, Jacob Piatt, "Alexander Taggart," *Indiana and Indianans* (Chicago: American Historical Society, 1919), 1777–1778. Esarey, Logan, *History of Indiana from Its Exploration to 1992, with an Account of Indianapolis and Marion County* (Dayton: Dayton Historical Publishing, 1924).

2 "American Biscuit Company and U.S. Baking Company," *American Federationist* 3, no. 1 (March 1896), 6–7. Hyman, Max, ed., "The Taggart Baking Company," *Hyman's Handbook of Indianapolis: An Outline History* (Indianapolis: M.R. Hyman, 1907), 278.

3 "William Louis Taggart," *Princeton Alumni Weekly* 46, no. 30 (May 1946): 26. "Bakery News," *Northwestern Miller* 62, no. 5 (May 1905): 276.

4 Taggart's. Advertisements. *Indianapolis Star*, February 19, 1912; May 10, 1914; January 27, 1921; May 5, 1921. Taggart's. Advertisement. *Logansport Press*, November 1, 1921.

5 Hohmann, Charles, ed., *Official Report and Proceedings of the*

Sixteenth Convention Bakery and Confectionery Workers' International Union of America (Boston: John C. Burmeister, 1917), 57.

6 Cline, Elmer L., "How Taggart's Salesmen Sold Themselves on Advertising," *Printers Ink* (July 1915): 25–28.

7 Taggart's. Advertisements. *Fort Wayne Journal Gazette,* May 23, 1922; July 22, 1922.

8 Hostess. Advertisement. *Salt Lake Tribune,* September 7, 1928. Hostess Cake. Advertisement. *Waterloo Evening Courier,* November 8, 1929. Continental Baking Company. Advertisement. *Good Housekeeping* (1929).

9 Taggart's. Advertisements. *Indianapolis Star,* May 18, 1921; May 20, 1921; May 21, 1921; May 23, 1921; July 9, 1921. Taggart's. Advertisement. *Indianapolis Star,* June 19, 1923.

10 Taggart's. Advertisements. *Indianapolis Star,* September 29, 1921. "Sevigne Wrapping Machine," *Nashua Telegraph,* May 26, 1923.

11 Continental Baking Company IPO. Advertisement. *Waterloo Evening Courier,* June 15, 1925. *Combination in the American Bread-Baking Industry* (Palo Alto: Stanford University Press, 1926), 9, 144.

12 *Bulletin of the Merchants Association of New York* 14, no. 2 (January 1925): 27. "Alexander Taggart, Jr. obituary," *Toledo Blade,* December 14, 1972. *Princeton Alumni Weekly* 25, no. 28 (April 1925): 694. *Princeton Alumni Weekly* 47, no. 24 (May 1947): 17.

13 Hostess. Advertisement. *Waterloo Daily Courier,* September 25, 1931.

14 Hostess. Advertisement. *Kansas City Star,* May 22, 1931. Hostess. Advertisement. *Oakland Tribune,* April 17, 1931.

15 Twinkies (Buster Brown). Advertisement. *Corona Daily Independent,* December 13, 1927. Jay O' Donnell Meets Buster Brown," *Inland Printer* 65, no. 5 (August 1920): 637. *Factory and Industrial Management* 78, no. 2 (August 1929): 461. Twinkies (Buster Brown). Advertisement. *Spencer News Herald,* March 21, 1929.

16 Hostess. Advertisement. *Waterloo Daily Courier,* September 25, 1931.

17 Hostess CupCakes. Advertisement. *Ogden Standard Examiner,* April 19, 1949; May 24, 1949.

18 Hostess/Howdy Doody. Commercial. (Accessed via Youtube July 2013.) Hostess/Howdy Doody. Commercial. (Accessed via Youtube July 2013.) "Inventor Honored on Birthday of Hostess Cupcake," *Daily Union,* May 11, 1989. Hostess Cupcakes. Advertisement. *Life* (June 1956): 136.

Chapter 6: Puddings

1 Webster, Noah, "Pudding," *An American Dictionary of the English Language* (Philadelphia: J.B. Lippincott, 1857).

2 "Vanilla Pudding," *Table Talk* 14, no. 4 (April 1899): 141.

3 "French Cream Cake," *Sterling Standard,* July 9, 1874.

4 *Jell-O, the Dainty Dessert* (New York: Genesee Pure Food Company, 1905).

5 Jell-O. Advertisement. *Life* (April 1944): 46.

Banana Pudding

1 Gillette, Fanny Lemira, *The White House Cookbook* (Chicago and New York: L.P. Miller, 1887), 367.

2 Means, Mary Pinckney, "Banana Pudding," *Atlanta Woman's Club Cook Book* (Atlanta: Atlanta Woman's Club, 1921), 177.

3 Nabisco shareholders report, December 1951. Vintage photograph in author's collection, dated June 10, 1948: "J. Weingarten #10 Houston, Texas."

Chiffon Pie

1 "Good Food," *Kingston Daily Freeman,* October 25, 1929.

2 "Lemon Chiffon Pie," *Brooklyn Daily Eagle,* May 26, 1931.

3 Knox Gelatin. Advertisement. *Odessa America,* March 5, 1941.

Pillsbury Cinnamon Rolls

1 Whitehead, Jessup, "Hotel French Rolls—An Inquiry into Their Origin," *Whitehead's Family Cookbook and Book of Breads and Cakes* (Chicago: Jessup Whitehead, 1891), 134–135.

2 "Good Rolls," *Semi-Weekly Wisconsin,* February 23, 1869.

3 Chase, Alvin Wood, "Parker House Rolls," *Dr. Chase's Family Physician, Farrier, Beekeeper, and Second Receipt Book* (Ann Arbor: Ann Arbor Printing and Publishing, 1873), 155.

4 Whitehead, Jessup, "Hotel French Rolls." "Parker House Rolls," *Cuba Tribune,* September 2, 1926. "Parker House Rolls," *Good Housekeeping* 6, no. 6 (January 1888): 173.

5 Goff, May Perrin, *The Household* (Detroit: Detroit Free Press, 1881), 391.

6 Jones, Mary Chandler, "Cinnamon Rolls, Parker House Rolls," *Lessons in Elementary Cooking* (New York: Sully and Kleinteich, 1913), 119. The Fawn (bakeshop). Advertisement for Parker House Cinnamon Rolls. *Oakland Tribune,* September 4, 1931. Richards, Paul, "Pecan Rolls," *Baker's Bread* (Chicago: Baker's Helper Company, 1918), 141. Evans, Edna, "Icing for Drop Cakes," *Home Baking* (San Francisco: Golden Gate Compressed Yeast Company, 1912), 42.

7 Pillsbury. Advertisement. *Life* (November 1955): 77. Pillsbury. Advertisement. *Life* (September 1960): 72.

Pop-Tarts®

1 The International Central Services Toaster Museum, Kettwig, Germany. (Accessed Online, toaster-museum.com, July 2016.)

2 Grocery. Advertisement. *Hubbard News,* August 16, 1962. Snowcrop. Advertisement. *Ogden Standard Examiner,* December 22, 1954.

3 Downyflake. Advertisement. *Charleston Daily Mail,* May 2, 1961.

4 Pepperidge Farm. Advertisement. *Lowell Sun,* September 17, 1958; *Eureka Humboldt Standard,* November 8, 1960.

5 Flavor Kist. Advertisement. *Life* (October 1961): 102.

6 "Pop-Ups," *Official Gazette of the U.S. Patent Office* 770, no. 2 (September 1961): 63. Taylor. Advertisement. *Ebony* (October 1960): 70.

7 Schulze Company History (accessed online, June 2013).

8 Country Squares. Advertisement. *Logansport Pharos Tribune,* September 18, 1963. Country Squares. Advertisement. *Logansport Press,* September 19, 1963. Country Squares. Advertisement. *Daily Sentinel,* August 12, 1964.

9 Prichard, James, "Pop-Tarts Turn 40," *Luddington Daily News,* April 5, 2003.

10 Keebler. Advertisement. *Oneonta Star,* August 25, 1955.

11 Pop-Tarts. Commercial. 1964. Accessed via YouTube July 2013.

12 Prichard, James, "Pop-Tarts Turn 40," *Luddington Daily News,* April 5, 2003.

English Muffins

1 *The City Cries of Philadelphia* (Philadelphia: Appleton, 1850), 84–86.

2 Braun, Emil, *The Bakers' Book* (New York: Emil Braun, 1901), 194.

3 Rorer, Sarah T., *Mrs. Rorer's Philadelphia Cook Book: A Manual of Home Economics* (Philadelphia: George H. Buchanan, 1886), 326.

4 "Table Talk's Bills of Fare," *Table Talk* 14, no. 1 (January 1899): 35.

5 *Cassell's Dictionary of Cookery* (London: Cassell, Petter, Galpin, 1883), 35.

6 "English Muffins and Crumpets," *Everyday Housekeeping* 15 (April–September 1901): 101.

7 Ronald, Mary, *The Century Cookbook* (New York: The Century, 1895), 355. Tyree, Marion Cabell, *Housekeeping in Old Virginia* (Louisville, KY: John P. Morton, 1879), 37.

American Muffins

1 Marks, Susan, *Finding Betty Crocker* (Minneapolis: University of Minnestoa Press, 2007).

2 Betty Crocker. Advertisement. *Working Mother* (June 1988): 19.

3 "Muffins on the Rise," *New York Magazine* (March 1987): 16, 19.

Crunch Bars

1 Loft (Milk Chocolate Covered Crackers). Advertisement. *Fitchburg Sentinel,* March 5, 1936. Chocolate Crunch. Advertisement. *Sioux City Journal,* December 12, 1925. "Chocolate Crunch," *Syracuse Herald,* December 21, 1933. "Chocolate Crunch Sundae," *Harrisonburg Daily News Record,* January 8, 1937.

2 "Krackel," *Official Gazette of the U.S. Patent Office* 407, no. 1 (December 1938): 590. Aaseng, Nathan. "Milton Hershey," *Business Builders in Sweets and Treats* (Minneapolis: Oliver Press, 2005), 17–39. Krackel. Advertisement. *Oshkosh Daily Northwestern,* October 21, 1938.

Peanut Butter Cups

1 Callebaut, Barry, "Chocolate Prices in the Early 20th Century" Accessed (online July 2013).

2 McRobert, T. B., "Nuts and Their Uses—Peanuts," *International Confectioner* 23, no. 1 (January 1914): 48. Neil, Marion Harris, "Peanut Butter Candy," *Candies and Bonbons and How to Make Them* (Philadelphia: David McKay, 1913), 186. Peanut Butter Centers. Advertisement. *Confectioners Journal* 46, no. 551 (December 1920): 3. Rigby, William O., "Peanut Butter Chocolates," *Rigby's Reliable Candy Teacher* (Topeka: Rigby Publishing, 1920), 97.

3 "Peanut Men and the Tariff," *Oil Miller* 12, no. 6 (February 1921): 17.

4 Carver, G. W., *Tuskegee Normal and Industrial Institute Bulletin*, no. 31 (March 1916): 26–33.

5 "Blue Bird Candy Shop," *Greater Harrisburg City Directory* (New York: R. L. Polk, 1939), 88. Willhide Johnston, Laura, *Descendants of My Great-Grandparents* (Harrisburg, PA: Evangelical Press, 1924), 326. Reese, Andrew R., *Reese's Peanut Butter Cups: The Untold Story* (New York: iUniverse, 2010).

Mars® Bars

1 "An Aid to the Collection of Tax on Soft Drinks," *Hotel Monthly* (1919): 67. *The War Tax* (War Revenue Law of 1918). H.R. 12863 (Washington, D.C.: Federal Trade Information Service, 1919). "Ohio Adopts Soda Fountain Plan," *National Drug Clerk* 6, no. 4 (April 1918): 305.

2 "Shakes," *The Dispenser's Formulary* (New York: D. O. Haynes, 1915), 70–75.

3 "Milk Replaces Suds and Soda," *Milk Dealer* 10, no. 1 (October 1920): 49.

4 "Revises Rules," *Albert Lea Evening Tribune,* July 24, 1918. "Use of Invert Sugar," *International*

Confectioner (July 1917): 78. "Malt Sugar Syrup," *American Druggist* 68, no. 2 (February 1920): 44.

5　Dale, J. K., "Malt Syrup," *Sugar* 22, no. 6 (June 1920): 381–382. Crampton, C. Ward, "Give Me a Malted!" *Boys' Life* (June 1940): 26.

6　Mars.com. accessed online July 2013.

7　Brenner, Joël Glenn, *The Emperors of Chocolate* (New York: Broadway Books, 2000), 54.

8　Milky Way. Advertisement. *Waterloo Evening Courier*, August 5, 1924.

9　El-Hai, Jack, "Candy Bar Combat," *Minnesota Monthly* (March 2007). Aaseng, Nathan, "Frank and Forrest Mars," *Business Builders in Sweets and Treats* (Minneapolis: Oliver Press, 2005), 55–65.

10　"Mars Bars," *Kiplinger Magazine* (July 1947): 20.

11　Snickers. Advertisement. *New Castle News*, December 26, 1930.

12　Snyder, Clara Gebhard, "Bon Bons and Eggs," *United States Egg and Poultry Magazine* 37 (January 1931): 17–21. Mars. Advertisement. *Boys' Life* (February 1932): 35. "American Eggs Every Day," *Poultry Tribune*, no. 38 (1932): 52.

Cracker Jack®

1　Haskell, H. F., *The Housekeeper's Encyclopedia of Useful Information for the Housekeeper* (New York: D. Appleton, 1861), 193.

2　Croly, J. C., "Molasses Candy," *Jennie June's American Cookery Book* (New York: Excelsior Publishing, 1878), 190. "Taffy Candy," *The Home Cook Book: Tried and True Recipes* (Toledo: T. J. Brown, Eager, 1876), 238.

3　Beard, Lina, and Beard, Adelia Belle, "Rag-Balls," *How to Amuse Yourself and Others* (New York: Charles Scribner's 1893), 427.

4　Pop Corn Crispettes. Advertisement. *Catalogue of the Brooklyn Library* (1877), 13.

5　*Annual Report of the Commissioner of Patents* (Washington, DC: Government Printing Office, 1884), 383.

6　"Philadelphia," *American Mail and Export Journal* 20, no. 1 (July 1887), 75–76.

7　"Machine for Coating Pop Corn," *Official Gazette of the U.S. Patent Office* 59, no. 5 (May 1892): 1297.

8　Leonard, John W., ed., *The Book of Chicagoans* (Chicago: A.N. Marquis, 1905), 182.

9　Handy, Moses P., ed., *The Official Directory of the World's Columbian Exposition* (Chicago: W. P. Conkey, 1893).

10　Flinn, John J., "Pop Corn Privilege," *Official Guide to the World's Columbian Expositions in the City of Chicago* (Chicago: Columbian Guide, 1893), 230.

11　*Proceedings of the Annual Convention of the California Bankers* (Los Angeles: Times Mirror Printing and Binding House, 1891), 58.

12　Bunting, Henry S., *Specialty Advertising: The New Way to Build Business* (Chicago: Novelty News Press, 1910), 12. Cracker Jack. Advertisement. *Confectioners Journal* (September 1922): 85. Cracker Jack. Advertisement. *Boys' Life* 10, no. 6 (June–1930): 4. "Manufacture of Cracker Jack," *Pure Products* 6 (1910): 589. Cracker Jack. Advertisement. *Chicago: The Great Central Market Magazine* (January 1907): 139.

Rice Krispies Treats®

1　Quaker Oats. Advertisement. "The English of Advertisers—Essential Elements," *Productive Advertising* (Philadelphia: J. P. Lippincott, 1915), 283.

2　Quaker Oats. Advertisement. *Delineator* 97, no. 1 (July–August 1920) 61.

3　Evans, Mary Elizabeth, "Rice Crackle," *My Candy Secrets* (New York: Frederick A. Stokes, 1919), 16.

4　*Interstate Commerce Commission Reports* 49 (February–May 1918): 568–569, 571.

5　Rigby, William O., *Rigby's Reliable Candy Teacher* (Topeka: Rigby Publishing, 1920), 171.

6　Hoffman, David, *Breakfast Cereal Gourmet* (Kansas City, MO: Andrew McMeel Publishing, 2005), 37. Longden, Tom, "Famous Iowans: Mildred Day," *Des Moines Register*. (Accessed online July 2013).

7　Kellogg's. Advertisement. *Marshall Evening Chronicle*, November 11, 1940.

Heath® Toffee

1　Karamel Korn Shop. Advertisement. *Chicago Heights Star*, March 22, 1935.

2　"John Mackintosh, of Toffee Fame, Dead," *Printers' Ink* (March 1920): 153.

3　"Candy Advertising in England," *Ad Sense* (July 1903): 189–190.

4　Forby, Robert, "Toughy," *The Vocabulary of East Anglia* (London: J.B. Nicholas and Son, 1830), 353.

5　Burg, Judith. *A Guide to the Rowntree and Mackintosh Company Archives, 1862–1969* (York: University of York Press, 1997), viii.

6　Mackintosh's English Toffee. Advertisement. *Bookman* (November 1906).

7　Mackintosh's English Toffee. Advertisement. *Out West* 22, no. 1 (January 1905): throughout.

8　"Lollipops," *Chambers's Journal of Popular Literature, Science, and Arts* (February 1889): 76–77. Whitehead, Jessup, *The American Pastry Cook* (Chicago: Jessup

Whitehead, 1894), 54. "Taffy," *Chicago Daily Tribune*, October 21, 1876.

9   "Candy in England," *Daily Courier*, July 8, 1913. *The Art of Confectionery* (Boston: J.E. Tilton, 1865), 55.

10 Whitehead, Jessup, *The Steward's Handbook and Guide to Party Catering* (Chicago: John Anderson, 1889), 461.

11 Webster, Noah, "Scotch," *An American Dictionary of the English Language* (Philadelphia: J. B. Lippincott and Company, 1857), 889.

12 Crutchley, George W., *John Mackintosh, a Biography,* (London: Hodder and Stoughton, 1921).

13 Wilkins, Mira, *The History of Foreign Investment in the United States* (Boston: President and Fellows of Harvard College, 2004), 144.

14 Trail Candy Shop. Advertisement. *Oregon Daily Journal*, April 5, 1916.

15 Wieda Bakery. Advertisement. *Hutchinson News,* May 11, 1910, January 15, 1912.

16 Peggy Pan. Advertisement. *Reform Advocate* (December 1920): 505.

17 *Official Gazette of the U.S. Patent Office* (1936): 1040.

18 *Ice and Refrigeration* 61, no.1 (July 1921): 57.

19 Karamel Korn Shop. Advertisement. *Chicago Heights Star*, March 22, 1935.

Sprinkles

1   Weschcke, Emil, "Materia Medica and Therapeutics," *Pacific Medical Journal* 47, no. 10 (October 1904): 613. Braithwaite, J. O., ed., "Granules, Pharmaceutical, Preparation of," *Year-Book of Pharmacy* (London: J. A. Churchill, 1902): 236.

2   "Sugar Granules," *Pharmaceutical Era* 20, no. 15 (October 1898): 493. "Sugar Granules," *Pharmaceutical Journal* 62, no. 1501 (April 1899): 322. "On Methods of Securing

Accuracy of Dosage," *Druggists' Bulletin* 3, no. 4 (April) 1889: 126. Strauss, G. L. M, *Reminiscences of an Old Bohemian* (London: Downey, 1895), 154. Hamlin, Mont M., Ed., "The Form of Drugs," *American Medical Journal* 31, no. 1 (January 1903): 470. Edes, Robert Thaxter, *Text-book of Therapeutics and Materia Medica* (Philadelphia: Lee Brothers, 1887).

3   "Definition of Terms," *Confectioners Gazette* 36, no. 397 (October 1914): 16.

4   Boericke, F. E., *Three Lectures on Homoeopathic Pharmaceutics* (New York: Boericke & Tafel, 1878), 20–21. "Rotating Confectioners Pan," *English Mechanics and the World of Science* 30, no. 757 (September 1879): 74. "Composite Cake and Confection Apparatus (pills)," *Definitions of Revised Classes and Subclasses of Subjects of Invention* (Washington, DC: Government Printing Office, 1912), 199. Hausner, A. "The Manufacture of Dragees," *Manufacture of Preserved Foods and Sweetmeats* (London: Scott, Greenwood, 1902), 161–162. Richards, Paul, *Paul Richards' Book of Breads, Cakes, Pastries, Ices, and Sweetmeats* (Chicago: Hotel Monthly, 1902), 8.

5   "Cane Sugar Tablets" and "Milk-Sugar Pellets," *The American Homœopathic Pharmacopœia* (Philadelphia: Boerick and Tafel, 1911), 477.

6   "Apothecaries' System," *Understanding Pharmacy Calculations PDF* via Pharmacist.com. Accessed July 2013. https://portal.pharmacist.com/source/images/samplechapters/9781582120959Calc2dCh01_bookSample.pdf.

7   Scoville, Wilbur, "Pills," *Art of Compounding* (Philadelphia: P. Blakiston's Son, 1914), 121.

8   Assorted Advertisements. *Druggists Circular* 62, no. 11 (November

1918): 246. Saccharin. Advertisement. *Virginia Pharmacist* 29, no. 11 (1945): 167.

9   Lathrop Candy Company. Advertisement. *Northwestern Druggist* 19, no. 1 (January 1918): 66.

10 Skuse, E., *The Confectioners' Hand-Book and Practical Guide to the Art of Sugar Boiling* (London: E. Skuse, 1881), 67, 192. National Candy Company. Advertisement. *Confectioners' and Bakers' Gazette* 28, no. 304 (January 1907).

11 A Boston Housekeeper (pseud.), "Jelly Cake," *The Cook's Own Book and Housekeeper's Register* (Boston: Munfoe and Francis, 1840), 27.

12 Howell, Edgar H., ed., *Pacific Coast Journal of Homœopathy* 26 (1915): 462.

13 "Wood and Selick," *Illustrated New York: The Metropolis of To-Day* (New York: International Publishing, 1888), 216. "Wood and Selick, Manufacturing Chemists, Importers, and Wholesale Dealers in Bakers' and Confectioners' Supplies," *New York's Great Industries* (New York: Historical Publishing, 1885), 183. Wood and Selick. Advertisement. *Ice Cream Trade Journal* 47 (1951): 47.

14 Neil, Marion Harris, *The Something Different Dish* (Philadelphia: David McKay, 1915), 56. Assorted Advertisements. *Confectioners' and Bakers' Gazette* 30, no. 325 (October 1908). "Almond-bread Cake," *Peterson's Magazine* 59, no. 4 (April 1871): 322. Magee, Katherine E., "A Bre'r Rabbit Party," *Table Talk* 28, no. 3 (March 1913): 143–144. Jenkins, E. H. "The Druggists' Relation to the Pure Food and Drugs Law," *American Druggist and Pharmacist* (June 1908): 337–338. Vine, Frederick T., *Biscuits for Bakers: Easy to Make and Profitable to*

Sell (London: Hampton, 1896). Simmonds, W. H., *The Practical Grocer* (London: Gresham Publishing, 1907), 241. Frost, S. Annie, "Trifle," *Our New Cook Book and Household Receipts* (Boston: People's Publishing, 1883), 250. Wyvern (pseud.), *Culinary Jottings* (London: Richardson, 1885), 345.

15 "Child Culture," *Phrenological Journal and Science of Health*, no. 5 (November 1891): 217. Hudson's Bay Company Candyland. Advertisement. *Lethbridge Herald*, December 4, 1924. "Birthday Cake," *Boston Cooking School Magazine* 17, no. 9 (April 1913): 776. Hirtzler, Victor. *The Hotel St. Francis Cook Book* (Chicago: Hotel Monthly Press, 1919), 275.

16 Hahnemann, Samuel, *Organon of the Art of Healing* (Philadelphia: Boericke and Tafel, 1904), 223. "Eating His Way," *Church Standard* 82, no. 24 (April 1902): 904. Porter, Eleanor H., "A New England Idol," *New England Magazine* 29, no. 1 (September 1903): 18.

17 Hill, Janet McKenzie, *Cakes, Pastry, and Dessert Dishes* (Boston: Little, Brown, 1917), 62. Hill, Janet McKenzie, *Cooking for Two: A Handbook for Young Housekeepers* (Boston: Little, Brown, 1919), 339. Mott, Hopper Striker. *The New York of Yesterday* (New York: G. P. Putnam's Sons, 1908), 425.

18 "Sugars," *Bulletin of the New York Botanical Garden* 11 (1921): 133. Richards, Paul. "Macaroons—With Butter Cream, etc.," *Bakers' Helper* 38, no. 460 (October 1922): 685. "Wife Preservers," *Hamilton Daily News Journal*, February 2, 1935. The Great Bull Markets. Advertisement. *Kingston Daily Freeman*, March 13, 1934. "Orange Jumbles," *American Cookery* 25, no. 10 (May 1921): 760. Grocery. Advertisement.

Marshall Evening Chronicle, November 28, 1940.

19 Gordo, Ben, ed., *Chain Store Age* 24, no. 7 (July 1948): 23.

20 Grocery. Advertisement. *Alton Evening Telegraph*, October 9, 1958. Wood and Selick. Advertisement. *Ice Cream Review* 34 (1950): 23. "Christmas Trees," *Connellsville Daily Courier*, December 22, 1956. "Decorated Cupcakes Will Please Children," *Bakersfield Californian*, January 4, 1951. Dixie Bouquet Cup. Advertisement. *Life* (April 1959): 62. Schlottag's Grocery. Advertisement. *Sandusky Register Star News*, December 1, 1950. Rainbow Orna-Mettes. Advertisement. *Berkshire Eagle*, December 9, 1969. "Our London Letter," *American Stationer* 39, no 12 (March 1896): 489.

21 Venz.nl. Accessed September 2013.

22 The Chocolate Factory Lofts website (http://www.275park. com/residential.html). *Delicious Decorette Desserts*, The Alan and Shirley Brocker Sliker Collection, MSS 314, Special Collections, Michigan State University Libraries; available at http://www.lib. msu.edu/exhib its/sliker/detail.jsp?id=5025. Eby, Margaret, "History Lessons: Sweet Spot," *New York Times*, June 5, 2009. Rockwood Decorettes. Advertisement. *Frederick News Post*, July 23, 1925. Rockwood Decorettes. Advertisement. *Suburbanite Economist*, November 19, 1925.

Ice Cream Saloons

1 Twain, Mark, *Mark Twain's Own Autobiography: The Chapters from the North American Review* (Madison, WI: University of Wisconsin Press), 261–262.

2 Welsh, Donald H., "Sam Clemens' Hannibal, 1836–1838," *American*

Studies Journal 2, no. 1 (Spring 1962).

3 "Ice and Salt Method in Practice," *Ice Cream Review* (August 1917): 14.

4 Nelson Ice Cream Cabinets. Advertisement. *Ice Cream Review* (August 1917): 9. Nelson Ice Cream Cabinets. Advertisement. *Ice Cream Trade Journal* 4, no. 1 (January 1908): 28.

5 Kennedy, Ridgway, "Standardization of Ice-Cream Cans, Brick Molds, and Cartons," *Report of the Twenty-First National Conference on Weights and Measures* (Washington, DC: Government Printing Office, 1928), 24–29. "Care of Ice Cream," *Druggists' Circular* 64, no. 9 (September 1920): 358.

Cookie Dough Nuggets

1 Sneller, Beth. "The Scoop on Cookie Dough," *Daily Herald*, January 10, 2003. Benjerry. com (accessed online July 2013). Goodman, Susan. "The Scoop on Ice Cream," *Syracuse Herald Journal*, July 5, 1992. Barber, Cathy. "Fitness, Fun Food Trends," *Elyria Chronicle Telegram*, June 26, 1991. Marter, Marilynn. "Ice Cream Survives Diet Trend," *Kokomo Tribune*, September 10, 1992.

Ice Cream Sodas and Floats

1 "Mix Your Business," *Meyer Brothers Druggist* 19, no. 9 (September 1898): 238.

2 "Soda-Water: What It Is, and How It Is Made," *Harper's Magazine* 45, no. 267 (August 1872): 341–345.

3 G. D. Dows' Drug Store. Advertisement. *Guide to Boston and Vicinity* (Boston: 1867).

4 "A Glass Worth Drinking," *Rhode Island Schoolmaster* 9, no. 7 (July 1863): 183.

5 "Float Ice Cream Sodas," *Ice Cream Trade Journal* 5, no. 6 (June 1909): 27.

Ice Cream Sundaes

1 "Short Answers," *Bulletin of Pharmacy* 18, no. 9 (September 1904): 396. "The Sundae," *Druggists' Circular and Chemical Gazette* 50, no. 6 (June 1906): 204.

2 Payson, George, *Totemwell* (New York: Riker, Thorne, 1854): 356.

3 "Commonwealth vs Burry," *Pennsylvania County Court Reports* (Philadelphia: T. and J. W. Johnson and Company, 1888), 481–487.

4 Blaikie, W. G., "American Notes—Sabbath Observance," *Catholic Presbyterian* (London: James Nisbet, 1883): 140.

5 "Gastric Ulcer," *Medical Times and Register* (November 1888): 119; (January 1889): 282.

6 "Sunday Soda Water," *Central Law Journal* 26, no. 15 (April 1888): 382.

7 Jones, Alfred H., "Soda Water Flavors," *Annual Report of the State Food Commissioner of Illinois* (Springfield: Phillips Brothers, 1903), 138. ("A sundae is an ice cream soda served without the carbonated water.") "New York's Soft Drink Bill," *Practical Druggist* 38, no. 8 (August 1920): 62.

8 White, E.F., "The Fountain and Its Accessories," *Spatula Soda Water Guide* 4, no. 8 (May 1900): 409.

9 Cedar Rapids Candy Company. Advertisement. *American Druggist and Pharmaceutical Record* (July 1912): 95.

Chocolate Syrup

1 Scudder, John M., "On Syrup of Chocolate as a Vehicle for Quinine," *Eclectic Medical Journal* 29, no. 5 (May 1869): 221–222. "Pharmaceutical Uses of Chocolate," *Canadian Pharmaceutical Journal* 32, no. 9 (April 1899): 418. "Chocolate Flavored Emulsion," *Spatula* 5, no. 12 (September 1899): 602. "Syrup of Chocolate," *American Journal of Pharmacy* 40 (November 1868): 517.

2 Wood, Horatio C., "Chocolate Syrup," *A Year-Book of Therapeutics, Pharmacy, and Allied Sciences* (New York: William Wood, 1872), 328. Adkins, William S., "Chocolate Syrup," *Practical Soda Fountain Guide* (St. Louis: National Druggist, 1911), 151–152. "Chocolate Syrup," *The Techno-Chemical Receipt Book* (Philadelphia: Henry Carey Baird, 1887), 135.

3 Hershey's Chocolate. Advertisement. *Druggists' Circular and Chemical Gazette* 40, no. 12 (December 1896): 49.

4 Hershey's Syrup. Advertisement. *Berkley Daily Gazette,* April 12, 1929.

5 Rigby, William O., *Rigby's Reliable Candy Teacher* (Topeka: Rigby Publishing, 1920), 225.

Ice Cream Sandwiches

1 Green, Ralph, *Green's Receipt Book* (Concord, NH: Republican Press Association, 1894), 122. "Ice Cream Sandwiches," *Western Druggist* 23, no. 12 (December 1901): 690.

2 "A New Sandwich," *American Kitchen Magazine* 13 (April–September, 1900): 34.

3 State Assembly of New York, *Eighteenth Annual Report of Factory Inspection* (Albany: Oliver Quayle, 1904), 95.

4 "Sandwich Originator Quits," *Ice Cream Trade Journal* 6, no. 1 (January 1910): 38.

5 "Supposed Death from Eating Ice Cream [Sandwich]," *Boston Medical and Surgical Journal* (May 1911): 764. *Ice Cream Trade Journal* 8, no. 12 (December 1913): 26.

6 United States Public Health Service, "Milk and Milk Products—Permit Required for Sale of Ice Cream [Sec. 8: Sale on Streets]," *Public Health Record Weekly Newsletter* (December 1913): 2868.

7 Ridgely's Pure Juice Stand. Advertisement. *Evening Independent,* July 1, 1921.

8 The Sanitary Ice Cream Machine Company. Advertisement. *Ice Cream Review* (October 1917): 19.

INDEX

Note: Page references in *italics* indicate photographs.
⋆ Indicates a recipe that is gluten-free or has gluten-free variations.

ABOUT THE AUTHOR

Stella Parks is a graduate of the Culinary Institute of America, and was named one of America's Best New Pastry Chefs by *Food & Wine*. After more than a decade in the restaurant industry, and a brief stint attending language school in Japan, she now works as senior editor at Serious Eats, exploring the art and science of American dessert. Her work has appeared in the *New York Times*, *Southern Living*, and the *Wall Street Journal*. When not in the kitchen, she can generally be found at the grocery store, as she is perpetually out of butter.